James Bowling Mozley

Letters of the Rev. J.B. Mozley, D.D.

James Bowling Mozley

Letters of the Rev. J.B. Mozley, D.D.

ISBN/EAN: 9783337012663

Printed in Europe, USA, Canada, Australia, Japan

Cover: Foto ©ninafisch / pixelio.de

More available books at **www.hansebooks.com**

LETTERS

OF THE

Rev. J. B. MOZLEY, D.D.

LATE CANON OF CHRIST CHURCH, AND REGIUS PROFESSOR OF
DIVINITY IN THE UNIVERSITY OF OXFORD

EDITED BY

HIS SISTER

RIVINGTONS
WATERLOO PLACE, LONDON
MDCCCLXXXV

ADVERTISEMENT.

In preparing the present volume the Editor admits to having included in her selection a few letters of a more private character than are often given to the world, and to having some misgivings in so doing. If it is a grave mistake, an apology will do little to excuse it; but in the course of selection it has constantly seemed that the more intimate the letter the more justice is done to writer and reader.

A series of letters in chronological order insensibly grows into a biography without any such design in the selector. Perhaps by admitting letters of the character indicated, the nearest approach to a true biography is reached that the life of a retired scholar can furnish.

The Editor's warm thanks are due to those friends of Dr. Mozley who in a few cases have allowed their letters to be inserted, as throwing light upon his own.

A. M.

Barrow-on-Trent,
September, 1884.

INTRODUCTION.

WHEN a friend of Dr. Mozley's maturer years—one to whose judgment all would defer—suggested to the possessor of his papers and home correspondence the publication of a selection of his letters, saying, that having had occasion to look over old letters, his stood out among them as full of force and interest; the idea, which had never suggested itself before, became at once interesting; finding encouragement in the fact of the large number of his letters that have been preserved. The habit, in some members of his family, of keeping letters, has preserved James Mozley's letters to his home through the various shifts and changes that time brings about: the vicissitudes of life and death sometimes laying question and answer, comment and criticism, side by side in startling conjunction.

In the attempt to form a collection of letters which are to illustrate a character as well as a course of events, the difficulty starts at the outset; how or where to begin: for it is impossible not to feel, when a character is looked into, how much the early childhood of a mind affects its whole subsequent development. Those who care for letters in this light, and not merely as records of events, do care to know under what circumstances and influences the manner of writing has been formed; and if these are to be shown, it must be by means outside the writer's own knowledge and consciousness. Advantages are subtle things. Great men's sons are supposed to be benefited largely by early initiation into great ideas; but it must constantly be the fact that the father's greatness, and occupation in great affairs remove his children from his indirect influence—the most powerful of all influences. It is the private family-life, in which each member follows his course in obedience to necessary rules of order and convenience, that often furnishes the advantages we speak of. James Mozley, as a child, heard public matters discussed before him in the family circle. His father was public-spirited and strong and undoubting in his convictions. He was a Tory, and believed Tory principles the safety of the State. Men may change opinions thus imbibed as time goes on—that is, they may think for themselves; but it is a good thing for the heart and intellect to have been zealous for a cause while yet too young to understand all its bearings; it is a good thing not to start life by being eclectic, good to feel one of a party; especially—and this is one advantage of a private station—to have its interests at heart without a thought or dream of personal or family advantage. Intelligent children who have to listen, not talk, while their parents and elders discuss general, public topics and public men, learn to think about them in a different spirit, and with different consequences from those children who are allowed to interpose and lower the subject to their level; who are, perhaps, encouraged to give their opinion on subjects above them. Public events, great questions, startling incidents take much more effect on the mind of children, if their interest in them does not exhale in chatter, in the liberty of interruption, perhaps in argument. Deference to authority, the sense of ignorance, should come before criticism. In this spirit public questions come to the child with the feeling of duty connected with them, and also with what one may venture to call the wholesome sense of partisanship; of being on the right side with the nobler actors and thinkers of the day.

It happened, too, that in this family circle letters were a great interest. Any member of it, away from home, was expected to write a report of his doings. Postage in those days was heavy. It was a matter of conscience to fill the letter, to make it as full and interesting as time and circumstances would allow; thus letters were a social power, as much so as personal intercourse. They were read aloud for the general benefit, when their subjects permitted it. The family was fortunate in some clever correspondents; friends, living in a remote parsonage, with the post reaching them but twice a week, but full of the keenest interest in what was going in the world and in the new books coming out; with an insight, too, into bright social life, as well as the religious thought of the day. Looking back forty years, Dr. Mozley wrote, on reading an old letter from this parsonage, sent to him to recall some incident: "It was quite a treat to read a letter of Mrs. Wayland's; such perfection of statement, the thought so full and clear." His eldest sister Jane, who died young, and to whom many of these letters were addressed, wrote good letters, and was complimented on her Richardsonian style. If it be asked how the art of letter-writing may be fostered, perhaps here may be found some answer, though in James Mozley, of course, the gift was there. With him, if he took a pen in hand, it was to think; whether the subject were persons or things. A name suggested thought about the bearer of that name. His earliest letters show the beginning of the habit; but naturally, when a boy, he accepted the judgment of others; and many of the following letters are given more as records of Oxford in his early days, than for any felicity of thought or expression. As time goes on nothing is more entirely his own than the judgment, whether of passing events or of character, that is found in his letters, to whomsoever addressed.

James Mozley was born at Gainsborough in Lincolnshire, September 15, 1813; his father removing his family and business to Derby in 1815. In seeking records of James in the early family correspondence, it is really necessary to include other names in the revival of so distant a past. As the eighth child of eleven, he has to take his chance of mention in the letters of the more important members of the family. Thus his name closes the mother's happy letter to her eldest daughter at school in Kensington in 1820, who had written, with great depth of feeling, an account of her confirmation by the Archbishop, and the previous examinations and preparation:—

"The impression your confirmation appears to have made on your mind, could not but afford us the most heartfelt pleasure. It is a ceremony too little thought of in the present day.... It is now five years since there was a confirmation in Derby. James was by when I read your letter; when I had finished, he exclaimed with great earnestness, 'I should like to see Thomas à Becket, Archbishop of Canterbury.'"

In a later letter (let it be borne in mind it is a young mother, married at seventeen, writing to her daughter at school):—

"We have given up all thoughts of sending Charles to Merchant Taylors'—he is too old to be on the foundation, and consequently cannot derive any future advantage from it. We are told if a boy at *eight* years old could read the Latin Testament and Ovid's Epistles, he might stand a good chance at Merchant Taylors'. I fear this is what none of my family will ever accomplish. Mine are not early blossoms. Perhaps James might be *forced* to this, but I think no probable advantage could compensate for the risk of sending so young a boy from home. From eight to twelve is a time in which a great deal of good or bad may be instilled into a child, and I fear he is more likely to acquire the bad amongst boys, unless he have some fixed principles of his own to make head against evil examples."

Probably it was because his elder brother Charles was already placed there, that James at nine years old—a "pretty little fellow," as his brother in after years recalled him— was sent to Grantham Grammar School, then under a Mr.

Andrews. Whatever control of temper Mr. Andrews ever possessed—and my brother Charles said the boys always regarded his punishments not as judicial, but as ebullitions of temper—was now rapidly on the wane, and circumstances, and something in James himself, were adverse to a good mutual understanding. A school-fellow, looking back, after reading of Dr. Mozley's death, says, in writing to my brother Arthur, "I remember him well; he was very sensitive, and our head-master, an excitable man, did not treat him judiciously:" going on to speak of his sharp, sarcastic tones. On the same occasion of the revival of old memories, another school-fellow, then in failing health, recalled him, as my sister Maria writes in 1878 :—

"He asked me if James was living, and I told him we had just lost him. 'Oh, then it was his death I saw in the papers' (he had not been sure it was the same clever little fellow he remembered so well at school). 'He was such a clever little fellow; he knew more at ten than any of us, but the boys bullied him; they were jealous of him, and I—.' 'Well,' I said, 'I hope you did not bully him?' 'No! no! I tried to protect him from them—you see they were jealous, and he was such a clever little fellow!'"

These memories throw light on a passage in his letter to me when at school near London; showing what he meant by "masters."

GRANTHAM, *April* 1, 1826.

I often think how much more agreeably you spend your time than I do mine, since I'm surrounded on every side by masters. So I think I may complain in the words of the Psalmist, "many oxen are come about me, fat bulls of Basan close me in on every side." . . . School boys have very seldom much news to tell. We hear just as much about banks breaking and failures, as if we were shut up in the Black Hole of Calcutta.

At the end of 1826,[1] his mother writes to James: "It gave me great pleasure to know you were in the First Class in Latin. We have no doubt you will be so in Greek soon." It was this forwardness that no doubt suggested to his brother Tom at Oxford, the idea of his trying for a Scholarship at Corpus, when only thirteen—an idea most delightful to the schoolboy, which stimulated his mind to great exertion, and would make school life more irksome to him than ever. This proposal coming from a brother, an undergraduate, may account for the growth of irritation on Mr. Andrews' part; he might feel himself, as the time drew near, second in estimation and authority, and be tempted to revenge himself, as his position enabled him to do. I give the correspondence between the brothers as at least characteristic of both, and perhaps a little out of the common in fraternal correspondence.

In the spring of 1827, James writes to his brother, on hearing from home that it was settled he was to try for the Corpus Scholarship:—

March 30, 1827.

DEAR TOM,—This letter, I assure you, however selfish you may think me, is entirely for my own interest. I have just now been in to Mr. Andrews, and what he told me was this: that I was to do as much Homer as ever I could, that I was

---

[1] The year 1826 is distinguished in the home correspondence by the introduction of a name that has had a large family influence as well as an influence since widely felt in the world. James Mozley's brother, Thomas, the third of the six brothers, went from Charterhouse to Oriel in the spring of 1825. The first mention of the name comes without any addition or comment: "Jelf, my tutor, is gone to Germany with £900 a year; Newman is appointed in his place." Then April 28, 1826, to his mother: "I have at last had an interview with my new tutor, Mr. Newman, who gave me much good advice on the subject of themes, and gave me a manuscript treatise on composition, written by Whately, who is a famous man here." And again, in the same year, before the Long Vacation, writing to his father: "Newman, my new tutor, has been very attentive and obliging, and has given me abundance of good advice. He has requested me to consider carefully what information and instruction I require for my course of reading, and also to determine what books to take up, and he will have a little conversation with me before the vacation."

to learn, and that well, as much Horace as I could; I then mentioned the theme—that that would go a great way if written well. He said I might do a theme two or three times a week, and also said that if I did it without grammatical mistake, it was all they could expect. Now although Mr. Andrews must know what I ought to do very well, yet I confide in you as much, if not more than in him. So I beg you will write as soon as possible, and tell me all you know about it. I think that Greek verses are to be composed by those that try. I shall therefore be required to know how to do them in some way or other. I have not done a single Greek verse in my whole life, much less an epigram, which I think is the hardest thing to be done that can be. I also told Mr. Andrews that Euripides and Demosthenes, and all kinds of works were set before us. But he said that the ground-work was the chief thing with me, and that if they perceived that I knew Homer and Horace well, they would of course think that in time I should be able to do any other book well. Now while I am writing this letter, I'm thinking—"Let me see; Virgil, Horace, Homer, Cicero, Demosthenes, Sophocles, Euripides, Menander! How can I be able to know all these?" But that you may know that I have learnt something from reading Xenophon, I remember that once Cyrus forbade his soldiers the use of too many weapons (taking away the arrow and javelin, and leaving only the sword), for fear that having so many things to attend to they should know very little of the use of any of them. It is the same, I think, with me; for if I tried to learn something of all these books, I am afraid I should know very little of any. But when you write to me you will tell all that I'm to do—how to write my theme, and how to make verses, both Latin and Greek, particularly epigrams: I have not the slightest idea how to put the salt, as they call it, in epigrams. I shall also want some books to tell me everything I ought to have, and what you think I can't get here send in a parcel from Oxford. I am asking a great deal too much of you. Hear, then, the highest degree of my selfishness: I should like to go up to Oxford about a week before the time. I would then write you a theme, and what you might think proper; you would also open a Horace and Homer, and other books in a place or two, and see how I get on. If you think well of this, I wish you would write to mamma about it, but if not I'll drop it, but not without some reluctance; write, however, what books I'm to read. I should like to have a Greek Gradus, if there is such a book... I have not the *slightest expectation* of gaining this, but I should like to get through my examination as well as possible.—I remain, your affectionate brother,

J. B. MOZLEY.

To Mr. JAMES MOZLEY, the Rev. —— Andrews, Grantham, Lincolnshire.

ORIEL, *Friday, April* 27, 1827.

DEAR JAMES,—I am sorry I could not answer your letter earlier; you must take up with the excuse of my College Collections, which have really occupied all my time. In the first place, let me recommend you to acquire, if you can, a less boyish hand; if you set up for a forward boy you must have a forward hand. I have had a letter from home in which they ask my advice about your coming to Oxford a week before the time. I have assented, so I suppose you will come, but remember you must expect to be kept very close till the examination; for a week's wandering among fine buildings and such novelties will have a dreadful effect in driving all your learning and your verses out of your head. If you can't see how this is the case you must take it for granted. I know it is the case. I suppose Mr. Andrews is in the main right in what he says about the theme; but a theme must contain something, and a great deal more than the themes you gave me last Christmas. In an English theme at least they expect more than grammatical accuracy.

The best, the easiest, and most natural way of acquiring ideas is reflecting on all the facts you hear or read of, all the incidents either in poetry or history, and trying to draw a moral from them—that is, considering of what common failing, or propensities, or what virtue are they instances. This will appear at first quite childishly easy, but if you store up these morals in your head, with the instances from which you drew them, you will turn them to great account when you happen to have a thesis given you on the subjects. The same method will do for getting a stock of similes. I mean that whenever you see or hear anything beautiful or curious in the changes of nature to consider what actions or passions of mankind may be compared to them. This will at first appear stupid work, but remember that although, when your thoughts are engaged on some interesting fact, it will seem rather dry labour searching for a moral application, yet when you are writing a moral essay you would find the interesting fact come in much to your satisfaction, and appear very beautiful. But it is not only from the facts of Nature, etc., that you should draw similes. The ancient mythology and fabulous history is a very fertile field. Indeed, they are even supposed by some to be allegorical representations of moral truths. Lord Bacon wrote a book to prove this, and, whether he succeeded or not, he showed great ingenuity in applying moral truths to them, and the consequence was (mind James), that one of the greatest beauties of his essays and other writings is bringing in constantly beautiful similes from those fables. As instances of what I have said, if, when reading of Narcissus, I added: "Thus the man who is conceited of his talents, by doing nothing but admire himself sinks into insignificance;" or in the story of Atalanta, if I said: "Thus the great mind, by stooping down to the temptations of riches or honour, fails of the nobler end of existence;" or if in reading the story of Memnon's Statue (I mean the music that always sounded at sunrise), I said: "Thus all the types and prophecies of the Jewish dispensation remained silent and obscure till the light of the Christian revelation fell upon them" —all this you would think very dull prosing. But it would come in very beautifully, when you were writing about a conceited man, to say "he becomes an intellectual Narcissus, pining away in the comtemplation of his own merits;" or, in talking of the desire of fame, to say, "like Atalanta, he loses the race by stooping for the golden apple;" or, lastly, you would think a dissertation on the Jewish rites somewhat enlivened by this simile: "They are like the statue of Memnon, which contained some musical chords so artificially wrought that when the morning light dawned on the statue they were no longer secret and silent, etc." If I were not in a hurry, and moreover, confined for room, I could give you a thousand such.

As for Epigrams, don't trouble your head much about them; but if you happen to see a good English one, or happen to hear a good *repartee*, or a good story, it would be useful practice to put it into a two-line or four-line Greek Epigram. But don't make a regular exercise if it; depend on it, the Examiners don't go by Epigrams. I should think, as Mr. Andrews says, they go by Homer and Horace more than anything else. You should prefer getting up a little perfectly and grammatically to a great deal tolerably. Because, of course, the examiners make great allowances when you have not read the passage (which they always inquire), and you would be rather mortified if, when the passage was pointed out, you found that you had read it, and therefore could not get the credit of a first sight construe, but had not read it enough to construe the better for it. Besides, remember that closely studying a small quantity will, of course, of the two give you the greater grammatical knowledge, and a better memory for the words, and, consequently, better prepare you for first-sight construing. Most of the books you mention are in the same dialect, so that learning one book must enable you to read the others. After every lesson recall all the words and new constructions, and you are going on all right.

So far from sending a Greek Gradus, I *strongly* advise you never to use a Latin one—only when you cannot possibly find out the quantity any other way; never for any other purpose. I would collect all the words of difficult quantity I could think of, look them out in the gradus, and learn off all the lines quoted as authority, or else any line you meet with in your reading. You will thus have a gradus in your head; and remember in the Corpus examination you will be locked up in a room, with nothing but pen, ink, and paper. I would also strongly advise you to use your dictionary as little as possible. Scaliger, one of the greatest scholars that ever lived, used neither lexicon nor dictionary; but if, after long trying, he could not find out the meaning of the word by its context, he kept it in his head till he found the word again, and again tried it by its contexts, and so on, till he discovered the meaning. I would advise you to learn by heart two or three hundred lines in Latin and Greek, and when you are writing in those languages, and in want of a word to express your meaning, run over these pieces (let them be prose as well as verse), till you find a word. You will find this difficult at first, but it will gradually become an easy substitute for either gradus or dictionary. Go on the principle of keeping as much in your head as possible, and trusting nothing to books and paper. I assure you, James, you have a good chance. I know several instances of great boys coming from the first forms of their schools and being beaten by some sharp little fellow from the lower forms, whom they had before laughed at. If the great boys you talk of are as old as seventeen, they must show something very extraordinary, or they have not much chance. —Yours affectionately,

THOMAS MOZLEY.

ORIEL, 17*th May* 1827.

DEAR JAMES,—I have delayed answering your letter longer than I intended, but I think it would do you no harm to leave you to your first instructions some time before I send any more. I am afraid you are learning too much by heart. I would advise you to learn no more, but frequently run over what you have already in your head, and use it instead of a dictionary, till you have every word at a moment's notice. Thus, when you have to translate anything into Latin or Greek prose or verse, and come to a difficulty for want of words, immediately consider in what passage which you have read or learnt would these words be probably used. It is from not adopting this practice—I mean the practice of ranging over your stores in search of good words and expressions—that so many men have read half the books in the Latin language, and yet can scarcely find words to express the simplest idea. There is, I think, no better plan of learning to write Latin than translating *loosely* into English each day about a dozen lines of Cicero, laying your translation by for a week and then retranslating it into Latin, and afterwards carefully comparing your Latin with Cicero's original; but remember this will be of little use if you do not store up in your memory each day the differences between your words and expressions and Cicero's, the probable reasons why his are better, and the general rules which you can discover by examining Cicero; and if you do not each day consider what assistance you can derive from your former labours. Do not omit this trouble at any rate,—if you find it too much with twelve lines translate only six. On reading over your letter I cannot help thinking you are learning by heart too much; certainly too much for applying to it all the rules I have mentioned above. Remember it is a thing of the most vital importance that you should continue to attach a pleasure to your studies; that you should think of them not only in school but in play hours and in bed. Whatever a person forces himself frequently to think of, he will soon like.

As for your themes I have already said much on the subject: but, by way of general advice, remember always, especially in English themes, not to consider how your thesis applies to the Greeks and the Romans, or to tyrants or conquerors, and not to talk about "the avaricious man," "the cruel man," "the idle man," "the sensual man," "the ambitious man," etc. etc., but consider how it applies to yourself, to your own secret wishes, your day-dreams, your studies, the things that cause in you pleasure and pain—your intercourse with your school-fellows, the causes of your various feelings towards them, your friendships, your hatreds, your envyings, your fearings, etc., their conduct and feelings towards each other, their parties, the idols of the school, etc. Be always examining your own heart and your own mind, and endeavouring to describe in words your internal feelings. I think there is no boy in England who would not soon have something to say on any given subject if he did this, instead of going off to Alexander and Socrates, and to similes of lions, and hawks, and ships, and rivers, and, worse than all, to stupid scraps of Horace and Virgil; for mind, James, whenever you find a good thought in another writer do not quote it, but express it in your own words with some attempt at improvement. Keeping in view all these directions, I would advise you to use always some such plan as this, which is recommended by one of our greatest Oxford writers: Make the four parts of your theme the answers to these four questions. 1. What is the state of the case—how in what cases, in what feelings, in what men, etc. etc., is the thesis true? 2. What are the *causes?*—whence is it so? 3. What are the consequences of this being the case, of these feelings being indulged in, etc. etc.? 4. What *practical* conclusions can be drawn from what has been asserted in the three first parts? what causes of injury are to be repressed? what things apparently harmless are to be avoided on account of their consequences, etc. Or, to be brief, 1. What is the case? 2. Why or how is it? 3. What follows? 4. What then must I do? You will perhaps find some difficulty in applying this rule to all subjects—you can, I know, to most—but, pray, always ask yourself the questions. I would advise you also to attend to your prose more than your verse; prose is infinitely the more difficult of the two. I will give you a few rules which have frequently been given to me. Aim at diffuseness, and do not care if your Latin is twice as long as your English. In Latin always give the *connection* of the sentences, whether that connection mark the cause, or the consequences, or the confirmation, or the instance, etc. etc. Do this whether you find the connection expressed in the English or not, for remember that very frequently where we understand the connection the Romans express it. If you cannot find one Latin word to express your meaning, use several; avoid as much as possible using adjectives without their substantives, especially in the nominative case; for remember that a Latin author will scarcely ever use a nominative case when he can bring in any other, and will scarcely ever use an active verb when he can alter the construction so as to supply its place with a passive.

Be continually breaking your words in sentences, and using every circumlocution you can think of. Indeed, you will sometimes not be able to translate an English sentence into Latin without giving in the Latin a full-length definition of every English word. Avoid all abstract terms; I mean such as honesty, virtue, humanitas, etc.—at least it is safer to do so. Be particularly on your guard against being deceived by the similarity of Latin words to English; for instance, "vitiosius," which I find in your Latin does not generally mean "more vicious," but "more rotten," and "communius" does not mean "more frequent," but more equally common to certain persons. "Genus" means sex "in propria quæ maribus," but nowhere else. Then I entreat you use a dictionary as little as possible, and when you do look for a word be sure you know the exact meaning you want to represent.

My father says that you must not go by London, at least as you go to Oxford, as that will infallibly drive all your Latin out of your head. I think that is true. If you cannot see yourself how this can be the case, you must take your father's word and mine for it, for there are many things which are perfectly true which yet could not be explained to you.—Yours affectionately, THOMAS MOZLEY.

May 22, 1827.

DEAR TOM,—I received your letter this morning. You appear from your letter to think that I have learnt all those lines off by heart, but I assure you I have only learnt to construe them. I shall do what you advise about writing Latin, for I really wish to know how to write it very much. I should like to see a specimen of your composition; I don't think I ever have. I assure you I don't think learning such a trouble as you imagine. I think I'm very different from what I was in this respect, when two or three holidays ago I used to hate any kind of learning, and be always going after novels. I do a piece of Homer now with pleasure, except now and then when I'm rather impatient. You'll see how I shall fag when I get up to Oxford. . . . I wish you would put the sentence about going in a postscript by itself, that I may show it to Mr. Andrews, and there may be no fuss about it. Put it with mamma's and papa's authority, for I can tell you yours won't be enough with *him*. . . . I declare I don't like Andrews at all. Every time I construe to him, he tries to put me in a passion by mocking me, but I always take it very coolly, with a smile of scorn and disdain. You have no idea what a sensation I feel when I construe to him; to be mimicked and derided, I cannot bear, and I don't think any of our own family ever could. I think you will pardon me if I wish to get away as soon as possible.

Early in June he went up to Oxford; the result is told in the following letter:—

ORIEL, *June* 15, 1827.

DEAR MOTHER,—James has not got the scholarship, but I am sure you will, or at least ought to be, much better pleased with things as they are. There were seven candidates, all of them about 17 or 18. James had been several times praised by the examiner; I believe the only one who was. When the thing was settled this morning the examiner, on bringing the news to the successful candidate (one Overton of Louth school) who was standing among the rest waiting in the quadrangle, told James the President ("and Fellows," James desires me to say) wished to speak to him. James accordingly went into the chapel, where the President and Fellows were, when the President told him they had been much pleased with his examination, that he had passed the second best, and would certainly have been chosen but for his extreme youth; since, on account of the number of vacancies in the College, he would be obliged to reside immediately after Christmas, which they said would do him great harm. It would indeed be ridiculously young. They then told him there would be another vacancy for Lincolnshire in about two years, when they hoped he would try. James was, as you would perceive, the only one to whom this was said, and, from all that I hear, the examiners never reject any one whom they have advised to try again. This, you will see, is a far more convenient time than now, if, indeed, that be not rather too young.[1]

James returned to school after his trial at Corpus in a state of mind to find his life there more irksome than ever. His

---

[1] He did not, however, stand again for Corpus: there was no election at the time expected.

master seems to have shown a certain triumph in his disappointment, as we gather from the recollections of a schoolfellow; and was in a temper to exasperate his somewhat unsettled pupil. Mr. Andrews' letter to his parents at Christmas of that year greatly disconcerted his mother. His brother had written from Oxford:—" I hope you will not be troubled by Mr. Andrews' report of James, as I think it very probable that he either thinks ambition the best of all motives, or that he has not thought on the subject at all—and that if he cannot see anything in James to remark and to commend besides ambition, it is his fault, and not James's." The state of things was so unsatisfactory that Mrs. Mozley was exceedingly anxious for James's removal from Grantham. His father, who was disposed in all such matters to take the master's side,[1] and who might probably be unwilling to remove a clever boy from a school which had good exhibitions, was difficult to persuade. At length, however, it was settled to give notice of James's removal at Midsummer.

In later days James Mozley used to contrast the boy's return to school of modern days with his own remembrances. Never, however, making allusion to the troubles these letters reveal, only how miserable the winter journey and all connected with the return used to be. It is as showing the influence upon character of this trying period, the deepening and giving reality to life, that the following letters are given. The sight of Oxford and his brother's friends; success in the College examinations, as far as the examiners' approval went; the self-reliance and hopes thus received; a new sense of power and intellect imparted to the boy of thirteen, followed by all this school tribulation and the home anxieties attending it, told with force upon

[1] Mr. Andrews had been recommended by very competent authority to my father—though some years before this date—and his own experience of school had been a very happy one. He had been a favourite with his master the Rev. William Grey—afterwards Minor Canon of Lincoln, and had left school with regret when called away to the business of life.

him. Trouble realised and dwelt upon in childhood and early boyhood, where there is power to grasp it and dwell upon it, leaves indelible marks on the character and manner. It is to illustrate this that we have dwelt upon this period.

His sister Jane writes to him on his return to Grantham :—

DERBY, *February* 5, 1828.

MY DEAR JAMES,—Mamma is desirous that you should be written to, because she wishes you to write soon to say how you are going on. As you are in rather peculiar circumstances this half year, we wish to keep up a regular and frank correspondence, which I can tell you is the only way of making mamma tolerably easy, for she is very anxious about you, and it is only from your letters that she expects to have any comfort: let them, therefore, contain your genuine feelings and a candid account of your proceedings. I know that yours is no easy task. You have not only to keep a strict watch over yourself, but you have to bear the strictest and not always the most charitable scrutiny from your master. . . . He wrote a most indignant letter in answer to papa's notice for your removal at midsummer, and I expect he will be cold and harsh in his conduct to you; but let not this discourage you in a resolution, I was very happy to hear you had made before leaving home, to try to regain Mr. Andrews' good opinion. You must not mind your endeavours to this good end being misunderstood, as they may probably be; but persevere not only for your own but mamma's sake, who suffers on your account a degree of anxiety which hardly a life of duty and obedience on your part will repay. You do not, you never can, know how deeply you are indebted to her. What struggles she has had to go through for what she has conceived to be your good. Therefore you should bear a great deal for her sake alone, even setting aside other motives; do not disappoint her hopes which have always been sanguine that there was that in your character that would, with your maturing sense, overcome the selfwilledness and other faults which perhaps you are less aware of than those about you. I do not wish to tease you with a sermon, but I think it my duty to tell you there is this anxious feeling for you at home, and that you will probably be most narrowly watched at school. . . . Yours affectionately,

JANE MOZLEY.

James's answer follows in a few days:—

February 11, 1828.

DEAR JANE,—I received your letter last Wednesday, which I assure you gave me much comfort, and so far was I from thinking what you said a teasing lecture, that I thought upon everything you said, and determined to do, as far as laid in my power, everything you advised me. Mr. Andrews called me into the parlour Saturday before last, and told me what he had written to papa; it would be no use my recounting what he said, as you know, I suppose, what he wrote; but I have not passed many such miserable hours in my life as those which I passed after that. I was continually imagining and making conjectures of what his letter would cause at home, and what a hardened rebel I should be thought there. But most of all I feared the agitation it would cause mamma. I have said nothing more than what I felt; and very seldom were my feelings so much excited as they were then. I received papa's letter last night; tell him to be assured that I will do my best to gain Mr. Andrews' good opinion. I can say with truth that I have not any bitter feelings towards my master hitherto; and I hope I shall pass the whole half year as reconciled to him in my own mind as I am now. Tell mamma to be assured that I will restrain myself as far as is in my power. I daresay you think this an odd sort of a letter; but I feel as if the power of expressing what I felt was gone. I go on now as other boys do, and am treated in the same manner. I have nothing more to say.—I remain your affectionate brother,

J. B. MOZLEY.

FROM HIS MOTHER.

MY DEAR JAMES,—I hope you are going on well in all respects; I have been sadly troubled about you. Mr. Andrews' letter made me perfectly wretched, and I have scarce been well since; I cannot help being in constant fear of some new complaints. There is always much to dread when such tempers as yours and Mr. Andrews' come in contact. You must be constantly on your guard, and let the recollection that you have not to stay very long bear you up under any fancied ill-resentment. Your papa would scarcely ever forgive your being sent away from school, and, depend upon it, Mr. A. will not bear much from you, knowing, as he does, that you will leave him at the end of the half-year.

[A few days later he writes :]

February 18, 1828.

We had a letter from Tom yesterday; he has read another theme in Hall. He does not seem much disposed to give up writing them till he is obliged; I am afraid they will take him too much time. [This refers to the question of his reading for honours.] Your papa has had a letter from Mr. Parker, of Oxford. He mentions Tom. The Bishop of Llandaff asked Mr. Parker if his son knew Mr. Mozley, of Oriel; and then went on to praise him in the most unqualified manner; talked of all his acquirements, and, more particularly, his English composition. He said "it was not only superior to any *young* man's at Oriel at present, but superior to any he ever remembered there." You may be sure we were all highly delighted with this. Your papa seems to think more of it than of any thing of the kind he has ever met with. I must leave Maria to tell you all the home news, for I am very much engaged to-day. Hoping to hear a good account of you soon, I am, my dear James, your anxious mother, JANE MOZLEY.

James left Grantham in the summer of 1828. When Dr. Arnold was appointed to Rugby, his brother Tom advised his being sent to that school.

CHELTENHAM, *February* 10, 1829.

MY DEAR MOTHER,—You must be uneasy at not hearing from me about James, and are, perhaps, thinking of letters miscarrying, and such accidents; but I have not received a letter either from Mr. Joyce or Mr. Arnold, who opened the school in person yesterday week, and ought, therefore, to have written to me long since. I don't know in the least what to do; I had a long conversation with Mr. Newman about James the last time

I saw him, but he could give me no assistance whatever. He said that he had been placed in exactly the same dilemma when he was fifteen, and had been sent to College at that age, merely for want of a better means of disposing of him.

When Dr. Arnold did write to T. M. it was to decline his brother on account of his age. I recall the term used—"superannuated." James therefore remained at home, under the tuition of the Rev. James Dean, until he went to Oriel.

The year 1829 was marked by what was felt a great family event—my brother Tom's election to a Fellowship at Oriel.[1] One of the first acts of the new Fellow was to send for his brother James to stand for a Fellowship at Trinity, for which, however, he proved too young to stand. James reports, with characteristic easiness, that Tom, having not yet got rooms in College, gives up his bedroom at his lodgings to him, constructing a bed for himself out of an easy chair: "This he prefers to a regular bed; for, being left to his own devices, his mind, he says, is so easy and comfortable that he is apt to sleep longer than is quite proper." Tom, on his side, conveys to his mother his estimate of James's personal advantages—his growth and fine looks, in terms that cautiously veiled his admiration: "What a prodigious fellow James is grown! I think he is improved in appearance. He does not lounge or heave, or roll, or hulk quite as much as he did."

---

[1] His sister Jane was from home at the time. She acknowledged the letters which had brought her the news with characteristic appreciation of the honour of an Oriel Fellowship in those days, and disregard of mere pecuniary advantage. Two letters in the same hand had given her a moment's alarm: "The idea of good sudden news never occurred to me, so it was with much trembling that I opened the one that bore the greatest marks of haste. 'Any bad news?' asked Mr. H. and M. 'No, good;' but that was all I could say for a few minutes, and when I *did* say that my brother was elected Fellow of Oriel, they would doubtless wonder that I could be so transported, the magic of these words being unknown to them. Mr. H. very naturally asked what the Fellowship was worth—*worth!* I quite stared; hardly comprehending the connection of pounds, shillings, and pence with the high honour of an Oriel Fellowship."

May 18.—James reports that it is ascertained that he cannot stand at Trinity, sixteen to twenty being the ages for candidates to offer themselves :—

"Tom, however, says it was not so much for a scholarship that he sent for me, as that I might read with him. . . . I called on one of my Lincoln friends to-day, and heard rather a gloomy account of Grantham school. . . . The school is falling off, there being now only thirty boys, and many of those going to leave soon."

As a testimony to his school teaching, as well as his early ability, it should be noticed that James must have been forward in every way, as well as well grown; for I gather from a letter, dated December 9, 1829, that his brother was endeavouring to effect his admission to Oriel in the beginning of next term—at the time when James was sixteen years and three months old. He gives to his mother the details of a call on the Provost (Dr. Hawkins) on this subject, and the many difficulties he interposed, of which it does not seem that age was one. He had pleaded that, as he should be in residence in Oxford, his brother might be with him in the lodgings he occupied, before entering upon rooms in College.

December 9, 1829.

I talked over the matter afterwards to Newman, and when I had done he instantly said : "But don't you see, Mozley, what his objection was?" I thought for a moment, and then it suddenly occurred to me that my brother entering on such reasons implied that I should certainly be made a full Fellow. Newman said, of course it was; and told me a story of Froude going to the late Provost, while probationer, and asking for rooms, when the Provost (Copleston) repelled him with indignation, and fretted and fumed for weeks after. It is, I must acknowledge, of great importance to keep up these suppositions, or by and by the Fellows would scarcely be able to reject an unpleasant probationer. Term ends on the 14th; before which day all matriculations for next term must take place. I shall stay in Oxford till that day for the chance of a vacancy, and James must hold himself in readiness to start for Oxford at a moment's warning, though, I confess, I have not great expectations. I shall probably stay a few days further, as Sam Wilberforce is coming up for his ordination.

Bonamy Price has got, or rather at this moment is getting, his Double First with uncommon *éclat*.

The idea was given up—or came to nothing—and the brothers corresponded, T. M. sending James geometrical propositions to prove, which James returns:—

FROM HIS BROTHER, T. M.

March 24, 1830.

I fear it will cost you some labour before you can learn the art of Deduction. For I would have you to know that the geometrical practice I am giving you is but one particular kind of process, which you will constantly have, and use in all kinds of knowledge. You do not seem to feel (as far as I can judge from your three proofs) the necessity of referring accurately to certain truths already proved. This is a matter of great importance, both for confirming and rendering accurate in your memory what you have already learnt, and because in all exercises of this kind in Oxford, whether written or spoken, the utmost verbal accuracy is always required.

Then follow instances. To this letter James replies with a becoming humility, exercising upon himself the analytical vein which made his subsequent studies of character remarkable.

March 31, 1830.

MY DEAR TOM,—I write, though I have only one proposition prepared. The first proposition that you speak of in your letter is indeed very badly proved, as I saw afterwards when I looked at it. And what you say in general about the looseness and vagueness of my demonstrations, I think I understand now, though at first I could not. If a problem is regarded merely as a riddle to be explained (and that certainly is its most amusing form), vagueness and indistinctness of expression must follow. And, as it is very difficult to prevent this; particularly as I know little of Euclid. I have not sufficient knowledge of Euclid for it to be a separate department in my mind, so that it is mixed up with my powers of investigation in general. This looking upon propositions as riddles is no more than what I have to combat against in almost everything I do. It is seizing upon all the interesting eminences and outlines of a subject without caring much how I connect them together, and hoping to understand the whole by catching at the general spirit of the history. For in this sense a proposition may be called a history, as well as a narration of events. Both in history and mathematics, it is curiosity which causes all this haste and negligence.

James Mozley entered on his first term at Oriel, October 1830, when he was just 17 (his birthday, Sept. 15). His brother's letter that speaks of his plans, etc., contains a notice of the difference among the Oriel tutors, which was exciting attention.

T. M. TO HIS SISTER JANE.

ORIEL, *December* 3, 1830.

DEAR JANE,— . . . All sorts of rumours have gone abroad respecting the differences among the tutors, and it has received a most amusing variety of versions. It has been described as a strike for advance of wages or more pupils, which of course has fitted well into the probable falling off of the College consequent on the Heresy: at Tunbridge, a friend of Christie's was told, the junior Fellows had combined to turn out the Provost. For my part, I think it no more use trying to send abroad a correct account of it, for it is not easy to make it obvious to the meanest capacities, and everybody now-a-days seems to feel himself justified in contending that to be truest which is the most consonant to his understanding. Besides, it is not to be expected that any one, for the mere love of truth, should be knight-errant enough to fight with blockheads about a few tutors, when it would be much easier to amuse them with something brief, intelligible, and false.

Newman's mother and sisters have returned for the winter, and taken a cottage at Iffley; I met them last week at Whately's. James has ˈmade up his mind to go home at Christmas; . . . he will doubtless be more communicative in College matters now than six months hence, when the freshness will have faded from his mind. . . . I take it there is little doubt of H. Wilberforce being elected here [to Oriel] next year, for there is no one yet talked of as likely to stand to compare with him. He is considered almost sure of his double first, and as likely as any one to get the new Mathematical Scholarship next June.—Yours affectionately, T. M.

About this time my sister Jane's health became an anxiety and a leading family interest. The eldest daughter, born when her mother was nineteen, she was from the first a power in the family. Her clear bright intellect, love of study, and ready powers of argument, eager temperament, social charm, and grace of person and manner, all gave her influence in the home circle, and constituted her the "star" of the family among our friends. The Derby riots, in 1831, were a trial to nerve and health. I was up-stairs on the third floor with her when the roar of the advancing mob gave us a moment's warning, followed as it was by a shower of stones, dropping with heavy thud from step to step of the upper flight of stairs. The brothers down-stairs, closing shutters against the missiles pelting in, found the excitement amusing. James happened to be taking a walking tour in the Peak, and regretted the fun. Nobody was much frightened, except the mother, nervous for everybody; but a house open in its whole front to the chill October night air was ill suited for delicate chest and lungs, even for a night, and told upon the invalid. My brother Tom was really the object of the mob's wrath, as he has intimated elsewhere. After the Christmas vacation, spent at home, James returned to Oxford, and writes to his mother the current news on Church affairs :—

OXFORD, *February* 1832.

DEAR MOTHER,— . . . What do you think of R. Wilberforce being made Bishop of Calcutta? There is a rumour got afloat; I don't know what foundation there is for it. Tom says it is brought down by some Balliol man. There is nothing so very improbable about it. The Bishopric has generally had to go begging a considerable time before any one will take it, and now, with the example of three Bishops in succession dying, each within two years of his appointment, it is not probable that its attractions should have increased. Of course, for all the influence the situation has, ministers would not care whether they gave it to one of their friends or enemies. Besides, Lord Brougham has for a long time been toadying Mr. Wilberforce, and he would have a considerable share in the disposal of such preferment.

Bulteel is progressing; he has published an account of three miracles of his own performance. One of them was in the case of his own sister-in-law, Miss Sadler, who had been ill a long time from some nervous disorder that kept her to her bed. He effected her cure by constant praying, and now she is, I believe, in good health. There is nothing very wonderful in all this. The prayers were going on in the room next to hers, she being all the time aware of it, and every one knows the influence of imagination in such cases as hers, which seems to have been a mere fanciful disease, as she always had the external appearance of good health. I don't know the other two miracles. Bulteel's sincere belief is that there is a new system of things in the course of revelation now, as there was in our Saviour's time, and that God has given him the power of working miracles for the same reasons that He gave it to the apostles, in order to convince unbelievers. He has also in this book declared his belief in the miracles going on at Mr. Irving's chapel—the unknown tongues, etc. There can be little doubt that Bulteel is partially deranged: I should not be much surprised if, before long, he attempts miracles of a more obvious kind, as curing blindness. These absurdities of his may possibly work some good, as showing the state that men come to when they choose to cast off all restraint. One man who used to be a constant attendant at his church, abuses him now without the smallest hesitation. . . . Dornford has expressed great indignation at the report about Wilberforce, and talks about juniors and seniors and undue exaltation, etc. Froude, the Fellow, is at home with a very bad cough.

The subject of the following letter relates to an affair of great parochial interest connected with the law of pews, in which my father had been concerned, and into which my brother Tom had thrown himself with ardour :—

TO HIS BROTHER.

OXFORD, *May* 9, 1832.

DEAR TOM,—Henry Wilberforce only went away this morning, so that I have been able to see something of him. . . . One subject that we hit upon is rather interesting to us. He immediately asked me whether you had been writing a strong pamphlet against the Bishop of L. and C. I knew pretty well to what he was alluding, but I was considerably surprised at the matter having got to his ears. However, he quickly let me know that he was acquainted with the grounds of the remonstrance, the arrangement of the pews, and the parochial quarrelling that had followed. It seems he had been dining at the Bishop's, where the subject had incidentally been brought out—I don't know by whom. The Bishop, he said, had acknowledged himself to have been in error. The notion they had about the authorship was that you had written one half and my father the other. Ryder had read it through, and he came to this decision. The first part he attributed to you, because it dealt so much in general principles, and also bore some similarity to what he knew of your style of writing. He had liked it very much, on the whole. Wilberforce asked me point blank how much was written by you. This was rather a hard, driving question; I made rather a bungling answer. He wished very much to see the pamphlet, and thought my father might as well send him one. I had one in my desk all the while, but as I did not know how far I might venture to lose

sight of it, I did not say anything about it.—Yours affectionately,
J. B. M.

Two months later his letters are full of the election for the Sanscrit Professorship, for which Mill and Wilson were candidates.

TO HIS SISTER.

March 9, 1832.

Newman, Keble, Ogilvie, Pusey of Christ Church, are all indefatigable in their labours for Mill. The contest will be a very hard-run one, and whoever succeeds will get it by a few votes. I have all this from Newman. By the by—[the passage is given not in the least for its truth, but as reporting the undergraduate impression of ladies, at all out of the common routine in intellectual pursuits and advantages]—Newman is going to introduce me to his mother and sisters. The Miss Newmans are very learned persons, deeply read in ecclesiastical history, and in all the old divines, both High Church and Puritanical. But notwithstanding this they are, I believe, very agreeable and unaffected. In fact, to have such a brother as Newman is a sufficient pledge of their carrying off their learning well. I walked out with Newman the other day, and had a great deal of talk, as you may expect, on things in general—political events, political men, political aims. I see more of him now than ever I did. I read an English theme in Hall yesterday. The subject was *Curis acuens mortalia corda*, which means "Sharpening with care the minds of men." I wrote chiefly on civilisation. You may not perhaps at first exactly see the connection, but when taken with its context it is very much that subject. The word 'civilisation' has a very political appearance about it, but of course while *in statu pupillari* we do not meddle with politics in public exercises. . . .

Some most puritanical-looking pamphlets have come out lately in the Balliol controversy; one against Bulteel, from one of his former friends, is entitled, "A hard nut to crack," and an answer has come out, "The Nut-cracker."

Early in 1832 his brother Tom had engaged himself to Mr. Round's curacy at Colchester. James writes that he had shown his letter to Mr. Newman, who was always anxious that his friends be up and doing:—

"I saw Newman to-day; he is very well pleased with Tom's curacy, and thought it would do him a great deal of good. He was particularly amused with his having to write two sermons a week."

Colchester, however, little suited my brother Tom's health; the work, into which he threw himself with great ardour, and the climate, and other things combined, reducing him presently to such a state that doctor and vicar were equally thankful to send him off to Teignmouth; where his eldest sister had been taken by her mother, to try the benefit of the famed Devonshire air. He looked like death when he came —that is, as if he had come to die, and at once recovered health and strength as by a miracle.[1]

---

[1] No such wonders were worked for the invalid for whose sake the journey was undertaken, though there was such amendment as led to the hope that a favourable turn had been taken. James had been anxious that the occasion should be used as an opportunity of seeing Oxford on the route. "I shall have the greatest pleasure in lionising you." It was thought best to take Oxford on the return journey—a delightful arrangement for Jane, but one that tried her strength more than she expected. The short entries in her Diary show the effort it was to her. Yet it cannot be regretted that she was by this means brought acquainted with the Newman family, and that thus a link connects her with the new influence which had such an effect on the family life; though Jemima, Mrs. Newman's second daughter, soon to be one of us, happened not to be then at home. Our party was most kindly received by Mrs. and Miss Newman, as well as by our brother's friends; all showing the mother in what high regard and value her sons were held. As a testimony to the singular personal influence of the two friends whose names were then associated, and the effect their look and bearing made on observers, I give a little extract from my sister's diary:— "*Saturday, July* 7.—Newman and Froude to breakfast. Striking entrance, the whole not to be described." The introduction of two gownsmen of such marked individuality, such unconscious dignity of aspect, with a sort of historical look about them, very naturally made its impression on ladies to whom everything was new and inspiring, who were the more open to impression for not having been prepared for this greatness of aspect. Others, no doubt, read in Jane's looks more than we, who were thinking of her as on the way to recovery. Much feeling was shown. The last entry, recording the kindness of my brother's friend, Mr. Christie, ends, "All soon followed—tea, and pleasant talk of Wordsworth—always repent of what I say. —Farewells: all seems now over in Oxford." She might have written

The following letter to me from my brother Tom, now in charge of Moreton Pinkney, bears on the state of things he has elsewhere described as immediately preceding the movement of 1833 :—

T. M. TO A. M.

ORIEL COLLEGE, *December* 22, 1832.

MY DEAR ANNE,—They are all here making up their minds to expect the very worst things. There seems no difference of opinion between Whigs and Tories as to what is coming—they are only blaming one another with having brought it on. The measure of Church Reform drawn up by Brougham and Lushington is to go beyond the expectation of all parties— it is to be a measure of *equalisation* embracing as one of its *least important parts* a change in the manner of collecting the ecclesiastical revenues. Ministers mean to keep it to themselves till ready, and throw it out to be carried by popular clamour without any alteration being allowed—in the idle hope (or rather pretence) that it is to be a "final measure." The Bishops have been met some time at Lambeth about it, and it seems generally understood that they are even more unanimous and decided than about the Reform Bill. They are most of them prepared, if it seems fit to the leading ones, and occasion seems to require, to resign their offices—and this they would be glad to do before they are embarrassed and stultified by concessions. The Whigs in London are quite horrified at the result of the Irish elections. In all *Ireland* there has not been one returned on their side. They are all Repealers or Conservatives. Now, of course, the Repealers will be glad to support the ministers in every work of destruction.

The opening of the year 1833 was saddened by the death of Jane Mozley, which took place in February. Shortly after, James Mozley escorted her devoted friend, who had passed

further, "All is now over for me of general intercourse with society," for few more opportunities for conversation with new and fresh minds were allowed her. The last seven months of her life were spent in her own room—first as a precaution, then as a necessity.

several weeks with her, back to her home. From thence he writes of meeting a leading, active member of the Liberal party, expressing himself at 19, with a strength which amusingly contrasts with his guarded, tolerant tone of later years, towards those who differed from him in opinion, wherever difference of opinion admitted of indulgent construction.

April, 1833.

DEAR MARIA,— . . . This reminds me that I must tell you something about Mr. ——. . . He is a regular built modern London barrister, and march-of-mind man, profoundly indifferent to exclusive systems of belief, withal very conceited. I suppose, however, he is a clever man; he has a good deal of humour and some wit, and plenty of anecdote and conversation; he has breakfasted here once, and dined twice. He is, as you may have heard, a friend of Lord Brougham's, and an active member of the Useful Knowledge Society. This intimacy with Brougham evidently gives him great satisfaction. . . . Tom Macaulay is another intimate friend of his, some of whose good stories he has given us; "very lucky man that Macaulay; he lives a great deal with the saints, and has capital things to tell of them." Can you imagine anything more disgusting than this style of thing? Here are these men who before the world cry up the saintly party as the only religious people in the kingdom, and who really think they are so, turning them to ridicule in their own private circle. Mr. —— knew Arnold, and has been acquainted with his schemes for some time. Arnold, he thinks, is one of the boldest men in the kingdom. His scheme of Church Reform, however, being this, is not practicable at present. There is not sufficient religious feeling in the country to carry it. Did you ever hear humbug equal to this? . . . Yours affectionately,

J. B. M.

Here these introductory pages come to a natural conclusion, the date of the last letter showing us to be on the verge of the Oxford movement, with its rapidly maturing influences.

LETTERS.

THE stir of thought which issued in the Oxford movement had already told on James Mozley. His interests were Church interests. The return of Mr. Newman from abroad, Mr. Keble's [1] Assize Sermon, and the Tracts which followed in due course, kindled in him, as in so many ardent minds, a zeal which found expression as it could. All who felt with the chief actors in the movement were admitted to the privilege and charm of their confidence, and derived energy from their example. The letters all report progress, and show one predominant interest.

OXFORD, *July* 12, 1833.

DEAR TOM,—Newman has at last come, and is looking very well, much better than when he went, and considerably tanned with his exposure to the southern sun. He landed at Brighton from Dieppe, and reached Oxford on Thursday. Frank

---

[1] In James Mozley's family the *Christian Year* had long been a household book. His brother T. M. had sent it, soon after its publication, to his sister Jane, with these words: "I should wish much that you would give a little study to the book I enclosed in the parcel. Study, perhaps, is too harsh a word, and savours too much of the dry critic. But, pray, do something or other with the book, and then tell me what you think of it. You may, with safety, declare any judgment you like, for I do not know poetry on which there are such various opinions. Some think it will outlive all other human poetry whatever, others that it will be unheard of fifty years hence; some think it simple, others far-fetched; some think it only requires a little pure feeling for the most unlearned to enter into it, others that it is utterly unconstruable to every one, and probably to the author himself; some think it breathes the pure spirit of 'our dear Mother Church,' others that it bears the 'mark of the Beast.' But if I would attempt to tell you all that has been or can be said concerning it, I must take up Johnson's Dictionary and go right through it, taking every epithet and coupling it with its opposite.—ORIEL, *May* 2, 1828."

Newman arrived the same day—a singular coincidence. It was only by a most fortunate train of accidents that Newman was able to come as soon as he did. The coaches from Paris to all the ports from which there are steamers to England were full. And if one of the passengers to Dieppe had not happened to vacate his place, he would have been detained some two or three days. By several pieces of good luck like this, he has travelled almost continuously the whole of the way from Palermo. Though looking well now, he was ill for a considerable time in Sicily. He stayed three weeks at Palermo waiting for a vessel to Marseilles, and dreadfully tired he was of the place. The Sicilian language is a dialect of Italian, but so different, that it was almost unintelligible to him. There were only three or four English residents there, and those merchants, fully occupied with their business, so that though they were very civil to him, and asked him to dinner and so on, yet by far the greater part of his time was spent in complete solitude. There were no books for him to read, none at least that were at all interesting to him. The English are very much looked up to there, both from the idea the Sicilians have of their wealth, and from gratitude for their conduct in the late war. Froude has just told me that Newman was most *dangerously* ill in Sicily, of a violent epidemic fever. At the time he was taken ill with it, there was no medical aid at hand. By one of those singular caprices which people in fevers sometimes take up, he fancied himself able to walk some way—he did walk a few miles, till he completely sank down, and was carried into a hovel. While lying there a physician happened to go past, and by his care he was so far recovered as to be able to reach the next town, where he got regular medical advice. But his life was still almost given up for three or four days. Perhaps the illness, on the whole, may have done him good. Slight weakness is all that now remains. . . . You will now think of coming up. Newman, now that he is once back, does not intend to leave Oxford in a hurry, so all his friends who wish to see him, must come to Oxford. Perhaps you'd as well come in harvest-time, as that seems, by all accounts, to be a time when clergymen can do nothing in their parishes. Newman wishes to see you very much.—Yours affectionately, JAMES MOZLEY.

TO HIS SISTER.

OXFORD, *Sept.* 3, 1833.

With this letter you will receive a considerable number of tracts, the first production of the Society established for the dissemination of High Church principles. Of course you have heard of this new thing set up. If I recollect right, however, Froude's letter was written at the first starting, not that there is much additional news to tell you about it; we must be content to wait patiently the effects of agitation. Answers, however, have been received from some quarters, and on the whole favourable. Keble has heard from Davison, the writer on the Prophecies—a great name, by far the most talented, I should think, of the old school of Oriel lights. He approves of the thing, though how far he is ready to go I have not heard. Then Ogilvie, he is a great addition, for his approbation implies that of the Archbishop too—it being a rule with him never to advocate any opinion or any proceedings which at all disagree with the Archbishop's views. So scrupulous indeed is he on this point, that he has narrowly escaped being classed with the timid party; by the timid party, meaning not those who are willing to concede, but those who are afraid to make a stir. The Archbishop [Howley] is thought here to be a man of first-rate principle, and one who would rather lay his head upon the block than commit himself to a connivance at a single unchristian measure which our present legislators may choose to adopt; but he has also been thought too deficient in active courage, to take an important part in public affairs. Perhaps he will show better when it comes to,—and Ogilvie joining himself is a good sign. Then Rose too has sent in his attachment to the cause; he will be a most valuable member, and will puff and blow about it in fine style in the *British Magazine* when the Society is fairly established. But for the present you must remember all these details I have been going through are secret.

What do you think?—you will accuse me of vast imprudence and perhaps impertinence, but—I have sent a sheet of Tracts to Mr. M. N., communicating to him at the same time the news of the formation of the Society, and asking him what he thinks as to the advantage of such publications being distributed. . . . The fact is, we must not be very scrupulous as to views or particular as to sentiments in the distribution of these things. Newman heard from Froude the other day. He was in high spirits when he wrote. His theory, he said, as to Parliament having been a lay synod before the repeal of the Test Act, and being now therefore completely changed in its constitution with respect to the Church, took very well. . . . You ought to know, by the by, that Newman is the writer of all the tracts I send you; Keble has written two, but they are not printed. Of Newman's things the two most important, as you will perceive, are the one on Ordination, and the one on Irish affairs. . . . Yours affectionately, JAMES MOZLEY.

In acknowledging the packet of Tracts his sister asks who is to distribute them; and adds, "it answers more my views of the Society, to circulate them all through the clergy. Therefore Mr. Dean has had nearly all ours."

OXFORD, *September* 20, 1833.

MY DEAR ANNE,—We muster rather strong at present in Oriel. Tom, Golightly, Blencowe are up, and Marriott has been up, but is now gone. You know, of course, what the meeting is about—the new Society. I cannot say, however, that this particular subject has been much talked about, or that anything new has been proposed, or that any more form and system has been given to the Society than it had before. However, it is something gained if people see one another, and discuss general topics that bear on the particular one. Actual business, it must be confessed, goes on rather slowly; but this must always be at the *commencement* of any work. The manifesto is not yet published, and perhaps may not be for some time. It is now undergoing Rose's examination. Keble's Tract, too, has only just come out; and I know it was in the press more than a week ago. When the former is printed I will send it you, together with some more Tracts, as you say more are wanted. What do people about you say of the style of these Tracts of Newman's? Blencowe says that some to whom he has shown them think it rather affected—I suppose from the sentences being so short, and so often interrogatory. One is not very much surprised at this in people who don't know Newman. Not that there is any ground for the charge of affectation, but the style is certainly singular, if one reads them (the Tracts) without bringing in one's personal knowledge of Newman.[1] X. finds some fault with them on these accounts, and says they look exactly like literal translations of the epistles of the Apostolical Fathers—but this is X.'s way. I don't believe he is thoroughly satisfied with anything throughout, except his own, of which he has very considerable admiration. He is an uncommonly good fellow, nevertheless, with all his conceit, and is now so brisk and active, arguing and unfolding his sentiment, and laying down the law in the most amusing manner. I don't know how it is, there is nothing in his conceit that at all offends one. It suits him so well, and is in such beautiful proportion with the rest of his character, that one would clearly pronounce him deficient in something or other if he was without it. He has been corresponding, as I told you, with a clergyman in Ireland, who turns

---

[1] This question on the subject of style was answered at once:—

"*September* 23, 1833.

"DEAR JAMES,— ... . It is both singular and disappointing that I have heard no remarks upon the style or contents of the pamphlets themselves. Mr. Dean and Mr. P. [the two active agents] seem to know what they are about, and, I suspect, put off the trouble of reading to a more favourable opportunity. Perhaps I ought not to say Mr. Dean; but I know Mr. P. does. One person, but I don't know who, said, I believe, that the style was not like Newman's, thereby showing he knew nothing about it; for it is, I think, most characteristically like him. He enters upon his subject in the first Tract—'I am but one of yourselves—a Presbyter; and, therefore, I conceal my name, lest I should take too much on myself by speaking in my own person. Yet speak I must; for the times are very evil, yet no one speaks against them'—with the same humble, quiet manner with which he enters a room before one is aware. I understand quite what Mr. X. means; there is certainly something uncommon in it; but this, I think, is a recommendation, as it excites attention." The letter goes on to protest against some strong language James, in the ardour of partisanship, had used towards Mr. N. M., a gentleman who had protested against Keble's sermon: "It is not from a man with such a training that you ought to expect much, and, therefore, you should not be angry when he merely acts as he might be expected to act."

out to be Mr. Magee, who has just written that address to the clergy of Waterford. It is an extraordinary coincidence (as he has fully impressed upon me) that this address was written at the very time that X.'s letter reached him, recommending that very proceeding. He read to me the other day the answer he received—a very noble and affectionate letter—though complaining, perhaps, rather too much of the apathy of the English clergy. What he says is very true; but the Irish clergy have made of their own accord most culpable concessions to Government, and so have themselves chiefly to blame, if their order falls into contempt. . . . I read some of N. M.'s letter to Newman, and he was far from setting him down as a hopeless case. Newman now is becoming perfectly ferocious in the cause, and proportionately sanguine of success.[1] "We'll do them," he says, at least twenty times a day—meaning, by "them," the present race of aristocrats, and the Liberal oppressors of the Church in general.

He is now in London superintending, I suppose, the publication of his book [*The Arians*], which is now printed. I have read a page of it here and there, as the proof-sheets came down. Full half of it is introduction, which is advantageous on the whole, as it touches on subjects which will soon come under public discussion—creeds and articles, etc. Parts of it are exceedingly hard to understand, owing to the subtlety of the Arian doctrines, and consequently of the orthodox answers to them.

The declaration of the Society is at last printed, but not published. Before that takes place it has to undergo innumerable criticisms, in addition to the six weeks' discipline and correction it was subject to before it was printed. It is completely different from the one originally proposed by Keble—a copy

---

[1] This passage curiously illustrates the description the author of the *Apologia* gives of his state of mind at this precise date: "My behaviour had a mixture in it both of fierceness and sport. They [certain acts] were the fruit of that exuberant and joyous energy with which I had returned from abroad, and which I never had before or since. I had the exultation of health restored and home regained. . . . I was amid familiar scenes and faces once more. And my health and strength came back to me with such a rebound that some friends at Oxford on seeing me did not well know that it was I, and hesitated before they spoke to me."

of which, I suppose, Tom sent you—and not half so interesting, though, I suppose, much more prudent. Mr. Hook, of Coventry, I believe, has had the chief hand in it. Then Rose, Palmer, Ogilvie, and a dozen more besides, have had a finger. Many cooks spoil the broth. People should remember that there is one important question which cannot but considerably affect the usefulness of the most prudent and nicely balanced publications—*i.e.* whether it will be read or not. Of course this single manifesto, being a dry affair, is not of much consequence. But a question has been raised whether *all* the tracts that come out in the Society's cause ought not to be the production of a committee, or at any rate be submitted to their alterations. Newman is against the theory, on the very obvious principle that intense stupidity cannot fail to be the principal quality of publications sent out under such circumstances. . . . There is—Tom has of course told you—a synod to be held here in the middle of November; it is particularly important that as many as possible should attend. If you want any more tracts I will send you plenty. You need not be so over-scrupulous as to the way of distributing them. Laymen are not excluded from having a voice in the Society—far from it. It is important that this should be understood.

To his Sister.

February 1, 1834.

My dear Anne,—The election of the Chancellor took place on Wednesday, and went off, as was expected, without opposition. As usually happens, however, on such occasions, people are now making up for their inactivity beforehand, by grumbling at what *has* been done. They say now that the Duke certainly was not the man—they have been taken by surprise. The Liberals declare they've been cheated, and many of them, Denison among others, affirm that they would have preferred the Archbishop, so the end of it is, nobody is satisfied. It really seems a great pity the Archbishop was not proposed. The majority of the country clergy would certainly have voted for him. However, when Keble and Newman put his name forward privately, which they did, some little time ago, it was received with such coolness that no blame can attach to them for not having pursued the thing further, though many now begin to ask, Why did not you propose the Archbishop? ... I don't know whether Newman told you, when he was at Derby, that he was going to stand for the Moral Professorship; he is, and has a tolerable chance of success if things go on as they are—for at present he is the only candidate.

The Duke of Wellington was always an interesting study to James Mozley. He liked to detect traits of nature in the great man, through all the ceremonial to which his greatness subjected him.

To his Sister Maria.

February 15, 1834.

My dear Maria,—. . . The chief subject of news that I can think of at present, is the Chancellor's official dinner-party in London, some of the details of which I have heard from those present. The Duke, I believe, cut rather an extraordinary figure in his Chancellor's gown, which is a very stiff and academical kind of robe, and which, moreover, had been made rather too long for him. However, he performed his part to the satisfaction of the company, and only made one false quantity on delivering his Latin speech, which was a very good one, and quite to the purpose, though it is conjectured, from various circumstances, that Dr. Bliss, the Registrar of the University, had a good deal more to do with the composition of it than his Grace. Some judges of character who were present are of opinion that the Duke, though a most inflexible person in his *general course* of conduct, does not carry his coolness at his fingers' ends in the way many great men do; since in the delivery of his speech he betrayed something not unlike confusion and awkwardness, and on one occasion addressed himself in energetic language to a servant who had made a mistake about a bottle of wine. The Duke had all his presentation plate on the table, as well as the Dresden China which the King of Prussia had given him. . . . So far so good. The only blotch in the whole affair was the presence of the Duke of Cumberland, who made no scruple of swearing every other word he said; and moreover subverted the order of etiquette by *himself* proposing the Chancellor's health, which properly belonged to the Vice-Chancellor to do. Lord Eldon was present in great force, and quite unable to abstain from talking about his consistency, while complimenting Dr. Kidd in a very short but enthusiastic speech, which no one understood till it was over. Lord Eldon is coming down with the Duke to the Installation at the end of next term. Oxford, I suppose, will be more gay than it has ever been since the visit of the Allied Sovereigns.

It is generally thought that the Church is looking up again. A year ago Ministers put forward definite designs against Church property. All these seem to have vanished. Articles are appearing in Radical journals proving that the House of Commons, reformed as it is, is fast losing its authority; and that when a party now has anything to accomplish, it does not address itself to the House of Commons, but to the public. The address to the Archbishop is *not* given as an instance of this, which is rather unfair; for it is in its more general character an unequivocal instance of a cause being effectually strengthened without any communication with the governing powers. Newman was closeted the other day two hours with Dr. Routh of Magdalen, receiving his opinions as to his work, which were very complimentary. Kaye, Bishop of Lincoln, has had a correspondence with Rose about it, particularly on the point of the *Disciplina arcani*, which is a subject the Bishop himself, Newman thinks, has touched in certain letters in the *British Magazine,* signed "Philalethes Cantabrigiensis." . . . Yours affectionately, J. MOZLEY.

It must have been after the two hours' colloquy mentioned in this letter, that Dr. Routh used to speak of that "clever young gentleman of Oriel, Mr. Newman."

TO HIS SISTER.

OXFORD, *March* 15, 1834.

Newman is *not* Moral Philosophy Professor, as you will probably have seen by the papers. Hampden offered himself the very day before the election; and, being a Bampton Lecturer, and an Aristotelian, and a Head of a House, and a Liberal, and, moreover, a stupid man in his way, he was of course the successful candidate. It is a pity the thing has turned out so, if it was only for the title-page of Newman's volume of sermons, which has just come out. Of course you will get it, if you haven't already.

The new Marriage Bill is making rather a stir here; Newman and all his party declare it to be quite unecclesiastical to give out the intention of certain people to enter into a purely civil ceremony during divine service, and in church. A small meeting was held to discuss the subject in Newman's room last night, at which it was resolved to get up a petition against it; and Harrison of Christ Church (the English Essay when you were at Oxford), has been intrusted with the wording of it. I see from a letter of Tom's to Christie, that John is thinking of something of the kind at Derby. It seems to me to be *just* the thing to petition about. It gives so little satisfaction to any party, that almost anything would upset it. Indeed Lord J. Russell has almost said as much. I suppose none of you think of coming to Oxford at the Commemoration. Newman has suggested to me one of my brothers coming. As Charles was invited at Derby, I should think this invitation of Newman's alludes more particularly to him. What does Charles say to it? The proposal, in my humble opinion, is not to be sneezed at. I dined at the Newmans' the other day—very pleasant; music, etc. etc. We had a splendid sermon from Sewell, of Exeter College, at the assizes, on the Origin of Evil. Not one person in the church understood one sentence of it. Sewell had threatened his friends with a metaphysical discourse on that occasion. According to M——'s definition it certainly was sufficiently metaphysical, and that was the only sense in which any one in the church could be sure it was so. Half the University are going up for Firsts. I am most unfortunate in my time. I have now got into that swing of reading, that if I had half a year before me, I think I could almost make myself sure of my first. I am conceited enough to think this. But it is a *very* different case when one has only a few weeks. After three years of idleness it is very long before one can chain one's-self down to a fixed course of reading. To be sure, you will say I ought not to have been idle; very true. —Yours affectionately, . J. B. MOZLEY.

TO HIS BROTHER JOHN.

OXFORD, *June* 16, 1834.

MY DEAR JOHN,—The installation has passed off very well. The only mistakes being the Duke's false quantities, which were treated very indulgently. The Duke himself, whether it was that his face was lighted up by the joyfulness of all about him, or whether he looked as he always does, I don't know; but his face had certainly a much kinder expression about it than I had expected to see. I should say that, dressed in a Court dress of black, with his Chancellor's robe on him, he was the most respectable-looking old gentleman I ever saw—not to mention any loftier qualities. He has a face that would suit any situation and character. In lawn sleeves, I have no doubt, he would look the most episcopal person on the Bench. He was evidently sometimes much affected by the enthusiastic cheering he met with, if one can gather anything from a certain tremulous motion in the mouth, which is a very sensitive part. The cheering, by the by, was more tremendous than anything I ever heard. The theatre was like a bell going. We all of us, of course, sported the most correct principles on the occasion. We hissed, groaned, and laughed at Dissenters, Whigs, Lord Grey, and his family in office. The people from London must have been astonished at finding themselves in a Tory mob. The feeling displayed will probably influence many in their votes in the House. One M.P. present, who voted a month ago for the Dissenters' Bill, has declared that, seeing the strong feeling in the University against it, he shall consider himself justified in not continuing to give it his support. The Duke, at a dinner at St. John's on Thursday, said that what he had seen here had put the thing in a new light to him; upon which the Duke of Cumberland stood up and said that he was glad to hear the Duke make such an avowal, as he was a person always to follow up what he had said. The Duke of Cumberland is the most grisly monster I ever set eyes on. He is fearful to behold. No wonder such odd stories get about him, like ghost stories about a gloomy house. He was well received, however, and I was glad of it. Old Lord Eldon was in the theatre the second day.

Henry Wilberforce has gone down with Tom to Moreton Pinkney, for two or three days. . . . Froude is staying at Barbadoes, and going on very well there. . . . Yours affectionately,
JAMES MOZLEY.

In the Long Vacation of 1834, James was one of a reading party, so called, in Wales, under Mr. Mitchell of Lincoln College, and writes home,—where Miss Newman was then paying her first visit,—at the close of his stay:—

To HIS SISTER.

September 12, 1834.

MY DEAR ANNE,—I am very happy to feel myself, with Tom, the joint cause of keeping Miss Newman amongst you a few days longer than she might otherwise have stayed. It has been raining here almost continuously for the last month, and the harvest is all but ruined. . . .

The gaiety of A. has at last come to an end, much to the disgust of many of our party, who now intend leaving as soon as possible. I intend leaving this day three weeks and going straight to Oxford. The gaiety has terminated chiefly from want of people to carry it on. Such has been the zeal of all, that I don't think any other cause could have stopped it. But the beauties of the place, the two Miss C.s, left yesterday. Two other beauties from C. are leaving to-day, besides numerous other departures. Things now look like Oxford in the Long Vacation. The Cambridge men, I think, I once told you, were remarkable for their matrimonial tendencies on expeditions of this kind; well, they have carried off the palm this year, though they are only two to our ten; . . . at least so it is reported on the best authority, though nobody knows how they intend to manage after the fatal stroke, for neither of them possess an atom of money. On Tuesday there was an evening party at Mrs. ——'s, which was to be a kind of break up, all intending to leave the next morning. Two of our party, who were favoured with an invitation, declared that towards the close of the evening the scene became quite affecting; absolutely tears, pocket-handkerchiefs, and everything that could be desired on such an occasion. Wednesday being a rainy day, none left—so there was a second winding up at Mrs. ——'s, to which we *all* went, myself amongst them. We had no second edition of the tears, but we nevertheless had a very pleasant evening and very good singing.... Yours affectionately,

J. MOZLEY.

This reading party was in preparation for the final examination, which resulted in a great disappointment. A *first* was what was reasonably hoped for; nothing less than a second could be contemplated, and a third was the upshot.

FROM HIS SISTER.

FRIARY, *November* 30, 1834.

MY DEAR JAMES,—I hope you don't break the seal with any apprehension of a home lecture coming upon you as a sort of appendix to your present mortification. I write because I feel tempted to give you my sympathy as soon as possible, and to assure you that some of us at least are not "immeasurably disgusted" with what we must consider your failure. It would have been an injustice to you not to feel very considerably disappointed at first, because I think that both from your reading and natural abilities we had a right to expect more from you; but the battle is not always to the strong, even supposing you were well prepared, and as Tom always lays the blame of any failure on the whole family, not on the individual, I suppose I must console you by saying that the family genius is not made for examinations; being too slow and deliberate—unable to call up its resources at a moment's warning. I shall, however, indeed be **very** angry with you if you allow yourself to despond on this, and do not rather consider this ill-success as a proof of the necessity for greater system and method in your reading.

My view is (but you may very justly think I know nothing about it) that you ought to read next year as much as you have done this last, and with more method, and then you may still have a good chance for a Fellowship, on which you know I had always fixed my affections for you.

December 1.

I wrote so far last night. . . . I find I have not mentioned either papa or mamma. You can guess, just as well as I can tell, their feelings on the occasion. Mamma said she had a right to feel very much disappointed at first, because she knew that in a day or two she should get over it and think no more about it. Papa is not very fond of talking on the subject, but he will, very cheerfully, on any other, and fell asleep after dinner just as comfortably as usual. So, on the whole, things are rather better than I expected. . . . Yours affectionately,

A. M.

To this letter is appended a little postscript, from a younger sister: " My love to you—though you are floored.—F. M."

To his Sister.

Oxford, *December* 4, 1834.

I have now received full and particular accounts of my third from different sources, all quite authentic. Cox, one of the examiners, told Christie that on Friday night (the class list came out on Saturday afternoon) my name was definitely down on the Second Class list. One might fancy that a settlement at so late an hour was surely a final one. However, the next morning it occurred to them that there were some men in the second class very little inferior to those in the first, and that, therefore, it was not fair to them that mine, with some other names, should appear with theirs. Accordingly the next morning they sent for me again, and gave me a piece of Latin. If I had been quick over it, it all would have been right. As it was, from natural slowness, together with being considerably fagged with the former day's work, and also an over-anxiety about being correct, the *viva voce*, too, dinging in my ears all the time, I am free to confess, as M.P.s say, that I was a very considerable time about it—more than three hours.¹

This passage is given to illustrate that "slowness" which, under certain trying conditions (only), was a characteristic of his mind, and which told against him in examinations.

February 16, 1835.

MY DEAR ANNE,— . . . Newman is particularly desirous of having some pamphlet on Suffragans written, and caused Dr. Burton to be sounded on the subject the other day. Burton, however, did not see it—he had written pamphlets enough, he thought. Burton has some reason to be cautious, as he is within an ace of a bishopric; as he *is*, he is just of all others, the man for the present Ministry—respectable, but not very strong. Newman does not write himself, because he thinks a pamphlet does no good without a name, and he is modest enough to think that his own is not sufficiently weighty. Rose has taken Arnold under his peculiar protection. In an appendix to his Durham lectures, he bestows several pages of comment on Arnold's advice to young clergymen, appended to his third volume of sermons. Arnold's advice goes to discarding all controversial works, which, he insinuates, have proceeded for the most part from men of "feeble and prejudiced minds," and substituting in their place Bacon and Aristotle, and such writers as expand the intellect.

. . . [After a list of names of men engaged to be married] Froude himself is beginning to joke about matrimony. He says in a letter to Christie, "There's nothing left for you and

---

¹ The following sentence, in a letter from home, shows that he did not allow his disappointment to weigh too strongly on him :—

"*December* 3, 1834.

". . . I think you have done wisely to set about something new; as fresh hopes, and objects of interest, reconcile one to the past more than all the thinking in the world. I am quite ready to believe all said about the examiners and their system, though I shall abstain from talking to other people of the reasons that have prevented your succeeding as you ought to have done; because the world is apt to put its own construction on the most profound reasoning that can be brought forward on such occasions. Mamma wants you to come home as soon as you have got all you wish out of your great folios."

me but to marry; for a wife sticks to you, but a friend may cut and run." This is a conclusion to certain complaints about friends not writing to him. He was heard from a few days ago. I read his letter to Newman; the first part is somewhat desponding, but he recovers his spirits toward the end. His cough, though not entirely gone, has gone off considerably. . . .

The Cambridge undergraduates have subscribed and made up a prize for the best account of Coleridge's System of Philosophy, open to the whole world. We here look certainly very small in comparison with such great doings. I had Hamilton to my rooms the other day; he is acquainted with many Cambridge men, and says their opinion of Oxford is, that we are gentlemanly, but shallow. Have you seen the Autobiography of a Dissenting Minister? It is a very amusing thing, though vulgar, rather. If you wish to have the whole series of Tracts, they are published now in one volume. . . . Mr. Philip Pusey is suspected of a leaning to Radicalism, because he said he would grant the Dissenters all that a *conscientious* Dissenter could ask. It would take some time to find out whether this is sound or not. It is an ingenious way of putting the thing.—Yours affectionately, JAMES MOZLEY.

TO HIS SISTER.

OXFORD, *March* 11, 1835.

. . . Sir Robert Peel, as you know, has thrown the burden of resisting the Dissenters entirely on the Universities, merely pledging himself not to force any measure on them. Accordingly, the Heads of Houses are expected shortly to take the subject into consideration. How their deliberations will end is not known, but it is feared they will propose substituting a declaration instead of a subscription. Newman was told by Pusey the other day that the Bishop of Exeter had come over to this view. His (N.'s) remark was that he liked seeing men come out in their true character. It signifies little what the Heads of Houses do, except so far as the name goes, if they only give a sufficient interval between their motion and the Convocation meeting to allow of bringing up the clergy from the country. These latter are most useful on such occasions, as, having but little actual connection with the University, they are not influenced by the same motives of expediency—the wish to keep things going—that many of the *residents* have. However, I should not fear much if the matter were left to the resident M.A.s.

Newman's pamphlet on Suffragans will be out immediately. It is astonishing the speed with which he composes; and that when he has a dozen other things hanging on his mind at the same time. It is certainly a good illustration of Rose's maxim, that those who have most to do are the fittest persons to take in hand any new work. The second volume of *Sermons* is also coming out. He dedicates it to his friend Bowden—an old college friendship—I think the author of a *Tract by a Layman*. We had a long discussion over the wording of the dedication the other evening. I have no more marriages to tell you of. The future Mrs. Keble is at present a Miss Clarke. I hear nothing of her, except a doubtless calumnious assertion that she is a blue-stocking. He, Keble, gave a most agreeable poetry lecture the other day, proving Homer to be a Tory (shall we say Conservative?), and finally stating reasons why it was that all real poets were Tories. It is a pity you are debarred by the language from either hearing them or reading them, should they be published, which doubtless they will be.

The assizes have been going on here lately—the judges, Park and Coleridge. The latter is an Oxford man, a friend of Keble's. Park's extreme respect for the University, not excluding even the junior members of it, was most amusing. One University man was brought up by an impudent javelin man, in open Court, for having made a disturbance in trying to force his way in, on which the following dialogue took place: "My Lord, I've brought up a man for ——." "A *man*, sir! A gentleman, you mean, I suppose." "My Lord, he was making a disturbance ——." "Sir, he was claiming his rights." "So, my Lord, I took him by the collar ——" "Collar, sir! what business had you to take the gentleman by the collar?" So the javelin man, in spite of all law and justice, was obliged to give up his captive, who was forthwith assured by old Park that he need not disturb himself at all about the matter.—Yours affectionately, J. B. MOZLEY.

At this time James Mozley was engaged on the English essay. I was visiting Mrs. Newman at Rosebank, and wrote to my mother, "Mr. Rogers was saying yesterday that Mr. Bridges had reported James's essay to be a very good one; the meaning was brought out clearly; and Mr. Newman said 'James certainly brought out his meaning very admirably in some things he did for us at the examination.' This is great praise from such a good and sincere judge."

To his Brother, T. M.

"My labours are now finished. I gave in my essay—that is, I put it through the nick in Dr. Bliss's door at six o'clock on Saturday morning; and that I got it in then is owing entirely to Bridges having stayed up with me the whole of that night and the greater part of the night before [to help in copying it out]. It is now over, and I shall wipe it off my memory as fast as possible."

To his Mother.

June 16, 1835.

MY DEAR MOTHER,—I have at last an agreeable piece of news for you. My essay has gained the prize, to my very considerable astonishment, though I do not know there is anything to be astonished at, for I should think I probably took more pains with my performance than any other who wrote, particularly as I had nothing else to do. But somehow or other success does astonish one—that is to say just at first. The feeling soon dies away, and joy subsides into a feeling of ordinary satisfaction, so that though I have only heard the news an hour ago, I feel now only a very moderate and chastened degree of pleasure on the occasion. This process in the mind is perhaps just as it should be, and prevents one from becoming conceited. You need not expect any particular pleasure from the perusal of the production itself, which is as stupid as need be, and as in fact it must be from the nature of the subject. Do any of you intend to see me spout in the theatre? You must write soon to congratulate me, for one chief pleasure on these occasions lies in these petty gratifications, as philosophers would call them. The day of Commemoration is to-morrow (Wednesday) fortnight. I have no more news for you. If any come up it will be a nice opportunity of arranging with Mrs. Newman as to the promised visit. I am glad to say Oriel has the English verse too; so we shine this year, you see.—Your affectionate son, JAMES MOZLEY.

There was a family gathering at Oxford to hear the essay. My mother and brothers came up from Derby, bringing my two youngest sisters. My father sends a few happy words, "gratified beyond what I can express," and quotes Napoleon's speech to his soldiers, "My children have covered themselves with glory." Everything went well; the weather was fine; the scene in the theatre beautiful; Mrs. Newman most hospitable; the party at Rosehill joining with ours in sight-seeing and all the pleasures of the occasion. Mr. Keble was up, and most kind to our party, speaking of the essay to my mother as exceptionally good and full of promise; and taking us into his old rooms at Corpus.

After the breaking up of the Oxford party, J. B. M. visited his friend Mr. Bridges, at Denton Court, near Canterbury, writing very happily of the days passed there. From thence he and his friend crossed over to Calais for a day—his first taste of Continental travel. After one whole day his letter shows how much he took in, both of the services in churches and the general aspect of the town, and the marked differences, extending to the smallest particulars, between Calais and an English town. Sight-seeing was always a strain on him: his mind worked hard; he was conscious of labour; so, on his return from this glimpse of foreign life, he writes:—

To his Sister.

August 24, 1835.

On Friday, Rogers lionised us over Woolwich, which was interesting enough in its way, and one is glad to have seen it; but really, after much and continuous sight-seeing, striking things of all kinds so pall upon one that I don't think the descent of a comet itself would excite more than the most otiose attention; and accordingly it was with the calmest indifference that I surveyed 27,000 cannon and some hundred thousand cannon-balls. This is a state of mind which one ought to be far from boasting of; on the contrary, I suppose if one had a proper degree of imagination one would be thunderstruck at such spectacles.

The name of Dr. Hampden has appeared already in these pages, but upon the death of the Regius Professor of Divinity, Dr. Burton, it figures in a more prominent manner, awaking a storm of controversy which was not to die out with the occasion that awoke it, but to be revived in the course of years with renewed force.

To his Sister Maria.

Oxford, *February* 13, 1836.

We have been all in a commotion for the last week, owing to the report of Hampden's appointment [to the Regius Professorship of Divinity]. The news first came out on Monday morning, and of course excited great astonishment. There was no doubt, however, about the fact; Shuttleworth had got it from the person himself; not that any official communication had come down; but that intimation had been given that it was to be so. Accordingly people began to bestir themselves immediately. That very day Pusey gave a dinner to the leaders of orthodoxy in the University, at which Newman, and Hook of Coventry, who happened to be up as select preacher, and others were present. A petition was agreed to, to be signed by the resident Masters, expressive of their condemnation of Hampden's tenets, and their entire want of confidence in him. However, a dinner-party was not to settle everything; and a public meeting was the next thing to think of. So the next day (Tuesday) was occupied in stirring up people. It was also thought requisite that an *exposé* of Hampden should be got up, especially as the length, stupidity, and obscurity of his Bampton Lectures, in which his chief enormities were contained, had deterred most people from ever looking into them; so that he might have maintained the Mohammedan system in them, for anything the majority of persons know about the matter. Newman took this *exposé* in hand, but was thrown back a whole day by a stupid mistake of Palmer's (of Worcester), who told him he need not trouble himself about it, as Dr. Bliss (the most unlikely person in the world) had taken it up. Afterwards it turned out that Dr. Bliss, as Palmer said, had taken up the thing, but differed from Newman "in the mode" of doing it; that is, he intended to send an article to *The Standard* on the subject, just as if a newspaper comment at all stood in the place of a grave and formal exposition of a man's theological opinions. However, the instant the mistake was discovered Newman commenced work again; and proceeded in a most miraculous way—day and night I may almost say, for he sat up reading and writing the whole of Wednesday night. He expected the thing [the *Elucidations*] to be printed and ready to send off to town yesterday afternoon, but it was not finished even last night. I suppose by this time it is; and some copies already sent to town to the Archbishop and others. However, I have not come to the meeting yet.

On Wednesday morning a meeting was held in Corpus common room, attended by about forty, a petition was read and agreed on, and by that evening had received forty-five signatures. The next evening, Thursday, it was sent up to town with seventy-three signatures altogether; which is a large number; half of the resident masters; especially considering how many would be prevented by *personal* considerations from signing it. It is astonishing how strongly men feel on the subject. Greswell of Corpus said he should consider himself guilty of an act of apostasy from the Christian religion if he did not protest against the appointment. Dr. Gilbert of

Brasenose declared the same thing. Dr. Cardwell, Principal of St. Alban Hall was going about for two or three days quite furiously, with a passage from Hampden's moral philosophy lectures in his pocket, and declaring that he ought to be turned out of professorship and hall, and house and home, and everything. It must be strong feeling which could raise the Heads of Houses: they had positively a meeting on Thursday to deliberate whether a petition in due form from the whole University in its corporate capacity should not be presented against Dr. Hampden's appointment, he himself being present at the meeting. This morning, to wind up the matter, H. gives out that he has withdrawn. Whether or not he would have been appointed against the almost unanimous feeling of the University, I don't know.... Yours affectionately,

J. MOZLEY.

To his Sister Maria.

February 20, 1836.

The last time I wrote, Hampden and the Regius Professorship was all there was to talk about; and it has been the grand theme of interest ever since. You will see by today's papers that he is finally gazetted. This is the present termination of all our struggles. Rose sent word of the event to Newman yesterday, officially as Chaplain to the Archbishop; to whom the petition against the appointment had been committed. The note was very strong, considering it was an official thing, and implicated the Archbishop. It deeply condoles with the University on the "great evil" that has befallen it, and could only suggest as a consolatory thought that no effort had been spared to prevent it. It seems the great argument with Ministers, and one which Rose admitted had a "deplorable strength," was the appointment of Hampden to the Moral Philosophy Chair, after the publication of the Bampton Lectures. I don't think myself we can fairly attach much blame to Ministers; indeed, as things go, it seems to have been a fairly conscientious appointment on their part. One person in the Ministry was strongly against it, and that was Charles Wood, an

Oriel man, and brother of the Wood who tried for the Fellowship about three years ago. The instant he heard of Hampden's probable appointment he went to Lord Melbourne and remonstrated, but was met with the answer that all was settled. Lord Melbourne himself had heard, it appeared, from some quarter or other, of Hampden's heterodoxy, and had forthwith consulted the Bishop of Llandaff, who assured him the charge was perfectly futile. This answer, as was natural, coming from a Bishop who had sometimes opposed the Ministry, and who had a character for orthodoxy, in a sort of way, satisfied Lord Melbourne, and he forthwith communicated his intention to Hampden; so Wood's remonstrance came too late. When the stir began at Oxford, and a petition against the appointment had made its appearance, Ministers were of course excessively angry with Copleston for having taken them in. Meanwhile Hampden wrote up to resign his appointment conditionally—that is, he was willing to do so if Ministers wished; and so the matter stood. I suppose, however, they did not think it worth while to break an engagement in order to gratify a party politically opposed to them. Lord Melbourne confessed to Charles Wood his astonishment at the number of heterodox names he had heard of as having started out of Oxford in late years. "Pray, Wood, how is it that in the bosom of your sluggish University, and out of a College by no means the largest in it, so many heresiarchs have lately sprung up: First there is Whately, Arnold, and Hampden, then there is Mr. Keble and Mr. Newman, who, I hear, are quite as great theologians as the others, only in another way." This anecdote comes in a letter from Samuel Wood.

Henry Wilberforce has been up this last week, and stays over next; his brother Sam preaches to-morrow at St. Mary's. Certainly H. W. is as little changed by being a husband and a father, as any one I know. He is just the same perfectly irresistibly ludicrous person he always was.—Yours affectionately,

J. MOZLEY.

The excitement upon the question was universal. A friend writes from Oxford, after a dinner party: "The guests sought no other subject; it furnished inexhaustible materials. The

Provost of Oriel, by your brother Tom's account, is quite worn out by the hard service that the M.A.s, by their frequent meetings, impose upon the poor Doctors. You will hear there is to be a Convocation on the 22d, to consider the proposal of the Doctors." The *Christian Observer*, commenting on the *Elucidations*, professed to have discerned Dr. Hampden's heresy as early as 1834. The *Watchman* assured its readers that "Protestantism was stabbed to the very vitals," and that if Dr. H. was appointed there was an end of all things. A "Tory Country Clergyman," to whom the *Elucidations* were lent on the condition of giving his opinion, remarked that "the Doctor is not fairly treated. These very men were quiet at the appointment of Whately," etc.

To his Sister Maria.

OXFORD, *Tuesday, March* 22, 1836.

We have had our grand meeting to-day. More by a great many came up on our side than I think were ever expected. There could not have been fewer than 450 in the theatre, out of which only 30 at the most were on Hampden's side. Two o'clock was the appointed hour for Convocation, so accordingly by that time the Convocation House and all the space about the theatre and Divinity School was crowded with Masters in black gowns, Doctors in red, some with caps, some without; some faces academical, others obviously clergymen fresh from the country: all collecting in masses and groups, talking and listening to one another; the former perhaps having the ascendency. In a short time there was a move for the theatre, the Convocation House being too small for the number. The bachelors and under-graduates rushed into the galleries, where we waited about half-an-hour before the procession appeared. Then the business went on in the usual form, which Anne, having been once present, may remember, though she may have forgotten a good deal of the Latin she heard on the occasion. On the Vice-Chancellor putting the question, Does any master wish to express his opinion?—Vaughan Thomas began a powerful address in the first-rate style of pompous Latinity, in which he supplicated the Proctors to pause before they put their veto, or, in case they were resolved, he insisted on the right of the Masters to have the thing brought to a division, and the number on each side counted up. This he proved from the wording of the statute, and he seemed to me and to everybody else to make out his case very clearly. However, neither his supplication nor his demand had any effect. After his speech was ended the Vice-Chancellor put the question *Placet* or *Non-placet*, which was responded to by a tremendous shout of *Placet* from the area. While the actual noise was going on, the Proctors pronounced their veto. Nobody heard them, and the procession moved out of the Theatre, leaving the Masters to stomach their temporary defeat as well as they could—if defeat it could be called; for while the Vice-Chancellor was marching out, the same division took place that Anne will remember last time; the *Placets* crowded together on one side, presenting a sort of wall or phalanx, by the side of which the Doctors passed in their movement out. Many of the Doctors left the procession and joined the Masters amid the shouts of the under-graduates. The minority appeared as contemptible as you can well imagine—certainly not more than 30, and one man, who counted, said only 25. One of the most pleasant sights in the whole scene was old Routh, the venerable head of Magdalen College, who appeared for the first time, I suppose, in these many years, in his place among the Doctors. At the first glimpse of his wig, a general acclamation was raised, which the old gentleman returned with several bows, in all the courtesy of the old school. On the meeting being broken up, a general cry rose up—"To Brasenose Hall." Thither the non-residents adjourned in a body, and put their names to a petition, requesting the Vice-Chancellor to call a Convocation next term for the expression of some censure on Hampden, and so the matter ends.—Yours affectionately, J. B. MOZLEY.

Mr. Rickards, the three Wilberforces, two Kebles, Ryder, Trower, Dr. Spry, and others, are up of our College.

In the April of 1836 he stood a second time for a Fellowship at Oriel.

To his Mother.

OXFORD, *April* 10, 1836.

MY DEAR MOTHER,—Yesterday's silence would doubtless give you by implication the result of the election; for which I hope you have been prepared. I am unsuccessful again: but I believe there was no helping the matter, the feeling in Oriel was so strong against having two brothers in the College. If I had passed an examination very much better than the one I did, it would have been all the same, those who voted against me, would have voted against me anyhow; that is, if I had not shown positively superhuman power in the examination. What sort of an examination I did pass, I do not know, and have not heard; but I should think it was superior in point of scholarship to the one I passed last time.[1] It seems certainly as if I was destined to be unfortunate in University matters. The essay last year is the only faint gleam of prosperity that has shone upon me throughout my course, and a somewhat unsubstantial one that appears to have been. However, I don't know

---

[1] Extract from *The Guardian*, Feb. 28, 1883 :—
"THE LATE PROFESSOR MOZLEY.

"SIR,—I venture to send you an anecdote, which, if you can find room for it, will interest not a few of your readers. In one of the Memoirs of the late Professor Mozley, which appeared in your columns shortly after his decease, it is mentioned that in standing for a Fellowship at Oriel he produced, as his English essay, just a sentence of a dozen lines, but such a sentence as no other of the candidates could have written. In an old commonplace book of my own, I find an entry made by myself, after reading the sentence. The subject given appears to have been 'Prejudice.' My note from memory, written the same evening, is as follows:—' Use of the principle of *Prejudice* in our nature: to create the feeling of *certainty*. The method whereby in so large a proportion of cases we have to arrive at truth—viz., our own research, in which we go on analysing, comparing, constructing theories—has a tendency to make us think the truth we so arrive at a thing that we have produced. But prejudice projects the truth from the eye, and gives it an independent existence, and objective face of its own. It is then a principle of our nature, a natural antagonist against a natural evil.—J. B. M. in to-day's paper.' My own memory may perhaps hardly have done justice to the writer's original thought; but you will judge how it interested
"ONE OF THE ELECTORS."

See p. xli. Introduction to *Historical and Theological Essays*.

that I have any right to complain, as long as one is enabled to preserve one's spirit and equanimity; which I certainly do to a greater degree perhaps than I have any right to, considering that my prospects are somewhat awkward, and that I ought to be looking about now to provide for myself. I feel that success has a far greater power to elevate me than failure to depress me. Whether this is an exactly proper frame of mind or not, I don't know. But one cannot help following one's natural temperament, and where that has such obvious advantages, as it has to me now, and saves so much present uneasiness, one is more inclined to make full use of it, than to be at all suspicious about its propriety. Well, what is to be done now? Newman has a scheme for me, which I will mention to you, though it does not bear out what I said just now, about providing for myself. Newman wishes me to stay up in Oxford still, and read. That was the only reason why he wished me to get in at Oriel; and that having failed, he has now this plan for me: Pusey, the Canon, finding his house too large for him, and thinking also that his house and income were never intended by the original benefactors of the Church to be used only for private convenience, is going to take in three or four men to give each of them apartments, and also the free use of his library. In return for this they are to read—divinity I suppose, or subjects connected with it; following at the same time the bent of their own minds as to the particular course of reading; and only referring to Pusey when they think they want advice and assistance. This is a liberal plan. Pusey, in short, only claims to give men an excuse and object for staying up after their degree; he wishes above everything to encourage the study of theology, as one great way of pouring in some light on this ignorant age; ignorant, that is, as to all sacred learning and primitive views. I cannot give the exact details of the scheme, or how we are to live together, and what we are to see of Pusey, and of each other—but there is the general arrangement. The only thing against it is, that it is not providing for one's-self. However, if there is no immediate means of effecting that, ... there seems, on the whole, much to say in favour of it.

You may consider if you like [in still supplying inevitable expenses], that you are giving money into the Church. You may fairly guess that I have no particular predilection for the thing, so far as one's natural hopes and fancies influence me. It is not a *very* pleasant thing—however one may rely on Pusey's perfect conscientiousness—to receive so much from an individual's liberality, but I suppose these are feelings to be got over. Will some one write to me on Monday? I am going down, I think, to Moreton Pinkney, where Tom has gone to-day. When is the ceremony? You have something there to console amidst these mishaps.—Yours very affectionately,

JAMES MOZLEY.

The ceremony here spoken of was his brother John's approaching marriage with Jemima, Mrs. Newman's second daughter, which took place on April 28, 1836. The day passed most happily, but shortly after Mrs. Newman became seriously ill; the attack, after some fluctuations, ending fatally on the 13th of May. This is not the occasion to dwell on the loss so keenly felt by all privileged to know Mrs. Newman, and especially by all members of the family into which her daughter had married.

TO HIS MOTHER.

OXFORD, *May* 21, 1836.

MY DEAR MOTHER,—Anne has not time to write to-day herself, so, as you expect a letter to-morrow, she has commissioned me to write instead. The funeral took place, as was intended, this morning at about nine. Tom and myself walked up to Iffley early in the morning, at a little past seven. They were to have left at eight, but, as it was, it was nearer half-past when we started. Some friends of the Newmans who had been invited, attended in church—Dr. and Mrs. Pusey, Copeland, Rogers, and others. Williams of Trinity read the service; I believe Mrs. Newman had expressed a sort of wish that he should. The vault was within the rails in the chancel of St. Mary's. The Newmans are as cheerful, now it is over, as one could expect. Newman himself is wonderfully improved in spirits. Up to the time of the funeral he was dreadfully dejected, his whole countenance perfectly clouded with grief, and only at intervals breaking out into anything like cheerful conversation. But whether it is that the funeral service, and the rite altogether, has thrown a consolatory colouring on the sad event, or that he does not think it right to go on grieving, now that all is regularly over, certain it is he seems much more like himself now than he has been for the week past. . . . Harriett does not go down to you immediately; she remains in Oxford [*i.e.* Rosebank] this term, and her brother keeps her company. When she purposes going to Derby I cannot exactly say; but I should hope it will not be long after the end of term. Newman too, I hope, will go down some time in the summer. It is really quite necessary that he should recreate himself every now and then—and I think he feels this; John, Jemima, Anne, you may look out for the end of next week. . . .

One quality Mrs. Newman had—a very admirable one in a person who had mixed much with the world—and that is, simplicity of mind. I cannot help thinking that she must have had considerable influence on Newman's character in this point; though one is generally disposed to think his a case where the maternal influence has been but slight in forming the man. If I know anything of Newman's natural character, I should say that he had lain under singular temptations to what goes greatly against simplicity of mind—that is, to "high notions," as we call it—a sort of leaning to the aristocratic world, which is a failing natural enough to minds of conscious power and refinement. Newman has steered clear of this, as we well know. I confess, in these days, when people indulge their own pride without scruple or restraint, and educate their children to be like themselves, and then cover it all with the surface of a religious education, with words and phrases, and spiritual professions of all kinds, it is really pleasant to find a person really moulding in some way the character of her family by the unostentatious influence of mere natural simple-mindedness. It is certainly true that one sees more in persons' character when they are dead than one did in their lifetime. We are apt to overlook real graces of the mind, merely because they may be unaccompanied with power and grandeur of character. Then we regret afterwards that one did not appreciate the person more. I am writing in Dr. Pusey's dining-room; I really flatter myself, I get on very well with the Puseys, which is something to say, considering the strangeness of the situation.—Yours affectionately, JAMES MOZLEY.

On Tuesday, the 27th of September 1836, my brother Tom, now vicar of Cholderton, was married at St. Werburgh's, Derby, to Harriett, the elder of the two Miss Newmans. On the dispersion of the family gathering, James paid a visit to Mr. John Christie, late Fellow of Oriel, now vicar of Badgeworth.

J. B. M. TO HIS SISTER.

OXFORD, *November* 12, 1836.

I left Badgeworth on Thursday afternoon. You seem from your letter to have expected me to be in Oxford two or three days before I was; perhaps I should not have been so late in coming up, and I rather reproach myself with it. But nothing disturbs me so much as your short bustling visits of a day or two; when you are come and gone again before you have got the din of coaches, porter, and packages out of your ears. I like to stay a sufficient time in the place to be able to have a quiet enjoyment of the scene about me, and be, as it were, an integral part of the household for the time being. Now I stayed long enough at Badgeworth to enjoy my visit extremely. We were a very sociable little family party, and seemed altogether to suit the small parsonage admirably. Christie is a most diligent visitor; almost every afternoon, from one to five, he is going about. In his walks with me, he called at several houses. ... This morning I should have gone with Newman to Littlemore, only it rained; I dine with him to-day, to meet Cornish of Exeter, who is rising into a member of the Apostolical party. Hampden has been preaching this morning at Christ Church, in his turn as Canon. There was an overflowing congregation, from some expectation, I suppose, that he might make allusion to his persecutions. However, he gave only a simple practical sermon, which was only remarkable for being excessively dry. . . . The Archbishop has been staying at Hursley with Sir W. Heathcote, where, of course, he saw a great deal of Keble. He pronounced himself afterwards more pleased with his visit there than any other in the course of his tour. Newman is working away at his new book [*Romanism and Popular Protestantism*], and finds it very hard head-work; he has written some parts four or five times over. Rogers comes up next week, and then we will have a consultation over parts of it, as well as on Froude's papers. I was at the theological meeting on Friday evening; Newman gave a paper with several quotations from Osborne—most dreadful passages. Their horror, I am ashamed to say, was somewhat lost upon me, from a circumstance that I need not explain.—Yours affectionately, JAMES MOZLEY.

This " circumstance," a tendency to be drowsy under sermons, attended him through all his later life. He *seemed* to sleep often in conspicuous places, where his companions would gladly have observed at least the *attitude* of attention, but he *heard* through the mist of drowsiness; and often came away in spite of appearances with a correct idea of the preacher's topic and manner.

OXFORD, *November* 26, 1836.

MY DEAR ANNE,— . . . Things have been very quiet this term. We have no condemnation of heretics, no pamphlets coming out, etc. The Provost just alluded in the most distant way to the sore subject, in his sermon last Sunday. He observed that it was a disgusting habit in persons finding fault with other people's theology. Nothing tended so much to make the mind narrow and bitter. They had much better be employing themselves in some active and useful way. This is laughable enough as coming from the Provost, who has been doing nothing else but objecting all his life. . . . Golightly told me, the other day, that this £1000 [given by him to the Bishop of London's fund for building new churches] has been rather a source of annoyance to him than otherwise. He finds himself talked to and appealed to in society in consequence. I should have thought more disagreeable things might have happened to Golightly than this; but there is a more serious nuisance still. People are so impudent as to think that having given so much is a reason for his giving more, or at any rate a sufficient ground for asking him. Accordingly, he had a letter from a person entirely unknown to him, the other day, asking him to give something to a church that was equally unknown to him, on the express ground that he had subscribed £1000 to the London churches. Again, he had a letter from a clergyman asking the loan of a £1000. What connection this person could discover between the want of churches in London and his own want of cash it is not easy to see, but Golightly gave him a settler in the letter he wrote in answer. As a set-off against this annoyance, he received the civilities and acknowledgments of the Bishop of London [Blomfield] when staying at Pusey's, and was asked to call at Fulham, whenever he came up to town. This was only proper. . . . F. has been at the Lakes during the Long, and seen a good deal of Wordsworth and Hartley Coleridge. Wordsworth spoke of Newman's sermons, some of which he had read and liked exceedingly. He spoke too of the *Christian Year*, of course admiring it, but, not with as much zest as one would have liked. The truth is, I believe, that is Wordsworth's weak point; he has no great fancy for other poets. . . .—Yours affectionately,

J. Mozley.

To his Brother T. M.

December 14, 1836.

I think of going home on Friday, on which day, Anne tells me, H. gives a grand evening party. Being a person fond of gaiety, I cannot of course resist being present on the occasion, especially after the sobriety and almost gloom of a term at Oxford. It seems laughable to talk about gloom in Oxford, where one sees all sorts of men every day, and meets with new views and fresh things and persons at every turn. But somehow or other the presiding genius of the place is not a merry one, after one's under-graduate days are over. . . . I suspect, after all, the truth is that when one's old friends have left Oxford it is a changed place, and that it is a very natural consequence to follow such a cause. The *Lyras*[1] are at last out; and I suppose the critique on them will be out too before long. S. Wilberforce finds fault with the hard and rash versification of some, and insinuates that the mind of the composer had probably lived too much apart from the tenderness and sympathies of domestic life. N. was considerably amused with this cut at him when S. W. sent him the critique to read over some little time ago. . . . Keble has been up delivering his terminal lecture. He dined on Tuesday with Pusey, together with Williams and Copeland, for the purpose of talking over the new translations of the Fathers. I was not present at their deliberation. . . . H. Wilberforce seems settling to his work (*The Confessions*) with diligence. I sent him down a *Vulgate* and a concordance to the *Vulgate* the other day. How are you going on? I suppose this is too early a stage in the business to put such a question. The Political Economy Professorship is vacant, and Merivale and Maurice of Exeter are the rival candidates.—Yours affectionately, JAMES MOZLEY.

I give the following as an early example of J. B. M.'s study of character:—

TO HIS SISTER MARIA.

March 1837.

You know —— is here. I don't think I have mentioned him in my letters yet. He is not quite so perfect as some of his relations, . . . not that I have really much to say against him; he means very well on the whole, but there is a certain want of delicacy about his mind, which prevents one from taking to him. I often suspected that A. was annoyed with his defect of manners, and it seems I was not wrong. . . . Certainly there is too little restraint about his manners; he is what one might call too free and easy as far as appearances go; and yet I have no doubt he means to be perfectly respectful.

[1] *Lyra Apostolica.*

But here his deficiency of mind comes in. He has not that delicate principle of respect in him which works insensibly in a person's manner whether he thinks of it or not, and is in fact perfectly consistent with great ease and freedom.

To HIS SISTER.

OXFORD, *March* 17, 1837.

You ask about ——. . . . He is the author of that article in the *Quarterly*, which contains most excellent views. Pusey's brother, the member, told him it was thought one of the greatest triumphs Newman had had, getting hold of the *Quarterly*. Lockhart finds he must have an infusion of Oxford principles, it takes with people now; that is, such people as read the *Quarterly*.

Newman has given me a copy of his book (*Romanism and Popular Protestantism*). He presented it with much grumbling and complaints at being obliged to give away so many; but, however, I should have that copy, because it was greased. I told him I should value the gift so much the more from seeing the sacrifice it was to him to make it. . . . There is to be another affray in the *Christian Observer* next month. H., of Merton, a leader of that party, preached in St. Mary's the other Sunday against the younger members of the University holding religious discussions on certain doctrines then much brought forward—alluding, of course, to Newman's and Pusey's views, which, nevertheless, he said he himself believed to be true. It is rather good these people objecting now to religious conversation. Not that I have ever heard any myself. I don't call talking about Newman and Pusey and the Apostolical Succession, or High Church and Low Church, religious conversation.—Yours affectionately, J. MOZLEY.

Shortly after he writes:—" Mathison told us that Murray had expressed his fears to him about that article—on the strength and ultra character of the thing. He would have given, he said, a thousand pounds to have it left out. However, he had been reconciled a little time after, on finding it did not give such general offence as he had anticipated."

To his Sister Maria.

OXFORD, *March* 29, Wednesday in Easter Week, 1837.

I have been uncommonly busy of late, but we are now enjoying ourselves, all of us. Rogers and Wood and Wilson are up for a few days. The two former came on Saturday, and with them Williams (the member) and Mr. Mathison, who left yesterday morning. It was disappointing enough to me that I could see so little of the party the first and larger half of their stay, my work taking up every minute of time till Thursday morning. We all dined here on [Easter] Sunday, Mrs. Pusey having engaged Newman six weeks beforehand to dine on Easter Day. We had also the whole party to dinner here yesterday, except Williams and Mathison, who had gone down. . . . Newman so enjoys a party of old friends coming up, it is quite pleasant to see it. It is only a pity those things are so short. Wood and Wilson go away to-morrow. Rogers staying over Sunday, and dines again at Pusey's, to meet Sir George Grey and Mr. Colquhoun, who are passing through, and staying the Sunday, principally to hear Newman preach. They are both Ministerialists—the former a nephew of Lord Grey. They are both Oriel men, and First Classes, and perhaps have a curiosity about the Oriel School. It will be funny enough to see how Pusey will manage with them; he has no idea of economising, and will surprise them a little. I am staying up the whole vacation, though when Wilson asked me to go down with him to Hursley, I felt strongly tempted. . . .

I must begin now to think of Thomas à Becket again; Pusey keeps telling me there are plenty of things for me to do when I have finished it, which is a consoling prospect. However, Newman pushes me on the subject every now and then, and Archdeacon Froude has mentioned the papers two or three times in his letter to N.—not that he seems in a hurry; but still, on the whole, there seems to be a call for it.—Yours affectionately, J. B. M.

Towards the end of 1837 James stood for a Fellowship at Lincoln. I feel I may give his own account of the affair, because it is more than confirmed by a note added in the end by Mr. Newman, which calls James the first confessor in the cause, and commends the "sweetness" with which he takes the disappointment; at the same time urging his stay in Oxford.

OXFORD, *November* 6, 1837.

MY DEAR MOTHER,—Bad news for you. I am sorry for it, but it cannot be helped. Of course, there is all that consolation for us afterwards which usually falls to the lot of unsuccessful candidates. They say I was the best of the whole set, and acknowledged so to be, which is not anything after all to plume one's-self upon, for there were only four candidates besides myself, only it allows one to take the present failure as a misfortune only, which is a comfort in a sort of way. We have a right to be composed and magnanimous on the subject, if we chose to be so, and can derive anything from such innocent consolations. I had the Rector's two votes, and three others, Michel, Atkinson, and Kettle. All my supporters, I hear, were very warm in my favour. The Rector commenced proceedings in chapel, declaring his intention. He said he should be very sorry for things to come to that pass, but if they did, he should certainly give me his casting vote. However, there were seven on the other side, so his casting vote was not called for. D., a school-fellow of mine, and one of the non-elected, called on the Rector immediately after to take leave. He (that is the Rector) told him he was very much astonished at the result of the election, and that it was very different from what he expected when he entered the chapel. . . . I have just returned from taking a run with Newman, and talking over what is to be done. Both he and Pusey wish me very much to stay in Oxford, and say it is my place. Newman is indignant that we should allow ourselves to be driven out of Oxford in this way by such a miscellaneous, irrational principle of decision as what seems to prevail in Lincoln College. In reality, one may say so without self-conceit coming in to the matter. From what I am told, the majority had nothing at all to say against the judgment of the minority. They were quite right, only they did not chose to have me. . . .

I heard a few days ago that some of them had a notion I was Radical, which was contradicted immediately. However, impressions last after the cause is gone, and Oriel is a suspicious place to come from; and, perhaps, there is a kind of confusion in some minds between the new principles and Radicalism, the only point of similarity being the newness in each—each wishing for something different from what had been. As for future plans, I suppose there is nothing just for the present better than staying in Oxford. I have pledged myself to prepare Froude's Thomas à Becket papers, and I ought to be near Newman while I am doing it—at least some part of the time. N. says I shall be able to get a curacy near.

There are reasons why the answers to this letter should be given, though with some apologies to the reader.

FROM HIS SISTER.

FRIARY, *November* 8, 1837.

Owing to the perversity of the Oxford post, we did not get your letter till this morning. But we had gathered that you were unsuccessful from your silence, and only supposed you were in no hurry to tell bad news. We give you now credit for more magnanimity, and are only sorry that our sympathy, for I will not say condolence, should not arrive when you expected. Of course we were a little disappointed at first, though we never for a moment doubted that you deserved success; but it is pleasanter to win than to lose. However, such disappointment is soon got over. . . . One can only regret it on a pecuniary point of view, and that, after all, is not worth thinking of. What stupid men they must be! I suppose John Wesley has frightened them from ever choosing a person of mind or energy. Mamma was very much pleased with your letter this morning, and with Mr. Newman's postscript, which it was very good of him to write. It would be very unreasonable in us to be dissatisfied when everybody says you did the best. Mamma has been reading papa your letter; he is "proud of having such a son," though perhaps he might have been willing that his acknowledged merits were more substantially rewarded. He wishes to leave your future plans entirely in Mr. Newman's hands, and would have you be guided by him. We of course all feel, as much as you can do, how desirable it would be, if possible, for you to stay in Oxford. I cannot think with satisfaction of any other place for you as yet, though I should soon be reconciled, if it were found necessary. . . . In Oxford you will be gaining experience and a right to teach; therefore a curacy near Oxford seems much the best, if it could be got by waiting a little. . . . Dr. Pusey is extremely kind, and mamma feels inclined that you should for the present avail yourself of his offer, though she leaves it quite to you. I know that you must feel some inconveniences in your present kind of life, and if you feel them strongly I would have you take lodgings. You are an economical person, and have the credit of being so both with papa and mamma. I do not mean to be ungracious to Dr. and Mrs. Pusey, to whom we all feel so much obliged, but still you may feel it would be desirable to be entirely independent; and their kindness, which does so much, perhaps can't do this. I have a message from mamma about your cold. If it is not better, she says you had better have some advice, and not let it hang about you. Miss Keen (our amiable and excellent Devonshire friend) desires her best thanks for your remembering her at such a time. She makes up her mind that there is something much better for you, and has visions of "fat livings," which are rather distasteful to mamma, who never fixes her affections on such things. . . . Yours very affectionately, A. M.

In the end of this letter are a few lines from my mother to Mr. Newman :—

MRS. MOZLEY TO MR. NEWMAN.

November 8, 1837.

MY DEAR MR. NEWMAN,—Accept my warmest thanks for the few words of kindness you were good enough to send me in James's letter. They would have been more than sufficient to console me under a keener disappointment. Many friends say, with you, that there is no doubt a greater good in reserve for him; but what greater good can he have, or can I desire for him, than the sympathy and zealous kindness of such friends as you and Dr. Pusey? I hope I can say that I never coveted riches or high place for my children. A reputation has been what I have most desired for them, and I am sure I am more in the way of my desire being granted when any circumstance strengthens the friendship of yourself and Dr. Pusey, than in obtaining a Lincoln Fellowship.—Believe me to be ever truly yours, JANE MOZLEY.

It may be said that the reputation here desired is precisely the reputation her son's works have subsequently gained for him.

To HIS SISTER.

OXFORD, *November* 9, 1837.

MY DEAR ANNE,— . . . Thanks for your most cheering letter. People seldom get congratulations and compliments on not getting Fellowships. I am, it seems, one of those fortunate individuals. I gave Newman his part to read, and, Pusey being with him at the time, left it there. He asked if he was to read the whole of it. I said certainly, if he liked, but the first part had no connection with *him*. When I returned again some hours after, he said he had been guilty of an act of ἄκροια, which Greek word means going against one's conscience. The act turned out to be that he had read the whole letter. Also it came out that he had read my mother's part to Dr. Pusey. . . . Of course I am staying on here for the present. Newman has a scheme for taking a house, and occupying it with a sufficient number of men without Fellowships, but who wish to stay up regularly in the University. He has written to W. Froude, who is threatened with his old complaint, and advised against going on with his profession, and he has spoken to Johnson of Magdalen Hall. I talked with the latter to-day; he has a strong leaning, I think, to the thing. These lodgings, the idea is, may be paid out of the Society's fund, and those who benefit by it in return give a portion of their exertions to the cause. I send you some memorials of the

Bishop of Sodor and Man; they were given me to send where I could. I believe there is a considerable chance of saving the bishopric, if there is only feeling enough shown for it.

Pusey's sermon is making a great fuss. I suppose it is the first time of the Revolution being formally preached against since Sacheverel's time. Newman has heard from Rivington, asking whether he will continue his support to the *British Critic* under new editorship, to which N. has replied that there must first be an editor that he approves of. I have set to again at Froude's papers, and purpose working steadily; it is more steady than hard working that is required for getting on with them. . . . —Yours affectionately, J. B. M.

In reply to this letter his sister writes :—

November 16, 1837.

. . . John, Jemima, and I have been talking over your concerns this morning. First we agreed that it would be well for you to stay some time in Oxford, then Jemima thought not too long, unless you had some fixed plan; as going on doubtfully from term to term gives people unsettled ways when they ought to be beginning the business of life seriously. Nobody quite understands this House, which I suppose is not a real scheme as yet. Of course you will be obliged to wait some time before you are ordained; as Christmas will be here too soon for you to avail yourself of that time. . . . While the [Oriel] exhibition lasts it seems an excellent reason for staying where you are, and mamma so much prefers it. She thinks it does you so much good; and you know her old ambition that you should write, which she fancies more likely you should do in the literary air of Oxford than elsewhere. . . . Miss Keen continues to wish for fat livings for you, and one night we had quite an argument as to one being desirable. She was so strenuous in its favour, and mamma in her indifference, that one might have thought your real fate hung on the decision of the question.—Yours affectionately, A. M.

1838 was distinguished by the change of editorship of the *British Critic*, which now became the organ of the party of which Newman, Pusey, and Keble were the recognised heads, Mr. Newman accepting the office of editor after some communication with Messrs. Rivington. One incidental use of the review was to furnish a field—a sort of practice-ground—for the younger members of the party.

To his Sister.

Oxford, *February* 6, 1838.

. . . I was with Newman on Sunday evening, talking over the *British Critic*. He is sanguine about contributors. Newman only took it after others refusing—first Manning, then Maitland. The latter was frightened by an article of Pusey's on the Church Commission, which he thought went too far for him in his present situation of librarian to the Archbishop. There will be four stiffly theological articles in each number—so Newman thinks to arrange it. The rest will be miscellaneous and literary. . . .

The article in the *Edinburgh* is, Pusey has heard, by Merivale. He rather likes it, on the whole; that is, he thinks the spirit good; but he will answer it, and enter into the historical question particularly. The article in the *Quarterly* is Sewell's. I should hardly have guessed it, though the beginning is like him. There is a bit, you remember, quoted in it from an article in the *British and Foreign Review*. That article is Price's. Arnold has been here, and called on Pusey yesterday—a visit of explanation, and kindly meant. They knew each other once very well. Arnold is on the Board of the New University in London, and is *for* the Greek Testament being introduced into the examination. He will not unlikely resign if it is carried against him. Pusey talked about this with him, it being a subject on which they could agree.

The river is frozen here so thick that they are going to roast a sheep on it, and everybody is skating. . . . Yours affectionately, J. B. Mozley.

From his Brother, T. M.

Cholderton, *February* 20, 1838.

My dear James,—I think since the days of my attendance at Pusey's theological meetings, he has delivered there some lectures on the inspiration of Scripture. Can you send me an account of what he then said, or does say, on the subject? It is to be the subject of the clerical meeting this day three weeks, and I wish to have something distinct to say upon it. I do not remember at this moment any place in Newman's published works where he has treated it.

OXFORD, *February* 21, 1838.

MY DEAR TOM,—Pusey sends you down his papers to look over for yourself, and collect what you can from. Though delivered only a year ago they were written, the greater part of them, several years since; so he would not hold himself strictly answerable for every word or phrase. Also the main subject is the Apocrypha, and the sense in which *it* is to be considered inspired. And Inspiration generally only comes in as introductory to this. Newman wishes you to pursue the thing, as some views are wanted upon it; and no one has taken it up yet in a regular way, or any way at all, if you except these very papers. . . . Little Philip Pusey is very ill and not expected to recover, though it may be some time before his complaint is decisive one way or the other. Pusey himself has been up to London just now to be a witness for Mr. Davenport, whose case you may have seen in the papers. His relatives choose to think him mad because he has given away £40,000 for charitable and religious purposes. Pusey met him at dinner in the Long: and went to testify to his sanity, as far as he could judge at the time. He was examined an hour and a half in rather a bullying way, and had seriously to give his opinion that the clergyman, seeking treasure in heaven, who gave £5000 to the London churches, was not mad. By the way, I strongly suspect this clergyman to be Pusey himself. If so, it is rather good. The question, however, was put by the counsel for his side, and perhaps might have been politic, before a London jury of money-getting persons; though to moot the question at all, of such a person, would rather be against than for such a case as Mr. Davenport's. Pusey, as is natural enough, is rather annoyed from thinking that he might have done better in the examination, and been more ready than he was; but I should think he did very well.

Sam Wilberforce preached yesterday his first sermon as Select Preacher. It was on the return of the Prodigal Son, and was *against* Pusey's views in his *Baptism*. He called on Newman afterwards, and, as Newman said, wished evidently to get from him what he thought of the sermon, but N., not having heard it, naturally evaded such hints, which S. W. would of course attribute to the subject of the sermon, rather than to so simple a reason as the preceding one. I suppose there must be something harsh in Pusey's statements, as they offend people so mightily—more than the same view expressed by the older divines—such as Jeremy Taylor. He hits people hard, and offers no apology or consolation for the blow. But I am speaking off the book, never having read his *Baptism* in a regular way.

Newman has been writing till his wrist is sore, and till he almost thinks of giving himself a holiday, though he does not know when. Pusey has just given me his papers, laughing all the while at their disorder, in which I joined him. They are written, as you will perceive, on odds and ends; the slips and backs of letters, and so on. I would caution you against trusting too much to the numbering 1, 2, 3, 4, which might be found to involve only the particular papers which bear them, not those which succeed, though you are at liberty to take the order as it appears till you have proof to the contrary. You will find the subject also in the second volume of the *Theology of Germany*, which will probably give you as much to your purpose as these papers.—Yours affectionately,

J. B. MOZLEY.

TO HIS SISTER.

March 4, 1838.

. . . Mrs. Pusey is much better than she was, and has come down-stairs to dinner for the last three or four days. The only danger is that she will overdo it and take liberties, now that she is no longer positively confined to her room. Little Philip goes on about the same. They think of going to some watering-place when the weather is fine enough—perhaps to Dublin. Pusey would wish to see the Irish clergy—those of them who are at all High Church—to establish a connection with them. But at present I believe there are only two High Churchmen in Ireland, Mr. Todd, and Mr. Gibbins, the editor of the *Index Expurgatorius*, so that there would be little to do in that way just now. Sam Wilberforce has been up preaching a University sermon. It was aimed very perceptibly at Pusey's view of baptism. This is uncommonly silly in S. W.; he professes himself of our party, and talks of *us* and *we* and so on, and yet splits from us in public. Pusey perhaps may have expressed himself harshly in his book, and one would have nothing to say if a person only sent his objections to himself; but it is a different thing to tell it to the whole world to please people by giving them the opportunity of saying "Ah! they are splitting among themselves."

In a letter of a subsequent date, April 7, addressed to James Mozley by a friend, we read :—

Henry Wilberforce, by the way, says that it would give Sam great pain if people thought he had been preaching *at* Pusey lately—that he only wished, without reference to existing persons, to express certain opinions of his own, the contrary to which he certainly was aware that Pusey maintained, but hoped no offence. Pusey does not conceal his disgust. . . . I am not surprised, by the way, at his growing fierce, for he is preached at every Sunday regularly. There is a hit at him in some hole or corner of every sermon one hears. Mr. Gresley this morning (or I would rather say Sir Nigel, for it must be the same, though he is put down Mr.) had a little fling at the 5th of November sermon. Last Sunday there was something of the same kind again. The Sunday before was Sam W.; and the afternoon preacher also fired a few shots. The Sunday before that Hampden gave vent a little, and Mr. Hill of Edmund Hall was almost bursting with spleen and ill-humour in a sermon he preached on St. Matthew's Day. Rogers is coming up again to reside, which is a pleasant thing for all of us, and for Newman especially.

I suppose by this time you have *Froude's Remains*.[1] It makes some people melancholy reading them, which I can easily understand in those who did not know him. However, the darker side shades off as you go on, and the whole ends in a cheerful character. Rogers' article on *Froude's Remains* (*British Critic*, No. XLV., Jan. 1838), is much admired and is certainly a great manifestation of ἦθος. The *Justification* is almost through the press. I shall be taking my M.A. in a few days.—Yours affectionately, J. B. MOZLEY.

TO HIS BROTHER, T. M.

OXFORD, *April* 6, 1838.

MY DEAR TOM,— . . . Your proposal of curacies does not quite come in with my views just now. . . . The truth is, I cannot make up my mind to leave Oxford at present. It is too much of a break to encounter all at once, and I happen to have a good reason for staying on. Newman intends putting some plan or other of a Society into execution next term, and I am to be a leading member—though whether principal or vice-principal I cannot tell you. But if there are only two of us, which seems likely at present, I must either be one or the other.

---

[1] *Froude's Remains* were so much discussed at the time that it may be well to give a private critique as representing the feeling among those most disposed to take the book for granted :—

"*March* 14, 1838.

". . . I have not yet said anything of *Froude's Remains*, though we have had them more than a week, and I have nearly read, in a desultory way, all the first vol. It is difficult to know what to say about it. Of course it is very interesting and very clever, but I must say I felt as if I was committing an impertinence in reading his private journal—probably the most really private journal that ever was written. For, conceive his horror while writing some of the confessions, to think that all that would be printed ! Then, I should imagine, there are many so little aware of their own weaknesses that they may look down upon Froude as having had more weak and foolish thoughts than others, or at least than themselves ; for people out of the habit of self-examination let thoughts of pride, vanity, greediness, and the like pass through their minds, and rest there without any thought or consciousness of the matter—that at least I fancy. I am afraid lest justice should not be done him, that people should not feel that the very fact of his noting them down proves they are not the habit of his mind but something strange, new, unfamiliar that he starts from. The letters are striking and in an odd style. I am very curious to know what kind of sensation his views will make, uttered so carelessly, instead of in Keble's, or Pusey's, or Newman's grand style. I think the journal *is* melancholy, but then every sincere thing of the kind must be so."

Johnson of Magdalen Hall will join; he is the only one we are certain of. But after the Oriel contest is over, others may be willing. I know Harriett laughs in her sleeve at all these schemes, but you must know I am grown quite a grave and reverend senior, and have a right to take a sort of part in these arrangements. I am an M.A., as you know, and I wear spectacles to a considerable extent, and this, you must admit, to be a powerful combination, and to make me altogether a much more important personage than I was before. Newman's *Justification* has been out a week. You must read Pusey's article on the Church Commission; it is a complete *exposé*, and gives the whole history from the first.—Yours affectionately,   J. B. MOZLEY.

In fact, James's decision to remain in Oxford was the right one. To write was his vocation, and the neighbourhood of libraries a necessity to him. The event justifies his resolve.

To MRS. THOMAS MOZLEY.

April 15, 1838.

MY DEAR HARRIETT,— . . . We are commencing our plan of a Society in real earnest, and are already in treaty for a house opposite Pusey's. We are forming arrangements as to details, and your brother is to order furniture forthwith from London; very plain of course—no sofas or arm-chairs. Your brother wished to have deal in the bedrooms; but I put my veto upon that on the ground of its being ostentatious. These things you are not to talk of, you understand, though I give you perfect leave to laugh at them internally as much as you please. I shall be glad to get a sight of you again at Cholderton, though I had rather it had been in summer-time, to enjoy the luxury of your woods. . . . Yours affectionately,   J. B. MOZLEY.

The next letter is written from Hursley, where he was on a visit to Mr. R. F. Wilson, Mr. Keble's curate.

To HIS SISTER.

HURSLEY, *April* 27, 1838.

It is certainly a considerable time since I wrote last, but I have gone on putting off, thinking I might have something to say after coming here. I came last Monday and shall leave next, after which I go for a week to Cholderton. I am enjoying the country and persons here uncommonly, and I find myself pretty correct in my expectations. Keble does not exhibit the *Christian Year* very prominently in his outward air or manner; and persons who came with the idea would be rather floored and perplexed, and not know what to make of him. It is neither amiable, nor civil, nor courteous, nor engaging, nor anything of the kind, but he leaves you pretty much to yourself, and speaks just when he likes, and what. Some persons might be put out by all this: somehow or other I cannot help liking it myself, and being amused by it. In fact, there, is something in the real and natural way of going on, which pleases one for its own sake, though it may not be personally attentive to one's-self in particular. We dined with him on Wednesday, and saw, of course, Mrs. Keble. There was Miss Coxwell and two ladies out of the village. Mrs. Keble is decidedly pretty and interesting-looking, very agreeable,—I should think clever. She looks delicate of course, but she has come to daily prayers with the exception of yesterday. I can hardly tell you what conversation was about; Keble lets everything take its course, and never sets any subject going of a continuous kind—probably would rather interfere with it if any one else did. You must not suppose by all this that I do not like K.'s manner or am disappointed. On the contrary, it really takes with me; only if I were a friend of his I should be afraid sometimes of *others* being offended by it and not understanding him. I was amused with a poetical sketch he drew of the society to be met in the club-houses in town. Wilson was saying that persons frequented those places in order to have fashionable or distinguished characters pointed out to them : There goes such a one, and so on. "Yes," said Keble, " there goes Lytton Bulwer, there goes O'Connell, there goes Jack Ketch, there goes Lucifer."

We are going to dine to-day with a Mr. Yonge of Otterbourne, a chapelry in Hursley parish ; he breakfasted with us the first morning, and seemed a kind of person to respect very much ; he is a great friend of Keble's, and superintends very sedulously the building of the new church at Otterbourne, which is much to his credit, especially as he has been in the army. We called at his house when we went to see the new church, and saw Mrs. Yonge and a family of cousins from Devonshire. He himself was at the church, where we afterwards found him all dusty from working and measuring and that kind of work.

Winchester Cathedral is very fine inside, especially the part where the shrines of Bishop Waynflete, Cardinal Beaufort, and William of Wykeham are. They rise up in a kind of area as if they were clumps of trees. . . .

I have told no Oxford news yet; really two or three days in the country is such a change that it makes one forget all little events before. One or two things, however, I do remember; Bridges is elected at Merton, which is very satisfactory; he resides, in consequence, the next year. Next, I must inform you that Newman has taken a house, to be formed into a reading and collating establishment, to help in editing the Fathers. We have no prospect of any number joining us just at present. Men are willing, but they have Fellowships in prospect, as R. And P., who stood at Oriel, and passed a very good examination—the best, as some thought —has a Fellowship at University in prospect, which would be interfered with by joining us, for we shall of course be marked men. It would, I have no doubt, seriously injure any one's chance at any College now being connected so openly with Newman and Pusey. My chances being over, I can of course afford to be cool and courageous in the matter. The house has to be put in order before we can go into it. I say *we*, but I really don't know of any one beside myself immediately and positively going there. . . . I have just seen H. Wilberforce and Ryder (the brother-in-law), who were calling upon Keble. Keble is certainly great fun, and I think I have been hard upon him in the beginning of my letter.—Yours affectionately,

J. B. MOZLEY.

I have given the impression of Keble's manner as it stands, in spite of the last sentence, as a very genuine, true piece of description. The manner is a poet's manner when off the fervour of inspiration. Of all things one cannot fancy Keble regulating his social habits by the *Christian Year*—by what might be expected of him as its author. The man stands before us as he was, his humour recognised, which in his " Life " finds little place. As for the second subject of the foregoing letter—the *Hall*, and those who entered into the scheme and took up their abode there being " marked men "—Mr. Newman, in spite of ascetic rule and disregard of personal advancement, which he inculcated on others and practised himself, was the last man to be indifferent on the point of spoiling other men's prospects. To be the means of doing so evidently dwelt on his mind and harassed him. On the occasion of James Mozley's standing at Magdalen in 1840, he threw his heart into the election, and had a good share in the success. Where the election was a near run thing, every friend, indeed, who brought his influence to bear, felt he had brought him in; but Mr. Newman had the feeling of responsibility which made it a personal matter, and success a personal relief as well as gratification.

On Trinity Sunday, 1838, James Mozley was ordained deacon. Some characteristic traits came out in the history of the preceding week. He had a certain coolness and freedom from fidget and worry that often amused his friends, and sometimes went too far, as on this occasion. Without adequate grounds, he had it firmly fixed in his mind that the deacon's examination would not be till the Wednesday and Thursday in Whitsun Week. It was an occasion to interest Mr. Newman. James had written to his brother Arthur, then an undergraduate at Oriel, with some inquiries. Arthur's reply had been that Mr. Newman did not know the time, " but you will very likely have to come to be examined very soon." Mr. Newman would not be able to understand a man's relying on anything but the most formal information, and the fact that James did not arrive from Cholderton, where he was reading for the examination, till the Tuesday evening after the deacon's examination was over, would seriously vex him, nor would he think it necessary to conceal his vexation. James had written home that, God willing, he was to be ordained on Trinity Sunday—"perhaps before you get this letter." To his brother he writes, after announcing the event of his ordination:—

> OXFORD, *June* 13, 1838.
>
> MY DEAR TOM,— . . . All's well that ends well; so mistakes do not signify now, but on coming up I found I had made a considerable floor as to the time of the examination, the two days for the deacons having been Whit Monday and Tuesday. Pusey instantly went to the Archdeacon, and explained matters to him; and the result was that I went in on Wednesday and Thursday, and had a private examination with the priests. The Archdeacon was very good-natured, and made no difficulty whatever, but I felt annoyed, especially as Newman took it into his head to feel hurt about it, not to say considerably enraged. However, I have made up the affair with him, and we are as good friends as ever, but he looked amazingly black at first, I can assure you, ἐρεμνῇ νυκτὶ ἐοικώς. I read prayers for him at St. Mary's on Sunday afternoon, and got through with one bad mistake and three minor ones. . . . They say I was heard pretty well, which I am glad of, for I did not strain my voice. But what do you think awaits me next Sunday, *if* I get a sermon finished in time? Newman positively intends me to preach for him. This is certainly starting rather boldly, I call it. However, Rogers seemed to think I had as well do it, and I thought it would be like mock modesty to refuse; and after all, if one gives a plain, straightforward sermon, there is nothing to affect one much one way or another. . . . Sam Wilberforce preached at St. Mary's on Sunday afternoon, but we were not out of the Cathedral in time to hear him. People say there were hits in it at Newman. . . . I do not take Water Eaton, unless the Bishop wishes it, instead of which, Newman has a plan for me to be his curate at St. Mary's.—Yours affectionately,
>
> J. B. MOZLEY.

It is interesting, after the story of missing the examination day, to read the following lines:—

"To James Mozley, Esq., Dr. Pusey's.

CHARISSIME,—I send you my surplice, not knowing whether or not you want it. It is that in which I was ordained deacon and priest.—With every kind thought, ever yours affectionately,

JOHN H. NEWMAN.

In fest. SS. Trin., 1838."

T. M's. letter in answer foresees for James the character of a bungler—How came he to be so positive it was Wednesday and Thursday?—Whose fault was it?—deriving also from James's history a confirmation of his view of a "family failing."

"From what I hear, S. Wilberforce does not confine himself to preaching in St. Mary's. He goes about talking against Newman and Pusey's views. It is to be hoped that he will publish, and so give N. and P. an opportunity of answering him. He taunts his brothers with being ridden by Newman, and boasts of his own liberty. Free, however, as he is, he is by no means happy—on the contrary, thoroughly discontented with everything about him, and his own condition and circumstances in particular. . . . Yours affectionately,   T. MOZLEY."

In the life of Bishop Wilberforce there is some mention of divergence of opinion from Newman and Pusey at this date. In a letter of his to Mr. Charles Anderson, August 18, 1838, there is a curious example of a certain blindness as to the probable effect of attacks on the persons he was constantly "hitting" in public and private: a blindness which perhaps was a natural concomitant of intense self-reliance and sense of power. "As to my agreeing wholly with Newman, etc., Newman has just, very kindly towards me, but, as I think, very unwisely, declined receiving more articles from me in the *British Critic*, because my sentiments do not sufficiently accord with those of Dr. Pusey and himself. This is to me another mark of party spirit, which I greatly lament seeing among such great and good men."[1]

[1] *Life of Bishop Wilberforce*, vol. i. p. 128.

To his Sister.

OXFORD, *July* 6, 1838.

DEAR ANNE,— . . . You must know I preached my first sermon at St. Mary's last Sunday, and had a much larger congregation than I should have had the Sunday before—more dons, and more strangers, too; the latter, of course, having come to hear Newman (who was in town). However, it cannot be helped. I wished to preach a sermon in St. Mary's, and that was a laudable wish, and therefore other things must give way. I believe I was not quite loud enough, and read rather too fast, and too monotonously. But the sermon was thought a *nice* one by my friends, though the Provost took the trouble the next morning to inform me that it was quite a mistake on my part—that I preached in Latin, and must have been quite unintelligible to the people in general. However, this is only the Provost's view, to which he is welcome. People must have been uncommonly stupid who could not have understood me, for I had neither hard words nor hard ideas, and as for going into the derivation of every word that one uses, whether it is Latin or Greek, one would be half a year writing at that rate. I should not think the Provost ever once thought of doing it himself. I take the sermon at Littlemore next Sunday.—Yours affectionately,

J. B. MOZLEY.

In July and August of this year he is at Cholderton alone, while T. M. and his wife are taking their holiday and visiting friends. The perfect solitude, of which he had now experience, encouraged his intellectual bent, though far from being congenial to his social nature. He writes to his sister, then visiting in Dublin:—

CHOLDERTON, *July* 30, 1838.

Thank you for your letter in the first place, which came in most opportunely to relieve the tedium of a long dull morning. They have treated me too disgracefully at Derby, never having written yet. I go on here pretty much as you might expect, and quietly enough; I have nothing to distress me throughout the week, or move in any way, except my sermon for the Sunday. This hangs heavy sometimes, especially as I am idle the first part of the week; and have, therefore, this cloud always before me. I intend to begin reading or writing something immediately, if it is only to give me something else to think of than my sermon. After all, I am afraid I do not write intelligibly for the people. One has accustomed one's-self to a certain style of thought and mode of looking at things, so long that one really cannot get out of it; and to write a good plain homely sermon would be a most unnatural exercise for me. I confess that I imitate Newman not purposely, but I cannot help it. I am not ambitious of being ranked among the servile cattle (*servum pecus imitatorum*), but one must follow in the track which has been laid down for one; so just as young Evangelicals preach evangelically, though they hardly know their own system more than they do any other, so I, forsooth, preach in Newman's way, with the same relation to him that the Oxford Newdigates have to Pope. However, I mean to try, for next Sunday, to write a steady practical plain affair, that even the Provost would approve of, though I cannot write pure Saxon, not having the pleasure of knowing that language. . . . Yours affectionately, J. B. MOZLEY.

The close of the Long Vacation he spent in Derby, where Mr. Newman also paid a visit to his sister: he, James, and Arthur returning to Oxford together.

TO HIS SISTER.

OXFORD, *October* 18, 1838.

MY DEAR ANNE,— . . . I have been busily engaged ever since coming up with making arrangements for the Hall—bustling about, calling at the upholsterers, giving orders for coal. The place is at present airing and warming. It will look decent enough when everything is in it. There are quite gay carpets in both sitting-rooms; as is natural in fitting up, one forgets the commonest things at first, till they come upon one one by one. I shall expect to find numerous deficiencies after all, when I come to the actual habitation of the place, and just at this moment, the thought of coal scuttles has flitted by me, and I have booked it in my memoranda.

I have not called on Pusey, as he does not see callers in the present state of his family [Mrs. Pusey in a most precarious state]; but I met him in the street yesterday, and had a little talk with him. He looked very pale and thin—quite ghastly— Mrs. Pusey is about the same; but little Philip is expected to recover. He is at Dr. Wootton's at present. Pusey's sermons at Weymouth are in course of printing, and will soon be out. They are very magnificent productions—so complete and solid; giving the whole history of our missions from the first, and verifying every statement by references. This is done in notes; I hardly know whether I like this way of giving information. They are at the bottom of the page; and so interfere with the text of the sermon. Pusey never does anything by halves. I understand he has made a great sensation at Weymouth; his mere appearance of itself would do this, especially just now—it is immeasurably apostolical. Arthur will fill the turn-over.— Yours affectionately,   J. B. MOZLEY.

P.S. [from Arthur].—James has left me to fill up, but I am not at all aware that one thing has occurred of more importance than another. We had a fair journey in point of warmth; the moment we got to Northampton, James and Newman set off walking. About six miles from Northampton the coachman stopped at the railroad station, on pretence of waiting for some passengers; but I believe simply for the amusement of seeing the arrival of the train. James and Newman, having walked on, missed the fun—there must have been passengers enough to fill twenty coaches; all looking exceedingly comfortable, without the wretched appearance people present in bundles of old clothes on stage coaches. All the ladies looked as if they were dressed for a fashionable promenade.

To HIS SISTER.

OXFORD, *November* 5, 1838.

MY DEAR ANNE,—I have a companion at last—S. He is up to take Harrison's Hebrew Lectures under Pusey, Harrison

of course being obliged to reside in town. I like him very
much; he has unwearied spirits, and will talk for hours on the
subject of old liturgies, breviaries, and rubrics. He knows all
the technicalities of them, and has them at his fingers' ends or
tongue's end, more properly speaking. I like hearing him go
on upon them, from the amazing zest and relish which he has
for the thing, quite amounting to epicureanism; though, I confess, I should be sorry to have to give an account when it was
over. He is decidedly clever, besides the immense information
he has on these points, and has a good idea of a joke, which
somehow or another he manages to introduce, even into his
liturgical conversation; though you would not think the two
very compatible. What do you think of my article having
been alluded to in a sort of way from the University pulpit?
It is absurd enough—but so it is—only very slightly, but
enough to recognise the allusion. Mr. Gresley (the author of a
book on preaching—*Ecclesiastes Anglicanus*), stuck up for the
phrase "ready-made apparatus," and thought it had been too
hardly handled.[1] We ought to *unite*, he said, the *lofty* and the
practical parts of our system. I quite agree with him; but
Dr. Chalmers *separated* them, and that in the broadest and
coarsest way. Rogers, who was behind me, declared he just saw
the tips of ears turning red. I confess to a temporary suffu-
sion; but it was only for a moment. There were not half a
dozen persons in church who knew either the article itself or
that I had written it; so I might have spared myself even that
piece of consciousness. Newman heard from H. the other day
—finding fault with Keble's article, that it was strained;
how he could really think so, I cannot imagine, Keble's theory
seems to fit Scott [Sir Walter Scott] so perfectly. Every one
remarks it as a case of extraordinary adaptation.—Yours affectionately, J. B. MOZLEY.

As a sequel to the portrait in the last letter, we give a passage from the home letter that follows in order :—

"I am obliged to change my tone a little about S., who,

[1] See *British Critic*, Palgrave's *Truths and Fictions of the Middle Ages*,
1838, vol. xxiv. p. 393.

though a very good fellow, is a decided bore as a talker; you know a week's additional experience is important on such a point. He talks so continuously, copiously, and pertinaciously on his own subjects wherever he is, that it is really no use asking one's friends to come to see one; if they come the result invariably is that they have come to hear S., not to see me, or each other. It is perfectly vain and useless any one trying to give adequate expression to any idea in S.'s presence—he is overwhelmed immediately. In spite of this, I like S. very much in many points; but he wants setting down—I have the will, but not the power."

Again, criticising his style of polemical writing:—

" S., you must know, is a most curious mixture of theology and erudition, with an immense taste for scurrility and the newspaper handbill style of literature; but, however, he is a capital person in his way—and all have their own way of doing things."

To his Sister.

December 6, 1838.

. . . Tom's pamphlet, of course, I have read, and think it extremely clever and amusing; there cannot be two opinions about that. Newman thinks the same, and is rather annoyed on that account; as he would like to have had it in the *British Critic* instead.[1] I think it would have been better too, perhaps; but persons have their own way of doing things. All here to whom I have shown the pamphlet are excessively taken with it. I was treated as one of the public. The first intimation at least I had of the thing, was receiving it from the bookseller, "with the author's compliments." . . . However, this does not interfere with the cleverness of the pamphlet. It is rather too clever if anything, that it has too much point in it at every turn. The plums are rather too thick; but this, I suppose, is unavoidable

---

[1] "A clergyman of South Wilts has written anonymously 'A Dissection of the Queries' of Lord John Russell on the amount of Religious Instruction and Education (Rivingtons), with so much cutting force and such felicity of expression, that it is a thousand pities he has not operated on a more public stage."—Notice in *British Critic*, vol. xxv. p. 255, January 1839.

with good writing, when the writer is fresh at his trade. He soon learns a little insipidity, and is more at his ease and less anxious about the opinion of the reader at every turn. . . . Newman's new volume (*Sermons*, vol. iv.), that he has sent, he intends to present to those who are employed on the communion-cloth. My mother is to be the trustee of the gift, so now your perplexity is settled.—Yours affectionately,

J. B. MOZLEY.

TO HIS SISTER.

OXFORD, *January* 16, 1839.

. . . Have you seen Gladstone's book? [*The State in its Relations with the Church*]. John should order it, if he can, into the library. It is a very noble book, I believe, and has damaged, if not destroyed, his prospects with the Conservatives. People are saying now, "Poor fellow," and so on. Hope of Merton told Newman this, as what he heard in town, and also said persons out of the political world could not understand the sacrifice Gladstone had made.—Yours affectionately, J. B. M.

TO HIS SISTER.

February 11, 1839.

. . . The Chevalier Bunsen has been here, staying with Acland at All Souls. Of course he has been made a lion, and dined and breakfasted at many places; among the rest, in our common room with Newman, where I saw him. He is a short, corpulent man, with a bright red face and sharp eyes, decidedly clever-looking, but you would not think him exactly a philosopher. He is a prodigious talker—literally talks unceasingly, and has a most amusing way of silencing others by lifting up his finger. If any one seems disposed to interrupt him, he says, "Oh, I'm going to that; I'll tell you that presently," and goes on swimmingly as before. However, he is really amusing, and therefore no one complains. He does give one positive gratification. The way in which he tells stories and describes persons is capital. He was a great patron of Bieni, at Rome, the Pope's composer, and told us very interesting things about him: how that he was a priest, and went about from six in the morning to twelve, hearing the prisoners' confessions in the different jails; and then set to at music. He (Bieni) was the great preserver of Palestrina's works and the old music, when the French came to Rome. The latter sold them out of the libraries—as they did numberless other papers—to the confectioners, and Bieni collected them by hook and by crook afterwards, with his own money, to the number of thirty-six folio volumes, all made up of bits and scraps, and restored again. Bunsen is a hard worker, and that morning he breakfasted with us had got up two hours before, and been reading Pusey's letter on the Sacrifice, which subject he discoursed upon to Newman. . . .

Mr. Gleig, the author of *The Subaltern*, preached at St. Mary's yesterday, a flowing, well-written sermon, with nothing in it. S. Wilberforce preached too, I thought a better sermon than ever I had heard from him, with high ideas in it. He is sadly pompous, though, both in style and delivery. Write before long, though I have no right to insist on a very speedy answer. When does my father go to Cholderton? He might as well rest here on his way when he does go.—Yours affectionately,

JAMES MOZLEY.

February 23, 1839.

We had a grand diocesan education meeting here on Thursday, when the bishop presided. It was for the new schools that are to be raised throughout the country for the middling class of people—that is, just above the labouring class—in connection with the Church. There is a society in town for the purpose, of which Wood and Acland, among others, are the delegates, and have been going about the country explaining the object of it. . . . Gladstone's book has come to a third edition, which is a great deal in so short a time.

TO MRS. THOMAS MOZLEY.

March 6, 1839.

DEAR HARRIETT,— . . . They say the greater sinner the greater saint; so Tom will beat all of us together in working when once he buckles to. We certainly are idle in Oxford; there

is no denying it; at least I am, and I will answer for several of
my friends. I think the advantages of Oxford lie in a moral
rather than in an intellectual direction. We are idle and
innocent, as Shakespeare says.¹ Either this is the account of
it, or else it is that J. H. N. works for all of us put together.
Here have I hardly done anything at all for my Article in the
next *British Critic*, though J. H. N. is particularly anxious
about it. How am I ever to string together, in anything like
method, all the bits and scraps and snips and snails, in the
shape of reports, messages, paragraphs, and the like, that have
come out on the subject of the Tracts? I have hardly an idea.
... Yours affectionately, J. B. MOZLEY.

TO HIS SISTER.

Oxford, April 3, 1839.

... The American Bishop [Hopkins, Bishop of Vermont]²
made his appearance yesterday just before dinner. I was

¹ About this time the idea seems to have occurred to J. B. M. of keeping
some record of conversations, probably of no common interest, in which
he was a sharer. He does not seem to have gone much further than the
thought, but one slight record is found among his papers, leaving no doubt
of the chief speaker, if there were no initial letter. The reader of Newman's Sermons will recall that on *The Invisible World*, where the brute creation is brought forward as an argument. "All is mystery about them. Is
it not plain to our senses that there is a world inferior to us in the scale of
beings with which we are connected, without understanding what it is?" etc.
The fragment is headed "Wild Beasts." "N.—White polar bear: what
a dreadful specimen of restlessness and impatience in an animal!—quite
miserable. Wild beasts seem a kind of fragment of some great world that
we do not see—such extraordinary developments they are, morally speaking.
P.—To see a lion suffering under the treatment of a common showman, the
lowest fellow possible—a lion, a creature that has a history of its own, as
man has, and done great actions that are talked of—is a degrading spectacle.
N.—I have not any great sympathies with those animals; I do not take
that view of them. They are sulky, unaccountable creatures." ... "The
Theatre." "N.—I think the notion of turning plays to moral purposes a mere
theory. They must be things to please the multitude. I believe plays do
not go down without a good deal of swearing in them. And there is something to be got over in the acting itself; the putting on a certain character,
dressing and showing-off before an audience. P.—Yes; but is not poetry
ἀνάμνησις, according to Plato? N.—Are we bound to take Plato?—however,
a poet works himself up in *his own room* by himself, which is a different
thing. P.—Ah, but he publishes. N.—Yes, *afterwards*. After he has
written, but the two acts are different."

² See *B. C.*, p. 281 : his work reprinted in London, 1839.

engaged, which was a nuisance. . . . However, we left soon and went to common room, where *his Lordship* was in great force, talking away to a circle about him on all sorts of ecclesiastical subjects. He is really a learned person, and very sharp too, ready in bringing out what he knows and arguing upon it. He was in the law for ten years before going into the Church, which may partly account for this. This morning he and Newman have been holding a long confab, which has increased Newman's idea of him. You must know, however, that to us who are accustomed to the baronial Hildebrandish bishops, or rather the descendants of them (unworthy though they may be), he is not a person one would take all at once for a bishop, having a slight approximation to the Methodist dignitary about him—say the President of the Conference or some such official. Not that he is anything of a Methodist in opinion. He has worked himself to quite the contrary—that is, to High Church views—in an extraordinary way, entirely by his own reading, which has been considerable, in the *Fathers;* and he is quite alive to what the wants of the Church are at present, and would introduce important changes into his own country, or 'our country,' as the American expression is. . . . I must not forget the *British Critic* amongst all these things, or omit telling the admiration I feel for Tom's *Church and King*, which I think beautiful, both in idea and in the way it is brought out. . . . C. Marriott is as serene and grave as ever amidst all excitement. . . . I forgot to say that Johnson of Magdalen Hall is standing for the place of Radcliffe Observer, vacant by Rigaud's death. It has hitherto been held with the Professorship, but need not be, the two being upon distinct foundations. Johnson has not even taken his degree yet, but any one can stand for the Observership, whereas it must be an M.A. for the other. The electors are the Radcliffe Trustees, who are quite independent of the University. Lord Sidmouth, Mr. Estcourt, Sir Robert Peel, Mr. Cartwright, M.P. for Northampton, are of the body. Johnson will have capital claims to show, having *erected* an observatory himself at the Cape, and superintended it as the temporary astronomer for three years, besides his book.—Yours, J. B. M.

The next letter tells of the election. From that time Mr. Johnson was a person of mark in Oxford.[1] It was at his house (as the *Apologia* tells us), that Mr. Newman passed his last evening in Oxford—"I slept on Sunday night at my dear friend Mr. Johnson's, at the Observatory,"—before leaving Oxford for good. I myself, with only a slight acquaintance, can well understand the feeling entertained for Mr. Johnson by intimate friends. I look back to 1849, when, sitting by him at dinner, he told me of having met in London, Newman and his friends, lately returned from Rome. Tears came to his eyes as he recalled the scene. One perceived that natural feeling had been allowed its full play unchecked by insular shyness.

In a few lines to his brother Tom, J. B. M. alludes to Mrs. T. Mozley's first essay in authorship. I may say here, that she inaugurated in the *Fairy Bower* the class of story or novel for young people of the well-trained thoughtful order which has been a characteristic of our day.

May 23, 1839.

. . . I heard of the new character in which she [Harriett] is going to appear before the world from J. H. N. before Anne's letter, which revealed it to me as a profound secret; giving also, at the same time, a very fine account of the impression the work itself had caused at home; which shows that they speak more good of it behind H.'s back than they do to her face. What surprises me chiefly at present, which is the only point I know about it, is the expedition of the performance. . . . Yours affectionately, J. B. MOZLEY.

TO HIS SISTER MARIA.

June 27, 1839.

. . . Oxford is fairly launched in this said Long now; and the caps and gowns have disappeared. Oriel is quite deserted,

---

[1] The reader is referred to the chapter devoted to him in the Rev. Thomas Mozley's *Reminiscences*.

all being gone except Newman and myself. The Commemoration, of which, by the way, I hardly have told you anything, went off very well. Wordsworth was enthusiastically received in the Theatre, and was, I heard afterwards, much affected by it, though he did not *show* the slightest feeling on the occasion. I was glad to have seen him, for really these great men are dying off so fast, that it is now or never with them. I sat opposite to him on the morning after, at a grand breakfast party given by Frank Faber of Magdalen, to which he was so kind as to ask me—a very good-natured thing of him, as I hardly knew him. Keble and all his party were there: Newman also; so it was really a galaxy that one has not often the opportunity of enjoying. Wordsworth did not talk much for the public ear: indeed one would not have liked it if he had, though it would have gratified one's curiosity more. Once he thanked Keble across the table for a compliment Keble had paid him in his Oration in the Theatre. I thought his style of acknowledgment rather more stiff than it need be, in fact a little inclined to pomposity. He is in private, I believe, an immense talker; and seemed to be talking a good deal during the breakfast, though it was only to his next neighbour, and in a low voice. Palmer's father-in-law, Captain Beaufort, had a D.C.L.; as also the Chevalier Bunsen. Arnold came from Rugby to see Wordsworth, whom he met at the Provost's to lunch, after the Theatre. Newman also gave a spread in the Common Room to the Kebles. The party consisted of Mrs. Keble and Mrs. Tom Keble, the little girl and boy, and Miss Coxwell, a cousin. Mr. Bowyer, the author of the article on the Discipline Bill in the *British Critic*,—for which article, by the way, he got his degree, having been recommended by the Bishop of Exeter in consequence of it,—was there. He is quite young, looks ingenuous and pleasing. I liked his looks. A degree is just the thing to have got for him, as, owing to his father's extravagance, he has not been at the University. . . .—Yours affectionately,

J. B. Mozley.

J. B. M. TO T. M.

July 10, 1839.

MY DEAR TOM,—I have been intending to write to you these several days past to congratulate you on your articles [in the *B. C.*] which I think are very successful, and out and out the best things in the review. Of course the Temperance one was the first to be read; and I should say that perhaps it is my favourite of the two, though it is absurd to compare when the subjects are so different. One naturally looks into a review for amusement first, and then edification in due time, and so is inclined to like best what satisfies the first feeling most easily. I fully expect to see it quoted in the papers before long. As I have begun to criticise, I will just say that I think the first part of the Evidences the most successful. The middle inclines to being too deep for a review, according to people's general way of reading. I entirely agree with it of course; and particularly with that part where you say you write at the risk of being misunderstood.

This is not very fine weather for John and Jemima; here at least we have April over again. Mrs. Small [mother of the Littlemore schoolmistress] is living in the expectation of seeing Jemima and little Herbert. Every time I go to Littlemore she asks me about their coming; and talks of it as the only important event that is to happen to her in this world.

Do you know of Pusey's having been thrown off the coach with little Philip, going from Brighton? There is a sharp turn of the road opposite Arundel Castle, and he was lifting up Philip to see the place, when the jerk caused by turning sent them both off, he having no hold at the time. They are not seriously hurt, though it is impossible to say what the effects will be in a person so weak as Pusey is just now. . . . Yours affectionately, J. B. MOZLEY.

J. B. M. TO H. E. M.

July 25, 1839.

MY DEAR HARRIETT,—I write to ask whether you will take me in if I go to see you for a few days. We are a party of us here going down to the consecration of Keble's church at Otterbourne. I had not thought of going myself; only, others going, one is drawn in by a kind of sympathy. Perhaps one or two of you may be there. Why not? I should think you could manage it somehow or other. That pony is a wonderful animal, and will do anything if his strength is brought out. J. H. N. is of the party to Hursley, but I am afraid he has no intention of paying you a visit; indeed we go post in order to save time. He comes back the next day to his children, whom he is preparing for confirmation; and Long Vacation is valuable, he says, for reading; he can spare less of it than any other time. Johnson also is going. He has been here for some time superintending his house fitting up. The rest are Morris, Bloxam.... Yours affectionately, J. B. MOZLEY.

TO HIS SISTER.

OXFORD, *November* 24, 1839.

... I am losing my last remaining companion in the House, Barker, who is going to be T. Keble's curate, and will be there till his ordination, in order to get a knowledge of the place before he begins. There is no one at hand just now that one can see to supply the places of all these desertions, so I feel myself to be inhabiting a whole house all for nothing, which is living in state indeed, but is not a very comfortable idea. The Lincoln Fellows are beginning to find out that they have done a precipitate thing, and say that they had no idea of electing a theologian, for which assurance one can give them ample credit, as perhaps it never entered into any of their heads that Colleges were founded at all for theological purposes.

Pusey preached last Sunday, the first time in Oxford since his wife's death.[1] When he came to the last sentence of the prayer before the sermon, in which the dead are mentioned, he came to a complete stand-still, and I thought would never have gone on. He has very little mastery over his feelings. In the course of the sermon there was a piece of friendly advice given to the Heads of Houses, for which they would not be much obliged to him. He had been talking of increase of luxury

[1] Mrs. Pusey died May 26, 1839.

amongst the under-graduates, of late years, from which he took occasion to say that those *in station* might do well to live more simply than they did. He dropped his voice at this part, which had the effect of course of giving increased solemnity to the admonition; for there was breathless silence in the church at the time. Pusey however meant the under-graduates not to hear, as he told Newman with the utmost simplicity after. It was to have been a sort of an aside from the preacher in the pulpit to the Vice-Chancellor over the way. The Master of Balliol was seen to march out of church afterwards with every air of offended dignity. The best of it was, the main body of the sermon had been quite in the general, on the vanity of human life, etc.—quite proper and unobjectionable. The heads were looking serene and composed, when, all on a sudden comes this highly practical turn to the subject.

So S. Wilberforce is the new Archdeacon of Surrey. I suppose his late speeches in Devonshire have done something for him. The Bishop could hardly keep him out of office after he had done himself so much credit. . . .

Rogers and Donkin have set up a few small private concerts, to be held in succession, at different common-rooms. Elvey and two or three other professional men will attend, and the rest are amateurs. Heathcote of New College, the splendid bass voice, is one. I am admitted of course only as a listener. The affair promises well. Donkin will take care only to have good music. . . . Yours affectionately, J. B. MOZLEY.

J. B. M. TO HIS SISTER, M. M.

OXFORD, *January* 10, 1840.

. . . We have had another Roman Catholic visitor here now, in the person of Mr. Spencer, Lord Spencer's brother. He is Palmer of Magdalen's guest, and is staying two or three days. Newman was asked to meet him, but declined; so he called on Newman and had a long talk.[1] Newman liked him, but thought

[1] I had an unspeakable aversion to the policy and acts of Mr. O'Connell because, as I thought, he associated himself with men of all religions and no religion, against the Anglican Church, and advanced Catholicism by violence and intrigue. When, then, I found him taken up by the English

him too smooth and staid. He is much more tolerant than most
of his party, and disapproves of the Irish Roman Catholics, but
hopes much of the English ones. He walked to Littlemore
yesterday. I do not know Palmer, so probably shall not see
him, which I am sorry for.—Yours affectionately,

J. B. MOZLEY.

The year 1840 is distinguished as introducing the Penny
Post. It is true in the case before us that, as the writer says,
the fact of writing a letter is all the same so far as the
process is concerned, whether it costs a penny or eightpence.
The change made no difference in his style, but perhaps it may
be doubted if the habit of writing full home letters would
have been formed under such altered conditions.

To HIS SISTER.

OXFORD, *January* 22, 1840.

I have not taken so much advantage of the penny postage
as I might have done. In fact, writing a letter is all the same,
so far as the process is concerned, whether it cost a penny or
eightpence. Term begins on Saturday, which I am really sorry
for ; you find all Oxford men complain of the change from vacation to term; never of the reverse. We have had a rather
pleasant interesting man visiting us this week ; a Mr. Bellasis,
a barrister from London, very High Church, a friend of Ward
of Balliol, who happens to be away now. Newman and others
have entertained him. It is amusing to see the variety of a
London barrister in Oxford. Of the London element he retains
enough to make a change from what one commonly sees here ;
though with none of the disagreeable features of it; for
example, he is so much more fluent, and can give regular
narrations with spirit, showing a person who has been accus-

Catholics, and, as I supposed, at Rome, I considered I had a fulfilment
before my eyes, how the Court of Rome played fast and loose, and fulfilled
the bad points I had seen put down in books against it. Here we saw what
Rome was in action, whatever she might be when quiescent. Her conduct
was simply secular and political. This feeling led me into the excess of being
very rude to the zealous and most charitable man, Mr. Spencer, when he
came to Oxford in January 1840. See *Apologia*, Part v.

tomed to argue and make speeches. . . . *Thursday.*—I did not send this letter yesterday from stinginess, because I should have had to pay twopence for being late, and pennies now are valuable things, which is one advantage of the penny post—it makes one richer. Newman has heard from Cholderton this morning. Tom is in a difficulty as to the two volumes [*Froude's Remains*, second series] being on such different subjects. Each is certainly worth a review in itself. Rogers, writing to Newman, says he finds it is the fashion at Cambridge to despise the vulgar clamour against Froude, and make out a common ground between him and themselves on the ground of intellect. Other points of course are inferior matters. They have formed such an extreme idea of his amiableness from his letters that they cannot imagine him able to be distant or severe to any one, even where principle was concerned. This is odd, as being so different from the common impression made. . . . Yours affectionately, J. B. MOZLEY.

OXFORD, *February* 15, 1840.

The theological meetings are set up again, having been only discontinued on account of Mrs. Pusey's illness. The first was last night. Newman read a paper on the Monophysite Heresy, which perhaps will not convey many ideas to you any more than it did to myself before the information I received last night. Pusey, Williams, and Keble are to be the other contributors this term.

To HIS SISTER.

[After dwelling on the circumstances of a sad death]—

OXFORD, *February* 25, 1840.

Things of a murderous character have been going on here also of late, though they have not terminated fatally, or are likely to end in anything else than a sentence on the culprit by the Vice-Chancellor of either fine or rustication. Ward (of Trinity) who has just published the Statutes of Magdalen, has been challenging Sewell (a Fellow of Magdalen)—they say not without provocation : only those who live in glass houses should not throw stones; and if a person cannot stomach an affront, he should not in the first place set the University against him by showing them up to the Radical public. A good deal of correspondence passed between him and Sewell on this business; the latter, who is a lawyer, having taken up the cause of his own College, though without any authority from the body to do it.... But the whole thing has been mismanaged from the first, the College not having done anything as a body; so that individuals in it have done what they liked. In this way the injunction was obtained, which was a most impolitic proceeding. Well, Ward and Sewell corresponded, and the latter, who is a thoroughly cool fellow, managed to irritate Ward by degrees, till a kind of ambiguous something about *satisfaction* was mentioned. Sewell writes back to say that had Ward clearly demanded the satisfaction of a gentleman in the obvious sense of that expression *he should have known what course to pursue,*—that is, *he* meant, have laid the note before the Vice-Chancellor; but Ward seems to have taken another view of the words, which was probably that intended for him to take; and accordingly the next answer brings a formal challenge. Sewell having gained his point proceeds to the Vice-Chancellor and gives him the note. Ward is Deputy High Steward of the University, which is a kind of judicial situation, though merely nominal; and therefore his conduct is so much the more unacademical. What will be done to him is not known, but probably he will be treated very leniently, from the provocation he had, and still more from the dislike there will be to seem to persecute. The Vice-Chancellor is very kind to him; and will give him every chance. Dr. Ogle is Ward's great friend, however: goes with him and sits by him in the court, and pulls his sleeve, and prevents him from breaking out into rages. This is excessively good-natured; but Dr. Ogle has always had rather a liking for him. He is, after all, more a weak intemperate person than a malignant; and people in general are rather disposed to take his part against Sewell. The President of Magdalen has come out in a way which makes people smile. Sewell called on him on receiving the challenge, thinking that he should of course have the warmest sympathy from the President, and commendation for his moderation. But the President was so obtuse or so malicious that he did not at all enter into the delicacy of the situation. "Well, sir, and do your friends object to your giving satisfaction?" Sewell could only say that the best friend he had in the world did; namely, himself. . . . Yours affectionately,   J. B. M.

Pugin at this date was a (perhaps *the*) great architectural authority, and his name interesting to the home circle as the architect of a new Roman Catholic Chapel in Derby, noticed in the articles on Churches preparing for the *British Critic;* the woodcut illustrations for which were then in the hands of his correspondent.

To his Sister.

Oxford, *February* 27, 1840.

My dear Anne,—Pugin came on Friday, last week, and stayed over the Sunday. I dined with him on the Saturday and Sunday. On the latter day Newman dined. It was his birthday, and Bloxam had asked him before Pugin's coming. However, he had no objection to meet him in a small party. Pugin was infinitely amusing, in his peculiar way, architecture of course, church ceremonies, liturgies, antiquities of all kinds being the subjects. He is the most unwearied talker, for a spirited one, that I ever heard. From six o'clock to eleven on Saturday was he on the move, never stopping, and when he left off he was quite the same as he was when he began. Plato would set him down as one of his irascible characters; for everything moves his wrath, especially in architecture. Such an one ought to be hanged for building such a steeple. He is never satisfied with half terms, but sends people to their final destination, the instant they become offensive. I said the Dean of York ought to be suspended—"In what way, sir?" as quick as lightning. His disgust when we told him of the new church in the *Arabesque* style about to be built at Wilton was most amusing. He will not admit any style of architecture for churches but the genuine Gothic, which he considers the maturity of the art, and all before it merely steps. So he could not bear even the Byzantine style being introduced at all here, or in India. When I asked whether he would allow any variety on account of the climate and situation, he said the pointed arch, and nothing but that, ought to prevail wherever Christianity existed. His summary judgments are as amusing a feature in him as any, and he has powers of language and quickness fully equal to express them; whatever extremity of disgust they may imply. So conversation, as you may easily suppose, is a delightful exercise to him. Before Newman he was not quite so vigorous. Lord Shrewsbury's not being present at the opening of the chapel in Derby was owing to him. Mr. Singe, it seems, is one of the old school of Roman Catholics who unite with Liberals, and want to attract people to their places by music and concerts. Pugin had all along solemnly protested against any other but organ music at the opening; but what was his disgust on the night before, when he saw a man with a fiddle-case making his way to the organ loft. He could hardly forbear knocking him over with his own fiddle. However, he forthwith wrote to Lord Shrewsbury to explain why he (P.) would not be present, and the latter, having the same views, withdrew also. The gaslights, that have been introduced since then, excited Pugin's displeasure immensely when he saw the place last. In fact he has washed his hands now clean of the place, and hardly considers it his own. . . . Yours affectionately, J. B. M.

J. B. M. always shows himself tolerant of great talkers. His temperament fitted him for the part of listener. The flow of speech, where there was fire and energy of expression, stimulated his speculative vein. The inexhaustible talker was a study on which he was content to dwell; he did not grudge him his monopoly. He could patiently wait his turn—resigned if it never came—while thought was busy on the man as well as his topic, on the phenomena that interminable powers of utterance were to him. Thus we see that, though architecture was not his line as it was his brother's, he could listen unwearied to Pugin debating on his one theme;—to a "scornful invective," for example, on the subject of *papier-maché* as a substitute for oak carving (one of the monstrous heresies of the day): "I never heard such a man—quite wonderful his powers of talking—both for endlessness and unflagging spirit."

TO HIS SISTER.

OXFORD, *March* 7, 1840.

MY DEAR ANNE,—I ought to congratulate Charles first on his birthday [February 29], that being so rare an occurrence in his life. We are remarkably quiet just now; the only thing that has made a stir lately being the affair between Ward and Sewell that I told you of. Sentence of *Bannitio* was pronounced on the offender, which sounds very awful; but it really only goes to exclude him from coming into Oxford for the rest of this term. As Ward does not live in the town, but at Headington, this will, of course, be no great infliction on him. They were purposely as lenient as they could be, on account of the provocation Sewell had given. Last Sunday the judges, Patterson and Gurney, went to St. Mary's to hear Newman—not in their wigs of course. This is a sign of things getting into notice. Bloxam is going to, or rather has given up, Littlemore, and Copeland is thinking of it. . . .

I will tell you some good things to read—though not sure they are quite in your way: viz., Carlyle's *Chartism;* the article on Lord Clive in the last *Edinburgh*, and the one on the Penny Postage in the same. Carlyle is a very striking writer; full of a sort of grim humour:—the grin-horribly-a-ghastly-smile kind of style; the subject, too, being one which develops such a power well. This is not an inviting or flowery description to give of an author; but for a variety he is wonderfully impressive. Lord Clive is Macaulay's. I recommend the Penny Post to John; it is very clever and sharply written, but not quite fair always. . . . Yours affectionately,

J. B. M.

TO HIS SISTER.

March 17, 1840.

DEAR ANNE,—. . . By the way, I have a book from Isaac Williams—a present to Jemima; a copy of his last volume of poems, which she shall have at the earliest opportunity. I hope she has not bought it. A modest author, like Isaac Williams, does not take this into account. How do you like the dedication to the *Church of the Fathers*? Williams was not in the slightest degree aware of such an honour coming till he saw his own name in print. It seems to me as if it were a translation of some old patristic dedication rather than an original one. . . . Yours, J. B. M.

To Mrs. Thomas Mozley he had written:—

"Your brother's *Church of the Fathers* is out, dedicated to Isaac Williams: 'The sight of whom reminds his friends of holy, happy, and primitive times,' which is more than one could say of the sight of a great many persons; I think those are the words. The book is to bring out the character of the Fathers, and show them as *men*, that they were not always *folios*."

TO HIS SISTER.

OXFORD, *April* 4, 1840.

MY DEAR ANNE,—Of course you have read half through the *British Critic* by this time. I have only read the Froude article [by T. M.]. . . . It gives too much the impression of Froude as a philosopher simply, instead of one who was constantly bringing his general maxims to bear most forcibly and pointedly on the present state of things; on particular classes, sects, and parties. It does not bring out Froude's great practical and almost lawyer-like penetration. The first two or three pages about Froude personally, I like very much.[1]

---

[1] The author of the article was as critical on its shortcomings, as a whole, as any of his readers. Some sentences, from the opening, one is tempted to give: "The contents of the present collection are very miscellaneous, and rather fragments and sketches than complete compositions. This, of course, might be expected in the works of a man whose days were few and interrupted by illness, if, indeed, that may be called an interruption which, at least all the period in which the pages before us were written, was

To his Sister.

The Altar-cloth arrived in Oxford on Thursday, and was despatched to Littlemore yesterday; I have not seen it yet, but shall take the earliest opportunity. I suppose it will be put up on Easter Eve, for the Sunday. Newman preaches at Littlemore that day, and comes to Oxford after service, after which Copeland takes the place. Newman's catechising has been a great attraction this Lent, and men have gone out of Oxford every Sunday to hear it. I heard him last Sunday, and thought it very striking: done with such spirit, and the children so up to it; answering with the greatest alacrity. It would have provoked some people's bile immoderately to have heard them all unanimous on the point of the nine orders of angels; the definiteness of the number being in itself a great charm to the minds of the children. He has been also teaching them to sing, during the week-time, and the fiddle has been brought into requisition, considerably to their astonishment; he found it the best way possible of keeping them in tune. St. Mary's, as you may suppose, during this interval, has been considerably thinned, though very good sermons have been preached there by Copeland, Ward, and Spranger. It was curious to

every day sensibly drawing him to his grave. In Mr. Froude's case, however, we cannot set down much of this incompleteness to the score of illness. The strength of his religious impressions, the boldness and clearness of his views, his long habits of self-denial, and his unconquerable energy of mind triumphed over weakness and decay, till men, with all their health and strength about them, might gaze upon his attenuated form, struck with a certain awe of wonderment at the brightness of his wit, the intenseness of his mental vision, and the iron strength of his argument. . . . We will venture a remark or two with regard to that ironical turn, which certainly does appear in various shapes in the first part of these *Remains*. Unpleasant as irony may sometimes be, there need not go with it, and, in this instance, there did not go with it the smallest real asperity of temper. Who that remembers the inexpressible sweetness of his smile, or the deep and melancholy pity with which he would speak of those whom he felt to be the victims of modern delusion, would not be forward to contradict such a suspicion? Such expressions, we will venture to say, and not harshness, or anger, or gloom, animate the features of that countenance, which will never cease to haunt the memory of those who knew him. His irony arose from that peculiar mode in which he viewed all earthly things, himself and all that was dear to him not excepted. It was his poetry."—*British Critic*, April 1840, p. 396.

see, however, how many continued to go out of habit, though knowing that Newman was away.[1]

The writer of the Magdalen Statutes article [in the April number of the *British Critic*] everybody thinks to be Hope, of Merton, whose name you may have heard. Oakeley is the writer of the first [the Church Service]; he is, as you observe, rather stiff and formal in his style, and wants spirit. Some good reviews, as you say, are wanted for the *B. C.* Essay after essay, however good each may be in itself, gives a prosing effect, viewed as a series. Rogers should write some more poetry articles; critiques are what keep up the *Quarterly*. Montrose is Le Bas's. . . . Yours affectionately, J. B. M.

The Altar-cloth mentioned in the last letter had been undertaken, under Mrs. John Mozley's auspices, for Littlemore Church. Mr. Newman had wished for one, and left it with his sister and her sisters-in-law, such near neighbours as to constitute in a sense one family, to work one. It may be said that zeal and ignorance worked hand in hand throughout the arduous task; nothing was known of the laws of ecclesiastical needle-work by any of the party. The youngest sister—now lost to us—whose taste would have ruled a few years later, was too young to have a voice; Mr. Newman had no opinions on the subject. It was his way to trust the good-will of his friends, and to hope the best from their endeavours. As one of the workers, I make these admissions, only pleading that the ignorance was not of the presumptuous order. There was no authority to be consulted—no formed taste in the matter of church needle-work anywhere; it had to be awakened; and, as far as I know, the Littlemore Altar-cloth was this awakener. It gave the start; though its own fate—the shape being altogether out of ecclesiastical order—was, when Littlemore Church came to other hands, to be banished to the colonies, as I have heard, giving place, no doubt, to something more in harmony with the new order.

[1] See *Apologia*, Part v.: "I meditated retirement to Littlemore. . . . I gave myself up to teaching in the Poor School, and practising the choir."

To HIS SISTER.

The Altar-cloth creates great admiration, with the exception, as of course you must expect, of a few criticisms; the chief of which is the one you suggest yourself. . . . Rogers seemed to have a few to make; but did not express them decidedly. Looking at the needle-work, I can easily understand the immense time it must have taken. . . . [Again, April 20.] You are quite right in saying that I have not seen the Altar-cloth. In the chapel it was quite another thing; I saw the whole first in a hurried way in Newman's little room. . . . Indeed, I can only say, and it is in perfect sincerity, not from any wish to please or flatter, that I think it a beautiful performance; there is a grace and splendour about it which is quite ethical, and which elevates and composes the mind to look at. . . . I went up to Littlemore to the morning service to-day (Easter Monday); the children were all dressed in pink bonnets and white tippets.

This last notice of Easter adornings is a sequel to the Lenten catechisings.

To HIS SISTER.

OXFORD, *May* 5, 1840.

DEAR ANNE,—Harriett has doubtless told you of all our Cholderton doings, but I have nothing else at present to talk about. I have enjoyed my visit very much. . . . On Friday morning we all went to Durnford. The greater part then immediately set off in two pony carriages to the C.s; why, I cannot imagine. Durnford is the most beautiful place possible now; besides which I did not feel disposed to cramp up my legs in a pony carriage any longer, having already taken two drives in the course of the morning. The people in these parts have no idea of any one using his legs; they are quite astonished at any one preferring a walk to a drive, though you only have to walk over the way. Legs have vanished altogether from their notion of the human shape; they are never taken into account, and in their place four wheels appear, two small ones in front, two large ones behind, converting man into a kind of centaur or large spider. I, as I observed, boasting a

pair of legs, declined taking part in the expedition, and proceeded with Tom to walk in the grounds. Tom went into the manor-house—the old building near the church—and began to poke about some old chairs and screens, on which I made off and had an hour's ramble in the woods; returned, and overheard Tom and Mr. Thurland talking in the churchyard; retreated again to the woods. It was a splendid day, and I never saw a place look better. Tom had a long argument with Mr. ——, on the subject of the old monks and hermits. His opponent prosed considerably; Tom was, as usual, victorious. Mr. Fowle was not well, and hardly opened his mouth. I have taken a great liking to Mr. Fowle[1] (vicar of Amesbury); his amiable qualities and frankness appear more and more every time one sees him. . . . I have not said about our party. Conceive the shock I had to endure. There were three ladies and a whole heap of men; the room was filled with men. Tom, by some exquisite management, made all *the three ladies sit together* at table [no doubt in his horror of draughts]. What more can I say? I did not recover myself for some time afterwards. I beg to say, however, that it was not from any selfish motive. I should have felt the same disgust if I had had to take a bird's-eye view of the proceedings. Luckily, Mrs. S. was opposite my part of the table, and talked a good deal; she is an agreeable person. . . . To be continued.—Yours affectionately,
J. B. M.

To his Sister.

May 9, 1840.

As soon as I came up from Cholderton, I found several persons expecting that I was going down forthwith to Christie's to help him for an indefinite period; I never having had the thing mentioned to me. I knew Christie was in rather sad case, and felt suitable compassion, and had really almost made up my mind to go yesterday (only for the term); but on mature consideration I am resolving it to be a bore to leave

---

[1] "H. E. M. has found that Mr. Fowle, whom you know, is cousin of our favourite, Miss Austin. Harriett, of course, asked a great many questions, and made out that she was an exceedingly nice, amiable, pretty person, just what one would wish her to be."

Oxford immediately, after one has come up to it again with the intention of staying the term. And Christie's, after all, is not a harder case than multitudes of clergy—not nearly so hard as Mr. Fowle's, for example. I daresay he works like a horse, but all one can say is, this is a troublesome world. [Proceeding to give good unselfish reasons for staying up]: I witnessed on Thursday the ceremony of laying the first stone of a school at Garsington, W. Pusey's curacy. The children all walked in procession from the rectory with long staffs—the girls with bunches of lilac, the boys with wallflowers. They formed a circle round the place, making a sort of large garland with their staffs: the effect very good.

The chief event of the past week was B.'s visit to Oxford, which caused quite a sensation and a series of dinner-parties in honour of him. He was of course in his element, and spent ten days exactly after his old fashion, in rushing from one man's rooms to another. He had only one answer to give for a long time to all questions, viz., how glad he was to be in Oxford again. So whatever he was asked, whether it was, How do you like your curacy? How do you like your rector? he had a deaf ear to everything that was not immediately connected with the fact of his actually there and then being locally and corporeally in Oxford.—Yours, J. B. M.

It had become clear that association with the writers of *Tracts for the Times* was a bar to election to a Fellowship in most Colleges. It was this that had reduced the Hall to the solitude described in a previous letter. One more trial was to be made by James Mozley, that he might continue in Oxford, so evidently the home suited to his taste and genius. I find a note from Mr. Newman addressed to him at Keele, where he was taking a friend's duty :—

"Monday will do for your coming. I have got your baptismal register and your College testimonial, and suppose you want nothing else; at least Bloxam tells me nothing else is wanted. I am sorry you have made up your mind to leave Oxford, but am sure that it is better for you to be settled than to be in doubt.—Ever yours affectionately, J. H. N."

To HIS SISTER.

July 25, 1840.

MY DEAR ANNE,—I have but just time to tell you that I am elected at Magdalen. It was the *nearest thing in the world.* However, on the good as well as the bad side of fortune, a miss is as good as a mile. The examination was considerably stiff, especially yesterday. The candidate who was set against me was Cholmeley of the Lincolnshire family, and of course great interest. A few of the Fellows, I believe, however, went by the examination simply. My great friends were Bloxam, Faber, and Palmer. . . . I should infallibly have lost the election if, most fortunately, two or three of my opponents had not been kept away from voting. Bloxam said that he expected, while the voting was actually going on, to see the doors open and these said Fellows to walk in. However, luckily it happened as it has. Touching the examination I passed, it is a matter of little consequence, but I believe it had the effect of enabling my friends to exert themselves and push me forward. But only a very few went by the examination itself. . . . I know you will all be pleased enough: and it is one of the greatest pleasures I feel on the occasion, to be conscious of that. The thing was so near run that Bloxam had actually written to Newman this morning, "Break it to Mozley that he will lose it by two votes." It seems to me a complete dream, and I am writing now as if I was asleep. A letter of Pusey's to the President had great weight, I believe.—Yours affectionately,

J. B. M.

A letter from my brother Tom opens the year 1841. His interests were so one with his brother's at this time, that there needs no apology for inserting such parts of the letter as concerned both equally.

T. M. TO HIS SISTER.

CHOLDERTON, *January* 11, 1841.

MY DEAR ANNE,— . . . It is now settled enough for me to

tell you that Newman has handed over to me the editorship of the *British Critic*. He takes the next number, and I begin with the July number. Rivington, at least, puts a good face on the matter, and expresses himself satisfied with me. In the written instructions I have received from J. H. N., I find one, "*make James write*," so let him know I expect something from him in July. You need not talk of this at present. . . . I have made great preparations in the way of lists of subjects, etc. It is of course a very serious responsibility, . . . and as for my opportunities and disadvantages, I think they are so nearly balanced that I have no need to complain. Very few people can write anything worth reading in London or large towns unless they possess *the* most popular and superficial qualifications. A crowd stuns and overpowers the mind, and great competition discourages those who have any tendency to diffidence. . . . Yours affectionately, THOS. MOZLEY.

Being in London when Oxford sent up an address to the Queen after the birth of the Princess Royal, November 1840, J. B. M. joined the deputation. All scenes stimulated thought in him, and the Duke of Wellington was always an object of interest.

TO HIS SISTER.

TAVISTOCK HOTEL, *February* 4, 1841.

I sit down with cold hands just to give you an account of our University deputation. We all met in the great room (Almack's that was), and waited about half-an-hour. I recognised a few faces that I knew; but most seemed to be London barristers or clergy. None except the deputation itself seemed to have come from Oxford, a thing easily to be accounted for in such cold weather. . . . It was funny enough to see one's-self in cap and gown marching through London. I tried to fathom the absurdity of it, but couldn't, for before one had moved twenty yards, it seemed quite natural; one had got an Oxonian atmosphere in the midst of London, and was carrying about the High Street at one's coat-tail. On reaching the Palace we proceeded up the great staircase, the Duke not having appeared yet. He brushed past us, however, as we were on the stairs, and put himself at the head. We waited more than half an hour in the ante-room. At last the folding-doors opened, and the Queen, or rather the place where she was, for we could not see her yet, was visible, with the Duchess of Sutherland on her right, and Prince Albert on her left. The Queen was perfectly immovable the whole time the address was reading : the higher you go in rank, the more people seem to possess this power of absolute immovableness. The Prince was, if possible, more so ; he might have been a cork man for all that one saw of his outside. The Duke read the address in a regular old man's voice, but very emphatically, though I think that as much arose from his want of control over his voice as from intention. The Queen read her answer very well, in a sweet distinct tone. I never heard a better speaking voice. When the deputation were presented by the Duke for kissing hands, she looked hard at every one as he came up, but her face as immovable as ever. She curved her elbow very gracefully as she held out her hand, which had no glove on it that I could see. The Queen was dressed in white satin, with silver facings, etc., a slight gold chain round her neck, and pearl earrings, the right foot on a stool, showing off her dress well. A long row of feathered men in scarlet supported the throne on each side, which added to the effect, but they were not seen till we backed out. The Queen seemed amused at the process, and laughed as we retired, saying something to the Prince. The Duke proclaimed each man's name in a loud voice as he presented him : Professor Wilson of Exeter, Professor Walker of Wadham College, Mr. Eden of Oriel, etc. . . . Yours affectionately, J. B. M.

In the following letter a subject is incidentally touched on, which, under the title Jerusalem Bishopric, was momentous in its bearings, though not effecting any of the objects for which it was designed.

To HIS SISTER.

OXFORD, *February* 25, 1841.

Manning was up yesterday to preach. He gave what one

might really call a powerful sermon; not controversial, but rather, as Coleridge would say, introversial, which is rather his line; that is, entering into and describing states of mind, struggles within; his subject being Judas gradually giving way to his besetting sin. He is certainly very deep, but not always in good taste, too nice and pointed in his style and his delivery; was so very emphatic in every little word and sharp thing that he came across, that he rather defeated himself and put everything on a level. Our Palmer [W. Palmer of Magdalen] is thinking of answering Hook, but has not got very far in it yet. As for F. Maurice, it is really no use to take him in hand. He is Mr. F. Maurice, an individual, and that is all. Hook's is a most amusing pamphlet, and takes everything for granted with such simplicity—that the Germans must be orthodox because they have certain creeds—and Bishop Alexander cannot think of doing anything uncanonical after Hope's pamphlet. . . .

I heard rather an amusing account of a young lady's visit to Oxford last term. The young lady, who had come to Pusey in such deep distress and religious perplexity, it seems was flaunting about with young gentlemen a good deal of the time, shopping, going down the river, and amusing herself very pleasantly—dear, good Pusey all the time being full of pity and concern for her painful state of doubt and anxiety. A certain young kid-gloved and scented gentleman of —— College was a particular favourite of the young lady, but she had several others as well, and used to go about quite *comitata caterva*, as we say in the classics, surrounded by a body-guard of handsome young gentlemen. . . . Pusey had ventured to suggest that she might dress a little more soberly, but had been answered by her sister, Would he have young ladies go about like nuns? . . . Yours affectionately, J. B. M.

Still more important is the announcement in the letter that follows.

To HIS SISTER.

March 8, 1841.

MY DEAR ANNE,—A new Tract has come out this last week, which is beginning to make a sensation. It is on the Articles, and shows that they bear a highly Catholic meaning; and that many doctrines, of which the Romanist are corruptions, may be held consistently with them. This is no more than what we know as a matter of history, for the Articles were expressly worded with a view to bring in R. Catholics. But people are astonished and confused at the idea now, as if it was quite new. And they have been so accustomed for a long time to look on the Articles as on a par with the Creed, that they think, I suppose, that if they subscribe to them they are bound to hold whatever doctrines are (not positively stated in them), but merely not condemned. So if they will bear a Tractarian sense, they are thereby all of them Tractarians. But whatever the view may be, there seems to be something brewing, and a man of this College told me just now that he had been canvassed to join in a public protest against the Tract. It is of course highly complimentary to the whole set of us to be so very much surprised that we should think what we hold to be consistent with the Articles which we have subscribed. Whether anything will really come of the matter I don't know. A hundred of the Tract sold in Oxford on Saturday. The Warden of Wadham is alarmed, but as yet we only hear of a vague impression being made, and have not got any particulars. . . . Yours affectionately, J. B. M.

To HIS SISTER.

OXFORD, *March* 13, 1841.

MY DEAR ANNE,—We are rather in a state of excitement just now, owing to the affair I mentioned in my last letter. You have probably seen in the *Times* the letter from the four tutors. This was followed up by meetings for two or three days running, of the Heads of Houses; the Warden of Wadham being the chief, instigated they say by Golightly—not that the Tract itself is not sufficient reason to account for the row, for it certainly is bold in parts. Newman expected it would create some disturbance, but not quite so much as it has.[1] I believe, however, the main cause of alarm is not this or that particular thing in it, but the whole subject being brought to bear on the

[1] See *Apologia*, 1st edition, page 172, 173.

Articles. Those who have always thought the Articles ultra Protestant, and been accustomed to think so ever since they were born, are naturally horrified at the idea that even their stronghold does not protect them, and that the wolf may come in and devour them any day. The Heads have accordingly met, and very furious they were. The first day, I hear on good authority, some of them could not condescend even to a regular discussion of the question, so entirely had their vague apprehensions overpowered their faculties. Dr. Richards, the Rector of Exeter, who is a strong man on our side, had a letter from Palmer of Worcester, in his pocket, in which he (Palmer) declared his full approval of the Tract, intending to lay it before them, in the hope that Palmer's known character as a theologian and a moderate man would have some effect upon them; but they were in such commotion that the letter would have been lost upon them, and he did not read it. Palmer sent this letter quite spontaneously, and it does him great credit, especially as he and Newman were rather on cool terms some time ago. They (the Heads) had a meeting again yesterday, but what conclusion was come to I have not heard. A virulent article has appeared in the *Oxford Chronicle* to-day, calling for the extirpation of the party from the University. The feeling of the residents, however, as a body, is either so strong in favour of the view, or, where this is not the case, so tied by personal connections and intimacies with others who hold them, that I do not think anything could be done here in the way of a public act of condemnation. The only possible chance we can think of is their bringing up clergy from the country on the No-Popery cry. This could not be done if any time were allowed people to reflect. But they get up a cry for the moment, and the excitement would last perhaps sufficiently long to bring up men by the railways and send them back again. I do not think that this will be done, but it is the only chance one can think of. Any proposal of the kind I mention would fall most exceedingly flat upon the residents. Some person took the trouble to write a note to *The Standard* to blazon the fact of that little disturbance about Morris's sermon in St. Mary's a year and a half ago. The name is not mentioned, but it is ill-natured to recall a thing so long past, especially as nothing official was done on the occasion. The Vice-Chancellor only gave M. advice privately, so the note is a misstatement of facts altogether. In our own common room the other day, when the subject was introduced, men seemed divided into two parts, those who felt with the Tract, and those who were entirely indifferent about it.

Keble saw it before it came out, and has since written to the Vice-Chancellor to claim a share in the responsibility of it. One hopes the thing will blow over after a little fuss. *The Times* taking the part it does is a strong fact; and attacks from Radical papers will only serve to mix us up with the Conservatives, and give us at least the toleration or the indifference of that party, instead of incurring their disgust too.—Yours affectionately,   J. B. MOZLEY.

Perhaps in the line of action that followed the publication of Tract Ninety, we may notice the first symptom of a difference in view between James Mozley and Mr. Newman. Though he might be classed among the young men,—he was now twenty-seven,—who took "the validity of their interpretation of the Articles from Mr. Newman on faith,"[1] and in his notices of the Tract in his home correspondence he seems to do so, his was not a mind or a disposition to repose such faith on any one implicitly. His defence of the line of No. XC. was *bona fide*. The Tract permanently influenced him, yet his criticism of Mr. Newman's mode of receiving the attack upon himself, as its author, shows that he stood external to the state of mind which prompted that mode. " Confidence in me was lost," we read in the *Apologia*, " but I had already lost full confidence in myself."[2]

---

[1] *Apologia*, p. 337.
[2] " Thoughts had passed over me a year and a half before, which for the time had profoundly troubled me—they had gone. I had not less confidence in the power and the prospects of the Apostolical movement than before, not less confidence than before in the grievousness of what I called the dominant errors of Rome; but how was I any more to have absolute confidence in myself? how was I to have confidence in my present confidence? how was I to be sure that I should always think as I thought now? I felt that by this event a kind Providence had saved me from an impossible position in the future."—*Apologia*, p. 173.

Mr. Newman was not one to infuse doubt by design, and as James Mozley had never any leaning towards Rome, or for a moment was shaken in his allegiance to the Church of his baptism, nothing passed to excite misgiving. He was therefore puzzled, and evidently disappointed at the line taken.

To HIS SISTER.

OXFORD, *March* 17, 1841.

. . . The storm seems to have blown over, and in a much shorter time than one thought of. The Heads of Houses issued a manifesto yesterday, which you will see in the papers. This expression of opinion is not of course invested with any authority. Neither the Heads of Houses, nor even Convocation itself, have the power of interpreting the Articles in a way to bind others, and there is nothing which can prevent tutors from lecturing in what way they please in divinity, except a positive injunction from the ecclesiastical authorities. J. H. N. has written a very polite answer to the Vice-Chancellor. But whether they will be provoked to think it humbug and concealed triumph, or be softened by it, I hardly know. Though admiring the letter, I confess, for my own part, I think a general confession of humility was irrelevant to the present occasion, the question being simply on a point of theological interpretation. I have always had a prejudice against general confessions, perhaps you may not have.[1]—Yours affectionately, J. B. M.

March 31 he writes to his sister :—

"J. H. N. is coming out with a letter to the Bishop, which is to be a final settler. The Bishop has behaved extremely well, and had some interviews with Pusey. . . ."

[1] A home letter of the same date (March 17) gives first impressions on reading the letter to the V.-C. in the newspapers. A sister writes : "I was entirely pleased with the printed letter to the V.-C. It struck me, on first reading it, to be exactly right, showing both confidence in his cause, and mistrust of himself as liable to error. There is a Catholic spirit of humility in it that one finds in some books, and longs to see practised. But I was sorry that it did not quite strike all others in the same light, especially H., who, though no judge of the question, is a good one of language ; and he thought it deficient in spirit. He would have liked something more like a retort."

J. B. M. TO T. M.

OXFORD, *April* 5, 1841.

MY DEAR TOM,—I really hardly know where to begin telling you news. The last and most important is a letter from the Bishop to J. H. N., in answer to published letter, thanking him most warmly, praising the spirit in which it is written, and says he will not have cause to repent of having written it, which is a quiet way of promising a continuance of his support to the views; at least this seems to be the real drift of his words. It is obvious that he would not have done anything if left to himself, and that he has been poked up by the Bishop of London, or Archbishop of Canterbury, to doing what he has. It is generally thought that the Heads of Houses have gone quite out of their sphere in deciding on the theology of a work; they are merely a committee for practical business; besides that, some of them are laymen. They rather feel this themselves, and say now that they condemn the *logic* of the Tract, not its theology. Wilson, of St. John's, has addressed a letter to Churton of Brasenose, against the Tract, and defending the view of the four tutors. It is excessively badly written in point of style; one has to read over a sentence a dozen times to see what he means, and as few people have the patience to do this, the pamphlet is not likely to be very effective. He cites two or three passages from the Homilies rather strong on his side of the question, or apparently so, and that is the most formidable thing he does. Ward, of Balliol, is coming out with an answer to him, part of which I have seen, and think it very conclusive. Hook is addressing a pamphlet to the Bishop of Ripon on the subject of the Tract. Manning was up the other day, preaching before the University. It was a good sermon, but not well delivered, and rather inclining to pedantry in the style; too polished and antithetical in the choice of words. He looked quite proper and archdiaconal, with the strait-cut coat and the gentlest shovel. He left on the Monday, to go to S. Wilberforce, at Winchester. Our President protested very strongly against the resolution of the Heads of Houses, of course, in writing; he never goes near them himself. I should

think he has had some influence over the Bishop, as the Bishop called on him lately on the subject. . . Touching your call for an article in the *B. C.*: since you wish me to write, I will write something or other, though the work I have been about for a long time is so different from reviewing, that I shall feel but awkward at anything in that way. I should rather prefer not taking a theological or even an ecclesiastical one. Your roof article will quite establish your architectural name here. Bloxam let out the secret of J. H. N.'s bust to him the other day,[1] quite unintentionally. It is finished now, so it is no matter whether he knows it or not. I rather think of going for a few days to town the middle of next week, and shall take an opportunity of seeing it.—Yours affectionately,
J. B. M.

April 20, 1841.

MY DEAR ANNE,—I heard from Mr. Wayland the other day, who gave an extract from a letter from Dr. Wayland [his American cousin, President of Brown University, who had been lionised in Oxford by J. B. M.], describing us a most agreeable, intelligent, gentlemanly set of men; but regretting that the advantages of the place were so confined to the aristocracy. He is, of course, perfectly mistaken here, and judges from what he sees on a first view. He meets with gentlemen and persons of superior manners, and forgets that it is the place which in many instances has made them such. For my own part, I think Oxford is the most levelling, democratical place in the kingdom. There are fewer distinctions, fewer *grades* here than anywhere. It is of less consequence to a man whether he is a man of rank here than in any other place in the kingdom. At Hull and Manchester, I believe, they are very aristocratic.

Have you got Palmer's pamphlet—it is rather tart, not to say harsh and abusive, but, at the same time, powerful in the extracts from Roman Catholic writers, which it brings against Wiseman. This was a part of the subject which the latter rather shirked, and, of course, he was open to a floor, as every

[1] A bust by Westmacott, now in the possession of his nephew, Henry William Mozley.

one saw. The only question was, who had really enough to floor him. Palmer has, therefore he floors him. Of course, passages without end can be produced from Roman Catholic writers tending to exalt the Virgin, only they say "You do not understand these; they are a different language to us from what they are to you, who are not in our system—you are not proper judges." This seems to be Wiseman's argument. We say words must have a meaning, and these words must mean so and so, and there the controversy ends. I do not see how it can go further. I thought Dr. Wiseman's an able pamphlet, and required an answer, but should have been better pleased with a more moderate one. It is not necessary to insult a man on the title-page with a soi-disant—" *Who calls himself* Bishop of Melipotamus." You may tell Jemima, Marshall has promised to send me a copy of the tune [for the Veni Creator] she means, and she shall have it for H. as soon as I get it. At the same time, I *rather* protest against using the tune for an ordinary Psalm. I rather like the idea of a tune peculiar to a certain time and place, as this I think is; something like the Miserere in the Pope's chapel. Everything of the sort, however, is published now-a-days, and if one does not, another does. So H. is perhaps right in getting all the good tunes she can.—Yours,

J. B. M.

J. B. M. TO T. M.

OXFORD, *May* 19.

The controversy is not yet over, as one thought. On the contrary, a very strong pamphlet is coming out by Ward, which I fully expect will create a row, though it is so impossible to tell beforehand what will be taken up, and what will not, that I will not pretend to prophesy on the subject. It depends so much on the peculiar state of the public mind at the time, what will inflame it, and what will not; and the public pulse is a very difficult one to feel. He says tremendously strong things against the Reformation and the English Church, so far as it has been influenced by it; but there is nothing which authorities can lay hold upon, as he does not meddle with formularies. It is, in short, a kind of strong interpretation of

No. XC.; just as Pusey's, which is also coming out at the same time, is a mollifying one, proving that No. XC. says nothing but what our divines have said before. Wiseman's answer is also just out, and, I confess, seems to me very powerful. He has greatly the advantage of Palmer in style and temper—though quite as *cutting*, yet more quietly so; and as Palmer's tone was certainly enough to provoke an opponent, one must let a man have his revenge; at least it is ὑπὲρ ἄνθρωπον not to give tit-for-tat. Wood, he who was Hook's curate, was up the other day, and described Hook as being bullied beyond anything by the Evangelicals at Leeds, so much so as quite to lose spirit. He had actually made up his mind to resign the living, but the Archbishop of York positively refused to let him. Keble was up yesterday giving his poetry lecture. We are beginning to talk of the next Professor now, and J. Williams is our man. Claughton, they say, will not stand against him. Kynaston, Master of St. Paul's, is the only antagonist as yet.

You are probably right as to Carlyle being too late for review now. I confess I proposed the book more for my own convenience than for that of the *British Critic*, having read it (the *French Revolution*) through, which is a compliment one comparatively seldom pays to a book.[1] However, I find now that, what with having promised to help Wilson (one of our Fellows) in editing the third volume of Bishop Andrewes (*i.e.* to look over proofs), and what with having commenced taking French lessons, I have enough to do for the present. So I will defer my valuable services to the *B. C.*—Yours affectionately, J. B. M.

His postscript, it must be remembered, is written before the days of photography.

"*P.S.*—They have got a most frightful portrait of Pusey out, which is stuck up in all the shop-windows. He looks wretched

[1] T. M. had written, May 5:—"About a year ago I proposed to J. H. N. to review Carlyle, and, for some reason or other, he very expressly declined, saying he would tell me why. I determined to ask his reasons, and I think I have, and that he assigned the uncertainty there was about the man. I suppose he is an unbeliever, and is likely to say things a great deal worse than he has yet said. Carlyle's *Revolution*, and other works, were reviewed in the *Dublin*, October 1838, with apologies for reviewing the first work so long after its publication."

enough *propria persona*, but this portrait quite makes one wretched to look at it—it presents such a picture of intense misery, age, and infirmity. I will send it to Harriett some day for her especial edification.[1] There is one of Sewell, too, much more fair; in fact, really a good likeness, and giving exactly his benignity and his pug nose to a T. Rogers has been heard from, from Venice. He is quite absorbed with the beauties of the place.

An allusion to an article in the July number of the *British Critic* is a reason for giving the following letter from T. M. to J. B. M. After some suggestions for the forthcoming number, he writes :—

CHOLDERTON, *July* 1, 1841.

DEAR JAMES,— . . . Things have been driven very late this time, owing to my many occupations during the quarter, to H. W.'s procrastination, and to your disappointment [due to a misunderstood suggestion]. For my own part I had made up my mind not to write anything myself this first time, if I could get contributors, but I perceive that if I am to have the Review in time I must prepare to do much myself. Faussett is a mere fill-up in this number, for that kind of stuff won't do for the staple of the number. If people tell me I have done that article too hastily and too sharply, I shall answer, Why did not they write for me instead of obliging me to write on the spur of the moment ? . . . You talked of coming here. We are quite ready any time, and shall be all the summer—at least so we hope. We have now the additional attraction of the church building, which is now about 6 feet above ground. I shall require the

[1] Mrs. T. M.'s letters at this time show that the strain was telling upon the physique of all deeply engaged in deed or in thought in the controversies of the time. "James," she writes, " says J. H. N. was considered wonderfully improved by his visit to Cholderton. I thought he did look so miserably thin when he came. It is quite shocking to see people look so. I do quite agree with a man who wrote to him the other day, and said the sight of such people '*made one sick*.' I am sure it does—sick at heart." And again, writing after the consecration of Ampfield Church, April 1841 : "J. H. N. is shockingly thin, and, set down on paper, would look as old every bit as that awful representation of him. Mr. Keble *does* get so old ! Mr. Williams [Isaac] looked sadly ill "—continuing her list.

breathing-time afforded me by making a two years' job of it, as by the 20th of August, when I stop operations, I shall be on the verge of bankruptcy. At present I don't see how I am to resume next spring, only somehow it looks too natural and *self-growing* a thing ever to stop. I can as little believe that the trees about me will not put forth their leaves next spring.—Yours affectionately, THOS. MOZLEY.

The Faussett article here mentioned is a review of the Margaret Professor's Lecture on the Thirty-nine Articles, "chiefly with reference to the views of No. XC. of the *Tracts for the Times*," delivered before the University, in the Divinity School, Thursday, June 3, 1841.

J. B. M. TO T. M.

July 13, 1841.

MY DEAR TOM,—Your squib, or whatever one is to call it, on the Margaret Professor has created a considerable sensation here. As you would suppose, I have not heard what is said about it among the Heads and authorities, though one may easily imagine. It is amusing to see the practical inference which the Professor himself drew from it. He went about forthwith canvassing for votes for his re-election, that happening to be just now. He got a good party together, some coming up a little distance from the country to be present. Of course they found all quiet when they got there. I certainly think it one of your most successful and amusing articles; in fact, I don't know any that I would place before it, though at the same time it is certainly a strong dose, especially for the Professor. I think we cannot turn the poor man out of house and home now that we have laughed at him so unmercifully, otherwise we shall be punishing twice for the same offence, which is against equity . . . The larking men here are wonderfully taken with the Apologue, and propose that you should edit it with illustrations by Cruikshank.

Writing home he says:—" I have heard only of two persons expressing themselves strongly about the article. One is Dr.

Daubeny. He took it for Newman's, and said, 'It was extraordinary how a person could appear so amiable at one time and so much the reverse at others.'" To his brother, T. M., he writes a few days later:—"I attended the Hebdomadal Board this morning, where there were two or three words let drop about your article on Faussett, which showed people to be considerably sore. Rather a vulgar letter, I am sorry to say, has appeared this week in the *Herald*, on our side, in which the writer lugs in your Apologue."[1]

TO HIS SISTER.

OXFORD; *September* 18, 1841.

DEAR ANNE,— . . . Bloxam is here, also C. Marriott and Copeland. Pusey is also back from Ireland. I accompanied him to his house from the Cathedral this morning, and had a long talk. He does not like the priests, from what he saw and heard of them. The Dublin ones were courteous and civil, but with nothing remarkable about them mentally. He said he only saw one who interested him at all. . . . Pusey did not go about much, but stayed at Kingstown. He saw Dr. Murray, who admitted—the only one who did—some faults in their religious books; all the rest stuck out for their system, both in doctrine and practice, to the lowest detail. He was interested, however, with some convents into which he went. We are a small party in College just now, and Oxford looks empty enough. Newman is at Littlemore teaching the boys to sing, but comes in tomorrow. . . . Yours affectionately, J. B. M.

TO HIS SISTER MARIA.

OXFORD, *October* 30, 1841.

We have had a visit from Selwyn, the new Bishop of New Zealand. He came only for a couple of days, to see the place before his departure. We all assembled—a large party of us— at Merton, to meet him at breakfast on Thursday at Hope's, who was his entertainer. Hope and Rogers are school-fellows of

---

[1] For further comment on the article and its apologue, "Growler and Fido," the reader is referred to the Author's *Reminiscences*, vol. ii. p. 245.

his, being nearly contemporaries at Eton; so you may suppose how young he is for a bishop. He is only, I believe, thirty-two; but not the worse for that—they want young men and minds in such places. He has, however, plenty of sense and judgment marked upon his face. It is quite the situation he likes, and has always fancied, and was, in fact, so disappointed at his *brother's* refusing the Bishopric, as he had set his heart upon accompanying him, that it occurred to the Bishop of London that he himself was the man. So the place was immediately offered and accepted. A large breakfast is just the place, of all others, where one does not see anything of a man. I did just see him, and that was all, but never heard him speak. He and Hope were talking together, as a matter of course, the whole time. In fact, to talk to twenty people at once is impossible, unless a man gets on the table and makes a speech. His wife was with him—a spirited-looking person, quite a young lady. She looked as if she would follow her husband through most things. . . . Mr. Edward Coleridge was with him; one of the masters at Eton, who was master when he was a boy; and Coleridge is comparatively a young man. Mr. Badeley, a barrister from town, was here also. He is a man who has come down to Oxford several times lately, a friend of Ward's and that set.

Keble has delivered his last lecture, which he wound up with a strong protest in favour of the connection of religion and poetry. People have begun some time to think of the next Professor, and Garbett's friends have established a committee in London, while Williams' have done nothing. From what I hear, even W.'s friends say his chance is not very good, but still sufficiently so to justify trying. There are several Colleges which to a man vote for Garbett—Brasenose, New College, and St. John's. We [at Magdalen] shall divide about equally, but perhaps rather for Williams than against.—Yours affectionately,

J. B. M.

To his Sister.

November 9, 1841.

Dear Anne,— . . . The new ordination of the Bishop of

Jerusalem is an event that is making a sensation. Our Palmer, who has been in Russia, and knows the state of feeling with respect to the Lutherans in the Greek Church, takes a very strong view of the matter, and wrote a letter to the Archbishop, which, however, was not put into his hands till after the ceremony—not that it would have made the least difference if it had. The Archbishop and Bishop of London rule everything, and do whatever they please—would not hear anything nor even communicate with the other Bishops on the subject. The Bishop of Oxford said he had no other information about the matter than the newspapers gave. Palmer is writing a protest entitled, "The Protest of William Palmer, Deacon, addressed to all good Catholics." It will be out in a few days after he has sent proofs to the Archbishop and Bishop, to correct misstatements if there should be any. It is very strong and very ably done; and, knowing the Greek Church, he can of course speak with confidence. Newman is about another, and I daresay there will be a more general one in course of time.—Yours affectionately, J. B. M.

The election of Poetry Professor to succeed Keble fell at a critical time. No one could for a moment doubt—it may be said that no one did doubt—that Isaac Williams was the obvious candidate, the fittest man for the office; but party spirit was roused; and rumours were afloat, which, with the majority of electors, threw such a consideration entirely into the shade. Some letters are given here to show the state of public feeling at Oxford and elsewhere. Amongst the alarmists, T. M.'s old friend, Mr. Golightly, stood prominently forward, and in the excitement of the moment certainly forgot himself in one flagrant instance, though time, that wondrous healer, brought about *more* than a reconciliation—a forgetfulness apparently on both sides of the old wrong.

The following letters allude to a general denunciation of the party in *The Standard,* in letters to Canon Faber, addressed to that paper :—

J. B. M. TO A. M.

December, 1841.

DEAR ANNE,—I have just time to write half a line. Golightly's letter has of course made a great stir. It seems to be agreed that though the letter, as a whole, is a great floor on his part (as producing *no sort of evidence*, even in the strongest cases, for quantities of people go to Oscot, and in Tom's case, not even pretending to produce evidence, but only saying "I *think I have ground for believing*"), yet that one or two awkward facts are let out—that is, that J. H. N. and Pusey differ as to Romanism, and that one was more disposed to think more favourably of Rome and more leniently of its faults than the other. This is, of course, a fact which we all know here, and which does not at all prevent the two acting in concert together; but this fact being put forward in that summary way may tend to create an alarm, and destroy that confidence in our party which unity alone can give. But this depends on how the public see it and follow it up. . . . Yours affectionately,   J. B. M.

T. M.'s letter to James on the subject is short and characteristic :—

T. M. TO J. B. M.

CHOLDERTON, *December* 3, 1841.

. . . Golightly's letter is beautiful. I don't know which most to admire—the negative or the positive part of it. I am chiefly amused at the way G. has tantalised poor Faber's (Canon of Durham) curiosity—*ten new* names as yet not blown upon—a regular Jesuit's College was the least I expected, when G. flings at him the old story of *British Critic* and the opinions of highly respectable friends, dignitaries in the Church, and Protestant bishops. As I lay in bed this morning, I thought over 30 pages of jokes at G.'s expense, but I suppose it is best to hold one's tongue.—Yours affectionately,   THOS. MOZLEY.

The question of the Poetry Professor to succeed Keble never came to the poll, but was settled by a comparison of votes.

Isaac Williams' party were so prepared for defeat that J. B. M. gives the history in his home letter in the spirit of making the best of it.

To his Sister.

Oxford, January 23, 1842.

People seem, on the whole, more satisfied than I expected with the conclusion the thing has come to, and think that with all the difficulties Williams' committee here and in London had to encounter they have done pretty well. The minority of 623 was a great blow to the opposite side, who had been counting on a majority of 3 to 1. . . . It seems to be generally thought that the Heads are strongly disposed to peace, and afraid to run any risk. The Master of Balliol gives out that he considers Garbett the most improper man in the University for the office. The Dean of Ch. Ch. is neutral, the Warden of All Souls very strong for Williams, to which, if we add Richards of Exeter and the President of Trinity, we have a good infusion at any rate of harmless materials in the Hebdomadal Board. The comparison of votes was a kind of half measure for which we are indebted to the President of Trinity—I mean as opposed to a mere withdrawal *sub silentio*. The Bishop of Oxford (Bagot) was persuaded to write several strong letters, urging a withdrawal, and among the rest a formal one to the London committee. The latter, who come out of the scrape better than I expected, were decidedly against it, but at the same time disliked the idea of opposing Episcopal influence, and this was almost the view of the Fellows of Trinity. Besides that, they were afraid that the known wishes of the Bishop of Oxford might actually prevent many voters coming up. In fact, they would have conceded the point most reluctantly had not the President been obstinate, and refused his consent to the acknowledgment of Episcopal interference; about which, I conjecture, he has some strong antiquarian theory as to the privileges of the University in that respect. So, as a middle course, something short of obeying the Bishop of Oxford, and also letting the world know as well as they could without a poll their real number, they acquiesced in a comparison of votes.

I see *The Standard* says that Dr. Gilbert produced vouchers for his 921 votes, whereas W.'s 623 were *certain* and *probable* ones —all that they had any chance at all of. That is simply a lie, and Haddan's scrupulous honesty is the sole cause of the report being spread. . . . The Principal of Brasenose, rather disgusted I suppose at such an imposing minority, commenced with saying something to the effect that if *they* (Garbett's side) were at liberty to reckon up all their chances they might swell out their list indefinitely. But he stuck short in the middle of his speech, and on Haddan's requesting to know whether the 921 was the *gross* number to be opposed to the 623 or a picked list to be opposed to the 500, Grove, a Fellow of Brasenose, admitted at once that it was composed in exactly the same way that the 623 was. . . . The Principal of Brasenose, being a sharp man in such cases, . . . instantly closed with the 921 to 623, and so the affair ended. . . . I omitted to say that the London committee had made a bargain with the Bishop of Oxford, and made him write a letter expressly stating that his sole ground was the peace of the Church, and even sent back his first letter to be corrected, but this would have been a poor compensation for a withdrawal *sub silentio*, and we are more indebted to the President of Trinity, as far as I have been able to hear, than to either of our committees on this matter.—Yours affectionately,

J. B. M.

To his Sister.

Oxford, *January* 27, 1842.

There is no more news as to the Poetry Professorship business. But there is a report that Gilbert and the Bishop of Oxford are to exchange Bishoprics, in order that we may have a resident Bishop to keep us in order. This is nothing more, however, than a report. In so far as it would look like a job to enable Gilbert to keep his Principalship, it does not seem a likely scheme for Sir R. Peel, though, as a check upon the movement here, it might be put in a popular point of view to the public. Peel told Lord Ashley the other day that he need not be afraid of the Oxford party, for he should take care they got into no preferment while he was in office.—Yours, J. B. M.

In March of this year J. B. M. was one of a deputation to the Queen, which after the ceremony dined at Apsley House.

To his Sister.

MORLEY'S HOTEL, *March* 19, 1842.

... The company besides the deputation, were the two Archbishops, Lord Redesdale, the two members of the University, Sir H. Halford, Lord Devon, Sir C. Wetherell, etc. The table was very wide, and round at the ends, each accommodating four or five. The Duke sat in the middle, with the Archbishops on each side. It was curious to watch the progress of conversation between them, though one was such a long way off that one could only see. The Archbishop of York was the favourite of the two, but as his line seemed to be only telling anecdotes, when he had finished one, he had nothing more to say, and a dead pause of some five minutes would ensue. The Duke seemed either not to have the power, or never to give himself the trouble of taking up the thread of any discourse, and seemed wholly dependent on what people chose to say to him. His whole interest is taken up in Parliament, and as soon as Lord Redesdale came, he immediately began to ask about what was going on. He was dressed in plain full dress, only short breeches, with the garter and the blue scarf round his shoulders under the coat. An ordinary blue dress-coat with brass embossed buttons, and a silk shawl waistcoat completed his attire. He seemed to enjoy himself most upon the ottoman after leaving the dining-room, with Sir H. Halford prosing things into his ear, which had the effect of a gentle stimulus, and one heard every now and then, Ah, Yes, Very well, and so on. Nothing can exceed the simplicity of his manner, which is of that kind that must have been acquired by *never* having cared about pleasing people, and being acceptable or popular. He treats complete strangers with the most utter and complete strangeness, but his manner to Dr. Bliss, who had seen something of him, showed that he acquired a liking for people by knowing them, and that his courtesy advanced in proportion to his acquaintance with the man, which is better than the

inverse ratio, as the more fashionable system is apt to be. . . .
Yours, J. B. M.

After a visit to his brother Arthur, then one of the Masters of King Edward's School, Birmingham, he writes :—

TO HIS SISTER.

OXFORD, *April* 12, 1842.

Arthur gave a dinner party on Saturday, where were Mr. Oldham, and most of the masters of the school. They were a pleasant set of men, very like College society, and keeping up that style. It is a pity they have not rooms within the walls of the school, instead of being dispersed through the town; it would make them quite a Collegiate body.

On Sunday he attended service at St. Thomas's (Bishop Ryder's) Church, Birmingham, and heard a sermon from Mr. Collinson, of Trinity College, Dublin.

What do you think of this notice being given out from the reading-desk between prayers and sermon ?

"The Rev. Martin Wilson Foy, curate of St. Martin's, will re-deliver, by special request, his introductory lecture, proving the coincidence between *Puseyism* and Roman Catholicism, in St. James's Church, Ashsted, on Tuesday next."

Now, one can stand a good deal in this way, because one has had a good deal of practice, but this was rather too bad. So after service I went up to the clerk, as he was proceeding to the vestry (not wishing to come in contact with the clergymen themselves), and asked for a copy of the notice. He said there was no *written* notice, but he would mention it to them—so at last I found myself ushered into the vestry, where I made known my request, and wrote out at their dictation the notice which had been given. When we came to that part of it, Mr. Collinson said, '*Tractarianism*,' etc., but the other, Mr. Wheeler, admitted that he said '*Puseyism*.' This constituted the whole of the scene. I made my bow and retired, I shall show the notice to Pusey to-morrow when he comes back, and suggest his writing to the Bishop of Worcester about it.[1] The Bishop can scarcely avoid taking notice of such a flagrant indecency when put before him. Mr. Lee was enormously disgusted with the notice in St. Martin's the Sunday before, where the word was "Tractarianism," but the use of such a mere piece of slang as "Puseyism," from the reading-desk, happily brings the matter to a head. . . . Yours affectionately, J. B. M.

OXFORD, *May* 22, 1842.

MY DEAR ANNE,—You have probably heard before now from Cholderton all about their visit here. . . . Mr. Bellasis, from London, came for a day, on purpose to see Tom, and he and Harriett had some pleasant talk. He describes the body of lawyers in town as changing rapidly; and really holds out a prospect of the old union between the legal and ecclesiastical bodies being revived. . . . As a *dernier* resource, the Exeter Hall gentlemen are going to send down some of their set, with Mr. M'Ghee at their head, to vituperate in the Town-hall here, and seem to suppose that they will really produce some effect upon the state of opinion here. Tom had a long talk with Pusey, chiefly about the *British Critic*, the latter recommending a few modifications of expression which had occurred there. The interview seemed to have been attended with some slight uneasiness to Tom, as I could tell from his manner afterwards, he not being yet used to take the passive side in criticism. *Entre nous*, I don't think it will do him any harm, and, to confess the truth, I had rather a malicious pleasure in seeing it.

The Bishop (Bagot) gives his long-delayed charge in St. Mary's to-morrow, which will be heard with considerable interest. He has been dreading it for the last couple of years, and ought to have delivered it long ago. They say he has a promise of the next translation, I suppose to York, and that he thinks he has had enough of care and responsibility in these questions lying upon his shoulders, and that he can claim fairly a little rest. It will be a perilous thing his going away—that is, for us.

[1] In the *Illustrated News* of this date there occurs a notice that the Bishop of Worcester had forbidden the use of the word "Puseyism" in church.

Archdeacon [S.] Wilberforce preached, they say, a very politic sermon before the Bishop the other day, and worthy a candidate for the episcopal honours. He attended the conference at Winchester between Mr. Wordsworth and Mr. Nicholson (on the subject of the former's sermon on renewing discipline), and seemed greatly perplexed what side to take, though he inclined of course towards the Low Church. This see-saw state must be a most difficult and agitating one to keep up, and he will require a bishopric for the benefit of his health before long, if for no other reason. The last joke from London is, that the two rival *Tablets* (there are two now—one Lord Shrewsbury and Wiseman's, the other the old O'Connellite one) station men with bludgeons at the Post-Office hole, to prevent each other sending off their respective papers.—Yours affectionately,

J. B. M.

In the collection from which these letters are taken, there is no mention of the action of Archdeacon Samuel Wilberforce, in the recent election for the Poetry Professorship, of which the details are given in his *Life;* but of course the tone towards him in the preceding letter is due to the part he took on that occasion. The following letter relates to the attempt by the Heads of Houses, who had appointed Dr. Hampden chairman of the new Theological Board, to free him from the censure passed in 1836, on his being appointed Regius Professor. His sister was then on a visit at Stow-Langtoft.

OXFORD, *May* 31.

The Convocation is on Tuesday, June 7, so Mr. Rickards should leave on the Monday morning. You see I take for granted he is coming. Everybody who wishes any remnant of orthodoxy to remain amongst us should come, and settle the matter once for all. The original statute against Hampden was a miserable thing, in this point of view, leaving it open to be removed whenever an Hebdomadal Board chose to liberalise. The censure ought to have been passed on the unsound propositions, not on the man, and then they could not have been retracted. We are going on very satisfactorily. To-day this circular is sent down to all the non-resident members of Convocation of every College. You cannot imagine the state of bustle and activity we have been in. The last week has been a complete dream—of interminable plannings, devisings, machinatings, talkings, walkings, writings, printings, letters for the post, wafers, sealing-wax, etc. However, the work is pretty near over now. In fact, when the circulars are fairly launched, there is nothing more to do. The new statute is expected to be thrown out by a large majority. Nobody sticks up a moment for the Heads of Houses. Respecting the point of inconsistency, tell Mr. Rickards that the statute of 1836 was generally considered only in the light of a *stigma*[1]—not as depriving him of those particular functions. That a man holding his opinions should have been allowed to go on lecturing and virtually exercising every position of his office, was indeed, and is, a most gross inconsistency. The statute just passed is only a slight addition to the great and acknowledged and systematic inconsistency. I voted myself against the measure upon that very ground—*i.e.* against Hampden; but, at the same time, to have raised a hue-and-cry would have been so apparently harsh and personal, that I am not surprised at the silence of men. You could not have raised a sufficient opposition without combining and making a noise; and though little additions to any wrong state of things are not to be despised, still, compared with the huge and monstrous inconsistency of heretical Professors allowed to lecture in an orthodox University, it was not much, and it would, in my opinion, have been straining at a gnat to have raised a formal war upon it.—Yours affectionately,

J. B. M.

---

[1] See article, "New Defenders of the Faith," in the *British Critic*, Oct. 1842 :—" Against the plain state of the case then—that Dr. Hampden did not retract; that Dr. Hampden *said* he did not retract; that *they* said Dr. Hampden *ought* to retract—what have they to set off as a counterbalance? We lack some very powerful ground, if this be possible, when the other side has swallowed up all. What is it? They '*felt* Dr. Hampden was, theologically, not the same man in 1842 that he was in 1836.'" "As the Regius Professor and Head of St. Mary Hall mixed more and more in society with his fellow Heads, the feeling of class would prevail, and the dignitary supersede and cover the latitudinarian," etc. Pages 431-435.

In reply to his sister's notice of his article in the *British Critic*, on "The Development of the Church in the Seventeenth Century," he writes:—

OXFORD, *July* 9, 1842.

I am sorry any part of my article seems hard upon our old divines. If it is so, it is owing entirely to my own bungling; I meant to be quite otherwise, as you yourself know my sentiments to be. I certainly think they, in common with their R. C. opponents, were much harsher in their language than they needed to be. It was an age of controversy, and everybody used strong terms. The R. Catholics were every bit as bad, if not worse. I certainly would wish to separate, for this reason, their *real spirit* from their controversial phraseology. Nor does this appear a refined distinction to draw, but one which one is making constantly in judging of historical characters or parties. This is positively *the only exception* I make against them; while, on the other hand, I claim for them every noble and catholic feeling, and consider them the great defenders of our Church, to whom we owe everything. I confess, however, I should not rank the Reformers *among* these standard divines, who seem indeed to have been a decided *reaction* upon them, *i.e.* very much more High Church. Compare Laud and Jewel. No time for more theology.—Yours affectionately,

J. B. M.

Best remembrances to Mr. and Mrs. Rickards.

J. B. M. TO T. M.

OXFORD, *November* 11, 1842.

MY DEAR TOM,—. . . Has Oakeley sent you the circular about the Welsh Bishoprics? They say there is a chance of keeping them if something is done. . . . I have hardly been able to show any civility to young ——. There is something very pleasing about him, though he has not fallen into the Oxford mould. Perhaps none the worse for that; but Eton and Harrow, etc., send such mature and formed gentlemen now-a-days up to the University (absurdly so, I think), that one notices deficiency of manner and rusticity, however slight. Hampden and Macmullen are keeping up the war, M. refusing to defend the heretical propositions which H. sent him for his B.D. exercises, and claiming the right to choose his own, which he has by statute, and H. resisting. The Vice-Chancellor has been applied to, and documents examined. Vaughan Thomas assists M., who is certain to gain his point.

Do you know the Provost has refused Arthur testimonials, except on the condition of rejecting[1] No. XC. I saw the letter (a copy of which A. sent me). . . . He talks about *we* and *us*, as if he were the College. J. H. N. suggested a short answer, that Arthur accepted the Articles in the sense of Convocation of 1562; of course it will come to nothing, and Arthur must wait another year, when he will be out of the Provost's power.—Yours affectionately, J. B. M.

P.S.—I enclose the Provost's letter.

Provost's Letter to Arthur.

My dear Sir,—Before we can send you the testimonial you desire, as we have seen nothing of you for a long time, I must ask whether you have adopted any new opinions or new methods of interpreting the Thirty-nine Articles. Whether you would interpret those, for instance, which relate to the controversy between the Churches of England and Rome, not according to the intentions of those who framed them, but according to some supposed view of the Catholic Church, and so, perhaps, very nearly in accordance with the principles of Rome herself—considering, for example, Ecumenical Councils infallible, and not objecting to the Mass, or believing in the intercession of saints.

I trust I shall hear you have not adopted any opinion of this kind; but to sign a complete testimonial for orders requires a good deal more knowledge of the person who desires them, than we can possibly have of you without this inquiry, after so long an absence from Oxford.—I am always, my dear Sir, yours very faithfully, Edward Hawkins.

A. Mozley, Esq.

[1] My brother Arthur took his B.A. degree Christmas 1840, at the age of twenty-one.

To his Sister.

OXFORD, *November* 24, 1842.

What do you think of the Provost sending Arthur's testimonials after all?

Mr. Caswell, the Mormonite, has been here collecting books for his College in America. Mormonism was, of course, *the* subject, and one he is never tired of opening out. His deafness prevents him from entering into conversation strictly speaking, so he is compelled to hold forth; not that he is averse at all to the advantage thus derived from his infirmity. His facts are certainly most curious, and he is so dry and quaint— so American with all his Churchmanship. He screws up his mouth in such a way, as he winds up a good story. Knaves are especially delightful to him, and that constitutes the great charm of the Mormonite subject. He considers Smith the greatest scamp that ever lived, and himself, of course, privileged in proportion in the acquaintance he has formed with him. He breakfasted with me this morning, and entertained the party considerably. He is evidently a person of thorough business-like habits, and most American spirit of adventure; cares nothing for journeys. He goes to Cambridge in a day or two.

The Heads of Houses are going to do a good thing in petitioning for the Welsh Bishoprics. This is an improvement on their ordinary proceedings, as the Church Commission is a child of Sir Robert Peel's.—Yours affectionately,

J. B. M.

To his Sister.

OXFORD, *December* 10, 1842.

I send you Palmer's and Ward's letters, which tell their own history. People are afraid that the former will do harm from its strength of language and anathemas. Palmer has a penchant for anathematising; he has been longing to do it for some time, and this was too favourable an opportunity to resist. Ward does not get out of the scrape very well; and his assertion about J. H. N. is too like a puff—*incomparably greater*, as if he was puffing off some quack medicine. Things are looking as favourable as one could expect; whatever be the event of the contest, we shall show such strength as will convince the world that we are not a mere clique. J. H. N. is disquieted at ———'s proceedings [alluding to some extreme proceedings by a young High Church incumbent]. He is a foolish fellow, and ought to be floored; not but that his seniors have set him the example, there is no denying.—Yours affectionately,

J. B. M.

To his Sister.

Oxford, *December* 20, 1842.

There is a quondam member of the College visiting us just now, namely, Sibthorpe [who had recently gone over to Rome]; he is with Bloxam, and dines with the President to-day. I have not seen him, and probably shall not; though, I believe, he is prepared to receive callers. I cannot say, for my own part, that I have any great respect either for his character or his conduct, and, as I do not know much of him, shall not think it necessary to run any chance of an awkward interview. The President always was fond of him, though how far it arose from a partiality for old families that had tenanted the College, as Sibthorpe's, from time immemorial, it is impossible to say. It is supposed that if Sibthorpe had not resigned, it would have been a long time before the President could have brought himself to cross his name out. It is rather curious that S.'s fall from his carriage seems likely, from what one hears, to have the effect of withdrawing him from a public and important position among the Roman Catholics. They say his head has been so much affected by it, that preaching will be a great exertion. Bloxam thinks that half from this, and half from not liking his new associates particularly, he will probably retire into private life. I hear Wiseman is much disappointed at the small chances of our all coming over. Mr. Phillips had misled him by extravagant accounts.—Yours, J. B. M.

Late in 1842, a Magdalen friend had gone over to Rome. J. B. M. writes to his sister:—

February 25, 1843.

I saw a letter from B. S. the other day, from Oscot. It did not seem to me written in spirits, and he seemed to have nothing to say about the *persons* there; all is system and routine, going on and on like a machine. I fancy there are one or two clever interesting men there, who probably would not treat S. with any particular attention after they had got him. Wiseman, I understand, is rather a don. The rest are mere second-rate teachers in the school. They had been having a burial, and the quantity of *Dies iræ* seemed to have oppressed poor B. S. not a little.—Yours, J. B. M.

To his Sister.

March 25, 1843.

My dear Anne,—I have got over my labours[1] for the *British Critic*, I am happy to say, although one is rather sorry at the same time to dismiss a regular employment of some months' reading and writing. Ward intimated to me yesterday that Tom could write a strong article when he chose, not referring perhaps to any recent communication, but some time back. . . . Ward is not a little touchy about his compositions in the *British Critic*. But I know nothing about it. I should say that most of Ward's articles were obnoxious to pretty strong criticisms. I hope J. H. N.'s criticism of my own, last October,[2] has done some good, and made the present article a better arranged affair than that.—Yours affectionately,
J. B. M.

To his Sister.

April 6, 1843.

My dear Anne,—Thank you very sincerely for your critical epistle. I see you know how to please an unfortunate author who wants a little bit of praise after the termination of his labours. . . . The fact is, history must be pictorial, or even theatrical to a certain extent, in order to effect its object. It

---

[1] "Strafford."
[2] "Development of the Church in the Seventeenth Century."

is all very fine talking about simple facts and *solid* narrative, and so on; you must have something more than solidity to give a true idea even of the facts themselves. I should like to know the parts that you thought obscure. I have one or two in my eye. . . . Tom has sent me a note, very complimentary, but intimating that my hero must be considered, after all, a despotic character, and that despotism rebounds upon itself. He says this as if it was half his own opinion, half what others would say. I confess I tried to make it clear that despotism (monarchy, that is) was constitutional *then*, and that a man might stick up for it, as he might for anything else established. Was this *clear* to you—*i.e.* my historical view on the subject? My view, I say—but really I thought every person except strongly prejudiced Liberals acknowledged it.—Yours affectionately,
J. B. M.

In the May of 1843 he was much occupied with the Welsh Bishoprics, the Church Commission being about to bring in a bill for the union of the two Sees of St. Asaph and Bangor, and the appropriation of the funds of the suppressed bishopric to other Church purposes.[1] Against this measure J. B. M. used his pen with effect, through such means as offered themselves. A packet of letters remains addressed to him from the Temple, by Mr. E. Badeley, himself very energetic in the cause and in communication with the leading opponents of the bill. His letters at first are not hopeful. He writes to J. B. M.:—

TEMPLE, *May* 6, 1843.

MY DEAR MOZLEY,— . . . I saw the Bishop of Bangor on Sunday, and from him I learnt that Lord Powis had had an-

[1] "It is not too well known that, among the recommendations of the Ecclesiatical Commissioners for England and Wales, which form the substance of the celebrated Act of 6 and 7 Will. IV. c. 77, is one which provides for the union of these two time-honoured bishoprics, as they are happily termed in a document now lying before us; in other words, for the suppression of one of them upon the first vacancy, presuming, of course, that the survivor agrees to undertake the additional responsibility. Nothing is required but an Order of the Queen in Council to give effect to this calamitous provision which has now become part and parcel of the law of the land, subject only to the aforesaid condition."—*British Critic*, vol. xxxiii. p. 237. Jan. 1843.

other interview with the Archbishop to receive his answer to the deputation which addressed him at the beginning of March —that the Archbishop was obstinate, and gave no hope of yielding—that there had been a meeting of Welsh Peers and the Primus at Lord Powis's house, where it had been agreed to make an attempt with the Government, and for this purpose to send a deputation to Sir R. Peel, with the Bishops of Bangor and St. Asaph at its head, and, after this effort to bring the Ministers over, to introduce the proposed bill into the Lords instead of the Commons, as before intended. . . . Ever yours sincerely, E. BADELEY.

The "proposed bill" here mentioned was a bill to repeal so much of the Church Commission Act as affected the two threatened Sees. Again, May 9, Mr. Badeley writes :—

The Welsh Bishopric question has been somewhat sleepy of late. I believe it is only by frequently repeated raps that we can hope to keep it awake. . . . I am rather anxious for a renewal of agitation. Might not a convenient road be opened, through this question, first to putting the Ecclesiastical Commission in its true position, and thence letting all people into proper views about *Convocation and Ecclesiastical Synods.* The ignorance on these subjects *is hideous.* You probably know Newman's articles on Convocation in the *British Magazine* some seven or eight years ago. I have almost wished for a separate reprint of them, with additions.

Again :—

May 12.

I have looked in vain, and asked other persons with equal bad success, for the speech of the Archbishop which you want. The North Wales Deputation are to go to Sir R. Peel tomorrow. They do not seem very sanguine of success, but the bill, I conclude, will be brought in, and it might be worth while to give it a start when it comes.

On the 17th of May, Mr. Badeley writes :—

I saw Lord Powis yesterday, and had a long account from

him of his interviews with the Archbishop and Sir R. Peel about the North Wales Bishopric. The Primate and the Premier were alike unsatisfactory. The former repeated his old absurd answers, "that he saw no particular reason for altering the Law now—that no objection had been made at the time," etc., etc. The latter seemed to think that if he concurred in any change of what had thus been decided by legislation and the Ecclesiastical Commissioners, he should be shaking the confidence of the country!! The Duke of Wellington puts himself with the Archbishop, and thus I fear there is very little chance of success this year. Of the Bishops, Lord Powis seemed to think there were nine with us, six against us, and nine more less doubtful. Perhaps your plan may be best—to omit the firing of shots at this time, and to resume the subject in order to another bill next year—though I confess I should have liked some very pungent articles on the Government and the Commission at once, in order to show them the unpopularity as well as the folly and iniquity of the course they are pursuing.—Ever yours, most sincerely, E. BADELEY.

Lord Powis means to move the second reading of our St. Asaph Bill next Tuesday, the 23d.

MR. BADELEY TO J. B. M.

TEMPLE, *June* 2, 1843.

DEAR MOZLEY,—Lord Powis has fixed the 11th of this month for his fight in the Lords about the N. Wales Bishopric, and a severe fight it is likely to be. If you have an opportunity, it would be as well to launch the forked lightning of P. H. S. at the Government and the Archbishop again, before the day comes. There may be some occasion for doing so, by noticing what has been done within the last few days at Oxford,—the Vice-Chancellor and Heads having agreed to give Lord Powis a D.C.L. at the Commemoration, in testimony of the sense the University entertains of his services on this question. The V.-C. sent a communication to this effect to Lord Powis, and he is much gratified with the compliment, and accepts. Peel and the Abp. are as obstinate as ever. Lord Powis had a more good-humoured and favourable interview with the Duke and the Bp. of London than he had with Abp. and Peel. The Abp. told Lord Powis that as he had now got archdeacons and saved the canonries of St. Asaph and Bangor, he might be satisfied. Lord Powis answered, that "archdeacons and canons were not bishops." (*N.B.*—This was a private interview.) Peel was dry and formal, and ill-tempered. The Bishops of Exeter and Sarum came up to town, on purpose to aid our bill. . . . I think our friends are put upon their mettle. You may aid the good cause by another preparatory shot.—Ever yours sincerely, E. BADELEY.

Dr. Pusey's suspension for two years, viewed in all its circumstances and his own behaviour under it, was certainly one of the most striking events of this eventful period. The stir that followed the announcement of the suspension, and the indignation amongst Dr. Pusey's friends, may be seen in the home letter written in the midst of all the work of protest:—

TO HIS SISTER.

OXFORD, *June* 4, 1843.

I have been writing day after day all this week, but something has just come to take me over the post time. You have heard, of course, of Pusey's suspension for two years, by the papers. It excites enormous indignation. All persons who are not quite with the Heads of Houses' clique are disgusted. It was really a sermon which people heard and went away, thinking it fine and eloquent of course, and giving high views of the Eucharist; but as for any doctrine, the idea never entered into any one's head, till the fact came out. The Heads will find themselves in the wrong, their mode of conducting the whole business has been so desperately unfair, not to say actually arrogant and tyrannical. What do you say to Pusey, in the interval between the call for the sermon and the judgment, actually receiving a note from the V.-Chancellor—a formal and official one—commanding him to hold no intercourse with his friends on the subject? The sermon is published, and now, I hope, something in the way of a general display of sentiment will take place.[1] . . . They have no notion of law—not an idea that there is anything *in rerum naturæ* to prevent them doing what they please. The Provost is in high spirits, so bland and courteous. He thinks he has done the thing, but it remains to be proved which way, for they have now made it a war *pro aris et focis*. If a thing of this kind were tolerated for a moment, we might as well take ourselves off with our tails between our legs. To show you the unrestrained, loose idea they have of their position, when Hampden first heard of his citation by Macmullen, he sent to his Proctor to say "he should have nothing to do with it—nothing to do with it." His Proctor advised him to change his mind on the subject, as in that case he should be reluctantly compelled to arrest him the next morning. This is a symptom of their state of mind. I send you a little thing of my own, and Pusey's protest, though of course you have seen the latter. Mine is a technical affair rather. You will understand, however, the main drift of it.

I should have written yesterday, but what with having to attend Convocation, lionising, and squibbing, I let the whole day pass. Three o'clock is the worst time in the world for the post to go out. Tom left to take his duty at Cholderton yesterday; comes back to-morrow.—Yours affectionately, J. B. M.

T. M. and his wife were at Oxford at this time. In a letter to her sister, June 12, Mrs. Thomas Mozley writes :—" James is

[1] The occasion is so very long past that a few facts may help the reader. The subject of the sermon preached at Christ Church, the Fourth Sunday after Easter, was "The Holy Eucharist, a Comfort to the Penitent." Objection was taken to it, and complaint made to the Vice-Chancellor, Dr. Wynter, by Dr. Faussett, Margaret Professor of Divinity. Upon this the Vice-Chancellor sent for the sermon, and appointed six Doctors in conjunction with himself—their names, Dr. Faussett, the complainant; Dr. Jenkyns, Master of Balliol; Dr. Hawkins, Provost of Oriel; Dr. Symons, Warden of Wadham; Dr. Jelf, Canon of Christ Church; Dr. Ogilvie, Regius Professor of Pastoral Theology. Sentence of suspension was passed, but the Vice-Chancellor steadily refused then, or at any subsequent period, to state the grounds of condemnation.

at the bottom of everything that is going on;" at the same time repeating that all the world was criticising Dr. Pusey's line. Clearly he was a man difficult to help, but the result proved that his own course of action fitted his character.

In this busy and exciting period, J. B. M. still found time for the *British Critic*, and was in communication with Mr. Badeley on certain legal points connected with the proposed Jerusalem Bishopric, on which an article of his appeared in the July number of that periodical.

To return to the leading subject of the day, he writes home:—

OXFORD, *July* 4, 1843.

I hope Arthur sent you a good account how things were going on. On looking back, the whole term is just like a dream, and one only has a vague recollection that one has been bustling about, both in body and mind, and doing nothing, as one ordinarily does, and that, among other things, there has been a sort of suspension of the ordinary communications home. The address to the Vice-Chancellor has not got on so well as might have been expected, so many who entirely disapprove of the Heads' proceedings objecting to the form of the address, or of an address at all. . . . The mysterious correspondence between the Vice-Chancellor and Pusey leaves a kind of *terra incognita*, which makes people feel not comfortable. Pusey has been most unfortunate in allowing himself to be caught so. He has absolutely got suspicion upon himself for what should have been indignation at the other party's injustice. I have just cast my eye over Tom's article, the *B. C.* being only just come. He seems to take a good bold straightforward line as to the total illegality and informality of the act, though what legal redress is practicable is another question.—Yours,

J. B. M.

Friends from the country had written, taking the same line. Mr. Rickards, of Stow-Langtoft, writes, on first hearing the news:—

MR. RICKARDS TO J. B. M.

STOWLANGTOFT, *June* 17, 1843.

MY DEAR MOZLEY,—Thank you for the papers which, one after another, you have been so good as to send me. We are all at a pause here, and in amazement too—waiting for the sermon; hardly believing that the Doctors can have condemned the doctrine of the Real Presence, and still less willing to believe that Dr. Pusey can have taught that by transubstantiation or consubstantiation. At present, in all this ignorance, the only thing I am shocked at is, the not saying to him outright, You have offended thus and thus. All the rest I can suppose accounted for; but this I speak not of till I know more, lest I should use hard words in vain.—Believe me, my dear Mozley, most sincerely yours, SAMUEL RICKARDS.

And, on the publication of the letter, he thus delivers his feelings:—

STOWLANGTOFT, *July* 6, 1843.

MY DEAR ANNE,— . . . This morning I have been reading Dr. Pusey's sermon with amazement at what has happened, and with indignation at the doctors. I cannot write the word with a big D while I write it of them. There is a good deal in the sermon of another sort which I did not expect—I mean, oddly and questionably expressed (I think); but as to the substance of it, and, most of all, on the point censured, if that be not true primitive and Church of England doctrine, I am much more astray myself than I believe myself to be. Indeed, I am shocked at the decision beyond, and far beyond, what I expected, until I read for myself.—Believe me, most sincerely, your friend, SAMUEL RICKARDS.

At the end of July, J. B. M. writes from Oxford:—

"I have seen hardly anybody here. 30,000 sold—the last account of Pusey's sermon; so said at least. [Frank] Faber had a note from Pusey yesterday, describing himself as receiving a great deal of sympathy from all quarters. The Bishop of Oxford has declared strongly in defence of the sermon. Ryder has just told me of an uncle of his, a strong Whig, who thinks the Doctors have behaved most unjustly. Whatever Pusey may get, they have got and will get nothing by the affair.—Yours,

J. B. M.

The following note is among the first in a collection of James Mozley's letters, to his friend Mr. Church (now Dean of St. Paul's), from which I have been allowed to select letters on subjects of the day, and on deeper or more personal matters, which will be felt to add greatly to the interest of the present volume.

To the Rev. R. W. Church.

12 Paper Buildings, *August* 1843.

My dear Church,—Have tidings of the correspondence between Badeley and the Vice-Chancellor reached you? The V.-C. has positively refused to receive the address, and attributed malicious and seditious motives to the signers of it!—says they are acting against their University oaths! You never saw such a document for unbridled folly. Gladstone, Judge Coleridge, and all are put together, and the whole set put down as boys; and the V.-C. acts as if he were the Vice-Chancellor of the universe. Badeley is amazingly on the *qui vive* about it, enjoying it more than I can describe. Gladstone is excessively indignant; Hook rages. The latter has dedicated a new work of his to Pusey; I question whether he has not written it on purpose to dedicate it. On the whole, it is a rich climax. . . . —Yours affectionately, J. B. M.

In the autumn of 1843 Mr. Newman resigned St. Mary's. James seems to have written to him either on the fact or the rumour reaching him; for the answer, dated September 1, thanks him for a "most kind note;" then, for the first time, confiding to him his reasons for the step. To his sister he writes :—

Oxford, *September* 6, 1843.

Newman giving up St. Mary's is indeed sad news. He says in his note to me he is very sick at the idea of it. . . . At

Westminster Abbey, on Friday, I met Captain Bowden, who engaged me to come to him at Wimbledon on the Monday. There I met H. W. Wilberforce. He is as amusing as ever. He gave us an accurate account of the paper got up in his own parish against himself and his curate (St. John) by a set of people, James the novelist among the rest. The Archbishop behaved very well about it, and took no notice. St. John was offered the living, on H. W.'s recommendation, but declined on finding he could not keep his studentship of Ch. Ch. with it.

It was a time of stir and agitation of thought—a time when persons were thrown upon themselves, to act no longer as members of a party under a leader, but each to consult his own judgment, experience, and character how best to work for the cause and principles he had at heart. The following letters recognise the importance of the crisis :—

To the Rev. R. W. Church.

Bearwood, *September* 11, 1843.

My dear Church,— ... Now I have a piece of news for you. My brother has given up the *British Critic*. This is not exactly public as yet, but will be soon. Both Rogers and myself think that you would be just the person to succeed. What say you? Of course Rivington has not made any offer as yet, nor do I hear of his having written to J. H. N. or any body; but if one had a name one might be at him in the first instance, and prevent the *B. C.* getting out of our hands altogether. For I think it just possible that Rivington may take fright now, and put the *B. C.* back into its old quarters again.

Things are looking melancholy now, my dear Church, and you and I and all of us *who can act together* must be bestirring ourselves. I feel as if a new stage in the drama were beginning, in which we shall have to do the uncomfortable thing, and take rather higher parts than we have done hitherto, or at any rate we must try our best.—Yours affectionately,

J. B. M.

Of another person unsettled by the aspect of affairs, and avowing a leaning towards Rome, he writes about the same time to a friend:—

September, 1843.

A. B. never cared much about the Church of England. All his very youthful days he was a Liberal, or something like one, and thought the Church system, and the Oxford system, and all systems established wrong, much on the Liberal system of change. Afterwards he altered in deference to Newman and Froude. But he never had any feelings for the Church; he never cared about her best men or her interesting periods. He never cared a jot for Charles I., or Laud, and all the rest of them. He has not, and never had, any historical, poetical, or romantic associations connected with her. All this is quite out of his line. He sees nothing but what exists practically before his eyes,—a bad diseased system. And the soul or essence of a Church, which lives underneath, it is not his character to see. We should take our Church as a whole, and look on her historically, and trace her tendencies. He would call this mere Toryism. You unfortunate High Church, as you call yourselves in the country, I can assure you, are not a bit worse off than we of that school are elsewhere.

We must all comfort one another as well as we can. I should like much to have some talk with you. I am melancholy, but do *not* despair. There is a spirit within the Church now, I think, that will work whatever individuals leave her.

Another of his letters, about the same date, ends—

" I for one must and will believe that this Church exists and may be appealed to, elicited, brought out, and developed in a course of time from amidst the mass of inconsistencies that encumber her."

In this state of feeling the retention of the *British Critic*, as the organ of the High Church party, was a matter of concern to him.

September 16, 1843.

MY DEAR CHURCH,—You are indeed a most modest person, as I always thought you, and as all your friends think you. I admire genuine modesty and humility. I have a penchant for it. Nevertheless I should like to see you editor of the *B. C.*, and wish it depended on myself. Unfortunately that is not the case. I called on Rivington the other day. He was very civil, even communicative on the subject of the *B. C.* Seemed less alarmed at the whole state of things than I expected; inclined to keep up *B. C.* on its hitherto footing, only dropping Oakeley. But he did not give any opening for my talking of a successor, otherwise I should have mustered all my delicacies and impudencies and ambages, and insinuated a certain individual who was the author of mediæval articles, and who seemed exactly to represent the tone that he wished to keep up. As it was, I departed, though perhaps something may have been done. I was studiously moderate, of course. I suspect he took my visit as an offer of myself. This was my fear at the first, but it could not be avoided.

I hardly expect to be in Oxford yet. I have not been very well lately—that is, have had a cold of a nastier description than my ordinary colds are, and should like to get home or to the sea-side if I could. I am about an article on Pusey's sermon, which I am sick of, though I only began it two days ago.—Yours affectionately, J. B. M.

TO HIS SISTER.

OXFORD, *November* 7, 1843.

We have been uncommonly quiet this term, one reason of which is that almost everybody is ill or invalided. [Frank] Faber wan as ever. Palmer has his eyes so bad that he cannot use them for anything. I am something of an invalid too, though Wootton says there is nothing the matter with me. Archdeacon Manning preached on Sunday, a testification sermon against the *British Critic*. I did not like either the matter or tone. He seemed really so carried away by fear of Romanism that he almost took under his patronage the Puritans and the Whigs of

1688, because they had settled the matter against the Pope. He did not indeed commit himself into a direct approval of them and the means they used, but talked of the whole movement as having had a happy event and being providential. Yet he went up to Littlemore and saw J. H. N. yesterday. I suppose he wants to disconnect himself regularly from the ultra party, and has taken this means. The Heads are immensely taken with the sermon of course. It had no merits as a composition, and was much inferior to his former ones. . . .

As for Y. Z., I do not think he means to cut the party altogether, but is one of those persons who are always thinking of their *own position*, just as invalids think of their stomachs; and if he signs an address to the V.-C. he must prop himself up by some counter step the next opportunity.

Sibthorpe [who had lately renounced Rome, and returned to the Church he had so lately forsaken] is expected here at Christmas. He has suffered, Bloxam says, amazingly throughout. But there are some persons who privately enjoy these spiritual uneasinesses and doubts, and I half suspect he is one. Mariolatry is the point on which he has started. I have no doubt there are things to astonish any one in that way, but he might have anticipated them. . . . Yours affectionately, J. B. MOZLEY.

In a letter home he writes:—

November 14, 1843.

R. Palmer is going to present his Fellowship to the College to buy new windows for the chapel, and we are going to rebuild our gateway in Gothic style. Pugin has sent in a plan which will probably be adopted.

Lincoln's Inn Preachership is now in the field. Manning and Palmer met, and had mutual complimentings and offerings to withdraw. Manning, I think, stands. Claughton is another candidate. They say Manning is too strong for the Lincoln's Inn men; if so, it shows the inutility of men making demonstrations, for his sermon here was thought quite low. You see Palmer [of Worcester], notwithstanding all his demonstrations, figures in *The Standard* as a Puseyite and introducer of

Romanism. *The Standard* professes to see through his protest. How unlucky! The world won't believe people, say what they will. All are put together in one heap. We are going on now in a sort of jumble-jamble way—differing amongst ourselves and attacked from without. No one can look very far into the future, and prophesy from such confused data. The clearest heads are puzzled, and our great strength lies in the anility and low principles of our assailants. It is to be hoped there is sufficient good principle at bottom left among us for people not to allow themselves to be ridden over by the Hebdomadal Board.—Yours affectionately, J. B. M.

The latter allusion is to a test or statute the Board was suspected of planning about B.D. degrees.

A letter, dated December 9, says that "Rivington has for certain offered the *British Critic* to Palmer (of Worcester), and Palmer is going to get up a meeting of Hook, etc., to know what he can do."

I am informed on the best authority that this statement is not correct. "It was decided to discontinue the *British Critic*. The editorship was not offered to any one. Mr. Palmer suggested another Church organ, which was issued under the title of the *English Review*."

In January 1844 I find a letter to J. B. M. from Mr. Palmer, asking for contributions to his periodical, and specifying the class of articles he would prefer, suggesting, for example, Prescott's *Conquest of Mexico*, *Travels in Ethiopia*, *Letters from Canada* :—a circumscribed range, which was not likely to offer many attractions; though there is nothing to show this from J. B. M. himself. In July of this year my brother announces to Mr. Church that the *Christian Remembrancer* is going to become a quarterly; and that in its new form he and the Rev. William Scott of Hoxton were to be joint editors. James contributed to the first number, which came out in October 1844, his article on Dr. Arnold.

Early in 1844 the Hebdomadal Board proposed a new statute for conferring B.D. degrees, a matter on which there had been a contention of some standing, between Dr. Hampden, whose office invested him with powers of conferring that degree, and Mr. Macmullen, whose Fellowship required him to proceed to B.D. in due course.

Against this proposed statute J. B. M. wrote a pamphlet, which Mr. Rickards congratulates him upon: "Thank you for the little pamphlet, of which the praise is that it does its work without becoming a big one—praise enough for any man or thing," and which receives the warm compliments of his friends, though no copy of it remains among the papers in my possession.

TO HIS SISTER.

OXFORD, *April* 1844.

... You see Hampden has rejected Macmullen after all. I only came late last night, and have seen nobody at all yet. I am glad that the question seems now brought to an issue, and put in an intelligible form before the world—namely, that persons who differ in opinion from Dr. Hampden are not now to be allowed their B.D., and to be deprived of their Fellowship in consequence. ... Macmullen is saved by a clause in the statute of his College, which allows his Fellowship to go on for a time if the *attempt* to get the degree has been made. ... Perhaps Mr. Rickards will send me a line before he comes up. ... Yours, J. B. M.

The next letter home tells the fate of the statute in Convocation :—

OXFORD, *May* 3, 1844.

MY DEAR ANNE,—I had not time to tell you yesterday of the event of the day. The majority was 341 against the statute, 21 for it, which makes a proportion of some 16 to 1. Nobody expected such a majority. There is no doubt that if the Heads had been united among themselves, and taken it up warmly, they could have commanded at any rate a few more than nine votes, for twelve among the Heads themselves must have passed the statute and voted for it in Congregation, which leaves nine Masters. Mr. Rickards dined with me on Wednesday, and a number of men looked in in the evening who had just come up. Bridges came up. X. was in high force, darting about, and speaking to almost six people at once, not having patience to get through any complete sentence to one individual before another became the object of his attention. Tom I saw for about half-an-hour. He went up to lunch at Mrs. Pearson's with Mr. Rickard and J. H. N. Dr. Hook looked remarkably majestic. There was a gay sprinkling of silk gowns in the theatre and quadrangle. The day was lucky too—a fine day is half the battle on such occasions. I hardly think any of the non-residents grumbled at having come up; they seemed to enjoy it.—Yours affectionately, J. B. M.

As one way of accounting for the smallness of the Heads' minority, a previous letter speaks of "the Duke" having had the proposed statute laid before him:—

The Duke's answer is considered a decided snub. . . . I cannot help thinking that Gladstone has been consulted by the Duke upon it. At any rate his character and known connection with the movement had not improbably an influence over a fellow Cabinet Minister. But the Duke's straightforwardness accounts for it without any other supposition. . . .

My patronage (as Fellow of Magdalen) is all over for an immense time. So my friends will care nothing about me, especially the dear ones from Lincolnshire and the stupid fathers of stupid sons, and all that class.—Yours,

J. B. M.

OXFORD, *May* 20, 1844.

I hear from Badeley that there is no hope of the Welsh Bishoprics Bill passing this time. Lord Powis and others had an interview with Sir R. Peel and the Archbishop the other day, and both were as obstinate as possible—said that the confidence of the country would be shaken if the decision of the Ecclesiastical Commission was upset. Nevertheless Lord Powis is to bring the bill into the House next week.

A letter two or three weeks later, from J. B. M., is in a different tone:—

Lord Powis and Serjeant Talfourd are to have D.C.L. degrees at Commemoration. The former should be cheered decidedly. I heard from Badeley this morning in high spirits at his success with the Welsh Bishoprics; the poor Archbishop [Howley], he says, was tamer than conceivable; seemed at last almost ashamed of himself. The Bishop of Exeter was very good.

In the same letter is a notice of Professor William Donkin, whose taste—or rather genius—for music was remarkable:—

Donkin played "Adelaide." There is certainly a *sui generis* character about his playing. He seems to personate a whole band—I mean all the variety and starts and flashes of it—in miniature. It is different from ordinary execution. Thus in the overture he played, the effect is not flashy or loud, but only very versatile, subtle, and varied.

In his *Life of Bishop Wilberforce*, Canon Ashwell gave a a page to the opposition raised to the election of Dr. Symons as Vice-Chancellor in succession to Dr. Wynter, on the ground of his having been one of the Six Doctors. The letters before us show how one or two eager spirits, confident in their cause, can override hesitation. Of course all the party were of one mind as to the fact that Symons was a most undesirable Vice-Chancellor. He was reported to have said the Puseyites had been treated too leniently, and ought to have been crushed long ago. His animus was bitter and unscrupulous. But the question was the expediency of the opposition. Mr. Henry

Wall of Balliol gave the chief impulse to the move. A letter from him brings out that J. B. M.'s first feeling had been against it. "I was not aware," writes Mr. Wall, " of the extent of your aversion to the measure of opposing Symons ;" so it is clear he had to be won over; but the letter shows a confidence of being able to carry the point, which had its effect. James is brought round, and writes to Mr. Keble. Mr. Keble answers :—

MR. KEBLE TO J. B. M.

I am sorry to seem to demur at any proposal of yours, but the truth is, I am not at all satisfied as to the *expediency* of such a move as this relating to the Vice-Chancellorship. I argued the point at Bisley with some one who seemed to think there were reasons of justice and dutifulness against it, and I said I had no feeling of that kind, but I doubted the expediency. However, if Marriott [Isaac Williams had written from Bisley strongly *for* the opposition to Symons] thought good to summon me, I promised to go. And then Marriott said there was little or no chance of a majority, but if we had only 150 votes against Symons, it would be worth while, etc. I will write to R. Wilberforce and some other friends, but I fear it will be very little that I shall be able to do. Your ground seems quite the right one, and I shall try to state it to people as well as I can. May I ask what would be the immediate consequence of our getting a majority, should so unlikely a thing occur ? *I* tell people, merely to make the next man, whoever he be, more careful.

Writing home, J. B. M. says :—

September 4, 1844.

Touching the V.-C. business, the thing is capable of being looked at two ways. Merely as an attack on Symons it is weak, but considering the whole of the present Vice-Chancellorship has been one continuous course of positive unconstitutional proceedings, it is a fair and solid ground to take to make a protest against it, and oppose a man as V.-C.

who is certain to continue it. And the time of a new V.-C. coming in is a definite, marked time to select from the show. It is certain to be done now, and, on the whole, I am glad for it. Keble, I. Williams, and R. Wilberforce are for it. The latter I was rather surprised at, but it proves so far that the idea commends itself to people.

R. Wilberforce, however, did not vote. Mr. Keble's letter was no doubt written when he had returned from Bisley to Hursley, and had thought quietly over the matter. An insight into the rise and progress of the affair seems to make some unaccountable things more intelligible. The result justified the less sanguine in their hesitation. Dr. Symons was elected by a majority of 882 to 183.

The first number of the *Christian Remembrancer*, as a quarterly, came out October 1844. Each editor contributed an article—James Mozley on Dr. Arnold, Mr. Scott on Mr. Keble's Prelections as Professor of Poetry. This article is described in the following letter:—

September 27, 1844.

MY DEAR ANNE,—It seems an age since I wrote home. I have been, as you might conjecture, tolerably busy lately. But the *C. R.* is all in the printer's hands now, and the thing finished for good or for bad this time. I confess my own article has been my chief work. I have not been very editorial. Scott's article on Keble is exceedingly good, thoroughly critical and scientific. It is an article it will do people positive good to read through. That is not perhaps the most captivating form of putting it. What I mean is that it points out a whole scientific view of poetry, and a whole field of criticism that will be new to many—of course gathered all from the Prelections. The translation from the Latin of Keble sounds quaint at times, but perhaps could not be helped. It is an odd situation to be translating from the Latin of an Englishman.

With respect to Arnold I have taken the line that I really and truly felt about him. And if any are offended I cannot help it. I depreciate more than condemn him; that is, I am conscious that my style throughout supposes him a less great man a good deal than what some think. However, it is no use heralding one's-self in this way.—Yours affectionately,

J. B. M.

A lady friend of Mr. Keble, in a letter of this date, tells me that Mr. Keble very much approves of the Arnold article, and speaks of James Mozley as a true son of the Church.

In October, after the number has come out and been read, he writes to his sister at Cholderton :—

I am glad to find my account of Arnold satisfies the Rugby men fairly. I did not want to offend them.

Our minority, small as it is, seems to be producing effects. Dr. Daubeny, calling on Bloxam, said that he and others were made so utterly miserable by such proceedings that they hoped they never would occur again. Bloxam said that depended on circumstances. The one fact of calling in question the rotation seems to put people out immensely. Their idea of the University is altogether disjointed by it. . . . Coleridge of Eton replied to some insults from some members of the majority rather well: "We have a saying at school that when a little boy fights a big boy, the big boy does not bully him again."—Yours affectionately, J. B. M.

Writing home he betrays a less cheerful tone on the same subject.

To HIS SISTER MARIA.

OXFORD, *November* 8, 1844.

Things look dark and cloudy just now. There is a general set upon us from all quarters, Conservative and Radical. The press never was so malignant. What is still worse is the utter indifference of a great number. Men who talk for you in a sort of way, and profess no sympathy with the attacks on us —*e.g.* on Pusey—yet take advantage of the first opportunity offered them, of coming up expressly to rivet the chain. A large proportion of the majority last time was composed of men with fair speeches in their mouths, who said they disliked everything the Heads had done, but thought this was not the mode or the occasion (or some periphrasis of that sort) of showing it. I can quite understand men being quiet and not liking to vote with us on such a question, but that men of professed High Churchmanship, and professing a strong disapprobation of the gross injustice shown to Pusey, should actually go out of their way, put themselves to trouble, come up in multitudes to perform a positive voluntary, gratuitous act, of swamping us, so far as mere weight could do it, is a fact that I cannot pass over; it seems *primâ facie* to show such heartlessness. . . .

For my own part, I feel that to be giving way to melancholy or disgust at the present state of things would be giving myself airs. I have no right to do it. Moreover, all movements have their dark times, and this may be only one of them, and one hopes it will pass off.

With respect to J. H. N., all I know about him is that he has been regularly down about things for the last year or two, and that he has expressed doubts as to the Catholicity of the English Church. I don't know anything more about it. He is hardly ever in Oxford now.—Yours affectionately,

J. B. M.

The test spoken of in the following letter was an alteration in the University Statutes proposed by the Hebdomadal Board, to be appended to the condemnation of Mr. Ward's book, *The Ideal of a Christian Church Considered.*

To his Sister.

There is a strong feeling against the Test in all moderate persons in Oxford and London, the only places I have been in. Badeley met Ernest Hawkins, who was not only against it himself, but said everybody else was he had seen. The ruse of the *piecing*—the joining the Test to Ward's business—only requires to be seen, to get us a majority. They could not carry a Test by itself. I hope it will be seen, though people are made strangely blind by a provoking book like Ward's.

With respect to Ward, I would simply tell Mr. Rickards [at whose house A. M. was staying, and who had expressed himself strongly against Ward], to think or not think about him, just as he likes. The Test is the thing we are concerned with—Ward can defend himself. The miserable state of things that will ensue here if it passes makes it almost a personal matter to ask one's friends to come up. Pusey will not take the Test—that he has declared publicly. What is the result? He will be liable any day to expulsion or perpetual banishment from the University. Every one who votes for the Test will be voting for his immediate liability to that punishment. Hussey the Professor, Eden, Baden Powell (!), and several Liberals, Price of Rugby, are all strong against it—a curious mixture. I distrust the Liberals, however, they hate us so. Gladstone is very strong, and thinks every exertion ought to be made against it.—Yours, J. B. M.

Towards the end of December J. B. M., as editor of the *Christian Remembrancer*, sent Dr. Pusey proofs of an article by H. W. W., to appear in the forthcoming number under the title "The Vice-Chancellorship of Dr. Wynter." The following remarks and comments, with the returned proofs, are honourably characteristic of the writer :—

DR. PUSEY TO J. B. M.

PRIVATE.

December 20, '44.

MY DEAR M.,—I doubt very seriously about all this invective against Dr. Wynter, because I was certain the whole was the proceeding of a timid, not of an unscrupulous man. He was afraid to commit himself, afraid to commit the University, afraid to make known why he condemned my sermon, or to let it pass uncondemned; unwilling to sentence me without giving me any chance of escape, yet afraid to commit himself to any controversy, and most unwilling of all that I should be able to say such and such propositions were given me to accept or reject. He thereby sacrificed himself; but, however, he became embittered, as it seems; and, although timidity often becomes the greatest cruelty, such was the key to his conduct, and so it is really wrong to speak of meanness, etc. These personal attacks always do harm to those who make them. I wish you would read over and amend these pages with this key. I think much would be better re-written. H. W. was in a great hurry, and has not put forth his mind. There are abusive epithets which do harm, but not much power. To say the whole, I involved myself so far, in my anxiety to obtain or force a hearing, that, though they took no notice of what I wrote, I committed myself enough to admit of a plausible *primâ facie* case to be made out, to give the *Record* and *Standard* scope for abuse. I am not anxious, then, for explanations. Of course, I know I am in the right in what I said; but there is enough in what I did to explain myself (though utterly useless), to enable them to throw dust into others' eyes.—Yours affectionately,   E. B. P.

P.S.—I have made two observations in the margin, but half erased them lest they should be printed. I have also altered one or two passages; if my substitution looks like my style you can retouch it.

In the midst of these exciting distractions, J. B. M. was engaged on his Article on Laud, which appeared January 1845, on which he writes to his sister :—

December 27.

I have been writing an article on Laud—my own biographical line again. He is a considerably more difficult character than Arnold—great, but twisty. It is difficult to follow him into all his corners. However, it is one good result of writing for a point of time—when the end of the month is come the thing must go in, good or bad, and it is over.

TO HIS SISTER.

LONDON, *January* 23, 1845.

They have got an opinion about the Degradation and the Test from Bethell and Dodson (Queen's Advocate), strongly against the legality of both. This was shown at the Hebdomadal Board, and oh! oh! d.; on the principle that any opinion could be got for two guineas. Nevertheless, it seems pretty certain that they will withdraw the Test. Almost the whole Board were giving their experience of the overwhelming majority of votes against it there was certain to be, the Provost alone declaring that his experience was two to one *for*; and that people's eyes were opening to its merits every day. Gaisford said he had been advised by a person of "very high consideration," supposed to be Sir J. Graham, to carry the two former [condemnation and degradation of Ward] with a high hand, but not to press the latter [the test].

At this time we gather from a letter of Archdeacon S. Wilberforce to Mr. Gladstone, the test was really given up.[1]

The statute, however, continued the subject of eager discussion beyond the date of this announcement. In one College several of the Fellows had declared their intention to the V.-C., to vote for the Test, when they were startled by the objection that it imposed an additional *examination*: "Very well, then, you want to saddle a new examination on the College." "Oh! Examination—I never heard anything about that." Second Voice—"That's quite a different thing." Third—"I'll be hanged if I'll vote for a new examination."

The Test being given up, the Hebdomadal Board startled the University by proposing the condemnation of Number Ninety—as a sort of second thought.

TO HIS SISTER.

OXFORD, *February* 1, 1845.

The Number Ninety move is a gross one indeed; I should

---

[1] "Since I wrote to you last, and told you in confidence the then decision, I have heard again (also in confidence) what much qualified that information. It is that—(1.) The Board of Heads will not withdraw the new statute solely because they will be beat upon it in Convocation; (2.) That they *will*, on address signed by men of known moderation; (3.) That they are certainly not averse to such an address; (4.) That I am esteemed a fit person to prepare it. I have drawn up this, and sent it to some friends."—*Life of Bishop Wilberforce*, vol. i. p. 356.

hardly think it can succeed. In the first place, there is not time for it now, to bring it on on the 13th; and it could hardly do to renew. That *da capo* plan seldom succeeds. There must be a week's notice, according to the rules of the Hebdomadal Board, before the discussion of the matter there, *after* the presentation of the petition. This, if the petition is presented Monday after next, which is the first opportunity it can, makes the simple discussion of the matter impossible at the Board till after the 13th, unless they violate their own rules, and, if they did, there is not, I think, statutable time from Monday to Thursday for the proposition that is to be brought before Convocation. Anyhow, it would have to be done with such disgraceful precipitation, that they dare hardly venture on it. Golightly is in thick communication with Dr. Ellerton, and is coming in and going out of College every day. He, and E., and F. are the trio on the subject. E. says nothing about it in public, which, if he was getting on well, he would certainly do; I asked him how he was getting on this morning, and he informed me that he had received the name of Mr. Hugh Stowell, at which I was not surprised. After all, it is really an impertinence for such men to head a movement, and think that the world will follow them. Their names will hardly do; at least, the fury of people must be tremendous if they can be caught by such.

Church [who, as Proctor, was member of the Board] describes the Hebdomadal Board as in a great fix about the opinion on Ward's Degradation; they hate giving way to it, and yet it bears its own solidity so genuinely upon it, that it will be a most disgraceful thing for them to bring on the measure in spite of it—and rush knowingly into an illegal act. I am clear for Arthur coming up, and voting against it; after Keble and Moberly and the rest have written against it, it should be opposed by all Churchmen. Besides, its illegality is quite a good ground enough in itself.

The Board do not relax one iota from their imperturbable self-conceit. All the world is wrong about things, and they are right. They are utterly incapable of understanding how the "Declaration" could be construed into a Test. Our Fellow,

Hutton, who is a friend of Ogilvie's, quite unconsciously mentions the "New Test" in a letter, not dreaming that it was not one, and received quite an angry answer, to say, that whatever way he voted, he *should* call things by their right names—it was *not* a Test.

Of course in the private correspondence between Archdeacon Wilberforce and Mr. Gladstone, it is treated simply as a test, and in all letters of the period. The statute could have no other use. The Test, under whatever name, was given up; but the No. XC. move grew beyond expectation.

The next letter is on the petition got up for the condemnation of No. XC.

TO HIS SISTER.

Ash Wednesday, 1845.

As you will have heard, the No. XC. move has mounted up tremendously. I confess it was so very low and ungenerous that I did not expect it; at the same time I was not, and am not, surprised, now it has happened so; one is surprised at nothing. If the University chooses to accept the guidance of such men as G. and E. and F., it is welcome, and much good may it do it. I cannot admire people's taste. It is remarkable, however, that among the 476 names only very few are resident, and *The Globe* acknowledges that it is bringing down the country parsons and the clubs upon us. The Hebdomadal Board are now fairly taking their line in putting themselves at the head of the non-residents, and determined to quash us one way or another. It is certainly owing to the Provost that the measure is passed; he was exceedingly bitter, and when men are bitter and strong, it becomes a matter of personal courtesy at the Board not to disoblige them.

I should have thought that the Provost, having got them into the scrape about the Test, would have impaired his influence a little. But a man who can talk is all-powerful.

We are sending down circulars with reasons against, and talking of the haste and precipitation of the measure. The present is a regular case, in which want of principle gives a party a positive advantage; only an exceedingly vulgar animus of a party could have brought itself to wake up a thing from four years ago, and *apropos* to nothing, to censure a man who has withdrawn from the University. Lord Ashley and the Bishops of Llandaff and Chichester signed the petition.

I am glad to hear so good account of my father.

Newman will take it very easy; but these things disgust and affect him more than he shows.—Yours affectionately,

J. B. M.

A few days later J. B. M. reports progress:—

To his Sister.

Oxford, *Saturday*, 1845.

We are very active here, and have been sending out circulars. I heard from Badeley yesterday; Judge Coleridge was fierce against the thing, and was for the Proctors vetoing. The Bishop of Exeter disapproved of it. Pusey heard from Gladstone, who was exceedingly indignant, and seemed almost to hint at some demonstration against it from himself.

Of course the thing will be carried unless the Proctors put their veto, but a good minority will tell in such a gross case. The Liberals were against it, many of them. Newman is of course very easy, though he feels such demonstrations more than he shows.

Rogers and Badeley are both writing, and I am engaged in a brochure.—Yours affectionately, J. B. M.

P.S.—You must console Mrs. Newman. Everybody who has any heart feels most indignant at this business, which is a consolation in its way.

This postscript refers to Mrs. E. Newman, an elderly lady, aunt to Mr. Newman, who had settled in Derby to be near her niece, Mrs. John Mozley, and who was greatly troubled by the whole state of things relating to her nephew, to whom she was devotedly attached.

To his Sister.

Oxford, *February* 1845.

The decision in Convocation will have come to you before you get this note: 777—386 on the first; 569—511 on the second. Some of our side were disappointed, and there was a general gloom thrown over us, for there really were strong expectations that the Degradation would not be carried. I never was sanguine enough to think so, and when I saw the full Theatre the affair seemed settled. But, after all, it was a near-run thing. A majority of fifty is nothing on such a question. The point is carried, and now a legal career is in prospect. Ward's speech was clear and fluent. He has a very good voice, and every word was heard.

The main line was that all parties in the Church did subscribe in a non-natural sense some parts or other of the Articles and formularies. His tone was too conversational, and had not effect enough. Mr. Blandy, however, was convinced by it, and consequently voted for him on the first point, on which he had not intended to vote at all. Mr. F. Dyson was up, and voted right. After all, I really am astonished at the number of men, and sort of men, who supported Ward after such avowals as he made. It is really a phenomenon to me. If he said once he said twenty times in the course of his speech, "I believe all the doctrines of the Roman Church," and 511 members of Convocation voted for him. Of course not half-a-dozen of these agree with him, but some think that Convocation is not the proper place to decide theological questions; others that Romanism is not worse than heresy, and that Ward ought not to be degraded when Hampden, and Whately, and a hundred others are let off. Still it is an extraordinary phenomenon to me that 511 should have voted so. Of course, we had a great many Liberals on our side, and all sorts of people on different grounds. But still it is considered on the whole a Puseyite minority.

Things are in an odd state, but we must take things as we find them. I heartily wish that Ward could have been gagged, but if he does say things, and come out, he is a fact and part of the state of things one has to cope with.

[A friend recalling the occasion, at which he was present, dwells on the proceedings immediately following upon Ward's speech—" The universal immense laughter with which it was received was one of the historical laughs of the world. I never remember anything like it."]

Gladstone came down on Wednesday night, and stayed with Hope, of Merton. I saw him, and breakfasted and dined yesterday with him at Hope's. He does not talk much. He is obviously exceedingly disgusted at the state of things here, and looked gloomy after the result of the Convocation, which he thought, however, "very fair for a mob." There is something very pleasing about him. Hope is a man one likes more the more one sees him. Sir W. Heathcote, Manning, Hook, D. Chandler, J. D. Coleridge, H. Wilberforce were the rest of the party.—Yours affectionately, J. B. M.

P.S.—Guillemarde, the Senior Proctor, delivered his veto with immense effect [this on the No. XC. question]. A shout of *Non* was raised, and resounded through the whole building and *Placets* from the other side, over which Guillemarde's *Nobis procuratoribus non placet* was heard like a trumpet, and cheered enormously. The Dean of Chichester threw himself out of his Doctor's seat, and shook both Proctors violently by the hand. The requisition has been renewed, as we expected. I don't know any more yet.

The requisition was, of course, to request the Board to renew the attack; but the following letter, written two months later, concludes the affair:—

OXFORD, 1845.

MY DEAR ANNE,—The matter about No. XC. was decided at the Board yesterday without a division—in the negative. There seemed to be no idea whatever of bringing it on again, and very little was said. A committee was appointed to draw up an answer to the requisitionists. The Proctors of last year thus stand in a somewhat triumphant position, having beaten the Hebdomadal Board. I suppose the answer to the requisitionists will be as high and mighty as it can be worded, but the fact remains.—Yours, J. B. M.

Immediately after the events of February 13, which have been given, Mr. Ward astonished the world by taking *The Times* into his confidence, in a matter generally regarded as of an essentially private character.

J. B. M. TO A. M.

March, 1845.

You do not mention Ward's letter to *The Times!* It is the general talk. I never read such a thing. The idea of a man writing to a paper about his marriage, and religious reasons. So complimentary to the lady!

Of course this was a circumstance to elicit comment among friends. One writes: "Ought he not to be 'poor Ward' for the future?" going on to say, "I can't quite analyse his last absurdity. . . . Egoism seems the predominant feature. Conceive a preacher of the saintly life expounding in *The Times!* . . . Will not the Heads accept it as a virtual recantation?" One asks, "What will Newman think of it?" Another answers J. B. M.'s letter already given: "An astonishing measure certainly. But I regard him as a sort of Frankenstein—a person made differently from other men; just to teach us how badly people get on who are guided, as they think, simply by reason; despising instincts, sympathies, and all the nameless humanities that make up a man." A letter from a friend to J. B. M., dated August 17, 1845, contains the following postscript:—

"Ward and his wife have formally, through Macmullen, announced their intention of joining Rome, giving a full month's notice 'not to take people by surprise.'"

The year 1845 was with J. B. M. one of extraordinary fertility and intellectual activity. In the midst of the distractions of public and private events he wrote five articles for the *Christian Remembrancer*, four of which, "Recent Proceedings at Oxford" in the April number, "Blanco White" in July, "History of the Russian Church," October, and "The Recent Schism," which came out January 1846, made large demands on thought and labour. This besides occasional pamphlets. Also this year *The Guardian* was planned by a few friends like-minded, among whom James Mozley was one prominent as writer and organiser. The Laud article, appearing in January 1845, was recognised at once as evidencing remarkable powers. Dr. Routh writes to him :—

February 19, 1845.

MY DEAR MR. MOZLEY,—I have read with interest and much admiration your development of the character of the great and good Archbishop. Pope said, after perusing the anonymous translation of the two satires of Juvenal, that the author would soon be *de terra*. Will you do me the favour of again accepting the office of Examiner for the Lusby Scholarship ?—I remain your obliged and faithful servant, M. J. ROUTH.

The heading of the article "Recent Proceedings in Oxford," in the April Number, is a curious illustration of the ferment that prevailed, being a list of thirty-three pamphlets and letters for and against the action of the Heads. The article towards its close has a touching passage on the attack on Mr. Newman, bearing out the feeling shown in the Private Correspondence.

What the feeling was under the pain and dread of impending change in the threatened loss of Mr. Newman to the English Church, the following letters show with telling force. My brother's letter to Mr. Scott (joint editor of the *Christian Remembrancer*) has been placed in my hand since Mr. Scott's death. His answer comes in its place in the correspondence of the year.

TO THE REV. W. SCOTT.

OXFORD, *May* 14*th*, 1845.

MY DEAR SCOTT,— . . . Now, to touch on a more serious subject, you mention Newman and the Littlemore company. I am afraid it is too true. Indeed, one can no longer speak in the ambiguous tone at all. It is actually to take place some time or other. One must be prepared for it. I ought to have written and talked about the subject with you before now; but it has been such a painful one to me, that I have never been able to do it, and even now it is a great effort to me to write about it. I have known of the tendency so long myself, indeed, that I hardly feel more acutely about it now than I did a year ago. I have got used to the idea in a way. But it is something like being used to being hanged. I hardly expect it to take place this year, but I cannot look for a much longer respite.

I had a note from Newman a month ago, immediately after the *C. R.* He wrote about my own article.[1] It had touched him much, he said. What he says of himself is, that he is borne along by an irresistible course of mind in the direction he is going—that he has withstood it, and yet it will take him. I don't know that there is anything very new in this. It is what most persons who go through religious changes describe themselves as undergoing. But it is the ground he takes; he cannot help the working of his own mind.

So now he has come to a point where I cannot follow him. It is a pain, indeed, to be in a church without him. But I cannot help that. No one, of course, can prophesy the course of his own mind; but I feel at present that I could no more leave the English Church than fly. What the upshot of this is to be we have yet to see. We are in a struggle. One's spiritual home is a stormy and unsettled one; but still it *is* one's home. At least it is mine.—Yours very truly,

J. B. MOZLEY.

To this letter Mr. Scott replied at once. It shows how deep a current of feeling flowed under a tone and manner characterised by an airy, half cynical humour.

May 17th, 1845.

MY DEAR MOZLEY,— . . . The mention of C. takes me (though, in truth, there is no taking, for my heart is always there) to J. H. N. Of course, in a way, one had for some time attempted to realise what must be, but it is just the same as

[1] "Recent Proceedings in Oxford."

attempting to realise losing wife or child. I for one have always, in my measure, leant upon Newman,—though I am scarcely acquainted with him—lived upon him, made him my other and better nature; so the crash is to me most overpowering. I dare not criticise any action of his; he is in gifts and acquirements and in all ways so infinitely above me that I cannot argue about the matter, only feel, and this of course selfishly. I cannot follow him. I have no calls that way. I cannot think that we are even what we are without God's especial providence, and this that we may be the better, not by individual but by corporate action and expansion. . . . Ever yours most truly, WILLIAM SCOTT.

In acknowledging a home notice of the Blanco White article in the July number of the *Christian Remembrancer*, James writes:—

. . . One's great feeling in reading through Blanco White was the singular antagonism in which his mind was to the doctrine of the Incarnation. All that part, by the way [criticising his own article], is somewhat clumsy, and if I had to write it over again, I would put it differently. I did not enter into what *was* Blanco White's religion enough. When I have written an article, and it is all printed, I feel like a schoolboy who has sent up an exercise with all sorts of mistakes in it, and cannot help himself: I mean with respect to arrangement and elucidation. You have exactly hit on the very parts that I meant to be the characterising ones as to B. W., which is satisfactory to me.

The President has had an odd accident—been bitten by a madman. His gardener at Tylehurst got into this state, and was secured in the arms of two men. The President went to him, to talk to him and soothe him, when the man, with a prodigious effort, meaning to embrace him affectionately, sprang out of his keepers' arms, and clasped the President to his breast, biting a great piece out of the back of his hand at the same time. The President has just been giving me an account of it, laughing enormously the whole of the time. The hand is going on well.—Yours affectionately, J. B. M.

On the 4th August of this year (1845), we lost our dear father, whose health had been for some time the cause of anxiety; every letter on either side conveying inquiries or reports, but the end came suddenly. For some time there is a blank of letters, James remaining at home with his mother and sisters. The first that occurs is the following to his sister, headed " *Private :* "—

October, 1845.

You will very likely have heard from Jemima that J. H. N.'s secession has actually taken place. I saw a letter or note of his to Keble, written just before he was going to be admitted. It said he was going to enter "the only fold of the Redeemer, the Church of St. Athanasius." Keble thought there was some excitement in the tone of his note, and was afraid for his state of mind afterwards. I only hope that the event having taken place, a good deal of what constitutes the anxiety and melancholy of the event, the uncertainty and expectation of something perpetually moving over one's head—that this part of the matter being at any rate over, we are relieved of something, though the fact is a bitter one. It is perhaps, on the whole, more comfortable to one's mind for a thing to *have* taken place than to be continually dreading it. J. B. M.

Writing from Winchester soon after, he tells his sister :—

" I spent a good part of the morning with Keble yesterday . . . Keble was in better spirits than I expected, and able to talk. Of course, you may conjecture the subject. He seemed very firm about the duty of remaining in our Church, and did not seem cast down, though exceedingly wounded by the recent events. Miss Keble is staying with him. I was much struck with her appearance. She has quite Keble's quick bright eye in the palest, most suffering face I ever saw."

It was on this occasion, no doubt, that J. B. M. consulted Mr. Keble on a plan for a devotional work he had then at heart, and which is discussed in the following thoughtful letter :—

REV. J. KEBLE TO J. B. M.

H. V., November 4, 1845.

My dear Mr. Mozley,—Excuse my not having written sooner. I have been very idle, and fancied myself very busy.

Such a book as you speak of is surely wanted; and to have it well done is exceedingly important. I suppose any one who entered on it, with the notion of compiling, ought to have his mind well impressed with this notion also, that *mere* compiling is a very dull thing; the passages one transcribes for such a purpose as this should flow from one's pen as naturally as if they were one's own. And this, I suppose, is one part of the secret of those R. C. compilations which you speak of. The several passages had been so meditated on and mixed up with the compiler's thoughts, that he could scarce distinguish the one from the other. And this seems to make a great difficulty in finding a proper person to do the work. It should be some one familiar, in the way I have now said, with our Andreweses, Wilsons, Taylors, Kens, etc., and also able to supply and connect where his text failed, in the same sort of way as Aquinas in the *Aurea Catena,* so as that the difference of material and workmanship should not be observable. On the whole, I think it almost more probable that a person may be found to do the thing well, originally, than such a compiler as I now speak of. Would it be a good plan to speak to two or three persons, to try what they could do for a certain time, either in the way of writing or compiling? If a certain number of earnest, thoughtful minds were employed thus for one twelvemonth, I can imagine a very good book or books resulting. It would be well, perhaps, to choose persons of different tones of thought and habits of life. But one essential requisite is that there should be no hurrying, nor any sensation of writing for a bookseller, or against time, or to counteract Rome, or to meet a call, or anything but pure desire to edify one's-self and others—love of the subject and of the work. I don't, of course, mean that we must wait till such purity of motive is to be found, but I do mean that in proportion as it is wanting, the book (I should fear) would fail. If anything else occurs worth writing I will write again.

I am anxious to know about the Leeds movement; more so from something I have heard this evening, as though things had fallen out rather to Pusey's discouragement.—Ever yours affectionately,
J. KEBLE.

TO HIS SISTER.

OXFORD, *November* 14, 1845.

The great event of the term has been the consecration of the church at Leeds. Pusey seems to be quite satisfied and impressed with the way in which it went off, and the good feeling and unanimity among the clergy assembled. Hook was exceedingly hearty, though very nervous beforehand, and apprehensive. He had a declaration against Popery ready to take off the effect of the meeting in that direction, but he gave it up. He was so exceedingly pleased when it was all over, and had passed off well, that his wife thought something was the matter with him; but it turned out to be simply joy and satisfaction. The Bishop, too, was dreadfully nervous, and, in fact, one would suppose Pusey was a lion, or some beast of prey, people seem to have been so afraid of him. The Bishop was afraid of being entrapped into anything, and objected to this and that. Among the rest, he saw on one of the doors the sentence—" Pray for the sinner who built this church," and required evidence that the sinner was *alive* before he consecrated. What was the greatest pity was, the sacramental plate did not appear at the consecration. There was an inscription on it that implied a prayer for the dead. It was, in fact, the gift of Lucy Pusey, and her name was, I believe, inscribed upon it. The Bishop says he will allow anything that the law allows; and I believe there is nothing against the law in this inscription. The point is not determined.

These little differences went on behind, and not in public, and Pusey was not annoyed, and took them very well. He and Hook seem to have been very cordial together. Henry Wilberforce, who was there, says he never saw Pusey come out so before. By the way, he does not preach this term, his turn not coming on till next February.—Yours affectionately,
J. B. M.

The last letter of this eventful year shows what new and strange duties were devolving upon him:—

J. B. M. TO HIS SISTER.

CLAYS, *December* 30, 1845.

I am working here at *C. R.* work—just seeing through the press the most disagreeable article I have ever had to write— one, namely, on Newman's secession.[1] It was absolutely necessary to notice the fact, and it fell to me to do it. I could not help myself. The article will, perhaps, have a decisiveness of tone to many ears, which (as being a new kind of tone to use in any sort of connection with Newman) will annoy some people. I expect it will, but the fact is not to be avoided that a new relation is begun between Newman and the English Church, and somebody must be the person to express that new relation. I have had the office, and a most disagreeable one it has been, as I say. But I feel strongly that, staying in the English Church, as I do, I stay to support her, and not to give her up, or stand loosely by her. There would be no excuse for staying on this latter ground, after this secession. The tone, however, of the article I have carefully guarded against being anything more decisive, nor do I think that N. can possibly complain of the view I take of him.—Yours affectionately,

J. B. M.

The article thus announced is read eagerly at home, and reassuring comments are sent. Mrs. John Mozley, reading and talking it over with his sisters, writes to J. B. M.:—

"I do feel so much obliged to you for the manner in which you have fulfilled your difficult and painful task. I had quite dreaded to see the case coolly discussed in print. Yet I felt, both from kindness and ability, you were the person to undertake it. . . . However, in some respects, J. H. N. would not agree with your view, I am sure he would estimate and feel grateful

---

[1] To this labour he had been impelled by his fellow-editor, Mr. Scott, who, writing on November 8, underscores the following words:—"*It is expected of us to take a line about Newman*, and WE CANNOT AVOID IT."

for the kindness and appreciation of his mind and powers, which the opening especially of your article shows. You must also allow me to express how much I admire and sympathise with the warm-hearted manner in which you stand forward as a champion of our poor assailed Church. It seems *a shameful thing* to have to assert even her very existence, and how painful to see people speak with only half a heart."

My sister Maria, staying then at Cholderton, delivers a message from Mrs. Thomas Mozley :—

" Harriet likes your article very much, and admires you in it— but she says there was a time before you knew him (J. H. N.) when he had a thorough attachment to our Church that you do not give him credit for; feeling himself completely in our Church. She mentions particularly a course of sermons on the Liturgy, preached, I think, about '29, which she liked exceedingly, and always entreated him to publish, but he never did."

To HIS SISTER.

January 16, 1846.

I have never thanked you and Jemima for your letters, which were very satisfactory to me. It was, of course, an anxious article to write, and one is very much relieved by hearing such opinions of it. I had a note from Wilson of Ampfield the other day, who tells me Keble is quite satisfied, which is a great comfort. He says " N. ought not to be hurt by it."

The following relates to Dr. Pusey's preparing to take his turn, after his two years' suspension :—

You see there is a dead-set made on Pusey by Golightly. The Heads are taking G.'s letters into consideration. I hardly think they will proceed to action, however, upon it. There is no tangible ground in the letter of Pusey in the *English Churchman*, and though they talk of a statute which requires a preacher to be *approbatus* by the Vice-Chancellor, it is very doubtful whether Pusey comes under it; because he preaches on a special statute, which commands all Heads of Houses, Canons of Ch. Ch., and

Regius Professors to preach in the course of the year. Anyhow it would be a consummate act of despotism which would be simply claiming the pulpit all the year round for the V.-C.'s own friends. Pusey is now at Brighton writing his sermon, very carefully. He intends to avoid giving any handle, if he possibly can. He is afraid it will be very long. I think that may be considered pretty certain; but nobody can complain after a two years' suspension. . . . Yours affectionately,

J. B. M.

To the Rev. R. W. Church.

Oxford, *Epiphany*, 1846.

My dear C.,—I read your article ["Brittany," *Christian Remembrancer*, January 1846], in the train, coming down. You have certainly managed to create a distinct image of Brittany. It is quite a whole. One has the idea that no other district in the world would have furnished that precise picture but Brittany. Also that view of Faith has so much in it, that you ought to make more of it, sometime or other. I could fancy it working up into something. The same of "the view of the powers which God's wisdom has in these last days placed in the hands of man." They are views which seem to explain our present state of things—the former, as showing that mediæval faith was not *so much* better than ours, as in one aspect it seems; the latter, as showing that our want of that aboriginal genuine faith has something to say in its defence and can point to a new dispensation of things which in some measure justifies or explains it.—Yours, J. B. M.

To his Sister Maria.

Oxford, *February* 1, 1846.

My dear Maria,—I have just come from Pusey's sermon. It was very grand, intense, and impressive—and went on with a great swing, as Pusey's sermons do. After nearly three years' silence, it was strange hearing his voice again. I should think the greater part of the audience had never heard him before. There was perfect stillness, and the mass was as dense as it could be. The procession of Heads was obliged to cut straight from the transept to their seats, instead of going all round, and down the middle aisle, as they usually do. There was nothing in the sermon to lay hold of, that I could see. The subject was Confession and the Power of the Keys. He had such a huge weight of Church authority with him, that he seemed to occupy the whole ground and possess the building for himself. He seemed to turn the vast tide of clamour, which has been trying to disconnect us from the Church so long, upon the other side. This in *effect* I only mean.

The sermon itself was simply practical, and put forward the plain statement in our formularies, and worked them out. The few I have seen since all think there is nothing to lay hold of. But that it will create great disgust I have no doubt. The only part I can fancy as being fastened on is where he spoke of College Tutors as men who might enter into more spiritual relations with those under them. He guarded himself, however, from any immediate, sudden application of what he said, and talked about time and waiting. I saw him just after the sermon; he was in very good spirits.—Yours affectionately,

J. B. M.

P.S.—The sermon will come out immediately.

To HIS SISTER.

February 9, 1846.

Pusey's sermon is not out yet. It is encasing itself, as most of his do, with notes, and making a regular fortification. What is said of it in high quarters here, is that "it is much to be lamented, but not to be complained of." Pusey is in high spirits—good spirits rather; and I think a little feeling of satisfaction at having silenced his silencers so effectually, might a little mingle with his feelings.—Yours affectionately,

J. B. M.

In January of this year *The Guardian* was launched into the world.

To HIS SISTER.

OXFORD, *April* 4, 1846.

... I mentioned *The Guardian* in my note, I think. It gains notice in good quarters, and that is all I can say. Professor Owen (a well-known man in the scientific world) was much struck with the review on *The Natural History of the Vestiges of the Creation.* Acland is very vigorous about it. But there wants the regular machinery for circulation. Then it does not appeal to any one class as other things do. Then people are so very touchy and peppery about a new paper, and think it a function of themselves, which the longer it goes on it gets the less to be.

There is an article in the *Dublin Review* in answer, in a great measure, to mine in the *C. R.* of last January. Its line is not an able one, which is rather to dissociate J. H. N.'s influence in the late move, and make it out to have been a coincidence in a number of minds equally at the same time. It would have been abler to have said Newman was the mover —and he was a providential one—as a line of argument.— Yours affectionately, J. B. M.

OXFORD, *May* 12, 1846.

DEAR ANNE,— ... I stayed in London till Saturday afternoon. I was unlucky in missing Dr. Mill, whom I called on at Lambeth. I had a long talk with Mr. Mathison at the Mint on the subject of education. He says the report is, the League, having succeeded in their Corn-Law movement, are going to commence an Educational one, and he was going to attend a meeting of the National Society, which had been summoned in the alarm of the report.—Yours affectionately,
J. B. M.

J. B. M. TO HIS SISTER.

OXFORD, *May* 20, 1846.

On Saturday I went down to East Farleigh, partly on pleasure, partly on business, to try to persuade H. W. to write an article I wanted written for the *Christian Remembrancer.* He was in London, and did not come till after my arrival. His mother was the only one in the house when I came. My ring at the door she supposed, of course, to be her son's; then, when I had sufficiently made it appear otherwise, another ring; and neither was this her son, but Mr. Spooner, the member for Birmingham, her brother-in-law, also an unexpected arrival. I felt I was going to appear awkward at finding myself interrupting their *tête-à-tête*, but found I had not much reason for it. For any one connected with the Wilberforces is used to interruptions and juxtapositions of all kinds. Mr. Spooner is a good-natured, violent Protestant—a mixture of an Evangelical and John Bull, very active, very talkative, and apparently exceedingly fond of business. He talked with great gusto of the committees at which he has to work incessantly, and enjoys it. He railed furiously at the whole House, declaring any 600 men in the streets were to be preferred to the present Parliament. On the whole, however, he enjoys his position. He is a strong Protectionist, but on some crotchety currency principle. All Sunday religious arguments were going on with good-natured vehemence between him and his nephew, who, by the way, I should say, came late on Saturday night with his Johnny, who had been sick on the way, after three days' dissipation in London, and was put to bed and slept eighteen hours, namely, till about five the next afternoon. Old Mrs. Wilberforce (Mrs. H. W. was in London) has to keep the old ground and the new one ;—her husband's and her sons',—and harmonise them ; which she does certainly very well. She is such an exceedingly mild, humble, pleasing old lady. I have met few like her. She was shocked at her brother preferring Unitarians to Roman Catholics. H. W. says she protests against him sometimes in private, and always takes his part openly.—Yours,   J. B. M.

OXFORD, *July* 1846.

MY DEAR ANNE,— . . . The fate of *The Guardian* is, I am afraid, sealed. The circulation keeps obstinately stationary, and B. has given his decided opinion that, after notice given, it must be dropped. I have a curious mixture of feelings on the subject, partly of humiliation at having to confess a most complete failure, and partly of relief that no more writing will be required for it.—Yours affectionately,   J. B. M.

The announcement that *The Guardian* must be discontinued for want of support excited warm remonstrances in certain quarters, where the need of a Church newspaper, and the satisfactory manner in which *The Guardian* promised to supply that need, was strongly felt. There survives a packet of letters from Churchmen of high name and credit, pressing its continuance. Amongst these letters are two of very urgent and friendly appeal from the present Bishop of Lincoln. Soon after J. B. M. reports :—

The Guardian, it has been resolved, is to go on, to complete its year of trial; but not till after much consultation and doubt. I think, on the whole, it is best it should, as it would have shown pusillanimity to give up before.

A turn of fortune, however, soon came. A friend and contributor writes to J. B. M. :—

October 23, 1846.

Sharpe and R. too are in great force about the *G. At last* we have got quoted in a morning paper, *Daily News*, by help of Le Verrier's letter. We may be caught out in some floor, but if we are not, I shall be very proud of the planet all my life long.

[If the writer of the letter is also the writer of the article in question, it may be said that he is not subject to "floors."]

A little book had been sent J. B. M., in which was the narrative of Gertrude Von der Wart :—

November 6, 1846.

MY DEAR ANNE,— . . . Gertrude Von der Wart is quite unique. I never read anything more beautiful. You have sometimes said you want to have an idea of what Homer really is. Now that is very like Homer, of course *mutatis mutandis*. There is the same sort of pure pathos, so very pungent, because so very truthful. I certainly get more and more to think that imagination is quite an inferior part of poetry. And Homer pleases because he exists altogether in a higher region than that of imagination—in that of absolute truth, the fact itself of high and pure feeling.

There has been a grand centenary at Ch. Ch., but dreadfully mismanaged, they say: the Dean not caring at all about it, and not letting those who did, manage it; so that hardly anybody has been asked. Sir R. Inglis came down, and I believe Gladstone.—Yours affectionately, J. B. M.

The year 1846 brings round, at precisely the same season, notice of another painful task completed: a task such as befell J. B. M. in 1845.

TEMPLE, *December* 30, 1846.

MY DEAR ANNE,—The *C. R.* will explain, when it comes out, why I have not been very communicative lately. You will see there is an article of prodigious length on a subject which it was absolutely necessary to notice, *i.e.* Newman's book. It is odd that such a task should have devolved upon me. There is a sort of fatality in these things; and Oriel seems destined to produce disagreement among friends. But so it is. The book must be noticed, and there was no one to do it but myself. Not that I have any delicacy on the subject, for J. H. N. has of course begun the difference, and that being the case, it is simply a fact that one is opposed to him; and whether one is silent or speaks it is all the same really. It has been most unpleasant work, however, not only on this account but from the argumentative style of writing one has to take up—most difficult and most dry. The thing has been hanging over me now for a year, and there is a relief that it is over. Not that the controversy itself is over, for controversy is in its own nature endless. But one may look about one a good deal before one has another call to enter the lists. . . . —Yours affectionately, J. B. M.

Such things cannot be helped; must be done; somebody must do them; and the line of thought was James Mozley's line: but such long task-work of antagonism towards a dear and most true friend leaves effects to be sighed over—effects which those escape on whom the ungrateful task does not fall.

To his Sister.

January 9, 1847.

My dear Anne,—I want to tell you how much pleased I am with my Stowlangtoft visit. Mr. and Mrs. Rickards are certainly a pair such as one does not often see—quite complete and perfect; such cheerfulness, simplicity, and cleverness, all going together, are quite a remarkable mixture. I had never seen Mr. R. before to have any continued conversation with him. He struck me much from the quantity of information he has, and his sharp neat way of always expressing what he wants, and bringing things to a point. The way in which he questioned me too, and got information himself (not much from me), was just the same. He puts just the right questions, and such as, if answered, would give him the best view of what he is asking about. Mrs. R.'s perpetual flow of spirits and benevolence is quite charming. I am glad I have been there . . . Maria will have told you about our doings and visitings.—Yours,
J. B. M.

To his Sister.

Oxford, *February* 9, 1847.

My dear Anne,—. . . I called on Pusey, who is looking tolerably cheerful after all his reverses lately. He is about a commentary on the minor prophets; part of a general commentary on the whole Bible, which is now thought of, not all from the same person, but one taking one part, another another. Pusey *intends* to make it a popular commentary, and to give the sense of the Fathers without references or (generally) extracts. Whether he will keep to his intention when it comes to, is perhaps doubtful, he is so fond of the quoting system. He says a new commentary is the proper way of meeting the Rationalists.

Mr. Hayes called on me the other day. He is a military-looking man, very simple, and hard in look and speech, but a man of respectable feeling, and well-disposed. He has been magistrate in India, and lived in stations where he was quite out of the reach of Europeans, who are a mere handful in India, and the great mass of the native population living by themselves, and with their religion and customs in full play, and nothing to disturb them. I asked him about Conversion; he said the great mass were absolutely untouched. The Europeans had not in fact come in contact with them. . . I asked him about the influence of the old superstitions on the Hindoo population as a whole, saying that I had understood it was less than it had been, and that the Brahmans were getting Liberal. He contradicted this, speaking from his own experience, and described the perfect immovability of a Bengalee Priest rather well, so soft and silky a person, that everything would melt like butter in his mouth, but you might as well try to shake a mountain as to persuade him. . . .

Sir Robert Inglis has written to the Heads of Houses, notifying on the part of the Government that they are going to look into the Universities. . . . Yours, J. B. M.

To his Sister.

May 20, 1847.

. . . I was in London yesterday on electioneering business, and Gladstone's committee seem to be in tolerable spirits. I did not see any of the great men, but only my own friends, the committee itself; the whole side are as odd a mixture as you can conceive. London Puseyites, who atone for their religion by their rank, mixing with Tyler, Hume Spry, Saunders of the Charterhouse, Hallam (the Whig historian), etc., and appended to this an Oxford committee of barefaced Puseyites, whom nobody in Oxford but themselves will join.

May 30.

The electioneering excitement has gone down a good deal. I have very little to do with the details of it, and do not know what the state of votes on our side is. I believe Gladstone is anxious to come in; and his dignity has so far given way that he goes about speechifying now at different places.—Yours, J. B. M.

P.S.—Whoever wants the book on painting [Ruskin's] to receive due notice, must write a review of it himself. I have got the experience by my *C. R.* labours, that nobody will write on a subject of another person's suggestion.

The following history of the Gladstone Election was written to his friend then abroad:—

OXFORD, *August* 6, 1847.

MY DEAR CHURCH,—You will have seen by the English papers the termination of our contest. We are of course elevated on the occasion. On meeting Michell to-day in the streets I was patronising and conciliatory; assured him that he would not regret the choice the University had made. It is rather curious that I do not think at any one time throughout the affair, which has now been going for three months and more, have the expectations of our side been equal to what they rationally might have been. The imagination was so strongly affected the other way. It was considered at first a sort of Tractarian puerility by many, our bringing forward Gladstone at all, so utopian did the chance of his success appear. Wall of Balliol was on Cardwell's committee. He laughed at the idea of Gladstone, and talked of 400 votes—more by the way, they say by 150, than Cardwell got. The most liberal set us at 600. Altogether a sort of stupor prevailed on the subject, in the midst of which, however, a most capital London committee was formed and began to work; Tyler being one of the first to join. Rogers described the melancholy meeting of three or four Gladstonians the first day or two, where they sat expecting. At last Tyler came—*advenisti o desiderabilis!* They felt as if they had caught the very largest salmon with melted butter, lobster sauce and all. Then Hume Spry, then Archdeacon Hale. I am telling you, I fear, what people have told you before, in all this. However, the London committee, which was out on the Saturday after the Tuesday of the first communication of Estcourt's retirement, was a great gain, and made an impression. I could see it producing an effect.

One of the most remarkable things was Gladstone consenting so immediately to be brought forward. The people in London had almost come to the resolution that he was an impossible card—*i.e.* too strong, I mean, in a party point of view for success. And they had sent down Bernard with Sir William Heathcote's name, to look about. In the meantime a carrier from us here—*i.e.* H. J. Coleridge, crossed Bernard on the road with Gladstone's name. Coleridge, as soon as he had arrived in town, heard of Bernard's mission with Heathcote's name, and was giving Gladstone up. But Hawkins and his father told him to go to Rogers. He went. R. sent him to Northcote. Northcote had an hour's conversation with Gladstone, at the end of which G. was a declared candidate. So the next day, Wednesday, we had a meeting here—*i.e.* in Magdalen—Gladstone's being the name. Sewell tried to extinguish us with a speech, and threatened his fiercest opposition. But nevertheless we kept to our man. I must confess to have felt some most uncomfortable qualms throughout the first outset of the contest. To have to choose between two men like G. and Sir W. H., gave a most uncomfortable responsibility. And one heard on all sides, Oh! we should have no objection to *Sir William Heathcote*. In fact his name was *mentioned* actually at the first meeting at Ogilvie's, who ultimately chose Round; so *apparently* certain we should have been of him, had we fixed on him. Of course it would have been a different thing altogether from having Gladstone; but he would have been a very good man. Let us hope for him one day as Gladstone's colleague.

You should hear Johnson; he says it is "the perfection of beauty." First, we have bowled out eleven Heads of Houses and Cardwell. Secondly, we have bowled them all out again, and Round. And thirdly—which is a spice for the simply malignant to relish—Round himself has lost his seat in Essex in consequence.

The Provost has behaved very characteristically. He has been for once in his life fairly perplexed; and he has doubled and doubled again, and shifted, and crept into holes; at last vanished up some dark crevice, and nothing was seen but his tail. One thought one was to see no more of him, when, on one of the polling mornings, he suddenly emerged, like a rat out of a haystack, and voted for Round. The Heads, in fact, have been thoroughly inefficient. The election has literally gone on *without* them. They have done nothing. Apparently they were sufficiently afraid of Gladstone's success not to like the chance of meeting him afterwards as declared opponents: and they could not bring themselves to vote for him, so they have been mere individual Roundites. One has hardly felt their existence throughout the contest. What do you think of Woolcombe of Balliol actually canvassing the Provost for Gladstone at the commencement! I should as soon have thought of engaging with a lion. Nevertheless, the Provost was most courteous. W. said we did not wish to make a religious contest. "Yes," said the Provost, "but Mr. Gladstone cannot help having his religious views." Then Woolcombe asked him, Whether he considered our position at all a factious one—a committee of M.A.s bringing forward their own man without any connection with the Heads? "Oh, no—not the least; it would be quite ridiculous to think so."

It is quite amusing to see how the contest has brought out some men: H. Coleridge, for example. He has been most useful throughout, and shown himself quite knowing. Then H. Harris has done a great deal among our young Magdalen men, and has quite surprised us all as a canvasser. Woolcombe of Balliol has been great too. Arthur Haddan is an old canvasser, and his experience in the Williams and Garbett case gave him a name. But he has kept up his reputation most decidedly. The astonishing perseverance with which he probed the *terra incognita* of names in the *University Calendar* was wonderful. There were only 600 at last of which he could give no account at all. I begin to doubt whether they exist myself. If they did, Haddan would certainly have got at them. Greswell was most characteristic, only his zeal was a too sanguine one. He was obliged to be kept in ignorance, as far as was possible, of the number of votes, and everything, because he went and boasted so immensely. As soon as we had got 800 votes he thought the contest over.

What a strange affair this is of the Nottingham election! John Walter was elected the day or two after his father's death, quite without his knowledge. The first intimation he had of it was in the report from the *Nottingham Reporter*, which came for insertion in *The Times*. It seems that the old gentleman's death produced a sudden sensation, and that out of gratitude they instantly resolved to elect his son. J. W. and H. W. were both here voting, though within two or three days of their father's death. The public-duty view prevailed. When shall we see you again? I send this by your brother.—Yours affectionately, J. B. MOZLEY.

W. E. GLADSTONE, M.P., TO J. B. M.

August 6, 1848.

MY DEAR MR. MOZLEY,—Your letter gives me peculiar pleasure by the announcement it contains that you believe many who voted against me in the recent contest are by no means broken-hearted at the issue. But I hope, in the anxiety to soften or remove adverse prepossession from the minds of any of those who are now become my constituents, I shall not lose sight of that deeper debt which I owe to my supporters, and especially, let me add, to my Oxford supporters, on account of the circumstance that there has hitherto been so little of personal acquaintance between them and the man to whom they have given their generous confidence, and their energetic and triumphant exertions. I am, believe me, truly thankful: the more thankful, I hope, from all that I know of myself, and of my own shortcomings, and of the tendency of my mind to make, some at least, of those shortcomings palpable in my public conduct; and from the high, the very high, conception which I entertain of the duties which should be rendered to Oxford by her representative. I am divided between the keenest pleasure upon finding myself so definitely and closely related to the University which I love with my whole heart, and the misgivings which, after having reflected a little on what I ought to be or to do, I turn to think of what I am. Of all the years of all the centuries which have made up her honoured existence, perhaps these now before us are the most critical—certainly they are among the most critical. I would that her interests were in stronger and in purer hands; God grant in His mercy that I may attain, after my election, to the gifts which I ought to have had before it. I rely most upon your assurance, which I am confident is more than verbal, that my weakness will not be forgotten in the prayers of those who bear affection to Oxford.

My hope is to be always there mentally, but much also bodily, and I have written to Mr. Greswell to ask *how long* a visit he thinks I may decently pay at the commencement of the October Term. So I will trouble you no longer.—Believe me, always very sincerely yours, W. E. GLADSTONE.

Rev. J. B. Mozley.

In the course of the next term the proposed visit was paid, and J. B. M. writes of the occasion to his sister :—

OXFORD, 1847.

Gladstone has been here this week. I met him on Monday at Greswell's. He did his part very well, but had to make a speech, which was somewhat gloomy in its forebodings. He talked of changes, and movements in a way not gratifying to established institutions; and the difficulties in which men in Parliament would be placed.

The fun of the evening was a speech of Greswell's, who congratulated us on our luck in winning the election; it was a series of the most lucky chances which had got it. He enlarged upon luck and chance to such a degree, as wholly to supersede the merits of the candidate himself as any part of the cause. And he went on so perfectly unconscious of this aspect of his speech, that, one by one, at last all the table were loudly tittering, which rose at last into unmistakable laughter —Gladstone, who had kept his countenance with the utmost rigidity for a long time, at last being forced to give way.

In November of this year Oxford was again thrown into commotion by Dr. Hampden's appointment to the See of Hereford. This is not a time or place in which to discuss the merits of the question, but a few letters may be given which throw light on the feeling and thought of the period.

TO HIS SISTER.

OXFORD, *December* 3, 1847.

MY DEAR ANNE,— . . . Thirteen bishops of the province of

Canterbury have signed a private memorial to Lord J. Russell against Hampden's appointment. This is a strong step. The opposition seems increasing too in the country.

I dined at the Bishop of Oxford's, at Cuddesden, on Monday. . . . I must say I was more pleased with the Bishop than I expected, for I rather dreaded coming into contact with him. There was less artificialness about him than I expected. A love of the humorous is a great leveller, and he can no more resist telling a good story, even though it a little compromises his dignity, than a dog can pass a tit-bone. He is exceedingly strong about this Hampden business, and thought it a subject on which the whole Church ought to make demonstrations. I am rather amused at the touchiness of the Bishops, now that there is a chance of their having Hampden on the same bench with them. They have very little respected our touchiness in Oxford on the subject, and have made men attend his lectures; —a circumstance with which Lord John will twit them, I doubt not. However, I am glad to see their orthodoxy—better late than never.—Yours affectionately, J. B. M.

Among letters and papers treating of the great Hampden question is one from Mr. Golightly to Dr. Ogle, with a message to J. B. M., "who cuts me now:"—of course on account of his recent denunciation of his brother in *The Standard*. It has something the air of an olive branch, and probably was received accordingly :—

"As Dr. Hampden's friends are making a vigorous attempt to persuade the public that the opposition to his nomination proceeds from only one party in the Church, could you take an opportunity of informing him [J. B. M.] that Vaughan Thomas, Lancaster, Trower, and myself, all members of Mr. Round's committee, have protested in some way or other. For myself, if my name can be of any use, I fully authorise the mention of it in *The Times, Guardian, English Churchman*, or any other periodical or paper."

A letter to J. B. M. from Mr. Charles Marriott—the most single-minded of men—throws a kindly light on the Bishop of Oxford's change of tone :—

BRADFIELD, *St. Stephen's*, 1847.

MY DEAR MOZLEY,—I have thought more about your letter on the connection of the Bampton Lectures and *Obs. on Rel. Dissent*, and am convinced that, though valid pleading, it is not really conclusive to the full.

The Bampton Lectures show so much confusion of thought, that their author is certainly capable of *thinking* for a time that a given view involves what it really does not. And so he might, in writing the *Observations*, *think* for the time that the principles of his B. L. must involve so much, and cease to think so afterwards. What he says of their being the same is his *own opinion* at a given time, but we know how much weight to attach to *it*.

I think, therefore, that if the Bishop clenches that withdrawal publicly, and expresses publicly his disapproval of the language of the B. L., while he allows the author to put an orthodox interpretation on it even at a little strain, and passes him under that interpretation, it is our business to acquiesce in his decision.

If the Bishop of Exeter presses for a more formal tribunal, I blame no one who co-operates with him, but I would allow the Bishop of Oxford's decision, though not exactly to my mind, to supersede my own opinion. I wish you to notice that in the passage on the Unity of God, Hampden calls this Unity a *fact*, thus admitting such a sense of the term. Don't try to set this aside, for you *ought* not. I have had a painful sense all these years, whenever I thought of Hampden, of his having been really misapprehended and misrepresented, though I still think, as I did from the first, that there was just ground for stronger acts than have been taken against him. I must say that my last conversation with the Bishop and subsequent consideration, have modified my opinion of Hampden's *honesty*. I used to doubt it much more than I do now. Pray excuse this rigmarole, and try to put as much ἐπιείκεια into the business as your dogmatic conscience will let you. Such a tiresome fellow is apt to put one's moral conscience to sleep.—Ever yours affectionately,   C. MARRIOTT.

A further reading of the lectures does not bring J. B. M. round to these opinions, but he recognises that much rests in *tone* :—

It is as clear as day what the theological system in them is, at the same time there would be great difficulty in proving it in a Court, especially such a prejudiced Court as Sir Herbert Jenner would make. You have a few passages where the system comes out strongly and decidedly, but these are very few, the rest lies in *tone*. For example he [Hampden] uses the words "heterodox" and "orthodox" throughout the lectures obviously with the most perfect impartiality between the two, thinking both equally wrong as being dogmatisers. I suppose no Court would take cognisance of *tone*. . . . Then the question would come to this, whether the few passages where the system does come out would be allowed to have their real weight assigned them as interpreting the rest.

The following letter relates to the confirmation at Bow Church, previous to the consecration of the Bishop-elect :—

TO HIS SISTER.

January 22, 1848.

I went up to London for a day the beginning of this week. Cornish (of Littlemore), who was there, described the scene at Bow Church as a more exciting one than the papers gave any idea of. He was certain that if it had not been in church there would have been a regular tumult. The *Second* "Oyez, oyez, oyez," of the crier, inviting opponents to come forward and state objections, ending with, "*and ye shall be heard,*" produced an extraordinary sensation of indignation. It added to the effect that the proclamation was delivered in the properly unconscious, sonorous, nasal tone in which criers deliver themselves; so that nothing of the ridiculous was lost. It was said Sir Fitzroy Kelly entered very keenly into the case, and was even sanguine as to the result. Lushington lost his temper at Bow, all seem to say, and behaved quite disreputably as a judge.—Yours affectionately, J. B. M.

A note from Mr. Keble to J. B. M., dated February 18, touches gently on the Bishop of Oxford's part in the whole business. A friend, under the initial T., had been endeavouring to engage his [Mr. Keble's] good offices for a friendly notice in *The Guardian.*

February 18, 1848.

MY DEAR MOZLEY,—... I explained to him that I considered the Bishop to have been carried away into weak and inconsistent behaviour through no bad motive, but from an earnest desire of peace joined to a fancy that he was the person to make it, as by a kind of special mission, which all must allow. I told him in substance that I thought Mr. K. had done more harm than good, and that the best line for the Bishop and his friends was to be quiet and leave it to his future conduct to show him the true and straightforward person which I have no doubt he wishes to be, and substantially is. . . .

Accept my best thanks for "Martin Luther," who I never expected could have been made so amusing and interesting as I find him—being now in my second reading.—Ever yours affectionately, J. KEBLE.

Writing soon after this correspondence, J. B. M. to his sister says:—" I have to dine—not an agreeable prospect—with the Bishop of Oxford on Wednesday, but he sent to ask me to meet his brother the Archdeacon, and I did not like to decline again." The Bishop's social charm was an influence he did well to rely on. He always seems to have been most himself when most pleasing.

TO HIS SISTER.

February 28, 1848.

. . . At Cuddesden there was not much of a party, and what there was was of the free and easy sort. . . . Robert

Wilberforce was there, and we—that is C. Marriott, myself, and he—went over in the same fly. The Bishop was as courteous and agreeable as ever. The subject of Hampden and the confirmation of bishops, etc., was fearlessly entered upon in the general, but I observed that *the* awkward point was always kept a respectable distance from. . . . The subject nicely moved round it, and never touched. Hampden's letters have evidently nettled him. . . . All, under-graduates included, made themselves perfectly at home, and certainly the Bishop has the art of making persons feel at home. He does not put on dignity. The Wilberforce nature prevails in him to a certain extent, notwithstanding his advancement.

What a tremendous affair seems coming on now! I never was so utterly astonished as at the first news of Louis Philippe's abdication. But this event, I suppose, will soon be left behind.

J. B. M.

Amongst papers, shortly after this date, is a little note signed with well-known initials:—"A pretty state we are in altogether, with a Radical Pope teaching all Europe rebellion! Every post brings a fresh argument for the duty of securing the middle classes if possible.—R. I. W."

J. B. M. TO HIS SISTER.

February, 1848.

There is a small excitement going on within a limited circle here in consequence of a Musical Professorship being vacant. There are some dozen candidates—among the rest, the two fierce rivals, Dr. Wesley and Dr. Gauntlet. Dr. Gauntlet made his appearance in my rooms on Saturday evening, and commenced instantly talking in a continuous flow about music and his own views. Before five minutes were over he was chanting a Psalm, in the style of what he conjectured to be the Temple service instituted by David. He has written a book, of which he produced the proof-sheets of Psalms with notation for chanting in this style. I was not fascinated by it. Dr. G. has one advantage—he is not a *loud* talker, though a copious one.

He is obviously too a clever man, and when he breakfasted with me the next morning talked sometimes about other subjects, and was amusing.—Yours,   J. B. M.

J. B. M. may be said to have had a passion for music, if that word is compatible with serenity of tone and manner in listening to it and talking of it. It stimulated thought. He had a correct ear and a fine intelligent perception of style and quality, a contempt for the commonplace and trash; he had strong tastes and dislikes, finding moral distinctions between different composers. He never listened indolently or unconsciously. It might seem strange that his share in the performance was never other than as a listener. But probably he had no singing voice (I doubt if any person ever heard him test his powers), and one may say that he never put his hand to any other skilled labour than that of holding and guiding a pen.

To his Sister.

Oxford, *March* 31, 1848.

... There have been some amusing struggles this term in the Union—*i.e.* Debating Society—on the subject of Stanley's Sermons. You know what they are—a new volume—which have been preached before the University, and represent the German School in England. Mr. Burgon, a Fellow of Oriel and a tremendous Churchman, who is librarian to the Union, and to whom it belongs to recommend books for purchase to the Union, refused to recommend this book; whereupon a certain Congreve, a Fellow of Wadham, and great Arnoldite, also a master at Rugby, came from Rugby on purpose to propose a vote of censure on Burgon, on the grounds that he had consulted his own private theological tastes in the matter, and not acted as the officer of the Society. The combat was conducted with great spirit; and Burgon, who is a great punster, fired off an enormous number of puns on Congreve's name—allusion to rockets, a man of fiery temperament, etc.—and whether his puns or his arguments carried the day, he won it by some hundred to some thirty votes.

Stanley is a very amiable pleasing man in himself, and one would not like him to be the subject of any rude triumph; —but the whole affair seems to have been without any acerbity. I have written a notice upon his Sermons in this *C. R.*—a thing I did not want to do, inasmuch as I meet him occasionally and am always good friends with him. But it would not have done to have omitted them altogether, so I made a notice of them —a tolerably long one, I allow. . . . Yours affectionately,

J. B. M.

OXFORD, *April* 14, 1848.

DEAR ANNE,—Palmer has a Chaldean visiting him here, quite a young man, and I should think quite a beau in his own country. He wears ordinarily our common dress, but will put on his Asiatic one if you want him. He dined with us in Hall yesterday in it, and really looked exceedingly handsome. He is a brother of a Mr. Rassam, who is, though a Chaldee, our consul at Mossul. He gives a shocking description of the Turkish governors in the provinces, and describes them as sending for the rich men immediately on arriving at their posts, and fleecing them as a matter of course. The expedient is, when they have exhausted all the man's wealth, and all he can beg from his friends, to put him to death, and suspend the body over the church door, till the congregation subscribe the rest of the sum pretended to be due from the unfortunate deceased. His uncle had his hand cut off, and died two days after from neglect and bleeding. The wonder to me is that people who can live elsewhere do not emigrate.

Lord Forbes is in Oxford. He is a most zealous Scotch Episcopalian, and is now engaged in a scheme for building a Cathedral at Perth, in which he has received all sorts of rebuffs, but he goes on, and is gradually getting money. Mrs. Sheppard, the President's sister, has given him £1000, and the President £100, and Mrs. Coutts he has hopes from.—Yours affectionately,

J. B. M.

At a dinner party in town—

"The talk fell upon Lord G. Bentinck. Everybody agreed he had killed himself by not taking holiday. He never had a holiday, but went straight from the exciting work of the House to Newmarket. W. said he kept a regular office in London for the transaction of his betting business with clerks. Mr. C. had met him at West Indian deliberations, and had been immensely struck with his calculating powers and his prodigious memory, not only for figures, but documents. He could remember a whole heap after he had been once over them. Those calculating minds, I suppose, always must be calculating; it gets to be a kind of disease."

Mr. Keble, writing May 11, 1848, on a proposed Tract movement ("Tracts for the Million"), ends a note to J. B. M.: " I see, or rather hear, that you have got the petition I sent you in *The Guardian*, and I am glad of it; also I see that some one of your Reviewers there has been abusing King Charles the First. He had need to be a very good man, that same Reviewer. —Yours in haste and affection, J. K."

The close of the year brought another excitement to Oxford and to society at large. The feeling raised by Jenny Lind is distinct from anything in one's experience. Recalling her voice we feel it a thing to hear once in a life; but it did not need musical taste or feeling to enter into her charm. She did without beauty, and needed no feeling for music in her worshippers—in fact, raising enthusiasm in persons who did not know one tune from another,—by whom she was only to be described by superlatives and the most violent antitheses. She visited the Bishop of Norwich, and a description from the pen of A. P. Stanley stands before me: " Jenny Lind has been here for three days, and leaves to-day. Of her musical powers I will say nothing except that they produced no impression upon me [he had no ear for music]; but her whole character and appearance is one of the most striking I ever saw—the manners of a princess with the simplicity of a child and the goodness of an angel. . . . The features are plain and homely, far beyond what you would infer from her portraits; but when animated

she is perfectly lovely, and her smile is, with the exception of
Dr. Pusey's, the most heavenly I ever beheld." Dr. Pusey also
is said to have been perfectly insensible to music, but there
was felt a fitness between the songstress and the divine that
produced quite a solicitude to bring the two together. Dr.
Pusey was sounded on the point. He declined all visiting, but
was willing to show her the Chapter-house. This task, however, fell to others. The way to introduce the name to her
would have been to tell her Dr. Pusey was Hebrew Professor,
and a man of saintly piety. J. B. M.'s report is in a calmer
vein, but every one who saw and heard her felt the need to
give his impressions. Every correspondence of the day had
its attempt to define what is perhaps indefinable.

TO HIS SISTER.

OXFORD, *December* 2, 1848.

MY DEAR ANNE,—I have seen Jenny Lind in her public
capacity, not in private. The Donkins were not successful.
Her first appearance is certainly not taking. She is plain, and
looked older than I expected. . . . Now for the favourable
side: I must say she had wonderful powers of making this face
of hers look very pleasing, and even lofty and noble occasionally. She had two great powers in her face; one of stiffening
it, and the other of resolving it, so to speak; I mean of im-
parting all sorts of active expressions, chiefly of the arch and
comical sort, to it. It was sometimes so perfectly motionless
and stiff as to be almost corpse-like, but not without a certain
grandeur, an expression of determined obstinacy, stubbornness,
and hauteur. Then when she changed to active expression, she
had all sorts of odd uses of her eyes, looking from underneath
and from the corners of her eyes, and so on, and was certainly
excessively arch; and one expression chased another, just like
waves over the sea. I say so much about her powers of expression in face, because it was quite obvious to me, before I
had been in the room a quarter of an hour, that her face was
half her singing. I felt sensibly that I lost full half whenever

I withdrew my glass. Her comic expression came out in the Rossini and the Swedish songs at the last. However, to go to her vocal powers, I cannot say that her voice was so full a one as I expected, or so powerful; her wonderful power over it seemed the great point. She could positively do anything with it. It was absolutely obedient; I never heard anything at all equal to its flexibility; she tossed it about as conjurors do their balls, and seemed to have twenty voices at once. She shook with such perfection that the note seemed self-undulating. . . . Then she imitated an echo, first a slow, then a quicker one, till the echo of the last note was, as in the case of the real echo, mixed with the succeeding note. Then she had astonishing powers of sustaining long slow notes, which she displayed in the song from Weber. [If this was the song I heard, it realised to me Milton's "divine enchanting ravishment."]

I have been writing a description of vocal machinery more than of music; but the fact is, a concert is almost necessarily a display of machinery. . . . I do not consider that I have heard Jenny Lind to advantage, though she showed off her powers astonishingly. Of course there was rapturous applause, and waving of hats and caps.

One amusing feature of the scene was, that being in an official University room—that is, the Theatre—the Vice-Chancellor and Proctors, who were all there, sat in their chairs of state, and with their caps on. So that Jenny Lind was performing before the University; just as we say, "a sermon preached before the University."—Yours affectionately,   J. B. M.

In the year 1849, J. B. M. was bursar of his College, and had accounts to keep—an occupation not much in his line. He reports himself as seeking relaxation under his duties in lighter fiction, for which graver literary pursuits did not leave him much time. After dashing off his thoughts on *Monte Christo* and *Wuthering Heights*—finding in the latter an element of truth and nature, however much it is spoilt—he touches on *Vanity Fair*.

To his Sister.

January 27, 1849.

Vanity Fair I was agreeably disappointed in; I found it less in the caricature line than I expected. It certainly is full of pieces of truth and nature—I think superior to Dickens in that, though without his exuberant powers of description. What he fails in is power of sustaining a scene; where feeling comes in he cuts it very short, and this has a disappointing effect on the reader, and it shows evidently want of power in the writer. It is clear he would make the scene longer if he could.

To leave criticism. Gladstone is here for a few days, seeing his constituents. He dined with me yesterday in our common room, and of course, as in duty bound, made himself very agreeable, and talked on all sorts of subjects, literary and political. The revolutionary movement has at last reached us, and a Tutorial Society is now in formation, embracing all those who bear or have borne College offices, for the purpose of discussing academical measures, and reporting thereupon to the Hebdomadal Board. Something of the kind has been wanted a long time, for the Hebdomadal Board never consult anybody previous to issuing a measure; then, when the voting comes, there is no distinction allowed, but the whole must be either accepted or rejected. This is a great stopper to all improvements. So some medium of conference beforehand with the Heads is a desideratum. This is only a form, in fact, of the original powers of Convocation, which have disappeared for years. Of course the Heads will not like it; indeed for us it is a somewhat revolutionary proceeding. But there is such solidity in the resident body of Masters that one need not be much afraid of excess.—Yours affectionately, J. B. M.

To his Sister.

Oxford, *March* 14, 1849.

I have dipped a good deal into the book you sent me [*Poetry Past and Present*]. The translations from the classics at the end are as good as elegant translators can make. Anstice has a considerable name. It so happened I heard one it gives of his recited at a party as a specimen of good translation, a few days before I had this book. I must confess, however, that to me all translations, without exception, appear failures. Cowley's, which is not a failure, is hardly a translation; it merely takes the idea from Pindar: —translations, I mean, from the ancients. Modern, I suppose, is feasible. Miss Donkin's, from the German, always strike me as being remarkable specimens of successful fusion —things that one would read without knowing that they were translations.

To his Sister.

Oxford, *May* 2, 1849.

We went our Magdalen progress last week—that is to say, two of us, myself and the college steward together, hiring a carriage at Oxford, which we put on the rail to Reading, and then posted. My companion is an excellent man of business, and formidable to farmers. His information and conversation were principally in that department, in which I was less at home than he; so that he, though generally taciturn, was the principal talker of the two. He is a brother of Mrs. Routh, one of the Berkshire Blagraves. The family is a good deal reduced; but Colonel Blagrave, his brother, is still a country squire of property. We drove through old family estates in the course of our travels, now passed away from them, but on which his father resided part of the year, in his boyish days; going from one hall where he lived the winter, to another where he lived the summer, with an immense train of servants and carriages, at a huge expense, there being no kind of difference between the two places, except that one was eighteen miles from the other. His kitchen bills may be estimated from the fact that his bill for malt for the year was £400. All the servants and all their friends ate and drank *ad libitum*; and post-boys were never known to be sober on returning from his house. Our journey was as otiose as it is possible to imagine, starting long after breakfast in the morning, and stopping long before dinner in the evening: precisely the same days and hours for meeting tenantry being kept that have been since the College was founded, when travelling was conducted over impassable roads, and on horseback, with College retainers, with large horse pistols and arquebusses behind.[1] It was, probably, a hard week's

[1] The old order in Oxford is so utterly changed that a glimpse into one scene of its domestic life may interest the reader. Dr. Routh, then in his 95th year, and his surroundings, even at the date of the following letter, were regarded as relics of a former state of things :—

"OXFORD, *June* 11, 1849.

"MY DEAR MARIA,—Yesterday we dined at the President's—such a curious interesting scene; Mr. B. congratulated Fanny on it, as what so few people do see. The President is more old and wonderful-looking than any one could imagine beforehand. He must always have been below middle height; but age has bent and shrunk him to something startlingly short when he walks. In his chair one does not perceive it so much. The wig, of course, adds to the effect—such a preposterous violation of nature. It seems quite to account for his not hearing what people say. His manner was most kind and courteous to mamma; and he took the opportunity of taking her into dinner to say some complimentary things of James, of whom I think he is very fond. It is really very nice to see his Fellows round him; they seem so fond of him. An indulgent respectful reverence, with a good deal of fun all the while, is the general manner; and he is very cheerful, and often laughs with the greatest heartiness. Mrs. Routh, in her way, is as unusual a person to meet; and harmonises with the scene;—extremely good-natured, probably had always something of the manner of a child, so wonderfully simple and unassuming. James says, what an absolute contrast their drawing-room presents to any other Head of a House in Oxford, in the terms of easy familiarity between the Fellows and their Head. Mrs. Routh is evidently not made for the stately. . . . She is so amiable and so thoughtful, in her way, for the comfort and amusement of her guests that one has quite an affectionate feeling towards her. She took us into many of the rooms, and into the College library. One singular addition to the party was Mr. Ormuzd Rassam, in full Chaldean costume, at Mrs. Routh's particular desire. This Rassam is brother of the Consul at Mossul, and himself was with Mr. Layard, and his chief help and ally in all his discoveries. You will remember the picture of this one in the procession of the Bull. James is always remarking his exact resemblance to the figures in the sculptures; and it is very true he claims direct descent from the ancient Assyrians, and says his nation has never been allowed to marry strangers, except just now, when his brother has married an English woman. Dr. Bloxam has spread it abroad that he is forty-fourth cousin of Nebuchadnezzar, and Rassam complains that he has been asked everywhere if it is really true. . . . Mrs. Routh laments his approaching departure: 'We shall go into mourning when he is gone! Oh, he is such a good man, such a very good man, I am so fond of him!' The President compliments him on his beauty: 'But as for such cousins as Nebuchadnezzar, they are nothing to boast of.'

"The look of things there was all so characteristic. The house full of books; the dining-room filled with folios and quartos, drawing-room, staircase, passages, etc., with smaller books. Mrs. Routh complains she shall soon not be able to get about, from the accumulation of book-shelves, for he still buys, and knows where every book in his library is. She took us into his dressing-room. The dressing appointments were of the most limited peregrination then. Herbert[1] came to me at Winchester to breakfast, after which we went to the cathedral; and then started to our manor farm at Otterbourne. There I left Blagrave, and called on Mr. Yonge with Herbert. Mrs. and Miss Yonge were not at home; Mr. Yonge having left them in London, principally, I believe, to come down to see me, in order to talk about Otterbourne school, for which he is anxious to procure a large subscription from the College. I was sorry not to see Miss Yonge. We then went to Hursley, and lunched at the Kebles', and went over the church, which I had not seen before. The piers are criticised as being rather too low, and I thought the altar end might have been more raised. But the architect was bent on keeping the village church style. It is impossible, however, to judge of it till the stained glass is in. Mrs. Keble looked very well, and Keble himself in good spirits. They have been successful with their ladies' petition against the new Marriage Bill, and have got nearly 10,000 signatures. Sir G. Grey, who is to present it to the Queen, was very kind and polite in his notes to Keble, and made allusions to former days at Oriel.

kind; but the walls up to the ceiling are covered with books, and there is a set of steps, which Mrs. R. said he could ascend quite nimbly, to reach any book he wants. As for the wigs, Mr. B. is in hopes of possessing one, and he communicates this hope to Mrs. Routh, who makes many characteristic exclamations. In the midst of all these venerable books, pictures of founders, and old-fashioned homely furniture—the Fellows in their gowns, Rassam in his flowing bright Eastern dress, and the President in his 'knees,' huge buckles, to his shoes, and robes, all as different from anything one is used to as may be—there was a gentleman commoner not much at home in the scene. He said he had never worn his gown so many hours together in his life. The bright moment of the evening to him was when Dr. Bloxam got a cup of tea (which he had stipulated with Mrs. Routh should be a *good* cup, not *husband's* tea) in his cocoa-cup. The management of these beverages was almost too much for Mrs. Routh, though she had Mr. B. and Fanny to help her.

"James was the one to talk to the President, and to draw him out. They talked of Hume, Adam Smith, Horne, Parr, Hurd, Jortin, Dr. Johnson (who, by the way, Dr. Routh remembered on his last visit to Oxford, describing him to us, as though seeing him, in a 'brown tradesman's wig'), and discussing style, etc. . . . I could not hear much distinctly; but knew what it was all about. . . . I did not say that Mrs. Routh calls the President 'my own.' 'Take care, my own,' I heard her cry out; she is very attentive to him, and protested much against Dr. Bloxam's satire on Husband's tea."

[1] His nephew, then at school at Twyford, before his election as King's Scholar to Eton.

The country about Selborne, where we were one day, is very beautiful. I made acquaintance with a man who remembered Gilbert White quite well, and had taken tea with him often.—Yours affectionately,   J. B. M.

To his Sister.

Oxford, *March* 15, 1850.

The Gorham decision is of course making a sensation; or rather it is not so much a sensation, as a graver feeling that a long and anxious struggle is commencing, of which people do not see the issue. I do not think that the body of High Churchmen are at all wanting to act in a hurry; but will be patient, and are prepared for years of contest and suspense. So I see nothing immediate coming to alarm people. There are a few who want to push matters to extremes at once, but the evident want of temper which such men show rather serves to make the rest deliberate. And such men are for the most part not men of weight or influence, intellectual or moral. Keble and Pusey are very conservatively disposed, also Marriott. I believe even Mr. Bennett is drawing back from his first movement. Maskell and Allies are for extremes.

With respect to the doctrinal question, and whether Mr. Gorham is really an actual heretic or not, I would not for my own part commit myself to an opinion. I have read enough to see that the doctrine of baptismal regeneration has a history appended to it, and is not to be decided upon wholly from the verbal statements in the Church Office, but that we are bound to go into the history of it. And I certainly see various changes and modifications as to the doctrine, coming out in that history, as allowable within the Church. I see statements made sometimes, which, if put into easy English and placed before some of our orthodox friends, would be set down at once as heresy, but which occur in undoubtedly orthodox authorities. It is possible that further reading might undo the effect of what one has now read; though I do not think that probable. But I know enough to see that people make very strong assertions on points on which they do not know much in reference to this question. Archdeacon Wilberforce's book is by no means satisfactory. He seems to me to make considerable flaws both in his reasoning and also in his interpretation of passages in ancient writers. He preached a stirring sermon on the Report last Sunday.—Yours affectionately, J. B. M.

In his letters home at this date, at each returning quarter, there is generally some mention of the *Christian Remembrancer*.

To his Sister.

OXFORD, *April* 3, 1850.

I hope the *C. R.* meets with your approbation; I think it a decidedly good number. . . . Church's article—the last one [Church and State]—is very good, and will I hope have the effect of quieting some minds who think so fearfully of our Reformation Erastianism. It had the effect upon me, as if one whole side of the truth, which had been completely suppressed throughout this controversy, and all the controversy of the last twenty years, had now fairly come out. Of course we shall displease our ultra friends who are eager for a convulsion. I confess I am not. Nor do I see anything in the temper of those who are which attracts me.

Southey's poetry I have not read for years, but I remember the impression it always produced upon me was that of a brilliant, lighted-up stage-scene. I allude to all that gorgeous Asiatic scenery and pomp piled upon pomp, all very powerful, but not an elevation of a material simply natural to begin with, as the highest poetry is, but starting upon an unearthly unnatural ground from the first. The change from his early Utopianism to his common sense content in after life, and satisfaction with his pursuits, and with the world because it supplied them, is a change, some modification of which thousands of people go through, but in Southey all comes out in black and white. The letter to Coleridge at the end is truly characteristic of him—that is in one of his best aspects:—a tremendous letter certainly.[1] . . . I was at the X.'s the other

---

[1] A letter reproaching Coleridge with his lavish display of all the signs of

day. She is rather criticised here in the form that men say they like her sister the better of the two. This sort of criticism is often unfair, for Miss X. is, after all, a more active contributor to people's amusement than the other. But all people profess to admire quietness of manner, and to make that their standard; though, when it comes to, they will pass by the quiet one, and go to the vivacious.

He comments on the news of an eccentric marriage, which excited stronger surprise in some quarters:—

The news about A. B. was a surprise, though I could not bring myself up to the proper standard of grief. There is something, however, almost grotesque, that prevents deep feeling, the oddness of choice is so much the most prominent feature. After all, he has done only what Richard Hooker did, but events that happen now strike one so very differently from those that happened three centuries ago. I hope he will bring her into some kind of shape, so as to allow of our seeing him again—for I find, after all, my opinion of him is not so very much altered. I have no doubt he would talk exceedingly well and interestingly about the whole affair, and show it in such a variety of aspects as would entirely deprive it of the matter-of-fact, ordinary incident of a man marrying his cook, and present us with a piece of poetry instead.

To his Sister.

Oxford, *May* 11, 1850.

A petition to the Queen and address to the Archbishop[1] are now in course of signature, generally among members of Convocation, resident or non-resident, though the canvass for non-resident names has not yet completely commenced. The petition is ably got up, and the points brought forward are good. The lawyers in town had principally to do with it. I send you a copy. You will see the President's name appears at the top. He looked over it and made some corrections

friendship to people he did not really care for. See *Life and Correspondence of Robert Southey*, vol. i. p. 266.

[1] On the threatened Royal Commission for University Reform.

before printing. The great apprehension felt here, even among those who are inclined to the cause, is as to Convocation. They dread the row and dissensions which will ensue. This apprehension is entertained principally by the officials of the place. I own I am not much surprised at this; for a formal move for Convocation is a serious thing—all parties have agreed so long to put down the idea, the High Church party quite as much as the rest; and in all the only champion of Convocation has been Whately. . . . Yours affectionately,

J. B. M.

In a letter written May 1850, James has heard from Mr. Gladstone on the Colonial Church question, who also tells him he is preparing a speech on the University question, to come on on the 30th of May. J. B. M. reports that "the document of the Hebdomadal Board in *The Times* was written (I hear) by the Provost." About this time my brother Tom spent a few days at Derby, when the subject of the Commission was entered upon. His sister writes to J. B. M., May 21:—

"I think that Tom regards the Royal Commission as inevitable, and that people will weaken their chance of influence and the weight of their opinion by opposing all change as the Heads are doing. Our argument was that people did well to mistrust Lord John. He seemed to say you did not commit yourself to him by allowing this first step. 'If a man comes with a pennyworth of watercresses to your door, and you buy them, you are not bound to buy a dead horse if he comes with it an hour after.' He will not allow it to be an objection that Lord John knows nothing of the University system, as possibly this deficiency deprives him of power to carry his point. He seemed both anxious and interested on the subject."

The Commission was appointed.

To his Sister.

October 17, 1850.

The Heads of Houses are in a state of considerable excitement about the new Commission, and the presence of Jeune at the Board led to a discussion as to the propriety of the same person belonging to two antagonistic bodies, as the Board and the Commission are. The discussion ended in the Board resolving itself into a Committee containing all the members of the Board with the single exception of Jeune.

Towards the end of the year 1850 Lord John startled the country by his Ecclesiastical Titles Bill.

To his Sister.

OXFORD, *November* 29, 1850.

. . . Everybody is expecting considerable difficulty from Lord John in the next Parliament. The popular feeling is thoroughly expressed for some bill against the Roman Catholics; but how can Lord John do it and retain his Irish members? And if no bill is passed, and these Roman Catholic bishops go on calling themselves Bishop of Northampton, etc., it will be a blow to the Queen's supremacy, for the whole world has agreed that the Queen's supremacy is involved in this matter. D., who is a considerable Romaniser, met Cardinal Wiseman the other day at Mr. Scott Murray's at dinner. There was a grand party of Roman Catholic gentry and nobility, ladies, etc., and converts. All went on their knees to the Cardinal. D. was disgusted with the man himself, and thought him vulgar. He began immediately talking about his pamphlet and its sale.

To his Sister.

OXFORD, *February* 6, 1851.

We had our meeting on the University Commission on Wednesday, and decided by 26 to 5 against giving any information. There was never known so large a meeting of Fellows. At the same time we carried a resolution unanimously that something was to be done for the improvement and extension of our College system of education. So we are going to reform ourselves.

Speaking of certain recent clerical converts J. B. M. writes:—

A. sets up now quite as a layman. He has taken a house, and furnished it in style, and, being a man of good family and fortune, he does not seem to have lost secularly by the change. B. takes advantage of his lay character, and goes to the theatre. C. has a stall at the Opera-house. No particular harm in this, if they really suppose themselves laymen. . . . And yet, under all the circumstances of the case, when men have put themselves forward as such tremendous theologians, these things are rather ridiculous.[1]

To his Sister.

Oxford, *March* 9, 1851.

The excitement of the political world has made up for the want of events in Oxford, of which there has been a dearth throughout the term, the most important fact I know being that Magdalen College is going to reform itself, and has appointed a committee for that object, of which I am one. We have nearly concluded our sittings now, and a report is being drawn up. We shall recommend to the College to found a Hall in connection with itself, and adapted for the most economical style of life for the students. Also the old corrupt system of nomination to demyships will be abolished. As I have had my share of the patronage of this system, it is no great sacrifice to me now to recommend its abolition.

The prospects of the political world are sufficiently unsettled. Nobody seems to imagine Lord John can continue much longer, and if he goes, one does not know why the Peelites may not come in. If they do, and Gladstone with them, the University will perhaps have cause to thank the Election Committee, which brought in the latter, as he is quite determined against the University Commission. At any rate, Lord John is not the person he was; his wing is cut short, and he can no longer be

---

[1] The eagerness of certain clerical converts to parade their emancipation from the restraints of Anglican orders was an irritating feature of the day. In my correspondence ladies describe with a sort of loathing encounters with old acquaintance whom they had known in all the decorum of clerical black, now garbed in showy waistcoats, or as one letter specifies in "blue neckties and ginger-coloured trousers."

energetically mischievous. A Peel Ministry will be favourable to the fair claims of the Church, and disposed to give up the old Royal Prerogative ground. Lord Aberdeen voted for the Bishop of London's Bill, and Gladstone and Sidney Herbert would both be strong on the Prerogative question. Gladstone, too, has great private influence over the Duke of Newcastle. As for Sir James Graham, he does not care a farthing for the Church, or for equity; but he would be obliged to make terms with Gladstone, if he was to have his services. So, on the whole, the claims of the Church are looking up. The Roman Catholics have done good service here, for nothing has so damaged the Prerogative prestige for years as this late affair. The real weakness of the whole claim has been so thoroughly exposed. At the same time, I am far from looking with unmixed satisfaction on a state of greater Church liberty. It will be connected with all sorts of nuisances, and the advantages gained will be much less than people anticipate. However, such a course of things is the order of the day, and the spirit of the age naturally brings it on. So, even if one did not want it, one has no choice in the matter.

I have kept very well hitherto, but should not be surprised if, as a measure of precaution, I took a run down to Malvern for two or three days. I have never been there, and have an idea that the air is exactly the thing.—Yours affectionately,

J. B. M.

To his Sister.

April 26, 1851.

. . . Our College politics have had a serious reverse since I wrote last. The President has summarily squashed the whole scheme, on the ground of being unstatutable. The committee, upon this, feel a little touched, just that gentle irritation being excited, which is rather pleasing than otherwise to the mind. His argument is the most ridiculous you can conceive, and this he probably knows; but anything that threatens to interfere with Magdalen as it is he cannot bear. Whether we shall proceed any further or not I don't know. The President has an absolute veto, or rather initiative, in College. Perhaps we may make a proposal to get the Statute question settled by an appeal to the Visitor. Meanwhile, it is a great triumph to the University Commission, who will, of course, say, Here is a college trying to improve itself, and cannot for want of an external impulse.

You would see Manning's and Hope's conversions in *The Times*. It is James Robert Hope, not the other. He has always had a strong R. C. bias, and was expected to go five years ago, when J. H. N. went.

I have been two days with my friend Frank Faber. He is always a pleasant person to go to, being so amusing a talker, and pointed and lively. He is far superior to his brother Frederick in this point, whose talk always seemed to me artificial and with effort, and, after all, nothing sharp about it.—Yours, J. B. M.

In July of 1851 his nephew, John Rickards Mozley, was elected King's Scholar at Eton, as on the same occasion his brother Herbert had been two years before.

TO HIS SISTER.

OXFORD, *August* 1, 1851.

I congratulate you all, and especially Jemima, on Johnny's triumphant success, which justifies the bold predictions of Herbert from the first, and is a well-merited reward to him after his exertions. I had been expecting for two or three days past to hear some news, remembering that this must be the time when the examination would have to be decided; the completeness of coming in on the spot is also a great additional satisfaction.

Oxford is so quiet that one really quite feels as if one was at some place away from it; it loses its identity; and a stroll in the deep shades of our walks in the evening has the effect of an entire remoteness from all human things.

We voted at a College meeting last week a portrait of the Bishop of Exeter to be placed in Hall, he to choose his own painter.—Yours, J. B. M.

Writing August 13, a postscript says :—

"The Bishop of Exeter has acknowledged our compliment in his usual polite style to the President; in a letter in which he also alluded to the chance of himself and the President having to suffer and be confessors together in the cause of the Church. The President, who remembers old times about the Bishop of E., was rather amused than edified by the allusion, and thinks it a capital joke."

TO THE REV. R. W. CHURCH.

DERBY, *May* 17, 1852.

I am going to give you a small commission, which I hope will not take up much time. There is a certain book called Stephen's *Collection of Ecclesiastical Statutes*, which contains all the Acts of Parliament relating to the Church specifically from Magna Charta downwards.

I want the period between the Reformation and the dissolution of Convocation in 1717. Could you run over the pages, and note the *sorts of Acts* which passed through Parliament relating to the Church during this time? I want rather to know whether any relating to diocesan or parochial organisation, or clerical residence or pluralities, and any of the sort of Acts which for the past fifty years have been usual in Parliament, passed during that time.

The reason I want it is for this. On looking over Lathbury's *History of Convocation*, I do not see that Convocation troubled itself at all with the temporal organisation of the Church, confining itself to canons about doctrine and ceremonial services, etc. So if any such Act passed Parliament then, it would show that the Convocation of that day left such matters to the Crown and Parliament, and did not think that *its own confirmation* in such case was necessary.

I see the London Church Committee object to Lord Blandford's Act, on the ground that assent of Convocation ought to be had in such a case.

I do not remember that any such Acts did pass Parliament in those times, for things were tolerably at a standstill in point of population, which has been the great reason of such Acts in later years. However, such a length of time would hardly pass without some interference of Parliament with Church temporalities.

It has occurred to me, and I think I have talked to you about it, that if Convocation does meet again, our friends will be disgusted to find these sorts of Acts passing through Parliament just as heretofore, without any reference to Convocation, or the least idea, on the part of any one member of the House, that its opinion is to be asked on the subject. One cannot expect the House to discontinue its present mode of legislating on such subjects, and then the Church will appear to many more subjugated than ever; for Convocation being met will be simply a spectator of such legislation, and not a participator in it.

So I think we ought to be raising up some image, if we can, of the practical future of Convocation, to tell men what they are to expect, and what Convocation is to do, and what it is not to do.

I rather purpose trying to get an article out of Gladstone, on the subject of the Parliamentary relation to Convocation.

As you have looked into the French Convocation history a little, perhaps you might know what were *its* general subject-matters. What powers did the Crown and Parliament of France exercise in the temporal organisation of the French Church? And did the French Convocation assent to or share in such organisation? . . .

I am reading Mill's *Logic, i.e.* judiciously—those parts I can understand. I am much impressed with the immense quantity of thought which he has put together, though one rather misses that very high sort of acuteness which one has in Hume and Pascal. He seems to get at his philosophy by patience and accuracy more than genius, though one would not say that he had none of the latter. And I cannot help suspecting that he makes considerable blunders in consequence of some defect here; for patience and accuracy cannot do everything, and will make mistakes for want of genius, just as genius will make mistakes for want of them; but I am talking prematurely.—Yours affectionately,   J. B. M.

DERBY, *June* 21, 1852.

MY DEAR CHURCH,—Your article is an important one,[1] as being a judgment on a question which has been raised so much lately, viz., the trustworthiness of Pascal's letters. And Pascal is such a book, such a centre and peg in the war theological, that it is highly important it should be kept, and the proper defence be made when it is attacked. M. Maynard is sufficiently clever to deserve an answer, and he exposes himself sufficiently to make him a convenient man to answer.

The article has suffered a little here and there from your having to do two things at once, collect information and arrange it. I think it is impossible to do this myself; so a point here and there loses by not being sufficiently brought out. But the idea you give of his arguments (M.'s, I mean) is very accurate and forcible. The view of the sacraments, as entertained in the Roman Church, will be new to people. At least I had never heard of it.

I have not exactly expressed what I think your article does, viz., that it lets one into a whole interior state of things in the Roman Church,—not of an exaggerated and horrible sort as the "*disclosures*" so called, which people do not really believe (I mean those who are bent on fairness to Rome),—but of a probable and ordinary stamp of commonplaceness and laxity and worldliness, such as people will instantly recognise as true. They have let the cat out of the bag, in short, and we have taken advantage of it.—Yours affectionately,   J. B. M.

In June of 1852, J. B. M. went abroad with his sisters. After taking the Rhine leisurely, he writes :—

TO THE REV. R. W. CHURCH.

GENEVA, *July* 11, 1852.

We have not been very expeditious travellers to get no further than here after seventeen days, but we professed to take it easy. . . . Nothing we have seen in the way of scenery is equal to the upper (I mean) Vevay end of the Lake of Geneva; it is truly Acherontian. It had that dark purple

[1] "Pascal and Ultramontanism :" *Christian Remembrancer.* July 1852.

mist on it when we first saw it, out of which the tremendous rocks on the Savoy side gloomed awfully. The opposite bank, too, is so mild and agricultural, with lonesome and quiet villages, that when you looked from your steamer, first on one side and then on the other, you might fancy the water dividing earth from Ἔρεβος. Such scenes must have suggested to Homer and Virgil their ideas on such subjects. I should think that when Ulysses, after rowing nine days on the ocean, at last reached the ζόφον ἠερόεντα, and saw the ghost of Achilles, Ajax, etc., it must have been some such place. . . . We took in the Lake of Geneva at the special recommendation of my brother Tom, who was wonderfully taken with it last year. . . . Geneva is certainly a taking place, and looks by no means Calvinistic.

I cannot exactly make out what sort of thing the National Swiss Church is. Where I have introduced the subject I have always observed an inclination to stick up for it, as against the Free Church, and that in religious quarters: *e.g.* travelling with a Moravian by diligence, a good sort of man—who talked of Scott and Newton—he said the Free Church of the Canton Vaud was but a small section, the mass of the people going with the National Church. I pushed him with the Geneva Church, asking if the National Church of Switzerland as a body had religious communion with the German Church?—a question which he parried by saying that each Canton had its own Established Church, which had not necessarily communion with the Churches of other countries. In an Evangelical bookseller's shop here there was the same kind of shiftiness. I saw immediately that the subject was an unpleasant one. What was the difference between the National Church and the Free Church? "Oh, pas beaucoup!" I confessed myself surprised, and said I understood there was a serious difference in doctrine. But the man shrugged up his shoulders higher and higher, and said "C'est suivant, Monsieur." He admitted, however, afterwards that the National Church of Geneva denied the divinity of Christ. The Free Church has only 5000 here.

The Roman Catholics on the Rhine are having vernacular

services at a great rate. They are more prominent than they were, I think. At Cologne the Grand Mass was very poorly attended, but perhaps that might be owing to the choir being blocked up. Again, at vespers, there was literally nobody except ourselves. The popular services were some vernacular litanies. At Strasburg there were two in the Cathedral, very effective, about half an hour each, with a sermon after them. The organ accompanied with full power, and the whole congregation singing in the nave. It was in fact little more than hymn-singing and a sermon. I sometimes wish our Church would adapt herself in the same way to the wants of the people.

The Germans being a nation of singers, the Church seems to make everything singing there. . . .

Best remembrances to Johnson and his wife, and the Ogles.
—Yours affectionately, J. B. M.

It was during this excursion, when the party had reached Como, that the news came to them of the death of Mrs. Thomas Mozley. She had been long in weak health; but when her sisters-in-law took leave of her in passing through London no fear of the coming event, so imminent, was in their thoughts. There had always been a strong mutual regard and appreciation between her and her brother-in-law, shown in many pleasant instances in the family correspondence.

J. B. M. TO T. M.

COMO, *July* 24, 1852.

MY DEAR TOM,—The sad news has just arrived. It is indeed a shock to us all. I feel all sorts of recollections crowding upon me now that she has passed away. It is a deep blow to one's spirits, yet I could truly wish always to be in the state of mind in which I am now, if one could be without the occasion which causes it. Such events are indeed wonderfully calming and subduing, and everything in this world seems of no importance, and the love of the world loses its hold upon one for the time, when they take place. I need not say how unexpected the news is. None of us were at all prepared for it.

We are, you may easily imagine, in no humour to enjoy any more Italian scenery, and shall leave this place by the quickest route for England immediately. I am glad to hear from Jemima that you bear your loss as every one who knows you would expect you to do.—Yours affectionately,

J. B. M.

On the death of the Duke of Wellington the vacant Chancellorship becomes an important subject.

TO THE REV. R. W. CHURCH.

September 26, 1852.

MY DEAR CHURCH,—In case Lord Derby should not accept the offer—an event which, I think, is on the cards—and Lord Redesdale is not put up, which appears certain, as one has not heard of anybody seriously proposing him, I should wish my name to be put to a requisition to the Duke of Newcastle; and so leave it with you. The more I think of Lord Derby's position as Premier, the more I see difficulties—or what should be such—to his acceptance of the Chancellorship. I cannot think, with *The Guardian,* that a statesman as such is cut out; for this would be simply driving us to take some stupid man every time. But a statesman and a Premier—under the present circumstances of the University—will certainly find himself in an awkward situation as Chancellor. For he cannot avoid, if he stays in office, acting in some way respecting the University. For to do nothing will be to act, and to act decisively. And he cannot act as Premier without coming into some collision with his office as Chancellor. The public will say, You are an advocate, not an impartial man to legislate. On the other hand, if Lord Derby does not feel himself at all sure of office, he may say that it does not suit him to reject a permanent position on account of so slippery a one as a Premiership.—Yours affectionately, J. B. M.

In 1852 J. B. M. visits his brother Arthur, then curate of Hingham, of which the Hon. W. Wodehouse was rector.

To his Sister.

HINGHAM, *November* 1, 1852.

It was a long time since I had seen your hand, and I was glad to see it again. I stayed three weeks at Yarmouth; through half of that time I had the advantage of Arthur's and Eliza's company. I do not know whether the reason is that there is nothing else to see, but I think the sea is seen to great advantage at Yarmouth, nor do I remember more enjoying walks on the beach. It comes in with considerable force sometimes. About sunset the lights on it were particularly good, especially when it was calm; then the nursery of bloaters really looked quite spiritual. I indulged in a few novels recommended by the Wodehouses: *Markland* and *Margaret Maitland*, by the same author, are very good, though with defects, and wanting incident and filling up. But there is a genial element of domesticity in the principal character in each, which is brought out very well; and there is a good deal of humour, which is a great advantage. Novels are generally very deficient in it. . . .

Mrs. Norton is to me a very stupid novelist, if one is to judge from a certain *Stuart of Dunleath*, full of drawling and exaggerated sentiment from beginning to end, without incident or humour; and depending really, as far as I could judge, on certain awkward positions of things,—as approaches to the vicious,—for its interest at all: there being, I suppose, some people sufficiently morbid to like the excitement of that, without absolutely approving it.—Yours affectionately,   J. B. M.

In 1853 a new election was called for on Mr. Gladstone's taking office under Sir James Graham's administration.

To his Sister.

OXFORD, *January* 9, 1853.

The election is going on well; Gladstone eighty-seven ahead. I hardly expect, with this majority and the fact of two defeats, many more will be brought up on Percival's side. . . . Keble and Moberly came up the first day, and dined in Oriel, where I met them. Keble seemed in good spirits, and not to care about the coalition—very angry with Denison. But Isaac

Williams is strong against Gladstone, I hardly know on what exact ground, whether political or some other. It must be confessed that all these charges have a tendency to increase a sort of Liberalism even in quarters most sacred from such intrusion. And a High Church Liberalism bids fair to be the order of the day. The regular Liberals, however, are only half supporters of Gladstone, and come up evidently with some reluctance. *The Globe* for some days hinted very plainly the idea that it would be a good thing if the University should turn G. out. This was not a good start for a coalition of parties. And the first two days' poll certainly looked very like the Liberals keeping back. However, *The Globe* and the Liberals have both come round. It is certainly surprising, and shows great power in Gladstone, the way in which he contrives to retain two large parties, who hate each other, both supporting him.—Yours affectionately,

J. B. M.

To Rev. R. W. Church.

Magdalen College, *Feb.* 10, 1853.

My question comes on on Friday evening, at the Tutors' Association, which is held at Oriel. I wish you could get your duty done next Sunday, and come up for a few days till it is settled. As far as I have sounded men hitherto, it is approved of, the only objections being as to some matters of detail, and how to work it with the present *viva voce* system. Some men too, otherwise favourable, rather cling to the Hebdomadal Board as the channel of communicating evidence to the public.

On the whole, I am disposed to leave these questions open. Let the committee, or committees, charged with the report settle with themselves whether they *wait;* they will know by thinking it over, whether their view is clear or requires information from others, whether they feel their minds made up. And as to the Hebdomadal Board, after we have collected the evidence, let us consider whether we shall send it on to the Hebdomadal Board to print, or print it on our own account. My main point is secured if the evidence is collected and published in any form; though it is of advantage that evidence should be *brought out,* and put in a good point of view by a favourable report, instead of being snubbed, as it may be snubbed, by the Hebdomadal Board report. My proposition is, that we *collect* evidence (which the Hebdomadal Board is not really doing) by asking for it, and drawing men's attention to particular points; when collected, then publish it in one way or another.

To his Sister.

February 15, 1853.

I find myself in the thick of,—where I was when I wrote last,—University questions, and shall remain so for some time. I hardly know what has made me gratuitously undertake such a subject, except I may venture to believe that it is public spirit. Certainly I came up to Oxford this time resolved to have nothing to do with them, and to pursue quietly my theological reading. But one cannot live in the midst of any world, and refuse all sympathy with its interests and agitations. At least I cannot; some can. Accordingly, I have now an article in the *Quarterly*, to which I am engaged. Gladstone introduced me to Lockhart, who was very civil and ready to have one:—this by writing; I did not see him. The changes recommended in the blue-book are so preposterous and unjust that one could not contemplate the shame of their being accepted without indignation; and in the meantime nothing is being written on the other side; and the idea has been gaining ground that the blue-book was being accepted. So, by way of offering my feeble opposition to such a result, I undertake this article. I have also induced the Tutors' Association to enter on the work of collecting evidence on the other side, it having confined itself hitherto to *viva voce* discussion. As all the productions of the family pen have an interest to the home world, I enclose a paper I sent out a fortnight ago, in addition to which I read a paper on the subject last Friday to the Tutors' Association, and the motion was formally discussed last night, and carried by a largish majority. I hope to get a good deal of valuable evidence, and on the side of moderate reform, without sweeping measures upon the Colleges *en masse*.

A pamphlet is coming out on the election by Sir S. Northcote; and the Provost has written a letter. The Bishop of Oxford preached at St. Mary's yesterday a University sermon, pronounced to be very useful for the under-graduates by the Fellows and Masters. Lord Derby and the President are exchanging polite pieces of scholarship. The President sent him a copy of a little tract, with an inscription in Latin, and Lord Derby has sent the President a copy of Greek verses written by himself *on* the President.

To the Rev. R. W. Church.

Oxford, *February* 16, 1853.

I carried my motion at the Tutors' Association on Monday, by a majority of 14 to 5. The meeting was not so large a one (there were three or four men who did not vote as I could have wished), but large enough perhaps for the purpose, especially as all knew of the scheme, and therefore if they stayed away could not have felt hostile to it. So now we must set to work. No committee is appointed yet; that, I understand, is my privilege to propose. I wish you would think over any questions that may occur to you, and give us the benefit of them. I must confess to a great hankering after rather an audacious effort; fairly asking (the reason might be modestly and solidly stated in a circular) the distinguished merchants, manufacturers, attorneys, barristers, and the representatives of the different professions in the country, *What are* the wants they feel with respect to a University education?—Whether they want it *at all* for their young men?—What modification in the teaching of the place would be required if they did want it?—How much time could be spared from business education? I gathered from S. Denison's evidence that there *was* a want felt of this kind by the *barristers*. But really, after all the talk there has been for some years about University extension, one feels one's-self almost entirely in the dark as to how far it is really wanted and will be taken advantage of.—Yours affectionately, J. B. M.

Early this year there was a gathering at Oxford on the question of petitioning the Parliament against the University Bill.

To his Sister.

Oxford, April 1, 1853.

I have been so much engaged in this last contest, that I have not thought of anything else for the last week. Very few of both sides have come up in proportion to the appeals made. I have been against the petition. I think the bill, on the whole, a good one, and there is no doubt that many modifications will be made in Committee. Its postponement, moreover, beyond this session would only have thrown the University on a more uncertain future, with less favourable administrators perhaps, and a reformed Parliament. Our line was clearly for an early settlement of the question. . . . The Bishop of Oxford was very nearly coming up to vote, and only prevented by the advice of his friends. He has been working up men. It is astonishing how impossible it is to produce anything like a large gathering on the most important question put before the University for two centuries. And yet it is easily explained: everybody knows the mind of Government and Parliament is made up, and that either assent or protest will not have any effect on the question of the bill passing or not. Gladstone has been surprising everybody here by the ubiquity of his correspondence. Three-fourths of the Colleges have been in communication with him, on various parts of the bill more or less affecting themselves. He answers everybody by return of post, fully and at length, quite entering into their case, and showing the greatest acquaintance with it.

Arthur came up at my summons, not on the whole sorry at a little change from Hingham, for a few days.—Yours,

J. B. M.

To his sister Elizabeth he writes of Lord Derby's Installation :—

June 15, 1853.

DEAR ELIZABETH,—My labours are not over, but are getting thicker as they approach the close. Church is up for a few days. Things are quiet again after all the bustle.

Lord Derby is considered to have carried off the Installation well. I attended his levee, and thought him certainly happy in his air and manner. But he has no right to talk of smiling and being a villain, for his face wrinkles into countless smiles at a moment's notice out of the most sour basis. I saw his reception of the Bishop of Oxford. At the levee a general smile went the round of the crowd, and only one quotation was in all memories.[1]

Disraeli was the great lion; but that worthy Vice-Chancellor at the Worcester dinner considered that the whole assembly, nobles and commons, had come there for the express purpose of hearing him talk on religion and morals; which he did, on the most lenient computation, for two hours. So Disraeli left without saying a word. Jeune, at the Pembroke dinner, was equally lengthy, with the addition of coarseness; as a specimen, he gave as a toast "the Church, the Queen, and the ladies of England!"—Yours affectionately, J. B. M.

To REV. R. W. CHURCH.

OXFORD, *November* 15, 1853.

... I have not told you how much we all of us enjoyed Scotland. There is such variety, the sea is a complete archipelago of small islands, many of them very fine in form, and with fine mountains. A view from a height on a sunny day is quite Grecian. Three of us, *i.e.* Arthur, young Kempe, and myself went to Skye, which was great fun—both the scenery and the characters we came across. The scenery is volcanic and Scandinavian, huge yellow mountains rising up with as sharp outlines as

---

[1] What occurred on the occasion of the Bishop's speech on the Canada Clergy Reserves was as follows:—"Lord Derby moved an amendment to the bill, and the Bishop of Oxford, speaking on the question, quoted Burke as having said that the Americans became intractable whenever they saw the least attempt to wrest freedom from them by force, or shuffle it from them by chicane. Lord Derby having taken exception to these words, the Bishop explained that the allusion was made with a smile, and was not intended to be offensive. Lord Derby then retorted with quoting, 'A man may smile and smile and be a villain.' Lord Clarendon came to the Bishop's rescue. Lord Derby's amendment was lost by 40 votes. He afterwards complimented the Bishop of Oxford on *his* power of taking a joke."—*Life of Bishop Wilberforce*, vol. ii. p. 186.

if they were cut out of brown paper, and looking for all the world like mountains on the stage. A cluster of them looked quite a fit place for an Odin Hades, where giants dance among copper kettles a mile high. I should like to have a talk with you, and compare Scotch with Grecian experiences of scenery. We are moving slowly here, the Tutors' Association preparing a College report; the Heads very taciturn. No sign of the report yet. I expect a tussle about the constitution point.

I do not envy you your task of reviewing Maurice in the *G.*, yet I have to do it in the *C. R.* It is a pity to see a man losing himself and becoming a ruin, from a radical mistake of thinking himself a philosopher. Some of the cut-up reviews did much good in this way. They put down a man at the outset. But Maurice has been petted and told he is a philosopher, till he naturally thinks he is one. And he has not a clear idea in his head. It is a reputation that, the instant it is touched, must go like a card-house.—Yours affectionately, J. B. M.

OXFORD, *Christmas Day*, 1853.

MY DEAR CHURCH,— ... So the first stone of the coalition is beginning to loosen, or rather is already out. Lake has been in London and seen Lawley, Gladstone's secretary, who is fierce against the unpatriotic conduct of Lord P., and also talks of Lord John's jealousy of the over proportion of work and power in the hands of the Peelite section of the Cabinet. The Reform Bill is his point, having pledged himself to one just before he was turned out. A report is going about to-day here of Lord P.'s return to office—not a very credible one. I suppose the Reform Bill will be the first thing when Parliament meets, and, as dissolution and fresh Cabinet depend on its fate, there is, after all, no knowing when our University matter comes on. Have you seen the report of the Heads? It is very weak, partly from the Provost's not being well, and partly from the awkward shape which was laid down for it by the Heads, a running comment on the recommendations of the Commission. So it is a sort of endless series of negatives and protests—very little arguing or good statement. It is the only document, in my recollection, in which they have treated the Masters with due respect. On the eve of their own dissolution!—a lesson to oligarchies, if oligarchies ever received lessons, or there were any oligarchies now—which there hardly are—to receive them. In the uncertainties of all prospects, one naturally fastens on the retributions which most gratify one's moral feelings.

Lake and Rawlinson have been seeing Gladstone. He is very strong against the religious animus of the Commission, but hints on more reconstruction than some of us like. Thus, he will both reduce the number of Fellowships, and also alter some of the others to terminable ones. No bill is as yet made out, and only the beginnings are as yet under the attention of Government. Jowett dined with Gladstone the other day, and was disgusted to find him strong against the Commission, and all the religious ideas in it, and talking against Locke and for Butler; that the loss of four Colleges would be less than that of the *Analogy*—in fact, quite incorrigibly bigoted. This is Lake's account—whose policy, by the way, rather is to impress one with G.'s conservative religionism, and on Lake and Rawlinson's side with G.'s collegiate reforms. . . .—Yours affectionately,   J. B. M.

To his Sister.

January 23, 1854.

We are likely to have for once an election without a contest, every candidate having declined on the other side. I am not, however, altogether contented with Sir W. Heathcote, and should much have preferred Roundell Palmer. The residents as a body are in his favour, the general desire being here to have distinguished men of some kind, who represent the spirit of the age in its unblamable features. It is rather a relapse to the country gentleman taking Sir W. H. However, he is Keble's patron and friend, and a very excellent man. It is certainly odd enough that, with every effort against it, Puseyites still get possession of the University representation—now the whole of it. . . . Roundell Palmer was formally asked to stand by a meeting of residents, and declined, in deference to the known bias for Sir W. H. among his friends in London. A second meeting asked him *again;* he declined again. But even at a third meeting a messenger was sent to lay the state of the case before Sir W. H. His answer was, that personally he felt disposed to withdraw, but that his friends had a claim on him. His friends advised him to stand, and so the matter ended.

The absence of a contest is a gain. Still I suppose we shall have the rather uncomfortable reflection soon of Roundell Palmer making a good speech on University matters in Parliament, and Sir William Heathcote a mediocre one, so that one man will do the work and another have the honours.

Scott stayed a day here on his way to Cuddesden, where he has been staying, consulting with the Bishop on Convocation matters. They are in doubt as to their course. Archdeacon Wilberforce was there, and attended two of the election meetings. The Bishop is a friend of Sir William Heathcote. Scott seems to get on with him very well, and is getting quite an *amicus curiæ* of the episcopal bench; though to see him in his travelling costume he is more like a foreign cavalry officer than an Anglican ecclesiastic, clad in bearskins and cloaks of the highest lay order.—Yours affectionately, J. B. M.

OXFORD, *January* 29, 1854.

MY DEAR CHURCH,— . . . So we are to have no contest. This is satisfactory, and justifies the return of Sir W. H., which I should have been otherwise somewhat disposed to grumble at, all my feelings being for R. Palmer. Why have you not come up? They have been expecting you at the Observatory.

We are in the midst of a College stir—a majority of one having carried at a meeting that it was allowable to ask for enabling powers to alter our statutes, in spite of the oath. I was one of the majority. The oath to ask for no change in statutes seems to me to be exactly on the same ground as the oath to observe them; and that if we interpret the one oath liberally we may the other. . . . Yours affectionately,

J. B. M.

Having the answer to this letter before me, I may use the privilege to insert here a comment on the last paragraph:—

To J. B. M.

"Your view of the oath is one I should like to see worked out. But it is to me a nasty subject, and there seems a difference between an oath directed to *one* particular point and an oath directed to a general matter comprehending a great variety of multifarious points of unequal importance. But it is clear that there ought to be some way out of a restriction which stops all improvement."

The year 1854 ends with the death of the President of Magdalen in his hundredth year.

To his Sister.

OXFORD, *December* 23, 1854.

You will have seen in the papers before receiving this the death of our poor old President. Long as it has been before us, it has rather taken us by surprise at last. He has been getting gradually weaker for some time; but so gradually that he seemed as if he might go on for another year or two. Last Sunday a change was observed in him; still he had his usual party at dinner, and, though he did not come down to dinner, saw them at tea. He was more sleepy than usual then. The next day he was worse, but on Tuesday revived so much that Bloxam lost all immediate apprehension, and the President himself said—"I think I shall be a little longer with you, Sir." On Wednesday, however, the weakness returned and increased till his physician, Dr. Jackson, thought it proper to call in Dr. Acland. They both entirely gave him up. . . . When I went to dinner in Common Room, however, on Thursday, I was surprised to hear all at once that it was a matter of hours with him. His head wandered a good deal till his death, with clear intervals. On Thursday stimulants were given him to enable him to do some little business that he had put off, but they failed. He thought, among other things, that Cholmeley was married, and had brought his wife to the President's lodgings, and was anxious there should be a room for them. He had little positive pain, but much uneasiness, which went off at last. He is to be buried in chapel. He had once intimated a desire to be buried at Tylehurst, but had never alluded to it for years, and so his family have it in the College. He has died, I hear, without any will, but only some directions. Whether this is delay, or no will was considered by him the best will, I hardly know.—Yours affectionately, J. B. M.

P.S.—Johnson is the President of the Astronomical Society next year.

OXFORD, *December* 28, 1854.

MY DEAR CHURCH,—The funeral is to-morrow, and will be largely attended. It is curious that the President left no will. . . . The President has by a deed of gift given his library to Durham, but the deed, though signed, has never been delivered; being brought to light for the first time after his death. So it will probably be unsound. . . .

The President did not think he was going to die so soon, but that he should linger. He was only in bed two days. He was wandering a good deal of the time, and within five minutes of his death was telling his old stories to an imaginary visitor by his side, whom he addressed every now and then in his usual way, known to all of us, "Do you hear me, Sir?" which he generally said when he suspected the wandering of his auditor.—Yours affectionately, J. B. M.

Writing the last day of the year he adds some further particulars:—

More facts came out about the President and his leaving no will. A will had been actually drawn up, and only wanted his signature when the last weakness came on and increased so rapidly that even this could not be given. The will would have left a large part of the property away from the family and left it to charities. Mrs. Routh is left with a very indifferent jointure, the interest of £12,000.—Yours affectionately,

J. B. M.

And in a letter dated January 16:—

The President's library, after all, goes to Durham. Counsel's opinion was taken. What determined it in favour of Durham seems to have been that the passing of the property to a corporate body would not have been any fraud upon Government, as there is no tax in such a case. If the gift had been to an individual, Government would have lost, by allowing the property to pass under that *form*, the natural tax upon a will.

The following letter, written after having been for ten years thrown upon his own thoughts, and upon the natural bent of his own mind and character, wears a serious air—a full consciousness of taking a step. Of course, to those near him, the step was no surprise :—

To his Brother, John Mozley.

Oxford, *January* 1, 1855.

The beginning of a new *C. R.* quarter is a proper time for my communicating to you a resolution which I have for some time come to with regard to the *Christian Remembrancer*.

I find that after four years of reading, interrupted indeed, but still carried on with some degree of system and considerable thought, I have arrived at a change of opinion, more or less modified, on some points of High Church theology; but to a very decided one with respect to a particular doctrine which has been the theme of great dispute, and on which the party in the Church which the *C. R.* professes to reflect has taken very strongly one side: I mean the doctrine of Baptismal Regeneration. I now entertain no doubt of the substantial justice of the Gorham decision on this point.

I have too been engaged, as you may know, on a book which is now arriving at something like completion; and part of which will express my views on this question, and enter into the whole argument connected with it.

I do not think it right under such circumstances to have anything more to do with the editing of the *C. R.* What I have had indeed has been of an imperfect irregular kind, and more belonging to the practice of an *amicus curiæ*. Yet it has been enough to make me connected with the Review, in the minds of that portion of the High Church party, and others to whom my name happens to be known; and I do not feel that in consistency I can continue it any longer.

I have written to Scott, some three weeks ago, to this effect. Will you, when you next write to Clay, tell him the same, and that he need not consequently send me any more proofs of the *Christian Remembrancer*.

This intimation of mine will not perhaps much surprise you, as you may have seen that I have been for some time undergoing a course of modification, and I think I have told you of the particular point on which I find myself coming into collision with the doctrines of the party.

Practically I have no wish to separate myself from those with whom I have hitherto acted. The Tractarian body is *now* the one with which, on the whole, I most sympathise. Nor does a modification on one or other point, or even a decided difference, make much substantial alteration in my feeling towards it. But when a particular doctrine has been made the watchword, and people have been considered to take their sides, according as they thought one way or another upon it, a disagreement with the party with which one has hitherto acted upon it cannot be ignored by one's-self. It affects one's official relations to the party, though one's present feelings may remain much as they were. It is now ten years since I commenced my connection with *C. R.* I might make my reflections on the advantages and disadvantages of it. It has made me write to a certain extent. I do not anticipate, now that the connection is over, that I shall do anything better with myself. Nor is my own future much brighter than that I have been conjecturing for the *C. R.* One must act, however, upon certain acknowledged maxims, and take what steps are imposed upon one by circumstances, or the course of one's own mind.—Yours affectionately, J. B. M.

To his Sister.

February 4, 1855.

There is nothing to talk of but the weather, which is more disagreeable than can be expressed, Oxford being peculiarly susceptible to all the damp of a foggy, misty thaw. At St. Giles's they have all had colds, Miss Amelia Ogle adding to her's a stiff neck, which obstructs her movements in that quarter effectually, and impairs their natural grace; for which it substitutes however (I am speaking of stiff necks generally) an unusual solemnity of manner; for persons having to turn right round when they speak to any one, the appearance gives to any communication that of a formal and dogmatic appeal. . . .

I have informed Charles Marriott of my altered relations to the *C. R.*, and the reason; to which he says, "For my part I object more strongly to the tribunal than to the decision"—that is, the Gorham decision—though he says he still *does* object to it. If people, however, cannot use stronger language than this, it seems to me that the ground for any strong separation of parties in the Church is rather gone.—Yours affectionately,

J. B. M.

To Rev. R. W. Church.

Oxford, *February* 11, 1855.

I have offered my book to Murray, who has accepted it. I find I shall have to split my subject, and devote one volume to Predestination and the questions connected with it, and another to the application of the subject to the doctrine of Baptism. I shall hope to get out the first before the Long, and the last by the end of the year. They will be separate books. There is one advantage in this division, that neither book will be portentous in size. The disadvantage is that there is not enough interest concentrated in each, Predestination of itself being a dry, crabbed subject, unconnected with any exciting feelings of the day. As I do not know, however, of any book which has formally gone into the subject in a fair spirit, there is room, I think, for such a treatise. . . .

I have communicated to Rogers and Marriott my withdrawal from the *Christian Remembrancer*, for which the reason is simply this, that I find, after reading and reflection, that I accept the Gorham decision, and that therefore, as the Tractarian party has so strongly committed itself against that judgment, both generally and specially by the protest of Pusey and its other leaders, I can no longer retain an official or semi-official connection with it, though one's private feelings towards individuals and the body may be much the same as before. . . .

We are congratulating ourselves on Gladstone's continuing in office. All the world is rejoicing over Lord John Russell. Independent of a triumph over an enemy, it is rather comforting to see what great mistakes sagacious and experienced men may make.—Yours affectionately, J. B. M.

March 22, 1855.

Things are more and more tending to Liberalism here. It is a progress which nobody can stop. The Council is obliged, though not itself Liberal, to join. The scientific Professorships are most of them now only to have a mild test of non-opposition to the Church—no *subscription*.—Yours affectionately,

J. B. M.

To his Sister.

March 12, 1855.

The only piece of news that there is for the last week is rather melancholy—the death of poor Craufurd, elder brother of the Ogles' brother-in-law. From the first moment they heard of his going to the Crimea, the Ogles in fact gave him up. He was not the least in a fit state of health to go, with a diseased liver, great propensity to rheumatism, and such general delicacy that he was always ill in England. However, his regiment being ordered out, he could not stay behind, or sell out. The first day he landed in the Crimea he had to sleep in the open air. But this passed off at the time better than he expected. However, a bilious fever shortly commenced, he was sent to Scutari, and there died. Such is the end of this heir of an old family and good estate, so little good have his social advantages been to him. He was at the marriage of his brother, and was much liked—handsome and gentlemanly.

Elizabeth is to be at the Ogles' to-day, and I go to dine there.[1]—Yours affectionately, J. B. M.

[1] My sister Elizabeth was at this time living with my brother Tom in London, and her letters contain many very interesting reports on the subject of the war; on the mismanagement of which my brother's London friends were so outspoken. She writes of what she hears, and testifies to the honesty of tone, to the absorbing feeling that prevailed amongst all with whom my brother was associated, and the intensity in his own case. Answering the attacks on *The Times* for its tone, she writes:—"The line of *The Times* may

To Rev. R. W. Church.

OXFORD, *May* 17, 1855.

. . . I have been dragging on through my *opus* since I last wrote, and now it is, I am glad to say, very near a conclusion. The book, I confess, is not what would be popularly called interesting, but if it establishes a point I shall be quite satisfied. My sisters Elizabeth and Fanny have been severally visiting the Ogles lately. The latter is here now, and I am giving a musical entertainment to amuse her. She has been for the last year nearly in constant attendance upon my mother during her illness; and she wants, in consequence, setting up again; and a little gaiety does her good. . . . Yours,   J. B. M.

To J. B. M.'s announcement of the approaching conclusion of his labours, he received the following reply:—

REV. R. W. CHURCH TO J. B. M.

May, 1855.

MY DEAR MOZLEY,—I congratulate you on the conclusion of your book. I have followed it, with great interest, sheet by sheet. It seems to me to have brought out very clearly the fact of the double and parallel lines of ideas, and to have confronted them with great distinctness and power. The subject is one which, I suppose, is not likely to tempt lazy readers. But you have not written for them. It makes one feel how one goes on, taking things for granted, both as principles and explanations, and as facts. I am very glad you worked the point well, about our ignorance. I never should be a meta-

be mistaken; it is a question of judgment how far it is wise to act on the accumulation of complaints that pour in upon them, but that they do come, and from quarters that must know, there is no doubt. Tom is quite sick with the accounts sometimes. People have such mysterious ideas of motives that influence *The Times*, whereas they often seem the simplest in the world; . . . I really think in this case a strong feeling that it must be done, and that a reform in the army is necessary. People feel so differently. Mr. Fraser [now Bishop of Manchester] wrote to Tom enthusiastically on their courage in laying the blame where every one felt it must be due, but dared not say." Each letter has passages in the same strain, on the same engrossing theme, sometimes reporting bitterer language, which, after all, subsequent history justifies.

physician; but the way in which assumptions excite no question, and people go on spinning arguments as if the whole of the invisible world was as easy to be understood as the theory of the steam-engine, has long been one of my standing wonders. . . .

I am glad that you have brought out so strongly the two-sided character of all our means of knowing, and the fact, that what we know in religious matters is but the tendency to know. The idea of perfect and absolute knowledge, which is involved in so much of what is said and taught on all sides, becomes daily more and more unendurable to me.—Ever yours affectionately, R. W. C.

TO HIS SISTER.

OXFORD, *June* 5, 1855.

What with Fanny being the correspondent while she was here, and my being in London, it seems quite long since I wrote to Derby. I had an agreeable week in London. The dinner at the Literary Fund passed off, owing to the Bishop of Oxford's spirited chairmanship, well enough. He certainly does everything with great go. Whately made an egotistical speech in celebration of his own liberality and judgment in his mode of patronising poor authors. Sir A. Alison was washy and flat, something like his book style. Neate made an elaborate speech, with a good deal of choice phraseology in it, which he had evidently prepared with care. It was all summed up in *The Times* as—"The Rev. Mr. Neate proposed Sir A. Alison's health in a neat speech." . . .—Yours affectionately, J. B. M.

TO HIS SISTER.

MALVERN, *August* 27, 1855.

I thought you would like to hear about Mr. and Mrs. Charles Dyson. It was seventeen years since I had seen either of them—not since that dinner-party at Tidworth, to which we went from Cholderton. Mr. C. Dyson is looking exactly the same that he always did, the alteration being that his hair has grown quite white. The contrast between the two brothers is as strong as ever. We had a very pleasant talk over various subjects, Oxford principally, and the recent changes in it, the war, Gladstone, etc. It is remarkable how an elegant and accomplished mind, as Mr. C. Dyson's is, overcomes the disadvantage of so plain a face. He is a very neat talker, and has all the courtesy and smoothness of the old school. It is pleasant to see two brothers sticking so close together through life. They differed about Gladstone, Mr. F. Dyson being scandalised by his course in the Jew Bill; but Mr. C. Dyson seeming inclined to go along a good way with him even in his war views. . . . It was a mere domestic meeting.

I never mentioned my evening with the M.s, where I met L. and his wife. We had a regular political and House of Commons talk; all sorts of gossip, such as floats about the lobby. M. describes Disraeli as popular with the younger members of his party in the House—very social and companionable, not stiff. The position of the Peelites is considered wretched and irremediable, and the Opposition glory over it.—Yours affectionately,
J. B. M.

Towards the end of 1855, J. B. M. was elected member of the newly constituted Council.

To his Sister.
October 26, 1855.

Thank you for congratulations on my new honours. There are, however, various reasons which must prevent my feeling altogether like the Head of a House. One is rather the fungus growth of a democratic movement, and probably the old Heads look upon me as a squire would look upon a respectable tradesman from the neighbouring town who had settled himself in his village. I can tell you nothing of my duties or experience of office yet, having had none. At the time when the news of my promotion reached me, I was just going to dinner in Hall, and so could not attend the first meeting *pro forma* of the Board, which was immediately after the election. The whole election was very quiet, no disclosing of the poll as it went on, and so no room for electioneering changes or combinations. . . . Cholmeley, the Proctor, described the first meeting of the Board at five o'clock, by candle-light in a dark room, as more like a cave of brigands than a council-room.—Yours affectionately,
J. B. M.

To his Sister.

February 1, 1856.

I am preparing a book, not a large one, for the press—a wind-up of my subject; after which my theological labours will rest—at any rate, probably, for some time to come. The title of it will be *The Primitive Doctrine of Baptismal Regeneration*. ... It will be an easy book, and only the development of one very simple position.

Shoreham will probably be settled in a few weeks, by which time it will have come down to me. The probability is that it will. I have hardly yet begun to realise the change it will bring upon me, and hope I shall not be seized with qualms and nervous fears about leaving a place I have lived in so long. The principal consideration is, after all, that, whether one goes or stays, *change* is necessary; and one cannot be the same in the future that one has been in the past. So that any sudden change of this kind is less really a change than it appears to be.

I am reading Macaulay. It is a new style of history, and open to criticism on that ground. But it is very wonderful the way in which he weaves all his innumerable details into the fabric, and brings in everything in its right place. I think he puffs and blows too indiscriminately about all events great and small, and that this destroys his perception often of the relative importance of events. Thus he compares the battle of Killicrankie in Scotland with that of Newton-Butler in Ireland, the latter being a very insignificant event compared with the former. His show-up of the Non-jurors is severe. On the whole, I find myself ready to agree with him in the main. It seems to me so very few of those movements which are attended with a certain romance, and so bias one in their favour for a time, will bear examination. There is often some gross offence against common sense in them, which was specially the case in the Non-juring movement.

Did I say in my last that I had met Elwyn, the editor of the *Quarterly*, an agreeable, very well informed man, and a fluent talker.—Yours affectionately, J. B. M.

To a friend whom he was advising to stand for the Taylorian Professorship :—

March 28, 1856.

With respect to the philological element, it appears to be plain from the wording of the statute that philology and literature are placed on an equal footing. Now, they will never get Professors to represent them both—that is, adequately. Indeed there is a kind of opposition in the two tastes. I mean that the same person who went into the spirit of a literature would not ordinarily be the person to investigate the philological basis of language. So that one or other element must always be in some degree unrepresented.

As for the work, Max Müller laughs at the idea, the vacation seven months of the year affording such ample time. I think that with respect to health even a good deal of work is by no means detrimental to it, so long as it is work congenial to a person's mind. What wears men is immoderate work and uninteresting work. There appears to me a real stimulus in interesting work to the health. I mean that if you are at all reluctant to face the prospect on this ground, this is a consideration that ought to be taken into account.—Yours,

J. B. M.

On Mr. Wheeler resigning Shoreham, then consisting of both Old and New Shoreham, the College divided the living; and Old Shoreham coming down to James Mozley, he accepted it, and, in July 1856, married Amelia, third daughter of Dr. Ogle, Regius Professor of Medicine, and twin sister of Caroline, wife of Mr. Johnson, the Observer; settling at once at Old Shoreham, to which he and his wife became greatly attached, and where, I may add, they were much beloved.

To Rev. R. W. Church.

Shoreham, *September* 9, 1857.

I don't think any communication has passed between us since the three days you were here. Since then we have been at Derby, Manchester, the Lakes, and Oxford, having previously too heard the Handel at the Crystal Palace. We returned five weeks ago, and shall now be quiet for a long time to come. Manchester was as agreeable a gallery of pictures as I ever saw; pleasant pictures to look at, good light, airy, etc. We were there four days. My sister Anne came with us. We took it leisurely, but not wasting our time. I was astounded, however, at the end of it to see, on looking over the catalogue, what a small proportion of the pictures I had even *looked at*—I think, on a most favourable estimate, not more than an eighth. Of that small proportion, how many I shall retain is another question. It was said the Manchester operatives did not patronise the place, but there was a good proportion of the common sort of people there.

I was glad to get a sight of the King of the Belgians; a quiet, shrewd-looking man, with the air of a gentleman, but not the least of a king; not an unpleasant countenance, showing considerateness, and the better characteristics of a man of the world. He seems to have managed their late rows in Belgium with great adroitness.

We were much pleased with the Lakes, especially Derwentwater. Grasmere, notwithstanding its high Wordsworthian reputation, is a little too small and basin-like. A great bulky hotel too on the margin, just built, obstructs your eye. Fox-Howe, Arnold's place (where Mrs. A. lives now), is rather too shut up for my taste. Wordsworth's house, where his widow now lives, is a respectable, rather ancient, sash-windowed one, not unlike an oldish parsonage of the more secular class; not pretending to the Gothic or ecclesiastic style. His old gardener described his nocturnal recitations of his own poetry, which had the effect of several persons talking. This rush of voices would pass his cottage about ten o'clock at night, as Wordsworth was returning from his late walk. . . .

What a horrid exhibition of humanity this Indian Mutiny is! It will of course end in a tighter English rule than ever. Only think of the nonsense of having allowed these natives a free press! How far will people not carry a theory? On the whole, with all its horrors, this row has its satisfactory results,

as being an unconscious justification of our position in India, showing that we are necessary for the people there. . . . Yours affectionately,
J. B. M.

In September of this year, while on a visit at Shoreham, Dr. Ogle was taken suddenly ill, and died there. The following letter relates to certain claims the Regius Professorship of Medicine had in the Ewelme Hospital, which, in the interests of the family, J. B. M. undertook to represent to Lord Westbury, then Attorney-General:—

To HIS SISTER ELIZABETH.

November 20, 1857.

I had an interview by appointment with the Attorney-General about the Ewelme affair. I had had some notes from him before, in which he plainly acknowledged the injustice of the former offer made, but referred to some steps which had been taken under the former Attorney-General, which there would be some difficulty in undoing. On calling, he gave me a very clear, lucid statement of the whole case, never stopping or retracing a step from beginning to end, just as if he were reading it out of a book. The upshot is, it will have to go through two legal references to Judge in Chambers, the result of which will be, in all human probability, that we shall get the whole six years' salary, amounting to £1500. After his statement, he began to talk about University matters, reform, extension; talked about his own academical life, having gone up at fourteen and maintained himself wholly at seventeen and a half old, or his father could not have kept him there. He remembered Dr. Ogle, but was a good deal his senior in University standing. He commented on the free-and-easy air of the present race of under-graduates, and was highly disgusted at the pretensions of Balliol in setting up a competitive examination for admission, the result of which had been disastrous to one of his own sons. There was a formality about his voice and pronunciation, but none in the substance of his conversation. As he did not appear to have suffered much from certain remarks, I felt quite easy, and had no particular qualms.— Yours affectionately, J. B. M.

To REV. R. W. CHURCH.

SHOREHAM, *January* 1858.

Arthur has been here a few days; he is quite a London clergyman now in his general acquaintance with things in the London Church-world. He goes about a good deal to morning meetings, evening meetings, to coffee and Scripture expositions at F. Maurice's, conferences on subjects of the day at the rectory, St. James's, etc. etc. He describes Liberalism as considerably advancing in some clerical quarters, especially on the subject of the Atonement, which is a complete bugbear to many. . . . Thought seems to be going in this direction lately, probably stimulated by Jowett's book just now, though Maurice has long taken this line. Indeed, S. T. Coleridge set the example. . . . Maurice, as I said, gives soirées, which are generally attended by some twenty of the younger clergy. He sits at a table with a Bible, and is asked questions upon difficulties, etc. His general line is to resolve everything into vagueness.

To HIS SISTER FANNY.

SHOREHAM, *May* 11, 1858.

. . . I heard Lord Palmerston at the Literary Fund dinner. I had never heard him speak. His speaking is a curious combination of perpetual hesitation, with a perfect type of the whole thing he is going to say—the construction of the sentence and everything—in his head. With his continual hesitation he yet never goes back a single step that he has made, but proceeds regularly on till the whole is complete. He is very choice in his words, and almost Addisonian—selecting the simplest, and never treating you to that fat, pulpy stuff which some speakers do. For a hesitating speaker, too, he has one remarkable characteristic, which is, that his sentences are very long and his constructions rather involved.

This makes his slow mastery of the work as it goes along the more remarkable. His appearance has very little in it; one might take him for anybody—a respectable grocer or alderman got up in good evening dress. He has nothing intellectual or aristocratic about him. He is stouter than I expected. *The Times* only gave his heavy speech on literature, and left out his lighter speeches, which were clever and characteristic. . . .
—Yours affectionately, J. B. M.

To Rev. R. W. Church.

Shoreham, *November* 1, 1858.

. . . We go to Oxford for a fortnight the middle of this month. The Observer has quite made up his mind to take a regular holiday next year in the shape of a Continental tour, of a half-business character, just sufficiently so to be amusing; visits to observatories, confabs with astronomers. . . . Goldwin Smith's duel with Froude is amusing. I suppose Froude's answer will be considered by his own friends rather good. I thought the tone of his [G. S.'s] article too supercilious, considering that Froude, whatever theory he may maintain on some subjects, has worked, and made solid additions to history, which are acknowledged. A man who writes simply as a critic, and with the great advantage of not having written any book himself, ought not to use his vantage ground too unsparingly, or forget that if he came to write a history himself, he too might come under the influence of some new theory or other.

They (at Finchampstead) see something of Kingsley. Tom says there is effort in his conversation and preaching, though very clever. His description was that he preached as if he was wrestling with an evil spirit. Keble has been preaching at St. Paul's. The sermon seems to have created a great sensation, though not having the advantage of being heard by more than a small part of the congregation. . . .—Yours, J. B. M.

Oxford, *December* 13, 1858.

My dear Church,—We have been making a longer stay here than we intended. It is the first time that I have really seen anything of Oxford since my departure, though I have been up several times for different reasons. Things look very unchanged except in Heads: everything very quiet. It is curious how completely controversy, in the Tractarian sense, has left Oxford—no allusion to it ever, even the most remote. What controversy there is, is wholly in the philosophical sphere. Mansel's Bampton Lectures are criticised a good deal. Wilson describes it as an attempt to defend orthodoxy on Kantian principles, and says that Chretien, Goldwin Smith, etc., do not like his ground. I have just looked into them. They seem to me to put forward the absolute unintelligibility of the Divine nature—even Divine moral character—too nakedly. This is his answer to the moral objection to the Atonement, Abraham's sacrifice, etc.: You do not know what *Divine* morals are. What Wilson says is, This breaks up the whole basis of revelation; and, how are you to argue with the Hindoo upon his immoral gods?—he will tell you, Divine morals are different from human. I give you the criticisms as I hear them. It appears to me to be one of those cases in which a man has been too confident of the strength of some grand general dictum, and has rested everything upon it, expressed in the boldest and most unqualified way. . . .

We have been out almost every day. *At homes* are the order of the day. The Vice-Chancellor gives crowded ones, as well as a succession of dinners. It is rather convenient for me who want to see everybody. I have had a long confab with Stanley —the very first I ever had with him. He has a generous desire to hear what everybody has to say, and made me develop myself on the subject of Luther, Justification by faith, a great crux of his [Stanley's], the Law, etc. I responded as well as I could. He is getting up the Arian subject, and has a sort of scheme in his head of separating the Arianism of the early times from that of later, on the ground of its (the former) dealing with the remote and mystical part of the subject— the eternal generation—while the latter comes into direct collision with the 'historical Christ." I did not quite understand his distinction, or rather I did and did not think it tenable, as I told him; for the *person* of the "historical Christ" and of the mystical one, or eternal Son, are the very same, and what you say of one you say of the other. I thought the idea rather Stanleyan.[1] He is a pleasant person to talk to, and one has a great deal in common with him.

How are you now? etc. etc. Remember we return home next Saturday.—Yours affectionately, J. B. M.

SHOREHAM, *February* 28, 1859.

MY DEAR CHURCH,—You will most probably have heard the sad news from Oxford before this reaches you. Johnson died quite suddenly this evening. A telegraphic message reached us here at half-past ten, about three hours after the event.

It was a complaint of the heart. I need not say what our feelings are. We start by the earliest train in the morning to Oxford. I was given to understand when I was in Oxford, by one of the doctors, in what direction the complaint was; but, though I felt alarmed at the time, there was nothing to show immediate danger; and one hears of those complaints going on for years.

This is of course a tremendous blow to all one's Oxford reminiscences, and makes everything quite different to look back upon. No one has been more completely identified with all that one has lived through for the last twenty years, than Johnson. At the same time, I almost feel a sort of impossibility in realising these very sudden losses.—Yours affectionately, J. B. M.

---

[1] Referring to this conversation there is a letter from Mr. Stanley, dated Christ Church, November 16, 1860:—

"MY DEAR MOZLEY,—I am on the point of publishing some lectures on the Nicene Council, in which I should much like to make use of what struck me as a very powerful defence of the Athanasian doctrine, or rather attack on the Arian doctrine, that you made to me when last I saw you in Oxford, viz., the simplicity of the Divine and human as opposed to the unphilosophical mythological elements which would have been introduced into theology by the notion of an Exalted Æon, Angel, etc. etc. etc.; as advocated by Arius.

"May I ask whether you have published such a statement in a form in which I could refer to it, or if not, whether you would object to my expressing my obligation to you for the argument.—Yours faithfully,

"A. P. STANLEY."

The following letter gives his thoughts on the death of a family friend of his whole life :—

To his Sister.

April 14, 1859.

I had seen Mr. Wayland's death in *The Times* before your note came. Your previous account of him, or rather his own account of his great weakness, had of course prepared one in some degree for the news. It has been, as you say, so very gradual a process, that the end came with as little change or surprise as it could do. Mr. Wayland was always to me a most pleasing person to think of. There was a finish about him which was not only external, but was really the expression of his inner self and true character. The perfect resignation with which he acquiesced during his whole life in the situation of a mere country clergyman, or in what is vulgarly called being "buried," without having anything even in his thoughts beyond it, was really a picture in its way in these pushing days,— though all days, I suppose, are equally pushing. Mr. Wayland's was the nicest form of a really humble man; there was not the slightest show of humility, but you found it out practically by nothing of the contrary kind ever coming out. I have always felt a great attachment to him, and should like much to have seen a great deal more of him than I did, but deafness is a serious obstruction. Except in the actual family circle, it seems to make all communication almost more or less necessarily artificial, and makes conversation quite a different thing. It was a particular misfortune in Mr. Wayland's case, for no one defect could have deprived so very social a person so completely of his principal ordinary pleasures as that did. Yet it is remarkable how perfectly he accommodated himself immediately to it, and made reading serve the purpose of recreation instead.

It is curious to compare his career with that of his contemporary [and early friend,] our Bishop. I consider our Bishop a good specimen of the class that "gets on;" he has always taken things quietly and never pushed. And yet, if you compare the two lives, I very much doubt whether Mr. Wayland has not, after all, got a greater quantity of natural happiness out of life than the latter. Three-fourths of the life of these dignitaries is passed in buckram, interchanging civilities or attentions which do not bring the mind into play, and might be done by automatons properly constructed. There is a sort of pleasure in the general consciousness that you are a great man, but, that allowed, the rest is really not *life* in any true sense. Whereas Mr. Wayland always seemed to me greatly to enjoy life in the best sense. When he was reading a good novel, for example, *he* was really living while his successful friend was acting some formality or other. Some persons seem naturally to develop into a sort of personified ceremonial —it is their destiny.

I find it very difficult to express my whole idea of Mr. Wayland, and yet I feel that his character has made a deep impression on me, and that, even when quite young, I involuntarily always thought a great deal of him. One reason, I think, is that he never *spoiled* any of his good qualities as so many good people do. They had all the advantage of being correctly represented, not pushed too far, or made hobbies or conceits of. For example A. B., the other day, made the remark that he never could like X., and he could not find out why, except it was that he was always thrusting his *honesty* into your face; a quality, by the way, which I do not know that he possesses to a greater extent than other people. But Mr. Wayland's good taste—or rather real naturalness of character—kept everything in its place, and yet there was a decided danger on the sentimental side if he had gone off in that direction. As it was, I think it was the *sentiment*—not sentimentality—in him which contributed to the general effect of his character more than anything else. It was the true thing as it ought to be, and not swelled out. There was a great deal of real philosophy about him, a true estimate of life, a way of taking things easily, as if they were to be expected. He had the good points of a man of the world. I think myself this is a rare character—at least I do not know many of it— what is called the man of the world " in a good sense." It is a very attractive character wherever met with. Our old

President had a good deal of it. It inspires a sort of confidence. You feel that your toes will not be trodden on in the course of the next hour. You know at any rate that he has not any divine commission to make himself unpleasant. There was a great deal of the softening effect of experience in Mr. Wayland, and there was a repose which is usually considered to be the accompaniment of rank where the person has never had to make efforts, and so never been in the way of forming restless or fidgety manners.

On the whole, I look upon his as a very valuable type of character, and the more so because so very pleasing a type. I like to have such an image before me, and am sure that as long as I live it always will be a pleasure to me to think of Mr. Wayland. If any of you are writing to Mrs. Solly [Mr. W.'s eldest living daughter], please give her my condolences and sympathy.—Yours affectionately, J. B. M.

To Rev. R. W. Church.

Shoreham, *June* 10, 1859.

. . . What do you think of the prospect of a new Ministry and the £5 borough franchise? Democratically it is a great step downwards. So Sidney Herbert is at last a declared Liberal. I suspect a little ambition in him. He seems now to stand next to Lord Palmerston and Lord John Russell, who must before very long move off the scene; so that, on the principle on which the Premiership is sometimes disposed of, being given to a sensible man of tact, under whom others are willing to serve—as in Lord Aberdeen's case—he may be the head of the Government not long hence. It is odd to see the old thing going on—the superficial flexible man rising, while Gladstone is apparently going down. . . .

July 4, 1859.

My dear Church,—Cobden's refusal of office has a touch of magnanimity about it. I suppose he won't take it without his friend Bright, and considers it a point of honour. I dare say, too, he is not sorry to show a set of exclusives who look down upon his class as purchaseable with certainty—if only they can lower their fastidious taste to swallow them—that he can do without it. From what I heard the other day from a cousin of his in Brighton, he appears to be setting up as a quiet Sussex country gentleman, buying land about his moderate paternal inheritance, which he bought back again, and building a new house on it.

It was a new fact to me to hear that he had had an uncle of his own name, once a Dean of St. Paul's.[1] He is not the sort of man whom one would suppose had connections in the Church. I suppose Cobden's refusal does not augur very well for the present Ministry's permanence. But a snatch of office is as much as any one expects now-a-days.—Yours affectionately,

J. B. M.

Shoreham, *October* 18, 1859.

My dear Church,—I am glad to hear you enjoyed your holiday and are the better for it. We have had our house full all the summer, and have been by ourselves now for more than a month. . . . I come across old faces occasionally—the Bishop of Oxford, at the Sussex Archæological, a month ago. He seemed much altered and thinner. Hook presided—a good speaker, and thoroughly self-possessed.

That review of Jowett in *The Times*—except on the audacious principle, which often tells—seems rather a mistake in judgment; the puff overdone, and the ground not judiciously taken. If the letter of Scripture is a veil, and Christianity is Jowett behind the veil, one does not feel very secure. It is curious to see two totally opposite schools talking of the difficulty of interpreting Scripture. But really this aboriginal Christianity which Jowett and his reviewer dig up beneath no end of strata, is as perfect an *arcanum disciplinæ* as ever was invented by tradition. Criticising as a looker-on, I do not, I must say, see much skill in the way in which the controversy has been con-

---

[1] The Dr. Cobden referred to was born in 1684, and might therefore be Mr. Cobden's great-great-uncle. He became chaplain to Bishop Gibson, a Prebendary of St. Paul's, Archdeacon of Middlesex, and Chaplain in Ordinary to George II. He published a volume of poems, and another of sermons.

ducted against him. Mansel's seems to me a blunder, though a clever blunder; and his, I suppose, is the best. The answer on the Atonement question especially, I should say, had been much mismanaged. When Jowettism recedes—as, in common with other fashions, it will before long—it will be before the grand *vis inertiæ*, rather than controversy. . . .

I met old Badeley in the Temple the other day, and went up for half-an-hour to his rooms, looking exactly the same as if it was yesterday I was in them; and he too, though I thought I detected a little melancholy in his air. I think he must miss his old cosy society and the traditions of his youth. He was quite Tory in his political talk. . . . Yours affectionately,
J. B. M.

To Rev. R. W. Church.

Shoreham, *November* 2, 1859.

If you read novels it is quite worth your while reading *Guy Livingstone*, as a disclosure of a sort of life and standard rather different from our own particular one. It is striking, and has great beauties here and there; but the main feature to me was the coarse, insolent *pharisaism* of the fashionable, hard-living set, who ride at everything, gamble, drink, etc. etc. I should have thought this antiquated. They are such tremendous swells of virtue on their own standard—sort of gods; and the author sympathising with it all and thinking it the thing: such rampant braggadocios, such insolent contempt of everybody whose happiness does not arise from a self-glorifying, bodily courage, rejoicing in the most vicious brutes, horses or men, as its material. It is the grandest crow over everybody, and I can only compare it—*in dissimili materia*—very dissimilar certainly—to the crowing of W. G. W. and Company, some dozen years ago, to the Pharisees and other respectable people.—Yours affectionately,
J. B. M.

Shoreham, *April* 2, 1860.

I am just returned from a visit to Derby, where I have been spending two days, while my wife was in Oxford. I left them all in spirits at Harry's having got the Newcastle. The victor brought down the news himself, which he bore with proper Eton magnanimity. John, the second brother, was very near getting it last year, but just failed, and was medallist. I took Frank Faber on my way to Derby, whom I had not seen for nine years. I found him very little altered, and abounding in the same interests and good stories; also particularly proud of a triumph he had just gained over all the established coaches in Oxford. A man who had to be got through the law school had baffled every resident artist. At length, as a last resource, A. F., of New College, sent him to his uncle, who, summoning all his old vigour in that line, got up Blackstone for the express occasion, and hammered it into the man so successfully that he passed through with *éclat* to the astonishment of everybody.

I have begun to read the new volume of essays from the Advanced School. I think it is a mistake their having connected themselves with Baden Powell. B. P. is certainly a cool fellow, the impossibility of miracles being his avowed conclusion now, put forward as a mathematical truth, which whoever does not see by intuition is simply defective in the rational faculty, and is unable to pass the Ass's Bridge of philosophy. He does not add to the ethical pretensions of the school. . . . I am a little disappointed with the intellectual merits of the compositions, as far as one is judge from turning over pages here and there, which perhaps one is not.—Yours affectionately, J. B. M.

To the Same.

June 6, 1860.

We had a very pleasant Oxford visit. It is a nice thing to see your acquaintances from time to time, especially when so conveniently collected as at Oxford, without too long intervals. It keeps up the continuity like a dotted line. Yet it is always rather hard work spending a week in a place after an interval of absence. I had rather a long talk with B., who was rather strong as to the Jowett element in Oxford, and the narrow line between it and positive infidelity. He was for renovating the Paley argument, which he thought had been much depreciated. Altogether things look as if there was to be an Evidence battle over again. . . . One feels after a stay in Oxford a twinge sometimes at a sort of involuntary hypocrisy one has carried on; first seeing one person and then another—orthodox and heresiarchs—and agreeing with everybody as much as one can. . . . Goldwin Smith lectured on Races, starting with a hit at Matthew Arnold's view in a recent lecture. Nothing very original, but capital writing.—Yours affectionately, J. B. M.

REV. R. W. CHURCH TO J. B. M.

WHATLEY RECTORY, *February* 22, 1861.

DEAR MOZLEY,— . . . So the row is begun about *Essays and Reviews*. Do you know who wrote in the *Quarterly?* Such things generally come out, but all I have heard is that S. O. disclaims it. I have not seen it, but I hear it galls. All these addresses, and circulation of extracts, and condemnations are of course inevitable. But it is uncomfortable work. One remembers how these things used to be done in former days. There is of course a certain coarse justice in such proceedings. There is a spirit and tendency about the book, as there was in Hampden and the Oxford movement, which is undeniable, whatever may be said about garbled extracts. And I suppose that it is quite possible and likely that a heavy blow may be dealt to the opinions—a much heavier than the writers dreamt of provoking. But unless there is also a strong argumentative answer to them, it is such mere provisional work. People will go on asking these same questions, and raising these same difficulties, and there is so much unfairness mixed up with and encouraged in these mere condemnations that really I revolt from it all. I certainly dislike the *Essays and Reviews* very much, for raising horrible difficulties which they seem to me to do nothing to relieve, but simply slur over, as B. Powell does about miracles and science. But I am afraid that the row will prevent for the present any quiet and hopeful pursuing of these questions, and certainly I should like to see some of them more fully examined, and even the real limits of the danger precisely drawn .... Ever yours affectionately, R. W. C.

To Rev. R. W. Church.

SHOREHAM, *March* 11, 1861.

MY DEAR CHURCH,—I feel much the same with respect to *Essays and Reviews* that you do. It goes against the grain to join an assailing mass.

Baden Powell spoils whatever element of truth there may be in his view by the desperate pell-mell hurry he is in, giving himself no time to distinguish. His view of course *admits* of the Scripture miracles being true as *facts*, though not *as* miracles—*i.e.* mutations of law. But he nowhere expressly states their truth as facts. It is all jumble and confusion when he comes to this point, which is of course the turning-point of the whole; "a region of faith," as he calls it (*i.e. not* of sight, as he must expect to be interpreted)—not of real fact.

It certainly appears to me that belief in miracles is upon an assumption; I mean the assumption of a personal Deity. Butler makes this assumption, which is strictly one of faith. But to believe in a miracle upon an assumption of faith is not counter to believing it as a fact of actual occurrence; for if the assumption is true, that which rests upon it is true, and true in its own sphere—viz., as a fact. B. P.'s tacit argument is that a thing is not a fact, because it rests upon a ground of faith in addition to that of ordinary testimony. However, all this is very puzzling. It does not seem to me that our divines were fully conscious of the immense assumption they were making when they assumed the existence of a God *in these senses* as the basis of the defence of miracles. It seems to me to be assuming everything; because if you suppose a Deity of such *a nature* as to interfere in human affairs, what difficulty is there in the fact of such an interposition? No man of sense would raise a question about it, if the testimony was good. The whole difficulty is in what the Bible *assumes*—a Deity of a particular nature and character—and not in its facts. For why on earth should not an ass speak, if there is some one to make it? But how do we get at

the nature of such a Deity ? By faith. Yes, but natural faith.
I suppose upon evidence. What is the evidence? That is
the difficulty. Everybody for years past has been giving up
evidence, instead of applying it; "We can do without this and
that and the other." The Paley argument of design is given
up; miracles of course assume and do not prove it. Then what
is evidence? It appears to me that people are very much at
sea on this point. The Provost can, when he is forced, make a
tremendous gulp of a disagreeable mouthful, but the process is
terrible to look at. . . . I should think the Principal of Jesus'
view of miracles in their metaphysical aspect would rather
puzzle that very respectable but not ultra philosophical body,
Convocation.—Yours affectionately, J. B. M.

P.S.—An absolute repose here must apologise for an argumentative letter, which is a very poor substitute for a "newsy" one.

To HIS SISTER.

March 20, 1861.

The excitement about *Essays and Reviews* still keeps up.
The best way of treating such a book would of course be for
everybody to hold his tongue; but one knows this is practically impossible, because people have the irresistible impulse
to testify. And if some testify, others must. The writers of
course go great lengths, but I think even they would shrink
from what their theology would practically become if taken up
by the mass. That is simple infidelity, and indeed atheism;
for Baden Powell's essay, popularly interpreted, could be
nothing else. A few subtle intellects may maintain really
to *themselves* a neo-Christian ground, retaining something of the
Scriptural system, but a congregation of such spirits is an
impossibility.

To HIS SISTER.

May 23, 1861.

So the Bishop of Salisbury [Hamilton] is going to bell the
cat. As a High Church Bishop he saves his party from an inconsistency; for though inconsistency is not the worst of sins, it
would as a matter of fact have been the grossest inconsistency

for the same party that tried to turn Gorham out, quietly to let these men stay in. Stanley, if he is the writer in the *Edinburgh*, deserves the knock he got from Jelf, not on account of the mistake, which is nothing; but because he had taken absurd advantage of a mere verbal mistake in Jelf—that is, as he thought it to be at the time. It is a piece of dishonesty which everybody seems to think fair now, to go off from the real merits of the question at any point, to discuss some trumpery verbal inaccuracy for whole pages, where your opponent has made one, in order to produce the appearance of a victory on the main question, when it has nothing to do with the main question at all.—Yours affectionately, J. B. M.

To Rev. R. W. Church.

Shoreham, *August* 4, 1861.

... What a melancholy event poor Sidney Herbert's death is! It has struck the whole world with a sort of gloom. I should think it was too late to think of anything like restoration when he took the move to the Upper House, but that if he had taken it a year or two back, and given himself a regular holiday, there might have been a chance. I suppose in such cases there must have been premonitory symptoms going on for some time.

To the Same.

Shoreham, *March* 31, 1862.

... We paid a week's visit to Tom at Finchampstead. It was the first we had paid. We were much taken with the house and whole place. I saw some of his neighbours, among others Kingsley, who dined there. He has a little the look, when he first comes into a room, of a lion—*i.e.* of one who knows himself to be a lion. But I thought afterwards the impression might be due to the natural restlessness of his eye and manner—something of the same that Keble has. He is a most continuous talker, but fresh and interesting, and without affectation; and his hesitation of speech is not so much of a drawback as you might expect. He gave one the idea of a man who had a real wish to be manly and simple-minded, and made that his standard. He is made, of course, an immense deal of.

To the Same.

Shoreham, *April* 26, 1862.

. . . I am glad to hear of your contemplated tour. As you are something of a traveller by nature, it becomes a void which requires satisfying from time to time, and such satisfactions are good things for the health and everything else. Our review was a fine sight—at least 200,000 people, I should say, on the Downs. I had the opportunity of watching two notabilities, Lord Clyde and Lord Cardigan—the latter very handsome, with quite a *beau-idéal* of a refined, well-chiselled face, but with a quiet yet vicious melancholy stamped upon it. I was struck with his absolute imperturbability, for he sat bolt upright on his saddle for at least two hours, without a movement of any kind, or even turning his head. Whether this was expression of an inward scorn for the whole genus *volunteer*, I cannot say. Lord Clyde had rather a Saracenic sit upon his horse, bending forward over his horse's neck, wriggling about in eel-like fashion, rather as Saracens are represented in pictures, as if he forgot he was upon horseback, feeling the animal so completely a part of himself. He had the look of performing all the processes of mind upon horseback. There was a decision in his own movements, shooting out his arms in giving directions like a signpost; and you should have seen him gallop up and *cap* the Duchess of Wellington, the white feather performing such a magnificent curve in the air. . . . Yours affectionately,

J. B. M.

In the autumn of 1862, J. B. M. published his *Review of the Baptismal Controversy*. He writes to his sister from London:—

Curzon Street, *October* 1862.

Thank you for the attention you have given to a book on so very professional a subject as mine. As you say, I should not have expected beforehand that I should have chosen such a subject, but circumstances dictated it, and in the great difficulty of choosing for one's-self, one rather too willingly perhaps acquiesces in the choice which circumstances make for one.

Of course no controversial book ever convinces anybody; what it does do, if its argument is good, is to enable persons, more or fewer, who were convinced before out of their own reflection, but shrank from avowing it, because they had not definitely looked into the facts of the case, to avow and express their previous judgment.

We have managed to see and hear a good deal, though the Exhibition is such a perfect infinity, that the more one sees the more one knows one has not seen. So that I do not profess to be proof against ignominious exposures of omission.—Yours affectionately, J. B. M.

This year the Rickards' party were at Brighton. J. B. M. writes:—

To his Sister.

SHOREHAM, *November* 21, 1862.

... Mr. Rickards took me to call on a Mr. Hircher, a converted Jew, who is reading Colenso's book, and full of the utter puerility of it. The text has never been considered by the Jews themselves infallible on the point of *numbers*, errors having crept into the MSS., or it being conceded that they *may* have.

Mr. R. entered a little on the subject of my book, the existence of which he knew, though not the contents. I told him the main positions of it, and specially the distinction between the grace of Baptism and the recipients of that grace (whether all infants are), upon which the argument is founded. So far from objecting he rather approved of it, and said the same distinction had occurred to himself at the Gorham row, only not with sufficient definiteness.—Yours affectionately, J. B. M.

James Mozley being part proprietor of the *Christian Remembrancer*, which took a strong line against his book, was desirous to dissociate the family name from the title-page of that periodical, and to make it over to other hands. This my brother John, not sympathising in J. B. M.'s modification of views, was unwilling to agree to. As recipient of both views, their sister has to make the best of things. "As you observe," J. B. M. writes, "the matter is not of very much importance."

To his Sister.

SHOREHAM, *December* 2, 1862.

I should describe our family politics as moderate High Church. I should describe myself under that term. I have said nothing but what recognised moderate High Church divines have said, such as the late Bishop Kaye, who was always regarded as *the* learned Bishop of the Bench in his day, and what the Bishop of Oxford openly says in his charges, namely—that our formularies were meant to include both parties.

But though moderate High Church, we don't go along with the spirit that breathes in the controversial reviews of the High Church party, still less should we be disposed to turn a clergyman out of his living for holding what is admitted on all sides to have been openly held in the English Reformed Church, from the first moment of its existence to the present moment. The Gorham judgment simply sanctioned a *de facto* state of things which had existed from the first—there being too, nowhere, any dogmatic statement the other way in our formularies. The High Church party practically gives up the case when it accepts as its leader the Bishop of Oxford, who openly proclaims the neutrality of our formularies. However, I am getting theological.

We have not quite made up our minds as to the time of our Derby visit. We think, however, somewhere about the middle of January.—Yours affectionately, J. B. M.

The question of the Articles coming up in 1863, J. B. M. wrote the Letter to Professor Stanley, which appears in the latest published volume of his works. We find allusions to it in the year's letters.

To Rev. R. W. Church.

SHOREHAM, *May* 12, 1863.

I am sorry the Oxford Liberals have taken to *aggression*.

For Stanley's attack on the Articles must be taken as such. It is very well to claim for their faith to be tolerated, but this is rather like an attempt to make you give up yours. It is evident it has been forced upon Stanley by the go-aheads of Oxford, and that he does not like his task. I have almost a mind to say something about it myself, but one's courage, like Bob Acre's, oozes through one's finger-ends.—Yours affectionately, J. B. M.

Writing to his brother Tom, to whom he had sent a copy :—

June 11, 1863.

I am glad you found my Letter readable. Anything connected with the Articles has a repulsiveness to the general reader, which it requires a strong effort to surmount. However, you seem to have got over the barrier by a strong exertion of the will. I do not think much of R——'s criticism, which would require us to read all the Reformers through before we could apply it, a task which would, I think, exceed the most Herculean strength.

Gladstone's speech was very clever in having something in it to please everybody, and excite hopes in all directions, and yet with the orthodox bent pre-eminent.—Yours,

J. B. M.

In July he writes from Cornwall, where he, his wife, and Mrs. Johnson were taking a driving tour :—

To his Sister.

Bude, *July* 14, 1863.

Our weather hitherto has been capital, and we have almost an excess of it now in the shape of a mist, which prevents us from seeing more than the rough outline of the cliffs of the magnificent bay on which we now are. On the north is Moorwinstow Cliff, the Raven's Crag, the finest in Cornwall, 450 feet high; on the south is Tintagel, the birthplace of King Arthur. This country is devoted to British romance, which, as it was a favourite subject with the archæologists of the reign of Henry II., may be regarded as doubly curious now. I must confess to vague notions upon this early period, but I bow to a name which has survived so many ages as King Arthur's, and can believe that he must have been something of a man. Earlier associations still accompany us everywhere. The Druids were great upon Dartmoor, and we passed by remains of circles and fragments of stand-up stones. We are resting ourselves now for a few days, and content ourselves with lazy walks on the breakwater, and to the cliffs close by. We have the advantage of a very nice inn, called the Falcon, in honour of the Aclands, who own all the land on this side of the river, and who have a falcon for their crest. Sir Thomas is idolised here. He has a cottage where he comes for two or three months every year, and he rules the place after the fashion of Haroun Alraschid, by finding out from everybody what grievances there are, and who have tyrannised in his absence. . . .

We like this place (Bude) better than Clovelly, which had some perfect pictures of views, but which kept you quite a prisoner in that steep corkscrew street, down the cliff, out of which you could only emerge by a determined effort, to go back to your pictures again, which were cut out for you in the woods of the Hobby and the Park, and were in fact in frames as really as if the latter had been gilt. There was something amusing, however, in the evening promenade of Clovelly, which consisted of the whole population, men, women, and boys, sliding and sliddering and twisting down the corkscrew of the street, catching hold of the handles and railings if a false step was made, which was easy enough, the houses on each side being within arm's-length.

To T. M., on the subject, he writes on his return to Shoreham :—

August 12, 1863.

Unfortunately times of enjoyment leave only general impressions behind them, and do not add much to the stock of human knowledge. I have several images in my mind's eye that I had not before, and I believe that constitutes all my acquisition. I can recommend the Cornish coast as having effects which I have not seen elsewhere, and more approaching sublimity than other cliff scenery, so that to the people who ask, Why did not you go abroad? I am prepared with an answer, namely, that you do not get *this* sort of scenery abroad; so that if you happen to be particularly fond of this one sort you must go where you can get it. I do not know of any near parts abroad where you can get it, though I daresay it is to be found.

To the Same.

Shoreham, *November* 13, 1863.

... Trench's appointment is a very good one, and Stanley seems made for the Deanery of Westminster, if one did not know that the appointment was only an intermediate position for him. I somehow had not anticipated another important event for him. It is one of those instances which shows how absurd it is to destine a man in one's own mind to be celibate. I had never connected Stanley with the idea of "settling down;" perfect freedom and going about indefinitely seemed to belong intrinsically to him. I will not associate any melancholy thought with such a subject, but it does somehow or other remind one of a tendency to subsidence which seems to exist in things, and which, though it may be kept off by vivacious acclivities for a time, has its way at last. Though of course he will be as intellectually active as ever, the Liberals of Oxford will find the loss of him.—Yours affectionately,

J. B. M.

T. M. writes to J. B. M., in return for his report, a full account of his own Irish tour. The answer speaks of my brother Charles, who was a traveller in the full sense of the word, one of his northern expeditions to Lapland, etc., taking him to regions in Finland where no Englishman had ever been before. Travelling, indeed, was with him a passion, rendering him perfectly regardless of the comforts of life in his journeyings—a disregard which told with sad force as the vigour of life waned.

To his Brother T. M.

October 26, 1863.

Your outline of your Irish tour gives so vivid and clear an idea of the main features, that I thought it a pity it should stop with me, so I sent it to Derby. Charles is going to give it a diligent perusal, in order to compare his own impressions with those of your sketch. He has been, as you may remember, a great Irish traveller, though of late years he has struck out bolder paths. . . . Charles's collection of Icelandic plants has arrived in London. John Ogle took them to the meeting of the Association at Edinburgh, and brought them back scientifically arranged by Dr. Balfour, with the request that any duplicates might be bestowed upon the rising Icelandic collection at Edinburgh. Charles has given the whole, and so goes down to posterity as a benefactor of science.

I had observed the defects of the *Saturday Review* article on Whately [written on the death of the Archbishop of Dublin] before you mentioned them. The writer did not know Whately's history evidently. He felt Tractarianism as a great sore through life, and was always hitting it, and in fact could not keep his temper about it. The writer in the *S. R.* can't have looked at his later writings, otherwise he would not have passed over this feature, and represented him as treating the whole subject with contemptuous silence.

Bonamy Price was enraptured with *The Times* article on the subject.—Yours affectionately, J. B. M.

To his Sister.

October, 1863.

I had a few days' reading in the British Museum week before last. A most pleasant place, and equipped with every artificial defence against sound that ingenuity could devise. Everything padded—floor, shelves, desk, everything you touch. Leather is the universal medium. The effect is very successful. As I do not want to refer to any very rare books, it will not answer my purpose to read there much. Did I live in London, however, I should prefer it to any Club library.

I dined one day with Rogers. I was rather amused with one statement he sported, namely, "How very few really useful people there were." I asked whether he did not consider himself a useful man? Upon which he explained that shoemakers, tailors, despatch-writers, etc., were useful in their way, but what he meant by useful men were those who did what other people did not do, and so filled a gap.—Yours affectionately,

J. B. M.

To Rev. R. W. Church.

Shoreham, *December* 3, 1863.

I had a long talk with William Pusey a week ago. He comes to his sister-in-law, Miss Freeman, who has a house for sick children in Montpelier Street. He was very little altered. I asked him about a report that Newman had written to his brother congratulating him on the comment on the *Minor Prophets*, and saying that such was the best way of meeting the scepticism of the day. He said it was true. Curious, among other signs of J. H. N.'s present state of mind. W. P. was very full of the Burial Service question, having himself had a case. He had had a talk with the Archbishop of Canterbury, who saw no chance of an alteration of the service.— Yours affectionately, J. B. M.

To the Same.

December, 1863.

So Stanley's friends at Oxford are getting up a parting compliment to him. It looks a little like an antidote to Wordsworth's manifestation, but it is so natural a thing in itself that one need not give it that interpretation. I suppose W.'s protest will have the effect of delaying Stanley's bishopric. One remembers the Hampden affair, and, though those days are past, people are never quite safe from revivals. If Gladstone ever is Premier he will have some difficult knots of this kind to solve.

Writing to Mr. Church after being appointed Bampton Lecturer for 1865, he tells him :—

April 13, 1864.

... I have chosen a subject on which there is not much new to say—Miracles. At least what there is new is not, unfortunately, particularly good or correct. Stanley writes to me to recommend to my attention *Middle Age* miracles. The suggestion is most amiable, but he could not have raised a more frightful vision to appal the rash adventurer upon a somewhat delicate subject. I had rather proposed to myself safer ground in the old established philosophical arguments, only content if I could give a fresh touch to one or two of them.

My brother Arthur tells me that Stanley's popularity is already commencing in London, and that relations with the young clergy are beginning to form, in connection with soirées at the Deanery, etc.—Yours affectionately, J. B. M.

In answer to this letter, his friend writes:—

"I wish I could come and talk with you about your subject, and then hear you. I don't think you need fear that your subject is one of which all that has to be said has already been said. Stanley's insensibility to the immeasurable difference that miracle or no miracle makes in our idea of religion has always struck me as the most singular mark of his want of depth. The course would be worth preaching if only to impress on people's minds how much turns on miracles."

In a note to his brother, J. B. M. alludes to a correspondence, then exciting much amusement, between Dr. Newman and Mr. Kingsley, following upon Mr. Kingsley's charge, in an article in *Macmillan*, that "truth for its own sake had never been a virtue with the Roman clergy," and that "Father Newman informs us that it need not be:" especially to the "brief analysis," with which Dr. Newman sums up the whole correspondence.

"R. was in a state of ecstasy upon the Newman and Kingsley correspondence; unable to contain himself. I think it is the best thing that has appeared on the stage since the *Critic*—in that line. *P.S.*—How does —— take Kingsley's fate?"

Father Frederick Faber died this year. In a letter after a visit to his friend, Frank Faber, after speaking of the wonderful influence Fr. Faber had in his new communion, and of instances that had been brought before him, James writes:—

The house abounds with photographs of him. I could not help myself, notwithstanding all these facts [quoted in the letter], discerning something of the *baby* in them—an absence of that solid intelligence which is the natural result of a thoughtful life. As for influence upon others, that is a question which I have not solved. . . .

In my short stay in London last week I was stimulated by curiosity to see how the Prince [of Wales] would carry off his chairmanship—his first appearance in public where he had anything to do. He was perfectly cool and quiet, and his voice admirable. There were only about three persons who were really heard, and he was one of them; only with this difference, that they had to exert their voices and he did not seem in the least to exert his. It was a strange contrast to his next neighbour, Lord Stanhope, who shouted furiously without the least effect.

SHOREHAM, *January* 31, 1865.

MY DEAR CHURCH,—We have been so perfectly quiet lately that I have hardly anything to say except that the approach of March has compelled me to put my B. L. thoughts into some shape. I find, as I suppose other writers must do, that the rough drafts create some dismay on first returning to them. It was the only subject that I felt myself equal to undertake, from previous thought and consideration, of all the subjects that engage men's attention now; but the conclusion is often less hopeful than the beginning when the prospect is vague. I begin March 12, and preach three; then start again May 7. The difficulty is in dealing with something so informal and unexpressed and indefinite as what constitutes the real objection to miracles in doubting minds. The formal, logical answers have been given over and over again, and with great force, but·the minds whom they intended to convince do not care the least about them. And yet no other answers can be given that I know of. Thus one is sometimes struck with the idea of the entire superfluousness of one's task, and can only take refuge in the necessity of the case, that people will be always attacking and defending as long as the world lasts. There is a pleasure in having definite work, and I have found the occupation in the main agreeable. The preaching I do not look forward to with much satisfaction, not having a vocation for it. The evidence part is tiring—so much in-and-out work with testimony, experience, laws of nature, and the rest, and qualifying of different kinds. I think I shall try to bring out in one lecture towards the end the argument that the practical force and success of Christianity has depended on certain motives, which motives have been supplied by certain doctrines, which doctrines could not have been proved without miracles.

It occurs to me that the enclosed may interest you a little.[1] It is an account of a paper read by Stanley at a clergy debating society, which meets at Edward Kempe's, which I had from Arthur. I am afraid Stanley is going great lengths; what I like least of all is the claim for sympathy—though only *ab extra* sympathy—with Renan. He forgets that Renan is not an unsettled heathen, but an apostate from Christianity, and that he (Renan) puts his own merit as an expositor on heathen ground.—Yours affectionately, J. B. M.

The Bampton Lectures took J. B. M. much to Oxford the earlier part of 1865, the delivery of the last lecture bringing him there at the time of Commemoration, an occasion on which the Bishop of Exeter, then a great age, so noted a figure in past ecclesiastical excitements and events, decided to be present.

[1] The "enclosed" was a letter from J. B. M.'s brother Arthur. It is acknowledged with a pleasant recognition of its truth of delineation. "Feb. 3.—Thank you for your brother Arthur's account. How very well he does it. He brings out so well the point of Stanley's manner—his rhetorical skill—his aggressive and defiant pluck—his desperate determination to claim everything and everybody with life in them as on his side. And then, after all, what *is* his side? What is the nineteenth century religion for which all things have been preparing, and to which all good things past and present are subservient and bear witness?"

To Rev. R. W. Church.

Oxford, *June* 23, 1865.

I met the Bishop of Exeter at lunch at Magdalen, at the President's, quite a quiet affair as he stipulated. On first coming into the room he was a sad picture of feebleness, but on sitting down he became talkative, but only to his next neighbour, and not attempting any general conversation. I told his daughter, who came with him, that his face struck me as having more flesh than his photograph gave it, and she said he had " gained " lately—rather remarkable at his age. When he prepared himself for the outer air, so far as a chair can be called that, he was, with his black blinkers and black spectacles, and black worsted oversocks, etc., a most singular object, exhibiting life under very unfavourable appearances. He travels three hours at a time by rail, but likes the utmost speed when he is on the road, and hates stoppages. His poor daughter looks clouded and depressed by anxiety, hardly speaking above her breath. Whether the disposition of the old gentleman had anything to do with it, I don't know. I am sending you an account of one great man in return for your picture of another, which was very interesting. J. H. N.'s good spirits are a striking feature in him.

The Commemoration passed over, it was thought, well as compared with former ones, the under-graduates subduing their ferocity a little. Michell from his rostrum defied them by his arm and looks, and as he did it good-naturedly he was occasionally cheered, amid the impertinence ; but he had a strong source of confidence in his son's Latin poem. Son and father represented the Latinity of our rostrum. . . . Yours affectionately, J. B. M.

On the 24th of August 1865, died Mr. Rickards of Stow-Langtoft ; a man most important to all who knew him, and with many of pre-eminent weight and influence—an influence perhaps peculiarly dependent on personal intercourse. J. B. M. writes to his sister a few days after his death :—

SHOREHAM, *August* 29, 1865.

I had heard only a few days before from Mrs. Rickards, about a temporary curate for Stow-Langtoft. She was relieved from the sense of present danger. The sad news therefore was a great surprise to me at least. I had always, from the quiet strength of body and mind which he showed at Brighton, his walking and talking powers, looked forward to an advanced old age for him. Perhaps the sea air set him up and showed him to advantage. He has been, one may say, one of the principal images that one has carried about in one's mind through life—I mean personal images. There was something about him that made one often think of him. . . . Mr. Rickards had weight, yet it is curious to see how gifts get divorced, which if combined would have produced great power. Had Mr. Rickards, with his *weight*, had forcible and popular gifts, oratory, or power of style, he would have been able to take a leadership of numbers, and sustain a situation of command. As it was, his sphere was confined. Yet, on the other hand, how little are the *other* gifts without that inimitable one of weight. What weak creatures people are without it! I cannot help therefore regarding Mr. Rickards as, in Carlyle's phrase, a strong man. He kept his ground through life; nothing displaced him. He had always command of himself, and could do what he aimed at doing, though he moderated his aim. I was looking over his fifteenth sermon the other day—" Godliness the ground of self-command." It is unconsciously self-descriptive. He talks of what he aims at, and, as what he aims at he attained, the image he draws is necessarily one of himself.

On the question of a memoir, J. B. M. writes :—

TO HIS SISTER.

November 21, 1865.

Mrs. Bayne's letter is equally sensible and feeling. Her idea of collecting family reminiscences and associations for preservation is much on the Mr. Rickards' type, and shows the sort of mind that would particularly appreciate him. About a memoir, the question certainly deserves considering, though there would be peculiar difficulties in this case, arising from the fact that Mr. R. was so especially a person who required to be *seen* in order to be understood. The difficulty of producing in the reader the true conception of the man without sight would be very great. It might not be amiss, if it could be done, to ascertain what amount of correspondence there was preserved. Letters to and from Davison, for example, supposing these to be forthcoming, on religious questions, would be interesting. In lack of correspondence, the substance of a memoir would depend on the recollections of those who knew him; things said on particular occasions, conversations of a definite kind. It would be anecdotal. Without *enough* material a memoir would do him rather injustice. The sort of career his was would not lead one to expect much quantity of this.

Mrs. Rickards sent me Keble's letter, which was characteristically worded. The *hand* showed much alteration. I liked it much, and thought the slight touches of description in it very true portraiture.

No memoir was attempted, but the view of what it should be, what should be aimed at, is applicable to the subject of memoirs generally. Writing to Mr. Church, J. B. M. says of Mr. Rickards:—

"It is remarkable what a large private circle he had, who all felt indebted to him for making them, so to speak. Mrs. R. has hundreds of letters from people. She is very sensible, however, and is aware of the difference between a large private circle and public life as the ground of a memoir. She has asked me to assist her in it."

To Rev. R. W. Church.

Shoreham, *October* 23, 1865.

My dear Church,—What an eventful week we have had! Odd that Stanley should so immediately succeed Lord Shaftesbury as the counsellor in Church promotions, as I suppose he will do now. At least if he does not absolutely, it will be curious to see what modifications of influence Lord Russell will allow him. *The Record* was in black upon the occasion. How studiously Lord Palmerston's illness, which seems to have been going on some time, was concealed, quite like some Eastern potentate's. ... *The Times* gave its *first* intimation that " Lord Palmerston was seriously ill," which it modified by the expression that it " did not wish to alarm the friends of the noble Premier," *when* he was dead. He was lying dead at the time people were taking up the *Times* at their breakfast tables. I suppose Gladstone will feel disappointed, Lord R. being so unpopular with the subordinates; still they prefer him to G. What up-hill work it is a man getting to the top—Alps on Alps, etc. I should think, however, that a little discretion, which he must learn *now*, will insure it to him, but when ? The articles on Lord Palmerston have been very poor, the writers unable to feign any surprise or solemnity. Yet surely such a disappearance is a great fact. It does not signify a man's age—he is *alive* till he is *dead*.—Yours affectionately,

J. B. M.

SHOREHAM, *November* 8, 1865.

MY DEAR CHURCH,—We have not, after all, gone our intended Paris trip. ... Our outing will probably be limited to a few days at Finchampstead, the end of this month. I presume the same literary theological projects that reach me reach you too. I was asked some weeks ago to write for a volume of essays, to be published by Longman, under the editorship of Mr. Orby Shipley, of whom I did not know much. I did not feel in a very writing humour, so excused myself. Another project reaches me to-day, and I also have no doubt yourself by the same post—the *Contemporary*, under Dean Alford's editorship. L writes to enlist contributors. I should have thought that L., as a man of the world, would have not meddled much with such breakdown undertakings as new reviews. He takes high ground, however, and urges the necessities of the times, and that something should be done to meet the " new school " in a Liberal quarter. I am sorry to say my stock of enthusiasm is rather low, and one acquires a kind of notion that certain movements die out of themselves, without so much writing against them. Though, if conscientious men think differently, one is ready to wish them all success in their plans. . . . And if one had anything to say perhaps one ought not to stand aloof, but that *if* is rather a puzzle.—Yours affectionately, J. B. M.

P.S.—The lectures will be out in a few days. I hardly know whether to be glad or sorry to have done with them. One feels a kind of blank. You are responsible for a paragraph in the first, and also for a note on the same subject—Patristic estimate of miracles as evidence—a note of yours having suggested the subject to me. The note has exceeded the proper limits of one.

To the Rev. R. W. Church.

Shoreham, *February* 19, 1866.

. . . I have of course many regrets with respect to the performance. One is, that I have not brought out Clarke's *Demonstration*, which is undoubtedly a very great book, and I think contains in germ the answer to the physical conception of a Deity now prevailing, and the proof of another world. I mean that it is the answer to the scientific people on that point. As a personal Deity was, however, assumed in my argument, I did not think of it, and his title of *Demonstration* has always given me a prejudice against the book. It is really, however, a mistake in the name rather than in the substance of the book. . . . Yours affectionately, J. B. M.

P.S.—What wonderful Parisian gaieties![1]

[1] The letter encloses a newspaper paragraph (the reference of course appended by the sender):—"The Paris correspondent of *The Morning Star* describes a novel costume at the fancy ball given at the Tuileries last week:—'The Marchioness de Gallifet, as the Archangel Gabriel, attracted all eyes; her short petticoat of white cashmere embroidered in gold, the glittering scale-armour of gold fitting tightly to her figure, her golden hair floating on her shoulders, star-lighted by an étoile of diamonds, invisibly suspended over her forehead, her wings of white feathers, which, in arching above her head, only terminated below her knee, and, above all, the golden sword clasped tightly in her fairy hand, and brandished even while dancing, formed a most bewitching *tout ensemble.*'" See 2 Cor. xi. 14.

To REV. R. W. CHURCH.

March 7, 1866.

... I have been staying with Arthur, and went to the St. James's clerical meeting on Thursday evening. Stanley on the *Irenicon*. It was a well-worded and clear paper, of course viewing the subject entirely on his own side of it. When questioned by Lord A. Hervey, Irons, etc., what doctrinal veto he proposed upon absolute universal comprehension, he diplomatised, and I understood him to say that was not the time for entering on that part of the subject. Pusey was expected up, but failed at the moment from a cold, Acland interposing. The substantial feeling of the meeting was against Stanley—though he is complimented by everybody, in such a way that he is not unlikely to be deceived, and to take it more as a sign than it really is. Mrs. Arthur Mozley, who was with a few ladies within hearing, in E. K.'s study, which enters into the vestry, said, as soon as the paper was over, a young man rushed up to Lady Augusta, exclaiming, "He is a prophet; He is a prophet." Irons spoke well. There was Oxenham, the convert. He spoke in favour of Rome as a conciliator—that she was ready to act on Wiseman's dictum, " We must explain to the uttermost." The facts don't look like it. All the world is talking of *Ecce Homo*.—Yours affectionately,   J. B. M.

In the spring of 1866 J. B. M., accompanied by his wife and her sister, Miss Ogle, took a well-earned holiday of two months abroad. The journey had been delayed, and even rendered uncertain, by the illness of one or two humble parishioners, who happily recovered in time for the party to leave home in comfort.

To HIS SISTER.

GENOA, *April* 12, 1866.

I date this letter from the city of palaces, but shall not be able to finish it here. I will put down a little, however, while first impressions continue. Genoa *is* a city of palaces. There are very large suburbs which do not partake of that character, but are entirely utilitarian, dirty, and ugly. Taking in the suburbs, it is an immense place, much larger than I had thought; these suburbs, however, figure as separate towns in guide-books, etc. In fact, the whole country from Voltri, about twelve miles off, is a suburb. But Genoa real is unmistakable, as soon as you enter. You are almost immediately in the Strada Balbi—itself, by the way, once a suburb to the very old town. You know where you are then. It is magnificent. We entered by a good evening light. I can give some idea of it perhaps, by saying that it is to the eye what a deep peal of thunder is to the ear. The stupendous size of the palaces, their enormous height,—with a good deal of dead wall about some of them, only relieved by rich and bold projected ornamentation—which you cannot easily take in, for you cannot see to the top of them but by stretching your neck back at right angles, all these giants, standing in a solemn row on each side, constitute indeed a sight. I do not know whether Emerson's friend [1] would call it "religion," but it has certainly as much right to that name as Mademoiselle Cerito's dancing.

The Strada Balbi is only the beginning of one long street of palaces, which goes through the Piazza dell' Annunziata, the Strada Nuovissima, Strada Nuova, and Piazza della Fontana Amorosa. The narrowness of the streets sets off the massiveness of the architecture. Everything is brought together in one mass of richness. I say *narrow*—but they are like Regent Street in width, compared with those of the old town, which are simply alleys. Yet in these too are congregated numbers of huge old palaces—the residences of the old families before they left for the new streets. In the darkness in which you walk, you do not see they *are* old palaces till you look up and see rich balconies hanging an immense height over you. The effect of some of the old streets is very fine—they seem, from their narrowness, constantly ending in a point, like the gorges of the Rhine.

We inquired at the Balbi Palace, but were told we could

[1] Alluding to the story of Emerson and Margaret Fuller at the opera, under the spell of Cerito's grace—" Margaret, this is poetry." "No, Ralph, it is religion."

not see it, the Marchesa Balbi having been ill for a month. We then crossed the street to the Durazzo Palace, and saw it; magnificent white marble entrance-court, white marble columns and staircase; the rooms all splendid in damask and gold. There were in one room two very fine vases of Cellini, made for the Durazzo of that day, with the Durazzo arms upon them. There was a portrait of the late Marquis, in his costume as a Genoese noble—a black velvet cloak—black silk cassock (as it seems), and a gold chain round his neck. In the other room the same person appeared in his ordinary costume, dressed like an English gentleman—frock-coat, and the choker worn some twenty years ago. The Durazzos live there always. There is something singular in the fidelity of some of the old families to Genoa. There they live, with suburbs like those of a manufacturing town within half-a-mile of them. The King of Sardinia's Palace is in the Strada Balbi—as long as an ordinary street itself.

We saw everywhere signs of a popular constitution—placards addressed "Elettori" and "Concittadini;" the style very magnificent. You cannot tell at all what they are about, the writers are in too inspired and expansive a state of mind to state anything definite. We found out, however, on inquiry, that one related to a national subscription which was being raised to supply the void in the taxes. We were told in the bookseller's shop that they were in good heart, and the sum considered sure of being collected. The Dorias have deserted Genoa, and live at Rome, calling themselves Doria Pamphili. Two rooms and a corridor alone are shown in the palace, four centuries old nearly, just the very beginning of the renaissance. The great Doria's bedroom is kept as it was—bedstead, etc., his portrait, taken after death, looking down upon the scene. His live portrait presents a grand shrewd old face. He was a friend of Charles v. He seems to have surrounded himself with boundless magnificence.

I have said nothing about the Cornice Road. We had good, not perfect weather—two sunshiny days, and two with good sky light and occasional rain. I need not say it is a land of olive trees, oranges, and lemons—sometimes growing wild apparently on the rocks. The succession of beautiful little bays makes a pleasing variety ; also, what is a great feature, the rapid succession of antique little cities, glittering with white and pink in the distance. Italy is certainly pre-eminently a land of plaster. But plaster does not produce the same ideas there that it does with us, where it is mean architecturally. You see it is the ancient rule and fashion. The gay white and pink, combined with the loftiness and good grouping of the houses, creates a kind of illusion as you approach. Every little fishing village looks almost palatial in the distance. It is as if Quorndon, Spondon, and Borrowash were suddenly seized with the desire of making themselves look fascinating and composed of marble palaces. Alassio is of another type—like a city on the Rhine. It is a very populous region. Were I to say the whole road up to Genoa was one street, I should be exaggerating, but there would be a foundation of truth. I am writing at a resting-place in the Apennines—Borghetto, where our voiturier rests his horses an hour. This is the *other* Cornice Road, on the other side the corner. It has grander features of scenery than the Genoese or *the* Cornice Road—the bays deeper and more strikingly shaped, and the mountains higher. We had a fine Italian sunset at Sestri last night, brilliant light yellow, and those hard, sharp outlined clouds you have in Salvator Rosa and the Italian school, with successive sudden darkenings, like those of a stage—a perfectly purple range of mountains, the sea gradually becoming pink—till all faded away. To-day our scenery has been all Apennine, with only occasional glimpses of sea—very grand; but no castles, and therefore no Castle of Udolfo. This evening we hope to reach Leghorn by rail, and thence to Rome to-morrow.

I observed, as we went along all the way, the priests seemed better friends with the people than they are in France. One sees them walking with and chatting with people. In France they seem to be always walking hurriedly by themselves through the streets, as if only some professional object took them out, and have a look of being pursued. Some of them here, too, look of a better class than the French priests. We have made a few purchases of Genoa gold work, and a rather majestic damsel tempted Amelia and Janet to invest in lace yesterday at Sestri, which is a lace place. I admired her voice and utterance, which reminded me of what the Opium-eater says about the voices of Italian women. They have nightingale throats. We are pursued, of course, by little boys and girls begging, but this is since we left old Sardinian territory. Here we are in new Sardinia. The Italian women are more striking than the men—handsome and expressive features. You observe their walk. They all walk exceedingly well, and all just alike; their figures very upright, while they plant their feet on the ground firmly, and with perfect regularity of pace, as if each foot felt a sense of responsibility, which, in fact, it does, for their walk results from their practice of carrying great burdens balanced on their heads, which compels these measured steps. But the habit formed continues when the cause is absent. Even little girls walk like soldiers. The children have animated vivacious faces. We have had a most moderate temperature hitherto. I could not have told we were not in England, all our wraps have been brought into use constantly. I suppose the warmth begins suddenly.

I have said nothing of the Rhone and its cities. They are wonderful specimens of hoary antiquity; and passing so quickly by the scenes of old Councils and Popes, one historical place after another, especially in the languid condition of a night railway traveller, when morning opens, was like a dream. But Marseilles rapidly dispels such illusions—an intensely modern citizen of the world place—all the men of the higher ranks discarding everything, even French, and looking just like men in London.—Yours affectionately, J. B. M.

To his Sister.

Rome, *April* 22, 1866.

We have been here now nearly a week, which has gone away quickly. We were shot here through the darkness by the rail from Civita Vecchia, so that our first impressions had to wait for the light. We went to the English service, and thence straight to St. Peter's. Now for the great question, the apparent size. My own experience is this. You are disappointed just the first moment as to the size, till you cast your eyes on the *floor*. Then it is no longer a secret. It is the largest expanse of floor you have ever had before you, there can be no doubt; and *from* the floor the size of the building then comes to you. I was not disappointed then. There was a true idea of immense size. If ever you find the impression of size diminishing, look at the floor again; that revives it. I think people make a mistake generally in looking *up* only; they ought to look down a great deal. The floor is the grand first element, which is outside of, and is not within the contracting influence of proportion. Then, too, English travellers, from the way in which our cathedrals strike the eye, are apt to look to the length as the great thing. In St. Peter's it is *space*—vast space on all sides of you. The huge masses of piers rise in seas of space on all sides of them, which your eye catches, as the segments appear—intersections of it on all sides. The richness of the whole effect is wonderful. It is not gorgeousness, for that is too heavy, but a most perfect blending of all colour. The whole is to the eye one mosaic. It seems as if designed to be a most costly and regal feast to that organ. I would not say it did not inspire religious feelings, and yet I think it would be nearer to the ocular truth to call it a palace than a church—such a palace as might be discovered underground or under the sea in some classical Arabian Nights' world. I need not go into particulars, all of which you have in Murray.

In the spirit of the whole structure, and of its monumental adornments especially, there is, of course, material for criticism. It is more of a glorification of the great Italian families than I expected. One was prepared for the Papacy being enthroned there, but not so much for the building being converted to the purpose of family exaltation, for Borgheses, Farneses, Medicis, Barberinis, Odescalchis, etc. The family names of the Popes appear on their monuments, with their colossal escutcheons in bronze or marble, so that a monument to a Pope is virtually an enthronement of the family in the place. Even round the high Altar itself the bees of the Barberinis go up the bronze pillars, and their coats of arms at the basement would make the floor of a moderate room. Before you enter, as you look up at the façade, the first words you see are "Paul Borghese." The Popes sit on royal chairs on their monuments, stretching out their right arms in an attitude of sovereignty and imperial power. Canova has the merit of making his Popes kneel—*i.e.* he deserves praise for his intention; but I doubt whether the other position does not best suit them. We attended vespers in the choir chapel on Sunday—the music and voices first-rate, in the operatic style. It is curious to see the minute proportion of the vast building which is congregational; the choir chapel would hardly accommodate more than fifty comfortably, leaving out the choristers, canons, etc. However, perhaps it adds to the dignity of the edifice, the very small ordinary use that is made of it. . . .

We find ourselves comfortable enough here. We are getting within the fascinating influence of the mosaic and gold shops.[1] The work is most beautiful. . . . The Vatican *was* a day's work. I was taken up by the guide into the entrance hall of the Pope's residence, where ladies are not admitted. In the corner was a door, which was explained by repeating several times "Machina! Machina!" It was a lift to pull the Pope up, and save him the ascending staircase, to his high lodgings.—Yours, J. B. M.

To THE REV. R. W. CHURCH.

ROME, *April* 30, 1866.

MY DEAR CHURCH,—I just write to you a line from the great city, where we have been a fortnight. The whirl of sight-seeing is against forming any general view of a place, and, as far as sentiment goes, it becomes impossible. *Getting* up one thing is very like getting up anything else. The first impression one had to account for was one's feeling so much *at home* in the place. It was not like other places in this respect. One had not that feeling of being a stranger and foreigner. I think old school-boy reminiscences had something to do with this. It is

[1] A pretty scene lives in the memory on occasion of their visit to his mother, on their return from this foreign excursion—Amelia suddenly descending on the home circle, laden with an arm full of offerings, hidden in jeweller's cases, which she distributed with a characteristic sprightly grace; every gift showing that the purchasers had had the destined recipient in their eye when the choice was made.

the locality of such very old familiar names and facts, everything that was hammered into one's head when one was twelve years old, that one cannot well feel forlorn or estranged. One seems to have a right here. Even the S. P. Q. R. on the municipal placards and the Senator's carriage is sufficient to put one at ease; and the Forum and Mons Capitolinus are such very old friends that one does not stand on any ceremony with them. If one had to choose a residence out of England, Rome would have great attractions on this ground—*i.e.* that one has in a sense belonged to the place so long that it would be next in point of domesticity to being in England. Even the severities of early school discipline, on the *olim meminisse* principle, form a basis of attachment.

Now for the place as it presents itself to the eye. I think its *tristesse* has been exaggerated. The number of huge blocks of public and ecclesiastical buildings—seminaries, propagandas, etc. etc.—impart a heaviness, so far as that goes; but the largeness and number of piazzas, the width of the streets compared with other continental towns, and the splendour of some of the palaces, produce a cheerful effect. One sees so much sky, and does not walk about with houses tumbling on one's head. I was not disappointed with the size of St. Peter's— the interior. Whatever people say, it does look very large indeed to the eye—naturally and immediately. The floor is obviously immense. The vastness of the *æquor marmoreum* upon which the pillars rest communicates itself to the erections upon it. The effect on the eye of the interior has hardly, I think, a word in English to describe it. If 'luscious' had a sublime sense, it would do in a way. It is a perfect feast to the eye, by its perfect blending and commingling of colours in connection with beautiful proportions and vastness. The eye has everything it wants, though, at the same time, the effect is palatial rather than ecclesiastical. It is, however, a kind of transcendental palatial, and you recognise it as sacred.

We have antiquarianised in the Forum and Colosseum, Capitol, etc., in the ordinary way, and received the last dogmas about sites and temples. One is astonished in the Vatican at the immense numbers of good busts and statues of the old world. Considering the plough had gone literally over everything, the quantity of recovery is enormous. There are so many actual faces of the old *distingués* saved—you know what they were. Even ladies' faces and fashions of dressing the hair—sufficiently ugly many of them—are a disclosure of the old Roman fashionable world. And the heads are so entire and clean—not a feature spoilt: *e.g.*, the bust of Cæsar, in the Palazzo Rospigliosi, one sees must have been an excellent likeness—something between Lord Brougham and J. H. N. Augustus you have every variety of, and see the change in his features as he became older. That handsome fat youth Nero must, as a beauty, have been criticised, though he is evidently quite satisfied with himself. I was struck with the English look of many of the faces: *e.g.* Pompey, in the famous Spada statue. We have not yet seen the Pope, though he has been seen. He goes out for his drive, they say, every day about three o'clock, or later, and sometimes gets out of his carriage and walks; but one has no means of knowing in what direction he drives. We saw Antonelli in the Rotunda in the Vatican, looking, at a spare moment, at the new Hercules. He is very polite, and gave us a sweeping bow, with uplifted hat, in passing. . . . W. Palmer has been most good-natured in showing us about, though, he says, this is an office he has had to do for so many, that he might as well turn cicerone, and charge his scudi. He has got up Rome in a way that only a Palmer could—exhausting every fact, speculation, and conjecture—Basilicas, Forum, Catacombs, everything. Though he only gives as much in his explanations as he thinks his hearers capable of receiving; the amount of the discharge is extraordinary. . . .

Palmer admitted that the exclusion of the upper classes of Italians from public business was a great evil, throwing them upon a volatile life as the alternative. They have not the idea of labour, he says, in their heads, and view life simply as a succession of amusements. One sees them on the Pincian. They dress quietly, and very much like Englishmen; but one's eye catches odd things occasionally one would not see in England; *e.g.*, a young swell driving round the Pincian in a most elegant basket-carriage, with a pair of horses and a postilion, himself alone in his carriage, smoking. That Pincian, by the way, is a most extraordinary scene—fashionable ladies and gentlemen, priests, clerical students in black, white, and red, friars with the cords hanging from their waists, sleek Monsignors, etc., all mixed together in the promenade-recreation of the day. Several families have managed to retain their pictures. It is, by the way, one of the features of Rome, which makes one feel at home in it, that it is such a centre and collection of originals of old familiar groups, and figures, and heads, that one has known ever since one was born.

We met the other day Mrs. Ramsay, the translator of Dante, a very handsome, intelligent woman, though talking with such extreme Scotch it was sometimes not easy to follow her. Her favourite here is Cardinal Andrea, now sent away from Rome for his liberalising bias. He is, she says, a really devout man, and a fervent man, but he cannot bear the political Papacy. He is a good Catholic, but says the Reformation was the fault of Rome: he is a friend of Mrs. Ramsay, who seems to have seen a good deal of him. They are very much afraid of him here, and there is a row going on now; and a fierce letter of Andrea's is talked about. The distinction is great between the streets of Genoa, placarded with addresses to electors and concittadini, and the streets of Rome, where, besides the municipal notifications, the only public notice I have seen is a Vendita dei Cavalli stuck up on the Palazza Doria—the Prince being announced to preside over it. Fox-hunting is a rising movement. Jockey-cap ladies' work-boxes are seen in the shop-windows, and the omnibuses call themselves Apollo, La Volpe, dividing themselves between the old and new claims. At Leghorn the engines were Petrarch, Boccaccio, etc. The lottery goes on with undiminished popularity.—With kindest remembrances to Mrs. Church, yours affectionately, J. B. MOZLEY.

To HIS SISTER.

ROME, *April* 30, 1866.

. . . We are charmed with the Campagna and its mountains, the distant pieces of bright green come out so in the spring, and the variations of lights and shades on the mountains in this clear air, which reveals the minutest slope and ravine, makes the whole like one of those pictures inserted in a crystal. I do not, however, remember a single passage in Horace in praise of Roman scenery, which he must have had before him every time he took his walk out of Rome, although he is full of the woods and cascades of Tivoli: from which I argue that the ancient eye for scenery was not nearly equal to the modern.

One is amused with the pedigrees of things one sees. The bronze columns of the Altar of the H. S. in the Lateran were taken from the temple of the Capitoline Jupiter; but the descent does not stop here—the Capitoline Jupiter took them from the beaks of the ships taken in the battle of Actium. The font in St. Peter's was Adrian's sarcophagus. The Popes take the old Roman Emperors' sarcophagi for their own. There is a system of accommodation and transference.

There is no wish among the English to see the Sardinian Parliament here, and certainly, as a tourist, I cannot but feel some sympathy with old Rome, classical and mediæval, which would be somewhat damaged by converting it into a modern capital with all its new offices, legislative chambers, new Court, etc.—in a word, making it a modern business place. There is a great deal to be said for Florence continuing the Italian capital even if the Papal State became absorbed in the Italian kingdom. . . . We just drove through the Ghetto, and made acquaintance with the features of the ancient colony, the very same identical one which St. Paul addressed in the Acts. In driving through the Piazza Navona—the large market—the man pointed with his whip to the line of pavement which separated the Christian stalls from the Jewish—Qui Christiani là Ebrei. . . . Yours affectionately, J. B. M.

To his Sister.

Sorrento, *May* 8, 1866.

My dear Anne,—Among the many things I have imagined myself seeing, I do not remember myself ever expecting to be a spectator of the miracle of St. Januarius. Certainly it was not a scene to confirm belief in miracles in any one who was shaky. It was difficult to make out at all accurately what sort of belief the religious section of the community have in it. Of course the world at large at Naples, as elsewhere, laugh at it. The procession was attacked by the students last year in the streets, so it walks now with an escort of bayonets. Bayonets stand on each side of the Altar, bayonets on each side of the Church door. The Sardinian Government, on principle, protects popular Festivals. People may think what they like, but they must not assault. This is fair. But to speak of the religious,—priests and good Catholics,—who were there. This was the most curious part of the scene. I suppose they would not acknowledge the thing *not* to be a reality. Yet the fact was they—even the religious—except for that interval, when everybody was struggling up the Altar steps to see the blood after the great event—they were all talking, laughing, handing their snuff-boxes, and enjoying the scene, like any crowd or fair. One ecclesiastic of rank, a remarkably intelligent-looking man, showed, we thought, some signs of suppressed disgust. He came in and sat in a large velvet arm-chair, in his undress garb, within the Altar-rails, some time before the entrance of the procession, waiting to receive it; during which time he was conversing with a number of people, laymen among the rest (it seemed to me) about general subjects. We admired his good address and grace of manner. At the first entrance of the procession his attendants robed him with marvellous rapidity; it was the work of a moment, and he was at his place incensing the images as they passed before the Altar. It was evident that they none of them in the slightest degree realised what a miracle was. It was old custom; it was *called* a miracle; it had the sanction of the Church. Beyond that nobody's mind went. I heard a French priest arguing with two sceptics about it, one of them a Yankee. He professed to be candid, but said he could not account for it. The fact *was* so. His opponents said the question was not about the fact but the cause; some heat was applied. He replied it was only just touched by two fingers. They replied, of course, it was chemical heat they meant. He did not continue the discussion. All this was close to the momentous vessel itself. The whole scene was a sort of miniature copy of the Greek fire at Jerusalem. It was a general *mêlée* within the Altar-rails—priests, laymen, soldiers, ladies, all talking and chatting. I was in the thick of them within the altar-rails. There was a prayer chanted for the performance of the miracle by an old priest, who, after he had closed his book, was immediately shoved down the steps by the eager crowd pressing up close to see the wonder take place. Some ten or fifteen minutes elapsed, during which everybody was talking, the amusement being only heightened by the hoarse cries of the old women—the relations of St. Januarius, who sat on the north side of the Altar.

These extraordinary weird-looking old creatures from time to time broke forth with their noises, which had much the effect of a startled rookery; Amelia said it was like frogs. Yet, when the sound of the bell announced the event of the liquefaction, I observed some young priests, either really, or because they thought it the proper thing, expressing a momentary fervent excitement, as if something really had happened. I did not press up to the Altar at first, but after some time I found my way up, when I was told that the blood had retired, but would come back again soon; and I had hardly to wait a moment when the points of the bayonets announced its approach, and an old priest came struggling up the steps, through the crowd. He then turned the glass case, containing the sacred phial or phials, round and round, with a candle before, and, as I was close to, I must certainly admit that liquid was inside.

Yet there were points of time at which the ceremonial was extraordinarily picturesque, if not imposing: when the procession, on its first entrance—priests, friars of different orders, and the figures of the saints (they call them silver) borne aloft on shoulders, moved round and round the Church, with banners and canopies; every figure being saluted by the venerable relations of St. Januarius, in their peculiar way. All this, with the gorgeous gilding and magnificent marbles of the church itself, composed a rich and rather grand mixture. The old women were certainly an immense addition. One was amused with the respect paid to heretics. We were the great persons in the scene, everybody giving way to us, and people on all sides being anxious to explain everything to us.

I have said nothing about Naples. We were unfortunate in having our first view under a Sirocco. On the land side, however —which was the way we came—the vast rich luxuriant plain, out of which Vesuvius rises, was very striking; and Vesuvius itself was clear. It is a most beautiful and majestic mountain, and it has the extraordinary advantage of rising up in an immense plain on both sides—for the sea is its basement on the other side. Tourist expectations of lounging, resting weeks, are disappointments. We had made up our minds for an open-air holiday at Naples, but the museum, Pompeii, and, in my case, the Castle St. Elmo, provided work for us. I obtained an order to see the dungeons of the latter, and can testify, with sufficient certainty, that they are horrible places. The outer circumference of the rock is galleried for cannon; the inner heart is hollowed out into caves and cells for prisoners. I was shown what they told me was Poerio's prison. If I remember right, Sir G. Bowyer, in one of his letters to *The Times*, asserted it was such an agreeable roomy apartment, with such a delightful view from it, that he should have selected it for his holiday season. Certainly it is roomy— a lofty large hollow in the rock; but when one has said this, one has said all that can be said in its favour. It is aired and lighted by a grating at the top of the roof, and, with that exception, is without communication with the exterior, and that is not the actual outer air. One or two cells, I observed, were lighted by small openings at the very top of their walls, to the outer air. On the whole, they are utterly barbarous places, and one is astonished when one sees them, that a European Government should actually have used them only half-a-dozen years ago. You would suppose their most recent use must have been in the thirteenth or fourteenth centuries. . . . There was a paragraph in the Naples English paper, stating, to illustrate the extraordinary political excitement now in the place, that nobody's pocket had been picked for two days. The furor had been too absorbing to admit of attention to baser things. The English banker Mr. Turner, who seemed a shrewd old gentleman, told me it was thought that, though the government humoured the popular excitement to a certain extent, there was an understanding at bottom there would be no war.—Yours affectionately,

J. B. M.

To his Sister.

Rome, *May* 19, 1866.

... We have been to some May sermons here. There is one every evening in a church in the Corso, close by, followed by a function and very beautiful Italian music. The sermons are simply declamatory and perfectly empty, but excellently pronounced in good Italian. I speak, of course, from Amelia's and Janet's report. I myself could only catch a half sentence every now and then. There is a studied elaborateness of *pronunciation*, to produce perfect clearness. The preacher walks up and down a small stage; sometimes sits down, and talks in an easy way with his audience. When the emotional part of the discourse begins, and the congregation are to be warmed into devotion to the Virgin, the preacher's voice suddenly bursts into a succession of high pitched sobbing utterances, as if he was almost choked with emotion, not forgetting, however, the pinch of snuff he is holding between his finger and thumb, which he takes in the intervals of his agitation. Or his voice adopts a coaxing affectionate whine. After this the congregation kneels and repeats some short prayers to the Virgin. Then commences the hymn, which goes through a long succession of stanzas, and is beautifully sung by trained voices in the organ loft, the congregation joining in a short chorus at the end of each verse. In the sermon we heard yesterday there was nothing about the Virgin till the very last. The subject of the discourse was the "Omnipresence of God." I saw nothing like real interest or absorption in the congregation. They listened quietly, but, as it seemed to me, with some indifference. I should observe that the emotion of both preachers was exactly alike, the sobs and everything. I do not know whether they are taught to preach, like our dissenters, and have to exercise before masters in classes, but the effect was rather like it.—Yours affectionately, J. B. M.

Throughout the whole of 1866 my mother's strength was failing. On his return to Shoreham, J. B. M. receives anxious accounts of her state.

TO HIS SISTER.

SHOREHAM, *June* 8, 1866.

I do not know what to think of my mother's state. There is a fall now both in yours and Fanny's estimate of her strength. . . . But even weakness as a symptom is uncertain, for old people may get very weak without vital danger. As I was sitting in the Salle de Lecture, at the Hotel Mirabeau, there came in a very old man in black, just able to put one leg before the other, with short steps like a child. He seated himself with great difficulty in his chair, feeling his way down in his seat every inch as he settled himself. He then put out a trembling arm, and got hold of a newspaper. That done, I saw that he worked away pretty well and got what he wanted. Then all at once I said to myself, I think I know you—you are Lord Brougham. But he was much altered, even from two years back, when I saw him at Ardingley laying the first stone of Woodard's School. Yet the manager of the Mirabeau, who talked to us about him, described him as still with an inner strength in him,—excessively irritable, jealous of all attempts to control him. He found himself in bed at half-past eleven one night, and was furious with his valet and everybody. Did they think him a child? He dined at the *table-d'hôte* every day. Though so muscularly weak, he has that sort of strength which enables him to travel, and had come up from Cannes to Paris in one day. I mention this to show that weakness wants defining—the sort of it—before it becomes alarming.

After this letter he paid a visit to Derby—a visit which was a great pleasure and comfort to my mother.

Writing to Mr. Church, he enters upon a great question touched on in a paper he (Mr. Church) had lately written :—

To THE REV. R. W. CHURCH.
June 7, 1866.

... Your remarks upon revelation, I think, hit the nail on the head. One feels that a religion, such as some would give us, which is a growth of the human mind, and a revelation, or religion in its true sense, are two totally different things, and that one cannot do what the other does, and has done. It is the idea, the belief that it *is* a revelation, which commands and inspires the human mind. People will not respect their own creation of religion; and it is mere folly to think that they will let it command and coerce them—or rather I should say a mere *dream*—for some do seem to think this whom one cannot call altogether foolish men. It is this essential difference in the two ideas which people pass over. As you say, such a growth cannot be a religion. The obscure rays of the spectrum is just the illustration I should have liked to have when I was writing.

To HIS SISTER.

SHOREHAM, *August* 20, 1866.

I think our events since our Derby visit have been almost confined to a visit from Church. We took him to Arundel and Petworth. The Petworth gallery was quite in his way, and as it really is a fine collection one knew he was not wasting time in seeing it; and that it was worth a headache which, with some satisfaction, he announced having received from it, feeling that he had *done* something. . . .

We talked over *Ecce Homo;* he reports that Jowett, etc., do not like it, though whether this dislike proceeds from opposition or rivalry is not clear. As there is something fresh in old-fashioned thought now, I have been reading the life of Scott—Bible Scott. I am wonderfully struck with the extraordinary energy and strong sense of the man, joined to his enthusiasm and disinterestedness. His discrimination and power of drawing proper distinctions, and of separating secondary from fundamental matter are very striking. Though a Predestinarian himself, he always insisted on its being a secondary point, on which people might differ without the least drawback. This moderation on a point which, where people do hold it, they think so very critical and testing, is a strong sign of his balance of mind. He seems to have spent a considerable part of the force of his mind in keeping doctrinal ultraism down in his own party, and it appears that the Bible Commentary was originally undertaken principally with that aim. Though, on minor points of social practice, rigid and somewhat narrow, his strong sensibleness on substantial points comes out. All this, with his great sharpness, immediate perception of humbug, shrewdness, and remarkable working power, make him certainly a great man. He has a perfect voracity for work, which in one of his letters he rather subtilely analyses and *excuses*. He says he does a great part of his work with the spirit exactly of self-satisfaction in it which a journeyman carpenter or bricklayer has. The thorough honesty of the man is so taking. He has a great appreciation of knowledge—various knowledge, and only restricted his own reading from a conscientious principle. But he was obviously, in his own tastes and inclination, omnivorous and wanting to know everything. Some of his letters, I think, show much more acuteness, analysis of human nature and motives, and such matter—akin to the intellectual power of the present day—than you would expect. His perpetual work was against this coming out in his published writings. Had he been a more idle man he would have been more original, for he had this latter element in him.[1]

To the Rev. Francis A. Faber.

September, 1, 1866.

My dear Faber,—I have not, I think, written to you since our return, or rather, I should say, since a few hurried lines from Rome, and now I hardly know how to begin a descriptive epistle. I must defer an account of our impressions till some opportunity occurs of a passing visit to Saunderton. Are not tourist epistles, by the way, out of date now?—and tourist conversation too? It seems to me everybody travels at such a

---

[1] The reader may remember the tribute to Thomas Scott in the *Apologia*, and the deep impression his character and writings made on its author in his early youth.

rate that travelling has become nothing, and all descriptions are become refuse articles. It is amusing, if people meet who have common travelling ground—cities, countries, nay continents, to see to what very small matters of fact, and bits of information, their whole communication is reduced, so that, after a tour is over, the tangible residuum seems nothing. One is aware of going through a certain experience, having been knocked about a little, tried one's eyes and one's legs—for nothing is so wearying to the latter as the hours of standing in the galleries—and of having acquired a certain facility in turning over Murray, and then there is little more that remains. Some great sights, however, are stamped on the mind's eye. We got to Pæstum, which was our farthest point. The great temple there is one of the grand buildings of the world, and should rank with St. Peter's, the Colosseum, St. Paul's, etc. I did not think beforehand such an effect could have been produced by simple Greek architecture before the Arch. . . .

Among sights I must not omit Pio Nono. I must modify, however, the melancholy sentiment which attaches to him. I believe he enjoys himself immensely, and likes being Pope. I see it in his face. He is as happy as possible. He has lived in threatening times, but they told me he was by natural constitution not sensitive, but took things easy. Then the triple crown is another sight. It did not look so awful as we expected; on the contrary, if there is any epithet I should apply to it, I should say it was pretty; the jewelled brightness makes it look quite white. You remember it, I daresay. . . .

The grandeur of the streets of palaces has almost excited my curiosity about the Genoese families. You know it is Stanley's principle—the aid of sight to history. There is a great deal in it. After one has seen a place, one wants to know about the people. . . . Yours affectionately,   J. B. MOZLEY.

TO HIS SISTER.

October, 1866.

Mr. Wilkinson's paper is a very clear exposure of the audacious exegesis of *Ecce Homo*. It is only too short, and one arrives at the end of it before one wants. I see the notice in the *Contemporary* is deprecatory, but does not deny the justice of the criticism upon such interpretation of Scripture. The unfair limitation in the area of the book and the range of facts which it takes cognisance of is very compactly stated.

I have been reading *Le Maudit*. It lets one into a new department of life and facts altogether, and I think something may be got out of it, though one does not go along always with the author, and has some doubt as to what his improved Catholicism is. His glorification of Paris, too, is fanatical.—Yours,
J. B. M.

The *Tablet* having quoted with commendation a passage from Father Faber's posthumous works, in which he makes a remarkable assertion about the Archangel Michael, J. B. M. writes :—

To HIS SISTER.

SHOREHAM, *October* 30, 1866.

Faber is certainly very amusing. . . . I may use that term because his spiritual world is so completely a region of his own invention that one ceases to connect it with serious subjects. The decision of a controversy by a fact about St. Michael, hitherto unknown, but assumed as an undoubted celestial fact because his pen knocked it off with perfect ease, is quite a specimen of Faber's reasoning. . . .

I have been reading *Felix Holt*. With all his honesty and artisan grandeur there is an odiousness about him which made me at his trial long for his transportation, and sorry when he escaped that peril. There is a want of reality about the character, however, which prevents one from treating him wholly as an actual person. He is the impersonation of ideas. Harold is a capital character, thoroughly natural.—Yours,
J. B. M.

To THE REV. R. W. CHURCH.

December, 1866.

I have written to Pusey. It appeared to me that somebody ought to call his attention to the real ground taken in that affair in *The Guardian*. Though I was far from the best person to do it, if it was to be done it had better not be delayed. I always feel, with respect to Pusey, that he does not make account of that necessary modification of relations which is occasioned by advance of years. This is a consideration over and above any particular ground one has adopted which he may disapprove.

So M. has Brightstone. It is a beautiful parsonage—at least as seen surmounting the churchyard wall; quite a model of the old creeper-covered combination of rusticity with refinement, whence issued, some thirty years ago, S. O. to the battle of life. What a brilliant storm out of what a haven!—but the former suited him better. . . .

I was glad to see *The Guardian* taking up the alteration in the *Christian Year*, and bringing out the weak point in the case of the alteration—that there was only an intention, not an *act*, of change on the part of the author. It seems to me a real distinction.—Yours affectionately, J. B. M.

In November James Mozley and his wife paid another visit to his mother. It interested and revived her. The beginning of December he returned to Shoreham: receiving constant reports till the end.

TO HIS SISTER.

SHOREHAM, *December* 26, 1866.

We like much to hear all that there is to say, though the very slow steps must make it difficult for you to observe and see the differences which really take place from day to day. I quite understand the sort of dreamy watching that must go on. To me who am absent, there is not of course this watching. The effect of it upon my mind I find rather to be an immense vista of the past, which is always either before me or close to me. At the approach of a great end and close, the past comes out as the past; it is separate from the present. It is a long reach, such a life, and goes back into such—to one's own imagination—early and primitive times. On looking accidentally at the title-page of Mr. Wayland's sermons, and seeing the date on it 1816, it came with a sort of surprise on me that my mother had then been sixteen years a married woman. And yet, compared with books of the day, the volume—its paper, print, and everything—looked quite an antiquity.

Do you remember the sermon on "The Greatness and Littleness of Human Life," in J. H. N.'s fourth volume? I read it to Fanny Winton[1] yesterday, who always expects a sermon on Christmas-day; there are so many natural points of view in the sermon, and it meets so completely the wants of a reader who happens to have the subject in his mind.—Yours affectionately,

J. B. M.

To HIS SISTER.

SHOREHAM, *January* 9, 1867.

There is only one announcement which we can expect now, and we shall expect it of course to-morrow. Nothing can be more peaceful or more suitable as a scene of closing life than that you describe. I am very glad that you mentioned me to her when you did, and elicited the notice and recollection of me at such a time, and the message, as I may call it, to me. Ever since those letters received from you about ten days ago, which obviously marked the last stage, and described a condition of such absolute passiveness and quietude, I felt for her almost as a person out of the world. So your note this afternoon has not made such an alteration in my state of mind. I have no doubt that the sense of the actual departure will be more forcible in a little time than it is now. And there is something in the death of the aged which makes it a more solemn event, though more natural than that of the young. I mean in this respect, that it is the fair working out of mortal life. In premature deaths there is an idea of something accidental—if this complaint had not been caught, if over-work, or climate, or something had not come in; but here one has human life before one in its fulness and completeness, and it is in its nature seen to be a transient state. Old people always look like barriers

---

[1] A poor parishioner, blind, and for many years bedridden, to whom J. B. M. and his wife were unremitting in care and spiritual attention to the end of her life.

between the younger generation and the end—a sort of defence, so to speak. When they go, a kind of protection seems to be gone, and one feels an alteration in one's position.

In my mother's case this is very strong. She has been such a centre of the family, keeping up its first and earliest form almost, through so long a course of years; for the Friary always seems to identify one with thirty or forty years ago. It is very seldom that the early type lasts so long. In most families it is scattered to the winds very soon, and not a trace of the original is left. The termination of such a state of things is a great change to one's-self, and seems in a way to make one a different person.

I shall retain her parting message to me as a solemn and at the same time pleasing recollection throughout my life.—Yours affectionately, J. B. M.

My mother died in her 84th year. After all was over he writes:—

To HIS SISTER.

January 10, 1867.

My letter yesterday was so complete an anticipation of your note this morning, that I seem to have already written what I am writing now. It is the end of a long, remarkably complete life—I might add patriarchal; for, having been the survivor of my father for twenty years, my mother included in herself all the parental relations. She was the sole centre all this long time; she was very fit to be; this is especially the life of a mother. She has had, one may say, no other life, and it brought her out extraordinarily in one region of a mother's feeling—namely pride in her children. This was indeed a great part of —if one may call it so— her power. She kept things together very remarkably, and there was something very effective about it. The feeling was a real influence. It is a great gift to people to be able to be proud of persons who are not themselves. It necessarily gives a parent great hold over her children. Of course all good mothers have it, but I think it was more of a strong principle in my mother, and had far more force and vigour than it has in the minds of most mothers.

It was remarkable that this feeling was not accompanied by any of the common worldly aims for her children. She never seemed to have advancement in life, in the ordinary sense, in her view. Nor did her own increasing years—nor, I must add, those of her sons—ever put the idea into her head. She was faithful to her own just, simple ideas on the subject to the very last.

That she should have lived to see the University careers of her grandsons was very happy for her. It gave a brightness to the decline of life; it was just what she would have hoped for. . . . Yours affectionately, J. B. M.

To his Sister.

January 22, 1867.

. . . Amelia went to Westminster Abbey on Sunday and heard Stanley. It was a sermon on marriage, taken from the Gospel of the day. He recommended it strongly, even earnestly and warmly, and Amelia said it almost amounted to a declaration of his own experience of the state. Among other things, marriage, he said, was a shelter from the tyranny of the world and the tyranny of the Church. It was her impression that the sermon would on the whole do good, the tendency being to induce a class of loose hangers-on upon general society to take that step.—Yours affectionately, J. B. M.

This letter à *propos* of Mr. Stanley encloses an extract :—

" Did I tell you," writes Mr. Church, " that Stanley dined at Rogers' when I was in town, full of talk, chiefly about Rome ? He did not seem to have seen Antonelli ; but there was a Monsignor Nardi, a man whom he described as being, like the Pope's face, charming and saintlike if you looked from one side, and heard of him from one set of people ; perfectly diabolical and malignant if you looked at him on the other, and heard what the other set thought. He took off Monsignor Nardi and his Italian gesticulations and tones with very accomplished action. He met the Bishop of Orleans, who told him of a visit he had from Pusey. Pusey came to talk *Eirenikon* and Council of Trent with him, just as he was going to sit down to a great banquet with all the dons and swells of Orleans; the General and Prefect and Chief Judge, and all the rest. He told Pusey that he could not wait, but that he should be delighted to take him to the dinner; to which Pusey went. '*Et pour me servir d'une expression mondaine, il y cut un très-grand succès,*' with the General, Prefect, and Co."

J. B. M. TO THE REV. R. W. CHURCH.

SHOREHAM, *February* 20, 1867.

... Have you seen the Bishop of Orleans' pamphlet? It is a fearful *exposé* of the French mind. He quotes right and left; of course Renan among the rest. I did not know before the outrageous speculative fanaticism of the man; it is beyond anything. He gravely suggests the idea of the general Resurrection being accomplished by physical science. Who knows? —he says. This seems a different element from the purely positivist in him. ...

Poor Lady Jersey's death was an interesting one to my neighbour Townsend. He and she were great friends once. I say interesting rather than melancholy, for he has passed the latter sort of impression. She was very fond of talking literature and poetry with him, and he went often to Middleton. She was very skilful in bringing *out* persons, and threw herself into what they said. But he said you could not help being uncomfortable rather, and saying to yourself, What is all this about?—why does she want you to talk? It was a problem that sat upon you all the time. Of course, she made use of Townsend's critical results, and retailed them in the next party as her own, being clever enough for anything. She aspired to the character of patroness of clever men, but I dare say there mingled some real pleasure in talking with a genuine mind, which people may admire on the outside, choosing the artificial line for themselves. He says she was artificial with all her grace. I suppose it was the fault of the George the Fourth epoch—the finest gentleman in Europe.

Writing shortly after :—

I have written to W. Palmer to prepare him for Sir J.

Colvile calling on him. I think they will be both pleased and amused with him. It must be confessed he insists on considerable continuity of attention, and does not encourage wandering thoughts. I heard from Frank Faber that he (W. Palmer) had been proposing to translate Newman's recent letter into Italian, but had been stopped by the Jesuits, at which he was irate and gave that body a lick with the rough side of his tongue.—Yours affectionately, J. B. M.

SHOREHAM, *March* 9, 1867.

MY DEAR CHURCH,—What an extraordinary state of the political world! R. Palmer certainly comes out as a prophet; he first uttered the dreadful word, "Household Suffrage," though Dizzy is the first Prime Minister that has. One sees Gladstone's tone altered, and feeling coming out. If one *did* want to be the granter of reforms to the country, it must be trying to have the prize caught just before one by Dizzy. On the other hand, how Dizzy must enjoy it! But we must wait. I hear of other moves—that J. H. Newman really *is* going to Oxford. This comes from Miss S. There have been so many oscillations in rumour, but this does sound rather authentic. Will Newman, under Coleridge's bill, really resume his M.A. and vote in Congregation? What a ghost to rise up before the old Heads —as many as survive! I have a pamphlet on the Colonial Church question on the stocks. It looks at it mainly in one point of view, viz., as connected with the Inspiration question; but I do not go *into* that question.—Yours affectionately,

J. B. M.

THE REV. R. W. CHURCH TO J. B. M.

WHATLEY RECTORY, *June* 6, 1867.

DEAR MOZLEY,—Will you notice Tyndall? He seems to me to lay himself open; and the *Pall Mall* comment on "unscientific criticism" equally. Just as if one mind is not as good as another, on the reasonableness and use of miracles, whether familiar or not with the *laws* of nature. And really Tyndall seems incapable of apprehending what the argument he attacks really is. . . . Yours affectionately, R. W. C.

To the Rev. R. W. Church.

SHOREHAM, *June* 8, 1867.

MY DEAR CHURCH,—I am not thinking of answering Tyndall, but the article certainly appeared to me to lay itself open on the point you mention. It seems to make such a claim to an esoteric infallibility in scientific men, and to put the thing on the ground of faith with regard to other men; " Your reasoning is nonsense ; you know nothing about it; you must believe *us*." Indeed, the esoteric intuition he claims for men of science appears to be even in *them* a land of *faith*. They despise reasoning. The "unscientific criticism" hits the nail on the head, as a phrase—all the better, of course, for witnessing as a phrase to its own Liberal origin. . . . T. is a friend of Beresford Hope, who, I suppose, is one of the "loving, candid," religious men whom he admires. There is a kind of genial tone in his writing which is amusing and rather attractive. He walks in Bedgebury Park during the hours of service on the Sundays, announcing to the company that that is his mode of worshipping the Author of Nature.—Yours affectionately,

J. B. M.

To his Sister.

SHOREHAM, *December* 4, 1867.

I suppose you are all of you congratulating yourselves on your new bishop. I must own myself to a certain tinge of regret that the Bishop of New Zealand should alter his name. It is a great name gone. Lichfield is a different thing. It rather divides the unity of his life and destroys the *whole* there was before. To the disbelievers in romance it is the sort of issue which tends to confirm their own standard, although this would not be quite fair, as certainly the great proportion of his life has been a romantic one. It is a pity, too, as far as it goes, to bring him into the party struggles of the Church at home, when his was almost a universal name as Bishop of New Zealand. However, your diocese will benefit by the loss of the Colonial Church.

The letter goes on to give his first impressions of a visitor who, to those who knew him, was one of the influences of their lives—Mr. Rose, Rector of Weybridge, and uncle of Edith Price, to whom our nephew John Rickards Mozley was engaged.

We were much flattered by Mr. Rose's kind account of his call here. It was a very pleasant one to us. He is evidently a man who keeps his eye open to everything that is going on, and he expresses himself easily and compactly, and introduces an agreeable succession of subjects, giving variety and liveliness to the conversation. It is the opposite character to what I have observed in some, who go on upon the first point that happens to start, and exhaust it in lesser and lesser remarks after the principal ones have passed, staying on the same ground perpetually. He was much pleased with J. R.'s Infinity argument with the Germans he met abroad somewhere.—Yours affectionately, J. B. M.

P.S.—This is my first direction to Barrow.[1]

THE REV. R. W. CHURCH TO J. B. M.

WHATLEY RECTORY, *February* 11, 1868.

DEAR MOZLEY,—I spent two or three days in London last week with Rogers. I did two things. I went over the Abbey with Stanley, who was good enough to give us a morning. He is a very good guide, and has it all on his fingers' ends. It is certainly a very impressive place. There is a sort of effect of being in a dream, and meeting all sorts of strange people, from Edward the Confessor to Thackeray, really brought close to you in actual existence, and yet only present by tokens and signs of the most heterogeneous kind; and we had a fine day, and the Abbey itself was very noble. The other thing was a lecture of T.'s, at the Royal Institution. It was said not to be one of his best; but his experiments were curious and

---

[1] A village near Derby, on the banks of the Trent, where his eldest and youngest sister had, after visits at Shoreham and elsewhere, now settled, their two sisters continuing to live in Derby.

neat, and uniformly successful. But all the time I could not help a kind of sense of the inconsistency of the man, such as he appeared to me, claiming to bring all truth within what he called science. There was hard-headedness, originality, and sometimes a touch of imagination. But there seemed to be also a hard and hopeless one-sidedness, as if nothing in the world would open his eyes to the whole domain of soul and spirit close about him, and without which he would not be talking and devising wonderful experiments.—Ever yours affectionately, R. W. C.

To the Rev. R. W. Church.

Shoreham, *February* 13, 1868.

Dear Church,—I always think the Abbey wonderfully adapted to Stanley as an historical building, but at the same time the building itself—the interior—must be greatly wasted on him. The architecture of the interior seems to me always extraordinarily designed to excite the sense of mystery in the mind. I know no interior in England equal to it in this respect. But I should think that a sense in which Stanley was singularly deficient. The account of T. exactly agrees with the character of his writings. There seems a tendency in these men to place the material world, as you say, in point of dignity above the soul which finds out everything about it. So it becomes literally a great wood and stone idol which they worship; the individual seems a minute insignificant thing in their eyes.—Yours affectionately, J. B. M.

P.S.—So poor Dornford is gone—an old Oriel recollection more to me than to you. He was my tutor at first.

To the Same.

April 9, 1868.

I had a letter from that queer fellow Rowland Williams the other day, informing me that he had devoted the first day of Lent to reading my *Bampton Lectures*, and proceeded to make some comment on them. The choice of the day was not complimentary to the gratifying powers of the author, but I was glad that he was orthodox enough to keep Lent in his own way. How quick the blow has fallen on the Irish Church! When the ground has been long preparing you seem only to have to strike. J. B. M.

P.S.—We meditate starting for Venice on Monday.

VENICE, *April* 28, 1868.

MY DEAR CHURCH,—We have been here a week from Milan, through 150 miles of mulberry trees. The approach by the railway is very striking—you seem to plunge, engines and everything, into the sea, and see nothing but sea and lagune around you for some three miles; so that Venice is still seen rising out of the water as you approach. I say this because one expected the approach to be spoilt. I do not know when you were here. Travellers, who were here several years ago, pronounce the place very little altered. The people are evidently cock-a-hoop and jolly at their freedom; the Piazza of St. Mark is full of a buzzing, smoking, ice and coffee enjoying crowd every night from 7 to 10. Ruskin's transcendental description of the interior of St. Mark's rather makes the reality fall flat. It wants general effect, though the details, tracing borders, capitals, etc., are exquisite. It struck me rather as a bronze church—the interior I mean—variegated and patched with gilt and other colours by the air, in course of ages. Ruskin, you know, describes a perfect vision of colour. I should say St. Peter's was this. But this colour is of that utter deadness in St. Mark's that you have to extract it by imagination. I do not know whether this agrees with your recollection. One knows half of Venice before one sees it, and the exterior of the Doge's Palace was what one had seen it in prints; but the grandeur and gorgeousness of the interior—the large hall and specially the ceilings—took me by surprise. There is something horrible, however, in the old workman sitting with all his tools about him, lions'-mouth, prisons, torturing irons, execution cells, aperture for throwing body out into the canal—all under one roof, and your civilisation sermon occurred to me; for certainly, somehow or other, in this very Venice, Government now, and a very good one, seems to go on quite spontaneously. So far from these frightful methods being needed, Government has almost ceased to be an art. It is simply public opinion. Government is restoring a good deal, among the rest Saint Donato and the Fondachi Turchi. We have been to Torcello, according to your recommendation. It is a wonderful little voyage through that archipelago of little islets, each with its campanile, church, or city some thousand years old. The old Duomo almost carries one back to the age of the fathers; indeed one seems here, generally, to live in an earlier stage of antiquity than one does at home—where age borders on the patristic; is more than mediæval. St. Mark's is more Eastern and Constantinopolitan than Venetian. Venetian sentiment comes out more, I think, in the Frari and San Zampolo, where the monuments of the old Doges are. The recumbent figures high up in the wall are a new fact to me. The equestrian statues in the same position were the same.

FLORENCE, *May* 16, 1868.

MY DEAR CHURCH,—I write a line to you from your quondam home. We have been here a week, having taken Padua, Vicenza, Verona, and Bologna on our way. There is of course an enormous deal to do here, and one becomes a perfect chaos of the contents of galleries, which test the weak framework of memory rather severely. One finds one's-self testing it by the photographs in the windows. The place is increasing in answer to the demands upon it. New piazzas rising up. . . . We have been to the Chamber of Deputies. There is a total absence of ceremonial, and a man in an easy morning-coat sits where our gowned and wigged Speaker sits; so that our House compared with this one represents the old *régime*. The great passion of the Italian public now is the Princess Margherita. The Government is getting capital out of her to cement the union of Italy. They work her hard; every morning at some public institution, every evening at the Prato, where she distributes her bows very gracefully and cordially. Her deadly pale complexion is accompanied with a very sweet expression, and, though not regularly beautiful, I can quite fancy her charming and fascinating everybody. For one who has to bow so much as she has, her lively flexible movement is advantageous. I observed especially that she bowed *back* so well, a difficult thing to do elegantly, but very useful to one who must find herself continually just catching people after she has nearly driven past them. They have sent her now to Genoa. The King [Victor Emmanuel] does not interfere with her, but keeps at a respectful distance, though we saw him too on the Prato. He is rather superior to his common portraits—not quite so truculent-looking.

We found ourselves the other day, on entering a church, San Lorenzo, assisting at a Mass for one of the Medici. But whether it was a Cosmo or a Lorenzo, I cannot say. The priests here are evidently a snubbed race. One never by any chance sees them speaking to a gentleman; always with each other, or with some common man. There seem, however, plenty of services and sermons. There is no appearance anywhere in Italy of religion having died away, and having less hold upon the people than it has in other Roman Catholic countries. Of the educated Italian Liberals, however, the only article of religion seems to be Dante. He reigns everywhere, statues multiplying; and yet I cannot imagine any real admiration of Dante without a religious belief of some kind.— Yours affectionately, J. B. M.

SHOREHAM, *August* 6, 1868.

MY DEAR CHURCH,—You were lucky in your two great mountains. I only saw the four tops of Monte Rosa, like spikeheads in the sky, between Lugano and Lucerne. I must see the Matterhorn some day, from your description of it, having a strong fancy for heights. We think of going to Dublin to the Congress; rather a dull affair, I am afraid, now that this Irish question has come on:—everything talked of except the one thing people care about. I met Neate in London the other day, much pulled down in health. He was much interested in the approaching Papal Council, anticipating a dreadful religious breakdown on the Continent, "the Catholic form of Christianity" crushed, and nothing in its place. He complained too of the universal "chaff" which religious questions had turned into here; that he could get no other answer from people, giving S. O. a rap on this point. . . . Yours affectionately, J. B. M.

In the autumn of 1868 James Mozley visited Ireland, and attended the Dublin Church Congress.

TO HIS SISTER.

SHOREHAM, *November* 21, 1868.

Our Irish tour was both pleasant at the time, and is also pleasant to look back upon. It is a gain to have seen some remarkable men, and to have made acquaintance with the Irish. It was a fresh kind of scene to me, and an agreeable and amusing one. In the absence of society here, such things are the natural compensation, and perhaps it is as good a form of seeing society as any. Archdeacon Lee was a most agreeable acquaintance to make; a man of perpetual readiness and quickness, and unwearied courtesy which always came quite fresh from him, and had not the look of any straining. It was the more striking in combination with a very learned character. Then Todd and Fitzgerald, both specimens of the student type not often equalled—Todd, in his deal-furnished study, surrounded with his Irish MSS. and Irish MS. dictionaries, was a curious picture indeed; himself just like a clergyman of an engraving a century and a half ago that you might turn up in some old book. It must have been the most genuine enthusiastic love which carried him through the rough materials he had surmounted. His bad health was but too apparent, and threw a shade of melancholy over the scene. Fitzgerald is more of the philosopher, but has still the quiet isolated stooping air and figure of the student, though joined with considerable ease and elegance of manner. There seemed to me a deeper vein of satire in him than he liked to reveal openly, but one caught glimpses of it. As for passing events, it would be very difficult to disturb him, and the perfect serenity with which he pronounced upon the certain prospects of the Irish Church, though he had only a couple of months before made his strong speech in the House of Lords, showed rather Mr. Wayland's type of passive non-resistance and great mastery over all anxiety.

I must pay a passing tribute to the cliffs of Moher—very grand; the finest specimen, taking height, colour, and conformation altogether, of cliff scenery I ever saw. Kilkee was not very striking; Killarney was—the metallic bronze colour of the mountains and their forms and interconnections. . . . Yours affectionately, J. B. M.

To his Sister.

Shoreham, *December* 9, 1868.

. . . I have obtained favour in an unexpected quarter, namely, with Kenelm Digby. He is such an old name, with his *Mores Catholici*, which one used to turn over ages ago, that one regards him almost as an old friend. I do not think, however, poetry, of which he has just published a volume, which he has sent me, is his forte; very good and serious, but in fact, as poetry, the queerest rigmarole you can conceive. However, in a poem on the supernatural, he versifies some passages in the *Bampton Lectures*. I need not say how eccentric a specimen of the Muse it is. There is a fine old fragrance however, about his reputation, and he is one of the learned names of the age.

Stanley will be a difficulty probably to Gladstone some day. The elevation of Tait has, as a Liberal precedent, cleared the way rather for him.—Yours affectionately, J. B. M.

Early in January 1869 Mr. Gladstone offered to J. B. M. the Canonry of Worcester then vacant. Amongst the official letters connected with the appointment, which followed on my brother's acceptance, is one touching on the office and function of Canons.

The Right Hon. W. E. Gladstone to J. B. M.

Hawarden, *Jan.* 17, 1869.

My dear Mr. Mozley,—When I had had time to receive the

Queen's approval of your appointment, I sent you an intimation of it; and I now think you will like to see the enclosed letter from the Dean of Worcester, which please to return.

Our neighbour Bishop here, the Bishop of Chester[1] (who is not our Diocesan), much approves of your appointment.

Among the Canons of our Cathedrals, even, and perhaps especially since 1840, there are but few who have contributed or are likely to contribute much to the theological store of the Church of England in this day of her pressing need. I rejoice that my first act in this province of my duty has been to promote the addition to their number of one who, as to both promise and performance, is sufficient sensibly to raise the average.

You will be grieved to hear that the Bishop of Salisbury lies *almost* at the point of death. Yesterday's account was a trifle better.—Believe me, sincerely yours,

W. E. GLADSTONE.

J. B. M. TO HIS BROTHER, T. M.

January 30, 1869.

Many thanks for your congratulations. We go to Worcester on Monday, and I hope to be installed on Wednesday. The Dean [Dr. John Peel] has welcomed me in most cordial and agreeable letters, but I am sorry to say his state of health is such that he will not be able to receive us. . . . The greatest part of the restoration of the Cathedral is accomplished. . . . The Dean, you know, is a most munificent public-spirited man, and has been himself the principal restorer.—Yours affectionately,

J. B. M.

TO THE REV. R. W. CHURCH.

WORCESTER, *May* 10, 1869.

What quick business they have made of the Irish Church Bill! I see the Bishops have ingeniously hit upon the expedient of diverting public attention from themselves and transferring it upon the Deans and Chapters. . . . Our Dean is in a great taking about it, and is going up, in spite of his gout, to the meeting at Lambeth. This proposal to abolish one

---

[1] Dr. Jacobson.

canonry out of four in every cathedral, in order to found suffragan bishoprics—*i.e.* to do their work—is about as cool a case as I have heard of.

I have made acquaintance with Mrs. Davison, the representative, after the interval of a generation, of Prophecy Davison. It is almost the resuscitation of an old generation. She becomes her associations, has a venerable, sweet countenance, a lively and quick understanding in conversation, and a musical voice. . . . She expressed, by the way, very quietly and gently, some surprise that Judge Coleridge had not asked her for letters of Keble's. I hope we shall know more of her. We have seen a good deal of the Dean—certainly a very accomplished man, one of those artistic talkers of the old school, with great poetical tastes, and one of those retentive and apt memories which illustrate conversation so well. We have had some most grotesque old Court anecdotes from him. He remembers Christ Church days of old, Lloyd and Bull, tutors, etc.—Yours affectionately, J. B. M.

To THE REV. R. W. CHURCH.

May 18, 1869.

. . . I do not myself agree with certain plans of reforms for Chapters which I have seen, professing to utilise them by attaching local employment to them; for example, inspectorships of diocesan schools, superintendence of diocesan church building societies, of S.P.G. and S.P.C.K. proceedings. This is the sort of thing. Such schemes would end in nothing but bringing forward a minor sort of practical local men who like this sort of work, and would lay themselves out for place in this way. It would, moreover, end in the Bishops having practically all the canonries in their gift. Government could not appoint local men of this sort, except simply from the recommendation of the Bishops. It would disconnect, meanwhile, the cathedrals from the great stream of theological and philosophical thought in the Church, and make them mere representatives of diocesan boards and committees. . . . But whatever one may think of Chapter reform, I object *in limine* to the subject being brought forward in this sort of way, merely as a tail to the episcopal question. . . . What right have the Bishops, at a time when public opinion was quiet, and nothing stirring against Deans and Chapters, to *get up* a cry against them ? . . . Everything now tends to drive this [the claims of learning and thought] to the wall—to give everything to busy men. A proportion ought to be insisted upon. I see Stanley and Mansel take this line ; there can be no doubt that G. has it in his mind to rectify the disproportion.—Yours affectionately,

J. B. M.

To THE REV. R. W. CHURCH.

WORCESTER, *June* 18, 1869.

Your sermon brings out the distinction in St. Paul's mind —wise and unwise—as an eternal distinction in the human race, very strikingly. One would not have thought beforehand that one needed to be reminded of the permanence of it ; yet we get such a habit of assigning a meaning *for the day* to New Testament phrases, that it is a surprise to feel that exactly the same persons are going on now, and the same state of things. I don't think persons realise the truly archaic aboriginal class the poor are, and you bring the fact home to them. All my experience is for the want of education being such an enormous want. I confess I fulfil my relations to them rather in the spirit of a debtor than that of an enthusiastic fraterniser. But you put the obligation in a fresh light to people. Indeed, this double element in society is a wonderful fact—the pertinacious primitiveness that, after all, adheres to the backbone or mass of the world's existence, the intellect being a mere fragment.

I am glad you coincide with my remarks on Copeland ; there is a certain satiety of the modern style that carries one back with pleasure to the old great men. So it may be to some extent a love of change that acts on one. But yet there is something more. The quiet statement seems to have more magnanimity and faith in it, as if to say, This is our view ; if you see it, so much the better for you ; if you do not see it, we shall not resort to violent modes of persuading you. However, practically there is a difference between admiring people and being able to imitate them. . . .

To the Same.

Shoreham, *August* 10, 1869.

. . . I spent a day with Copeland, the end of last month. He goes back to Nonjuring days, and brought back vividly to one the deep, ancient root of anti-state principles in the school of the Norris and Watsons; and how curiously this antiquated current mingles now with the great present rush in the same direction. It reads like a Sibylline prophecy. We were exceedingly pleased with his new church; such exquisite carving in the capitals of the pillars, and all representing and doing justice to a vast amount of work and tasteful consideration. We are just settled down again, having spent the month in a circuit of family and other visits. We were much pleased with my sisters' new home at Barrow.—Yours affectionately,

J. B. M.

The following letter was written on the death of a College friend and early intimate, whose name has appeared in these pages:[1]—

To Miss Bridges.

Shoreham, *August* 10, 1869.

My dear Miss Bridges,—It was with surprise and grief that I saw the announcement of your brother's death. I did not know that he had been ill. I had not seen him for many years, but letters passed occasionally between us, and we kept up in heart our old Oxford friendship, though circumstances had not favoured our meeting each other. Indeed it does not require meeting often, to keep up the feeling of an early friendship, begun in under-graduate days, when we were both at Oriel together, and continued when we were both Fellows of Colleges, residing at Oxford. The feeling is as fresh in my mind as if it were only a few months since. He had a generous, affectionate mind, which attached everybody to him, and there

[1] See pp. 48, 49.

was a liveliness and freshness in his views of things, and what came out of him in conversation, which made it very delightful to be with him. There was a brightness about his disposition and qualities of mind which give a vividness to all my recollections of him; and if we had chanced to meet anywhere of late, I believe I should have met him as if there had been no interval at all since our College days. I was hoping he might come to see me at Worcester, knowing his fondness for cathedral service. We used to go together to the Oxford chapel services, and he would ask the choristers to his rooms. I can hardly realise that he is gone, his death has come so suddenly upon me. . . .

Might I ask you to be so very kind as to acknowledge these few lines, and tell me what you are able to tell me about him. I have been quite cut off from hearing of him. The announcement in the papers is all I know.

I had the pleasure of seeing you and your sisters at Denton. This recollection mingles with sadness as I think of the occasion on which I now write. With my best wishes for all of you under this sad event, believe me yours very sincerely,
J. B. MOZLEY.

This letter drew from his friend's sister a full and very interesting reply.

J. B. M. TO MISS BRIDGES.

August 20.

MY DEAR MISS BRIDGES,—Accept my sincere thanks for your letter with the account of your brother, so deeply interesting notwithstanding its sadness. The sudden call, amid the activities of life, to face another world is a thought which, as it rises up before us in our ordinary state of mind, dismays us. But he was equal to the occasion. What a calm but strong spirit he showed! It is an encouragement to those who survive. There must have been a steady habitual principle of faith in his mind to have responded so remarkably to such a call. For my own part, starting as we did life together, I feel a peculiarly deep lesson in his closing scene. Yet it ought not to be only a lesson, only a memento of life's transiency, only a warning to make one wise and sad. It ought to inspirit in a Christian sense, and make one think of another world with more cheerfulness and hope. May the recollection of those last days be ever a source of peace and consolation to you, who saw his faith while you comforted his suffering. I wish the same to your sisters. I thank both you and them for your kind remembrance of me.—I am yours sincerely and much obliged,

J. B. MOZLEY.

To THE REV. R. W. CHURCH.

WORCESTER, *November* 1869.

MY DEAR CHURCH,—Thank you for the sermon.[1] I have returned the compliment in kind;[2] for, by a curious coincidence, we are both of us on Parker's table at the same time. Yours strikes me as quite in tune with Westminster Abbey, and harmonising with the *genius loci;* an historical portrait of the episcopate in the great historical church. . . . I should like to have heard it in the place itself; it would have held its own. It must have gratified Moberly, and just helped him at the time when a man wants helping with elevating thoughts. . . . We had a pleasant week at Oxford. The Bishop of O. [S. O.] preached at St. Mary's, but made no allusion to his diocesan promotion.[3] He strikes people in society as in a state of pleasure tinged with melancholy, in which, however, the former preponderates.—Yours affectionately, J. B. M.

To HIS SISTER.

WORCESTER, *November* 24, 1869.

. . . I have not told you of William Donkin's death.[4] He died while we were in Oxford, and only three days after we called, and I had sat talking with him some time. He was sitting in an arm-chair, looking attenuated indeed, but still not perceptibly different from himself in talking. He was always so very subdued that there was less space for change. We

---

[1] Preached in Westminster Abbey at the consecration of Dr. Moberly to the See of Salisbury.
[2] The Roman Council; preached at St. Mary's, November 7, 1869.
[3] To the See of Winchester.
[4] Savilian Professor of Astronomy and late Fellow of University.

talked about Church appointments and the practical spirit of the age, which turned every place into practical work and would not recognise study. But he was for a student claiming his right, and declining other engagements; in which case he thought his right would come to be acknowledged. We talked also about William Froude, who tenanted their house two or three times when they were in Madeira. There was so very little difference in him that when, three days after, we were told of his death, it seemed to throw an unreality upon the thing, and the change appeared like going from one room to another. Amelia talked with Mrs. Donkin, to whom obviously nothing immediate was at all present. She was considering the prospects of the winter, and the workmen were laying down water-pipes in the hall as we entered. The event came in so oddly and incongruously in our Oxford week, and yet I suppose the way in which one receives such pieces of news is oftener this than not.

His is a remarkable life in a sense—such a long uninterrupted neighbourhood to death, spent passively and contemplatively, with nothing to distract him. The Observer [Mr. Manuel Johnson] used always to allude to him as a remarkable instance of a sceptical, scientific mind by nature, kept in order and subdued. It is curious how his physical inability never took from his reputation. It tells well for Oxford. It was never doubted what he *would* have done if he had had strength, and this was put to his credit almost as much as if he had done it.—Yours affectionately, J. B. M.

In the year 1869 J. B. M. was chosen Select Preacher, and began the series of University Sermons since published.[1]

---

[1] There is something so characteristic both of him and the writer of the following letter (Mrs. James Mozley), that I yield to the temptation of extracting from it the adventures of one sermon :—

"COLLEGE GREEN, WORCESTER, *December* 4, 1869.

"MY DEAR FANNY,—It is time you should hear something about last Sunday's sermon, the success it had, the dangers it ran, the tribulation I went through, and James's astonishing calmness and resignation in very trying circumstances; but as I shall only require a very moderate sympathy with the troubles that are past, I will begin at the end, and tell you how much the sermon was admired. Miss Smith told me as I came out that one

To the Rev. R. W. Church.

February 24, 1870.

You ought to have been in Oxford to meet the Greek Archbishop and his archimandrites, who were with him three days of the congregation said to her, "What a shame there should be such a small number to hear such a splendid analysis of character!" . . . The Vice-C. said he hoped it would be published at once, while the impression remained, but it is not going to be. The Pharisees will keep unchanged another year or two, after all the centuries that have passed since they were denounced. . . . Now, I have told you all I can about it, because, of course, you like to hear. I don't go writing like this to other people.

"You must know I took my black hand-bag in the carriage with me, and put in it, for safety, James's sermon, money, etc. We arrived at Oxford in the dark. I had to wait on the platform a quarter of an hour or more before we could get our luggage or a porter, carefully guarding my bag with my foot, hands being full. Then, on alighting at New Inn Hall, it was carried to my room with the other luggage, and I sat down talking by the fire, till time to dress for Mr. Smith's dinner-party. Imagine my dismay when I opened it to find it was some gentleman's bag I had taken instead of my own; and mine, sermon and all, was gone on we did not know where, or with whom. How the change was made I can't tell; I took it from close by my side. Well, it was dinner-time. I felt turned topsy-turvy, obliged to go out at once, as this party was given for us. So James had to go off to the station, to telegraph to three addresses we found in the bag, and that was all we could do. I happened to know who the man was, when we found his card, so felt sure all would be safe; but no hope of getting the MS. in time for next day. Most luckily—all was most lucky—I had put the rough copy tidily altogether on the sideboard here, so I telegraphed to Rose to send it by post, and, having done all that could be done, went off to Balliol, determined not to say a word, for I knew how much the Smiths would sympathise. James came in late; but Miss S. feeling sure, as she said, that I was not a woman to send my husband posting off after luggage, except it was very important, questioned me, so I was obliged to confess, but not till dinner was over, what it was. Great sympathy; very little hope. We went home. I had, as you may suppose, not much sleep; but relying much on the invaluable Rose, I got up an hour before morning, and was up and dressed by seven, waiting for the post. Sermon arrived; sat down at once, wrote, without moving, till twelve, Alice Cornish doing a little, and had just reckoned I should have finished by one, when the door opened, in came the bag—all contents safe. When I got the rough copy in the morning, I was at peace, knowing I could write it out again. James had written it so badly, it was impossible to preach from his own writing. Nevertheless, I was glad to see it come in. Mr. Waller, the owner of the one I had taken, behaved in the *most extraordinarily* excellent manner; finding the contents valuable, he took such immense pains that we got the bag, as I said, at twelve on Sunday morning, the very first train it could have come by. The whole thing seems wonderful. What things telegrams are! I didn't say how well James behaved—not a word of reproach—only threw it entirely on the bag itself, which ought not to be black, every one being black. So I expect it will end pleasantly in my having a nice new Russia leather one, conspicuously trimmed with gold, to prevent any future mistakes."

at our President's, where he was staying. Unfortunately, the means of communication with him were difficult, as he only spoke modern Greek and German. There was an interpreter, a Mr. Timbres, a Greek merchant at Liverpool, of position, who attended the Archbishop in his tour for love. He found it dreadfully hard work, as he told me, and was quite knocked up. All his power was elicited by a conference between the Archbishop and Pusey, on Sunday, on the *Filioque*. You may imagine the difficulty of transferring the respective communications from the two theologians to each other. The conference did not end favourably. Pusey was Latin, and the Archbishop Greek; and they could not hit on any explanatory appendages to the word. Pusey was quite prostrated by disappointment, and wrote most downcast letters to Williams. I remember Palmer used always to tell me the Greeks were inert and pliable on the outside, but clung tenaciously to every bit of their theological position when the trial came. I liked the Archbishop, and he was universally popular—quite a man of the world, with good presence and address. The Liverpool archimandrite really made a good English speech, with great rhetorical effect, at the great dinner on Monday. But as conversationalist, he was slow, and not up to words. There was some difficulty in keeping all the party in proper humour, the Syra archimandrite being disposed to be sulky, thinking he had not sufficient honour paid him. The Archbishop pronounced him to G. Williams ἄνους, and that he should not take him out again. The Bishop of Winchester dined with us in the hall, to meet the party on Sunday. He had had a hard working day, and was dull at first; but brightened up in the evening, and was very amusing. Burgon was in good spirits, and had received a great many flattering letters on his Temple correspondence. Temple Chase was up. The Provost was fairly well, and was at the Monday's dinner; but Williams was down upon him for having taken the toast of the President's health out of his hands, for whom it was designed. However, an opening was made for W., who likes to have his say. He is a good man on the whole for such an occasion, but he ordered the poor archimandrites about in a way they did not like. . . .
—Yours affectionately, J. B. M.

WORCESTER, *May* 26, 1870.

MY DEAR CHURCH,— ... It is indeed a very slippery basis on which everything is standing now, and one hardly knows what to expect next. I extremely dislike the apparent determination of some members of the Upper House of Convocation to cram this new translation of the Bible down the throats of people. It ought, if it is ever sent out, to win its way gradually, and by the voluntary acceptance of it on the part of the Church at large. So much at least is due to the venerable prestige of the authorised version. I do not see well, moreover, how it can be otherwise, for Convocation cannot *authorise*. Yet some talked as if some definite act of authority was immediately to impose this new translation on the Church. . . .—Yours affectionately,

J. B. M.

In 1870 J. B M. and his wife took a tour in Scotland, carrying with them an introduction to Mr. Blackwood, then at his country house of Strathtyrum.

TO HIS SISTER.

DUNKELD, *September* 30, 1870.

We have just arrived here from St. Andrews, where we spent two days, dining yesterday at Strathtyrum. It is a large house, with grounds and woods, and the old part was Archbishop Sharp's country house, the very one he was journeying to when he was murdered. The Blackwoods are most hospitable. He is an uncommonly shrewd man, with much humour, and plenty of stories about literary men. . . . There was an authoress staying there—Mrs. O——. We both thought her very taking; with something of an arch expression, a musical voice, and inclined to be cheerful and merry, but with a very quiet way about her. She is almost one of the family there, Blackwood having known her from a girl, and first brought her out in print as a critic of Thackeray, Dickens, etc. The said Thackeray complained of some of her criticisms to him (Blackwood), with whom he was on intimate terms. So, after much arguing on T.'s part to prove that " Blackwood " had made a great mistake, B. said simply, " Well, Thack, I won't repeat it," which produced a tremendous laugh from Thackeray, and the retort, " You rascal ;" and so it ended ; the admission gained being that Thackeray was ready to take his chance, and have a little more such criticism if it was forthcoming. . . .

I should describe the Scotch service both Free and Established as ultra-cathedral, in the sense of being totally uncongregational. The hymns rise up out of an enclosure beneath the precentor's desk concealing the choir, and the congregation quietly listen *sitting*. The effect of this in a large, round, galleried church holding 2000 or 3000 people is rather absurd. The sermons were good compositions, *read* without any action.

I must not omit Abbotsford. Its gimcrack character is exaggerated. It is a nice place, and looks like a home. Hope Scott has built a new part for himself, *not* shown; it is well added, so as not to interfere with Scott's Abbotsford. . . .—Yours affectionately, J. B. M.

Did I tell you that at G.'s there rose a discussion as to the number of words a labouring man in the country had for all the purposes of speech ? It was estimated differently at 500, 300, and 100. I hazarded the remark that the women had a larger vocabulary than the men. L. did not accept the fact absolutely, but I think I am right.

SHOREHAM, *September* 1870.

MY DEAR CHURCH,—What extraordinary times we live in ! We are here enthusiastic Germans. How little one knew a month ago upon what an edge the empire was tottering ! I suppose the Emperor himself saw it only too keenly. Indeed, one cannot help thinking, if he had been a more stupid man and not been so conscious of the slipperiness of his position, he might have tided it over. There appears from all accounts to be a strong peace, commercial side in France, that would have supported him in doing nothing. But the danger of the other side, and all his own weak points, seem to have filled his mind. I came across Ranke's summary of the character of Clement VII.—a regular Italian type—which seemed to correspond rather curiously with the Emperor's. Of course, such correspondences do not bear pursuing into details, but there are some general features. I enclose it.[1] What a melancholy picture he presents now! I thought the inner paragraph going into such details about him very out of taste. What a good letter of Max M.! We have been here now a month; Caroline is with us. . . . There seem signs of an incipient row in Germany on the Infallibility question.—Yours affectionately,

J. B. M.

THE REV. R. W. CHURCH TO J. B. M.

WHATLEY RECTORY, *September* 7, 1870.

DEAR MOZLEY,—We have certainly lived to see wonderful things. It seems to be a part of the age of railroads and telegraphs that things are brought to such quick decision. But the incredibility beforehand of what has happened now, combined with its perfect naturalness and reasonableness, now that it has happened, is alarming, when one reflects that our own turn may come.

What is to come of France? The spirit of falsehood, and lying and bragging, at any rate, has not yet been put down; and with that spirit, and the rage and shame of such a humiliation, I look with utter perplexity as to what will be the effect of the continued disaster which I suppose is to be looked for. France, of course, is in a very different material condition from what it was in 1792, or even 1830 and 1848. But it never was in such danger and such shame as it is now. It seems to me that it will be more easy for the Germans to gain victories than to know what to do with them.

I wish I could be enthusiastic for the Germans. As far as the war goes, they have only dealt back in wonderful style what undoubtedly was meant in full measure for them; and so far I am entirely satisfied. But in spite of Max Müller, Bismarck sticks in my throat. I cannot doubt that he not

---

[1] Extract from Ranke's character of Clement VII.: "His acuteness sometimes seemed injurious to him. He seemed to be too conscious that he was the weaker. All possibilities of danger arose before him, and harassed his judgment, and puzzled his will. Some people are endowed with a quick and intuitive perception of what is the simple, the practical, the expedient in public affairs; he possessed it not. In the most critical moments he was seen to doubt, to vacillate, and to consider how he could save money."

only prepared, but wished for, this war as the one thing which would put the keystone on his work, and weld together the South and North Germans. His end has been a great one. But his policy in pursuing it seems to me simply of the same kind as that of the Emperor, when he sought the great end of a strong Government in France. He was determined to see Germany great and united in his own day, and cared nothing for the price or the means. First Denmark, then the Austrian war, then for four years letting the Emperor go on talking after the fashion of the *Projet de Traité*, instead of at once and in earnest stopping him. I cannot conceive an honest man letting even an antagonist go on believing that, with perseverance, the bait might take, and quietly listening to proposals which he felt to be disgraceful; and I don't see how, at the best, Bismarck can be acquitted of this.

Your extract from Ranke about Clement VII. is a striking parallel, and I have no doubt suggests the true explanation of the Emperor's mad move. I was reading about Clement in Guicciardini lately. When the Constable of Bourbon was advancing on Rome, Guicciardini was the Pope's officer, and wanted money to pay troops to oppose Bourbon, and he could get none; and he is in such a rage with Clement because the Pope would not adopt the obvious expedient of *selling* a dozen Cardinal's hats. He is indignant that a man of such lax views generally should let himself be overthrown for a mere exceptional and anomalous bit of scrupulousness.—Ever yours affectionately, R. W. CHURCH.

J. B. M. TO THE REV. R. W. CHURCH.

SHOREHAM, *September* 1870.

MY DEAR CHURCH,—I can quite enter into your remark about Bismarck, and can abundantly comprehend his being thought a very suspicious character. And yet I thought there was something natural in Max Müller's explanation of the private confabs, and the certainty that an abrupt stopper given by Bismarck to the French proposal would be a signal for immediate war. Under such circumstances it is like a pistol being presented at you, and you parley with the man without the same amount of scrupulosity that you might have under other circumstances, if only you can prevent him from firing. The complication in France seems growing worse, and I should think even Bismarck himself must have some difficulty in making out whether he had rather France had a Government or not. In the latter case, one does not see what is to stop the war at all, there being no power to treat with about peace. And if French anarchy goes on, one sees no terminus but that of Prussia simply drawing her own frontier, and occupying Metz, Strasburg, etc., as her own fortresses. But this would not be satisfactory.

How quietly Rome has gone! How little one could have prophesied such a tranquil end, as if nothing at all had happened. People do not talk about it. If they do, it is a forced recall of their attention. Immense armies do occupy the ground so, and create an imagery that fills the mind. The next thing is Russia occupying Constantinople. One really hardly sees what there is to prevent her just now. We are expecting the Empress to come to Brighton.

SHOREHAM, *October* 22, 1870.

MY DEAR CHURCH,—Many thanks for the *St. Anselm*. I have been very glad to renew acquaintance with it in its new form. I think the theological metaphysician and the statesman, in his own sphere of politics, are so striking a combination in St. Anselm. I hardly can point to such another instance. Augustine had dealings with the civil powers, but the Donatists' was an inferior local question in its civil aspects, and he had to deal more with proconsuls and the police than with chiefs. Looking upon Anselm on his student's side, the region of subject he takes is natural, he looks so intensely of the student type, and so naturally absorbed a man in his own thoughts. He must have had great power of breaking off one thing and taking to another as he was called upon—a most difficult thing, and an enviable faculty. On the side of the affections too he throws off the student type with great easiness. Scholars and intellectual men have not generally much expressiveness in that direction, but there is an elegance and flexibility in him which fit him for society and for popularity. One must certainly rank him as one of the most remarkable of the Church's characters. There is a great finish and completeness in your portrait, which very vividly sets off and combines the different and opposite characteristics of his mind, and gives the largeness and freedom of the type in which he is cast. His attitude on the Investiture question is described with precision, and the aspect of it as "positive law" separates him very definitely from the ground of a zealot. One sees how constantly a point leaps to a Divine law level unless watched; and even the steady thinkers that watch it cannot stop the impetus. His attitude on the miraculous claims of the Church is striking too in its guardedness. It is curious how many great Church minds have been in the position of checkers throughout. Gregory on the Roman claim, Bernard on the cult of the Virgin, even Hildebrand *doctrinally*—on the transubstantive point. Bowden shows that he protected Berengarius.[1] It would be curious to make out a list of the many that have been on the protesting side on some point of the day, their influence having been overruled by the strength of the popular will of lower and coarser thought. One sees the same thing in parties on a smaller scale. Thomas Scott, the man whom the Evangelicals are most proud of, was all his ministerial life fighting on the side of works, as against what

[1] Berengarius opposed the definite doctrine of "*change of substance*," i.e. Transubstantiation, maintained by Paschasius, Radbert, and Lanfranc. For this he was accused of denying the *Real Presence*, which he always affirmed. Hildebrand took his part: 1st, At Tours, 1054 (Bowden, ii. 242); 2d, More doubtfully at Rome, 1059 (*Ib*. ii. 243). Hildebrand, now Gregory VII., was induced to send for him to Rome, 1078; "but on the council assembling he acted the part of a friend to the accused. Berengarius, with his concurrence, in lieu of repeating the declaration of 1059, made the following in less stringent terms. . . . This confession was no sooner made than Gregory declared it was enough for the Faith, . . . that B. was no heretic" (Bowden, ii. 244, 245). When Berengarius's opponents still pressed for more stringent measures, Gregory allowed them to exact a further profession of faith from Berengarius; but he sent him home under protection, and forbade any further molestation of him (Bowden, ii. 247-8.) "Freed from his difficulties, Berengarius avowed, on his return, his original opinions, and ascribed his formal disavowal of them to the fear of instant death. But Gregory, however urged on the point by Berengarius's enemies, firmly refused—and to the end of his life persevered in the refusal—to take any further measures against him" (Bowden, ii. 248).

was considered the high Justification doctrine, and was in bad odour with a large section of his party.—Yours,

J. B. M.

To his Sister.

SHOREHAM, *Dec.* 1870.

We are Germans here. I think the right is on their side, and the alarmists, English as well as others, who practically deny their right to unite and form one nation, are totally in the wrong. The French obstinacy, in preferring dissolution as a nation to parting with two Departments, seems to me irrational and wrong. A thorough beating in war is a fact of Providence, and ought to be accepted, and it is impiety and rebellion to prefer national suicide to a moderate penalty. Yet some encourage them in it as if it were fine. It is considered heroism. It is really cowardice. They have not the moral courage to avow defeat. One hopes, however, that they are not thoroughly committed to the principle, and that if Paris gives way they will surrender.—Yours affectionately,

J. B. M.

To his Brother, T. M.

January 23, 1871.

DEAR TOM,—I have received a note marked "*Most private,*" offering me the Regius Professorship of Divinity, which is likely to be immediately vacated. . . . The offer is most sudden and unexpected. I dread the change at present, and do not feel particularly comfortable. My long absence from Oxford, my total inexperience in lecturing, and the difficulties of the times appal me when I think of them, and I could doubt a choice which takes me from the tranquil harbour of Worcester into the agitated sea of Oxford. But one follows a kind of destiny which antecedents form for one.—Yours affectionately,

J. B. M.

P.S.—This is, of course, a secret at present.

To the Rev. R. W. Church.

SHOREHAM, *January* 29, 1871.

MY DEAR CHURCH,—The ultimatum arrived yesterday, though not before the announcement in the papers.

I am glad you sympathise about Ewelme. I am clear myself as to the improvement that a separation would be, and that a parish of 700 population ought not to be joined to a Professorship, thus saddling a parish of such size with perpetual non-residence, while the Professorship, too, is saddled with the perpetual burden of so large a charge. It is a different case, I think, if you are already in a parish, and do not want to give it up. There may be reasons for not desiring a break from connections already formed, and the size makes a difference, Old Shoreham being a little more than a third of Ewelme. . . . A separation was attempted the last vacancy. I do not know what the hitch was.—Yours affectionately, J. B. M.

The connection which my brother had formed with his parishioners at Old Shoreham was of a very real character. While he was thoroughly acquainted with them all, their comparatively small number admitted of his pursuing his theological studies. His wife's heart was in the parish; both were lavish of all the aids that an open hand, and, in her case, exacter knowledge of the needs of the poor in illness could bestow.

DR. PUSEY TO J. B. M.

February 7, 1871.

MY DEAR MOZLEY,—How strangely different are the times in which you return among us from those in which you left us ! Now the fight is not for fundamentals even, but as to the existence of a personal God, the living of the soul after death, or whether we have any soul at all; whether there is or can be any positive truth except as to physics, etc. I asked a physical Professor about a R. C. book on geology and the relations of physical science to faith discussed in it. "No one," he said, "thinks any longer of this; the question is wholly removed to materialism," etc., and instanced some eminent person, or persons, who was entirely happy, having satisfied himself that he had no hereafter. Another or other physicists look upon revelation as an interference with the study of physical certainties.

But we have a great battle; I for whatever time remains to me, you during, I hope, many years of vigour. It is an encouragement that the battle is so desperate. All or nothing; as when the Gospel first broke in upon heathen philosophers; and the fishermen had the victory. Will you think about that transmitted plan of the Regius Professor giving men twelve lectures, which are to crowd all theology into a fortnight. They are the bane of theological study here. Parents and young men get through and get off as cheaply as they can. But now that, if they like, candidates for orders can begin the study after moderations, there is no excuse. I do not mean that you should not, κατ' ἐξοχὴν, sign testimonials for bishops, but I think that the testimonials ought to cost men something more than a fortnight. The plan began in my day, when Bishop Lloyd had to prepare lectures in a hurry, and began that system of private lecturing. But then we had at least alternate days on which to digest what we heard, as the lectures were spread over a month. Burton, in good nature, contracted them into a fortnight. You will think about this. God be with you in all things.—Yours affectionately, E. B. PUSEY.

In the summer of 1871 we—my sister Elizabeth and myself—had the great pleasure of receiving Dr. Newman at Barrow. He was spending a few days with his sister at Derby, and the family party adjourned to Barrow-on-Trent for two days. It was a happy and memorable occasion. Full accounts of it were sent to Worcester, where my brother was still residing. He writes a long letter in reply, greatly interested, dwelling on persons of the day and events—not, however, suited for present transcription. Dr. Newman had written a note to him on the occasion to which allusion is made.

WORCESTER, *June* 29, 1871.

MY DEAR ANNE,—Newman's week at Derby and Barrow must indeed have been a curious revival of the past. It would have been difficult to find any party where the enormous chasm of intervening events could have preserved still so completely the substantial identity of feeling and character. . . . J. H. N.'s note to me was very pleasant, and just what one liked. I could not but observe the hand so strong and very like its old self. . . . Yours affectionately, J. B. M.

P.S.—We spent an evening with B. lately. He knows everybody, among others J. H. N., and has called on him sometimes at Birmingham. He knew him a little in Oxford in old times, and has tried to get him over to ——, but not succeeded. J. H. N. does not much care about meeting celebrities at breakfast.

J. B. M.'s next letter to his friend and correspondent is addressed to him under a new designation:—

TO THE DEAN OF ST. PAUL'S.

CH. CH., *November* 12, 1871.

MY DEAR DEAN,—Thank you for your congratulations on the Doctrinate. I cannot say that I particularly affect the title, but as I am presumptuous enough now to pretend, in fact, to instruct others, I cannot reasonably complain of the title of instructor. . . . Yours, J. B. M.

CH. CH., *November* 1871.

MY DEAR DEAN,—We should like very much to see your new home, but we shall hardly be able to bring it in our journey back to Shoreham this time. . . . Oxford is certainly something of a whirl with its Convocations, Congregations, and meetings of all kinds, to which we have added this term special meetings of the Divinity Professors on the subject of the Athanasian Creed, to which the Bishop has called our attention. . . .

Have you read Goldwin Smith? The epigrammatic power wonderful. He is, in his way, and with all his bitterness, still something of a prophet. He denounces, and with a moral weight and force not wholly wanting. He has a true perception of public *sin*. And the English, both Church and nation, has in him a judge who tells the truth, though savagely.—Yours affectionately, J. B. M.

In January 1872 he received the news of Mr. Scott's death, his co-editor, in days past, of the *Christian Remembrancer*. Mr. Scott had been seriously ill for some time, and accounts had reached him of his state. When last in London J. B. M. had called, but found him unable to see callers. Since his connection with the *Christian Remembrancer* was loosened, communication had naturally become very rare.

January, 1872.

DEAR ELIZABETH,—I wrote to Mrs. Scott yesterday. I have often thought that there is a curious caprice in the arrangements of life, which makes one see absolutely nothing of some with whom one has been intimate, and whose society would make a difference in life, and a great deal of others who are nothing at all to one. For twenty years I have seen hardly anything of Scott, and yet there was no reason why I should not fall in with him any day, and have an intimate conversation with him. He was thoroughly good-hearted, and a cynic with it. This is not the incongruous combination which it might seem; if well tempered, it is a good one. *The Guardian* memorial is not well done—too taken up with externals, boards, committees, meetings, and other fussinesses. There certainly was something very sterling about him, a true ring; and that in spite of various seeming levities in him. I don't think I ever knew any one that I could feel more sure about behaving quite well to one in any complication and trying test, where he could not be found out if he behaved ill. . . . I have always felt that Scott possessed a character and had several features in peculiar combination. C. remarked the other day what was quite true, that he had an affectionate manner to his friends, though there was a considerable cynical element in him. He had a gentleness in all private communications with you, whether in writing or *viva voce*. It was a contrast to some who abound in honeyed modifications of expression in print, and are always on the edge of insolence in private life. Church and myself were comparing notes. He said he had seen nothing of him for years. One thing was, he was not a man that went down into the country—[he had a house at Maidenhead, and was devoted to fishing]—and many of his friends depended entirely on visits to London for a chance of seeing him; and seeing a man in London *is* a chance, unless you make a regular appointment, which is somewhat formal, and requires antecedent arrangements. On the whole, seeing people is one of those things which look excessively easy in all prospective and all retrospective views of life, but which are difficult in the present.[1]

Heavy personal anxieties were soon to press upon my brother; in fact, could not be wholly absent from him at this time. There is something, perhaps, in the praise of routine that occurs in a letter to his brother, T. M., which forebodes change.

"There seems, indeed, to be a providential design in making routine—which must be the life of the mass—such a satisfaction and repose to the mind. Country clergymen, for example, are a happy instance of its soothing power. I confess an enormous attraction towards a routine life. There is nothing happier than life passing quietly, and one day exactly like another—at least that is my experience."

In March 1872 James speaks of past engagements at the beginning of term, where "*we* [himself and his wife] met friends," etc.; but his letters soon became reports of his wife's health—making the best of it, never speaking of danger, to the family circle—leaving it, however, to be inferred. To his friend Dean Church, writing May 30, there are some touching words giving expression to the fear of what was coming, and ending, "pray for her and for me."

In June a house was taken in the Parks, for fresher air and quiet, to which the invalid was removed under the superin-

---

[1] A postscript to this letter touches on another life ended—a life in strong contrast with that on which his thoughts had been dwelling. Our young friend, Alice Wilkinson, younger daughter of the Rev. W. F. Wilkinson, late vicar of St. Werburgh's, Derby, and at that time rector of Lutterworth, died at this date. This event led to a correspondence shortly after.

tendence of her brother, Dr. Ogle. From thence the following letter was written when the end came:—

DEREHAM HOUSE, *July* 29, 1872.

MY DEAR CHURCH,—My dear Amelia died this morning. It was sudden. She had partially recovered, as I told you, from the prostration of her long neuralgic illness; but fainting fits had just begun to come on, the result of a disordered circulation. In the second of these she died at about two o'clock this morning. You will know my state without my speaking of it. She was all in all to me. Always close to me—so affectionate, so generous, so true-hearted. I tremble when I think of what I have to go through in parting from her. May God assist me. The vista of the past rises before me, so cheered and animated by her presence. I feel that, as far as what this world can give is concerned, my life is over.—Yours affectionately,

J. B. M.

I have some scruple in giving the following letter. The reader may feel that the privacy of deep feeling has been invaded; but it conveys a lesson; and as he had, to use his own words, in accepting his office undertaken to instruct others, I venture to transcribe it:—

DEREHAM HOUSE, OXFORD, *August* 7.

MY DEAR ANNE,—One looks back now on a death and on a funeral. Such is the order of things in this world that what is so long an uncertain future, doubtful and agitating, is changed in so short a time into a retrospect. As I look back, however, I see more and more what I have lost; and what haunts me night and day is the reflection that I was not sufficiently grateful to God for the gift while I had it. It would appear almost an impossibility sometimes to realise a source of happiness while you had it, and that the loss of it was necessary to make you feel it adequately, and as it deserved to be felt. There is such a way of taking for granted what we have, and only appreciating at its full worth what we have not. It is almost the great fault of human life. It would seem that all would be well if one could only realise the happiness one had. Some do this in a great degree—Mr. Rickards did. But it is very rare; yet not to do it is a certain source of deep regret.

When I think of Amelia, her great affectionateness and generosity of character is the charm of it; but there was so much substance in her mind; power of reading, entering into what she read, ruling her household, and all business-like gifts, which do not often go with intellectual quickness. And with all her openness and freedom from reserve, some parts of her character only came out in fragments.

It was a remarkable feature of the illness—the great cheerfulness of the sick-room. It was the only place which *was* cheerful; all was gloom out of it. She gave directions about herself with great clearness and rapidity, but Rose followed her perfectly, and this of itself gave life to the scene. Then she was cheerful in talk, and liked talking, though she preferred having one at a time to talk to. She was anxious that her illness should do good to others. She thought much of death, though it was uncertain to her how long her illness might be, and whether she might not recover from some symptoms. She had very intense feelings on catching glimpses of the green and sunshine, and said to Caroline, " You do not know what it is to look on nature with death in prospect. I cannot tell you. It is indescribable."

With respect to myself, some friends who write to me say that work will ultimately be my chief consolation; but I feel that some considerable time must pass before I can work naturally. A state of conscious deprivation of so deep a kind is a great depression of all strength and activity of mind, though it is attended by thoughts, I hope, more useful to me than any activity.—Yours affectionately,[1]   J. B. M.

Many thanks to Elizabeth for her very interesting letter.

[1] Perhaps some lines from the answer to my brother's letter—an answer written under the pressure of strong feeling, but of which no word need be retracted—may serve the purpose better than any comment written after the lapse of years:—

" BARROW, *August* 9, 1872.

"MY DEAR JAMES,—I do not know that I should have written to-day but for a little message from Jemima. I had just received your interesting and

A recent page records the death of a young friend. Her mother, in writing to J. B. M. on his own loss, showed such an intelligence of sympathy as touched a chord, and led him to enter, in successive letters, upon the uses and purposes of bereavement in its more poignant aspects:—

To Mrs. WILKINSON.

OXFORD, *August* 31, 1872.

MY DEAR FRIEND,—Thank you for your kind and true sympathy with me in my great sorrow. Your own great loss enables you to feel that of another. She was, indeed, a constant source of cheerfulness and happiness to me. She never lost her youthful spirit, and the warmth and affectionateness of a youthful character, whose self-sacrifice is not a laboured effort, but always a ready and cheerful gift to others. The loss of much valued letter, of which my mind was very full, and I gave it to her to read. She returned it to me, and, with a broken voice, asked me to give her love, and to tell you you were constantly in her thoughts. She cannot but feel that your loss may some day be hers. So I judged by the depth of her sympathy. [This foreboding had its swift fulfilment; my brother John died on the 23d of October, 1872]. I think all you say of the difficulty of valuing enough blessings while we have them is an inevitable sentiment on the loss of them. . . . One satisfaction must be yours, that those intellectual qualities you dwell on as so striking in Amelia, and which made her so charming to others, were much quickened by marriage. There is no doubt that her mind advanced and gained power in her resolution to care for and enter into all that interested you, to be your companion in everything. Many most happy marriages still fail a little in this; the wife is not her husband's intellectual companion. You have the happy power to be interested in the views of native good sense wherever you see it. All women feel stimulated to think their best with you; and it was, I am sure, one of Amelia's highest sources of happiness that there were no subjects that you treated as out of her range. One feels, indeed, that a very perfect marriage of minds has been dissolved. Regrets there must be, though *I* see no cause for them, but the lasting impression must be that you made her happiness; that, I think, she would say of herself, that she had been fortunate beyond the common lot of women in her choice.

"Elizabeth is saying that you cannot have many letters of hers, she was so seldom away from you. If so, you have a loss; there was always so much in her letters, such a large range of interests, and remembering all the things that would interest her correspondent—and all so brightly told. How few have her sparkle of wit, and what a gift it is to be remembered by. People who knew her ever so little have such a keen remembrance of her. Mrs. S., with whom you spent an evening here, has been so deeply touched by her death—speaks in such fond admiring terms of her look and air."

such a one is one of those deep deprivations which one feels throughout whatever one is saying or doing.

I always thought your dear child Alice expressed in her countenance and air a very interesting character. When she was silent they spoke for her. There was an inward poetry and retiring thought in her look which raised a curiosity in any one who saw her to know what she felt, and what was in her mind. I remember in her, as a child, something of an habitual mysterious look, as one might call it, of which her later face still preserved the record; but there was no gloom in it—it was only a token of the peculiar presence of the religious sense. When such an one is physically weak it only deepens affection for her, and the care of her possesses the whole heart. The loss is all the greater and more penetrating. May you be comforted under it. My best wishes to Mary and Mr. Wilkinson.—Yours, most sincerely, J. B. MOZLEY.

This letter drew from the bereaved mother an account of her daughter's last hours—a scene most impressive, as I had heard it immediately after the event from her own and her daughter Mary's lips.

TO THE SAME.

SHOREHAM, *October* 14, 1872.

MY DEAR FRIEND,—Your letter is indeed a beautiful picture of a serene deathbed, and the consummation of a life. For it was, doubtless, the simple reflection of a life. Everything was done. There was nothing to do but to die. There is nothing that reveals a life so clearly as such a death. The shortness of the last scene does not in the least lessen the effect of it, because it is just like a word or even a look in particular and critical circumstances of life, which may tell everything in a moment. There is such a sure foundation shown in her.

I cannot but think that the peaceful image of her last years will come back upon you after a time with more of a happy than a painful feeling. There is so much to rest upon, it will bear so much dwelling on. And losses, too, change *us*, and change considerably our own standard of happiness, purifying it; so that we are able to be more cheerfully affected by these pure retrospects and reflections than we were before. We are more sensitive to chastened sources of happiness.

I am struck with your account of her good judgment, and the naturalness and facility with which she used it. I suppose it is the disorder of our minds which makes acts of judgment so difficult to us, as a good deal has to be set to rights before the judgment can act. In some—very few, I think—the judgment seems to be always ready. There must have been an order and a repose in her mind. Mere physical weakness does not create this. But peace of mind and the quiet religious temper, of course, greatly favour the judgment.

In the case of a loss that penetrates very deeply into us, what we cannot master is the kind of contradiction that death is. I might almost say the fact of death. The person is only a moment gone from us, and yet she is no more in this world. It is a kind of discord in the mind. Certainly the reign of Death in the world must be said to begin first in survivors, and in their whole state of mind, which is *their* separation from the living—living up to this moment; *their* death to *them*.

May you have your great trial gradually softened to you, and retain, without the present bitterness of the loss, all the deep satisfactions which such a child's life and death leave behind. With all kindest recollection to your husband and Mary, your very sincere friend, J. B. MOZLEY.

J. B. M. TO MRS. WILKINSON.

CH. CH., *December* 20, 1872.

MY DEAR FRIEND,—I cannot but think that that peculiar and extraordinary contact with death, which is produced by the departure of some one very dear, is part of a providence which relates to the person's life—the one who suffers the loss. I mean that it is the will of God that he or she *should* come into a remarkable experience of pain for the departure of a human soul from this world, should be made to feel the full force of regret, and thus experience the power of death, and, as it were, pass under His hands and His stroke even in this life. If we consider how many near relations and friends, for whom we feel affection, pass away from this world, and we mourn them, but do not feel that settled hold of a deep regret which affects our whole minds—if we consider, I say, how much death takes place near us without bringing us into any deep inward contact with it, and making us feel the whole fact of the dispensation of death under which we live, we see a peculiar reason why, upon some special occasion, this extraordinary experience should be imparted to us.

Persons cannot perhaps fully account in *all* cases for the effect of a death upon them; in some they can; but in others they might ask themselves why there has been so remarkable an effect in this case, and they might not be able to satisfy themselves wholly. But even when we can, there yet seems to be a supplementary reason for the deep penetrating kind of regrets when they do come, in the thought that it is the will of God that we should at one time or another come into contact with the full reality of that dispensation of death under which He has been pleased to place us.

In no part of God's providence does the wisdom of its balance appear more strikingly, I think, than in connection with the fact of Death. When I say so many deaths take place, even in our own near circle, without strongly—I mean in comparison—disturbing us, I do not say it in the sense of blame. The business of life requires that, accompanied with all seriousness, there must be an easy natural recovery from these losses generally, even in our own circle of relationship. It is a part of providence that it should be so. But that seems to be so much the more reason for special visitations of sorrow, when they come. And these deep experiences of loss and of a departure, when they are imparted, may rectify a defect which may attach to our ordinary comparative immunity from the bitter kind of grief. Though even to these visitations there is a law of relief, and providence softens them when they have answered their purpose.

I suggest this consideration to you, as so great a sufferer from the regret for one departed, because it has a relieving tendency to feel that there is a purpose answered by any visitation we are under, to which we can give some distinctness and definiteness, and that we connect our grief with something special in the scope of God's providence for us, and bring it into clearer harmony with His plan of education for us. . . . Your most sincere friend, J. B. M.

After bereavement, or indeed any great absorbing trial, the power of reading—of taking an interest in books—is a step many have welcomed. The first book that engages their attention, after a long, troubled interval, is invested with an interest that it could hardly otherwise have won, and takes a stand in the memory as an event. With the opening of a new year my brother's correspondence shows that this step had been taken. He writes of books :—

TO HIS SISTER.

January 9, 1873.

The revival of the Hares, after so long a break, is curious, and says a good deal for the vigour of the family. I take to the book. I have only read the first volume. Maria Leycester is attractive in character and in style. In the early portrait I thought I detected a certain likeness to Jane; the hair of a certain date gives, perhaps, or aids a resemblance. It was village life and aristocratical clerical life put before one rather suddenly, as a re-awakened scene, and without any disagreeable features or pretensions to excite one's hostility. It was curious to think of her as Stanley's aunt.

The Hares were men of conversation, and won their ground by that power—wonderful life, vivacity, and affectionateness. Julius died just before I came into this diocese, otherwise he would have been my archdeacon. . . . His vicarage was filled with persons from London and the literary world : Bunsen often there—a sort of open house kept; he talking endlessly, and bringing out all his reading. I heard Augustus preach in New College Chapel, on Trinity Sunday, on my first visit to Oxford, when I went up to stand for Corpus. I remember his peculiarity of voice, and also the general quality of his sermon; its eloquent philosophical language, which I recollect inspired me with a sort of ambition. The subject was that of the day—the incomprehensible nature of the Deity.

We have just been passing through a time of the departure of great names. Lytton Bulwer recalls one's early days. I remember so well Mrs. W. describing him as she saw him from a house window, in a street procession at the Lincoln election. The very *beau-idéal* of youthful glory and intellect, and his costume the quintessence of fashion, his manners superlative in their unruffled ease and condescendingness. It was the absolute perfection of a certain kind of article. I was always, however, stopped in his novels by the want of humour. It is certainly a great want. And why so perfect a man should be without it is a mystery, and, what is worse, he tries, and fails. I have been told there is some in *My Novel*.

The news about Pusey was at first very alarming, and even now the idea of a vicinity to danger has not passed away. His loss would be a great event. He is one of those fulcrums and stays about which people gather. His departure would add to the unrestraint and disorder of the present state of things.—Yours affectionately, J. B. M.

To Mrs. Wilkinson.

Shoreham, *January* 31, 1873.

My dear Friend,— ... I remember when our President, Dr. Routh, died, making the observation to myself that one was more surprised at the death of old persons than at the death of young ones. I mean that, though the laws of nature prepare one for it, when it actually takes place it is more of a downfall, and what one may call a crash, than the younger death is. There is so much more fabric to fall down. A long life occupies so much more space in our minds; it is a large building which has gathered up into itself a quantity of material. When it falls there is so much more actual shock to our mental senses, it is so *great* a departure. I compare it, of course, to a shorter life in the same relation to us; it may be only that of a public man, or a member of the same society with us. The old man does, by his very length of life, root himself in us, so that the longer he lives, the longer, we think, he must live; and when he dies it is a kind of violence to us.

I do not know whether you at all recognise this aspect of the departure of a long life, or whether you partake of the impression. I recollect I had it very strongly when the whole College, with all its train of past generations that survived, followed the old President to the grave. The majestic music and solemn wailings of the choir seemed to mourn over some great edifice that had fallen, and left a vast void, which looked quite strange and unaccountable to one.

But what I want to say now is that intimacy, sympathy, constant care for another, constant affectionate observation of another, seem to have the effect of length of time in the deep root they give to a life within your own mind. The object of such watchings and tendings, so much thought and concern, fills so much space in your mind, that if it goes, there is a vast empty space, which appals by its strangeness.

It may be short in years, but it is a long life in the affections, in the quantity of care, acts of love, wishes, hopes it has called forth, the amount of mind in you it has exercised; what you have done reacts upon you, and forms an impress which stays, and which will stay, though there is no reason why it should not survive the painful stage, and enter upon a calm and harmonious one, when the great discord will cease.—Your very sincere friend, J. B. MOZLEY.

TO HIS SISTER.

March 28, 1873.

Your copy of *Middlemarch* was a great treat—so much character and humour in it. The satirical vein has, I think, grown upon the author; and I suppose it is in its nature to do so. She has a fine, or intended to be fine, character or two, and all the rest is for the purpose of showing up. She is certainly *au fait* at the whole vulgar side of the middle classes—all their customs of mind and thought, points of view, their sense of grievance, retaliations, etc. Especially does she take off their flatnesses and modes of speaking about subjects above them, literature, poetry, etc.; as, for example, Mr. Borthrop Trumbull, who is a clever fellow in his *own* department. She quite soars in flatness; and when one thinks she has got as far as can be reached, ascends to celestial summits.

I observe she has a favourite in a certain rather old-fashioned clerical character, as Mr. Cadwallader and Mr. Farebrother. She must have known them, and come across clergy in her youth. Mr. Brookes is excellent, and new. But Casaubon appears the most studied character. It is capital; all harmonises;—the sort of refinement he has, and his dulness and pitiable incarceration in his labyrinth and winding-stairs, unable to get out of the sepulchre in which he lives. Then the spitefulness of the latent sort, occasionally creeping out of its hole; and his inability to receive sympathy, and total incongruity to Dorothea gradually coming out; and his inward protest at the want of appreciation of him, and suspicion that the Archdeacon had not read his pamphlet. Altogether it is quite a whole, and it is new. As a piece of satire, however, it comes out rather late, as learning is now almost abandoned; and if a man begins to suspect he is getting into the mud, and to stick anywhere, he rushes out as quick as he can. Dorothea is striking in this point of view, that she is of the perfect type, and yet attractive, which perfect characters so very seldom are—generally being instances of the law that, humanly speaking, perfection is dry, and that you want faults to be interesting. And it is remarkable that she manages to make the character without the character saying much, as Dorothea is not much before us as a speaker. I must say, however, that she spoils Dorothea a good deal, if not degrades her from her high place, by her after-treatment of her, making her fall in love with what Mrs. Cadwallader very justly calls the Italian boy with white mice. For, although she makes him shake his hair and coruscate with electric sparks, Mrs. C.'s view of him prevails. He is too conceited and impudent a young fellow to be fastened on to Dorothea. It shows a *want* in the writer's mind. I take to Mrs. Cadwallader, and she is done to the life, but I daresay one likes her better in a novel than one would have done in reality. . . . All satirists, of course, work in the direction of Christian doctrine by the support they give to the doctrine of Original Sin—making a sort of meanness and badness a law of society. I have made this the subject of one of my lectures, but it is of the very roughest workmanship. Miss Evans's pictures will only end in aiding the Evidences of Christian doctrine, much as she may protest against it. I think her enmity to the middle classes must be partly from the fixity of their belief; being the class of all society least open to the disturbing force of new ideas whether of belief or morals.

TO THE DEAN OF ST. PAUL'S.

June 13, 1873.

I can hardly wish you too quickly over the convalescent state—the becoming well again—as it is, I think, a singularly enjoyable bit of life—far more than being actually well and vulgarly strong. I remember recovering from a fever a great many years ago, which took some two or three months; and there certainly was a sensation of life, and an extreme susceptibility to all natural enjoyments of mind and body, which one has not in regular health. . . . I see you are in the middle of the Cathedral reform subject. I thought Goulburn's pamphlet took the proper line, but he appeared to assume the existence of a strong movement in the direction of a coarser change, with official work and diocesan department to manage; in other words, to help the Bishops. The age seems to be quite set in this line, and not to be able to trust work of a less tangible kind. They will get a good deal of professional activity, but the whole will be a fall for the English Church.—Yours affectionately, J. B. M.

TO MRS. WILKINSON.

CH. CH., *August* 30, 1873.

MY DEAR FRIEND,— . . . It is strange to me to think it is a year since the great change in my life. I used to count the weeks, and feel that I had done a great deal when I had got over so many. But Time makes one feel one is in a machine which does not stop in joy or grief.

After dwelling on some points in his friend's letter—changes and losses of friends, and speaking of similar losses in his own recent experiences—Hope Scott and others—he ends them with :—

And Henry Wilberforce, whom I knew so well. There was a thorough natural force and brilliancy in his wit which I never heard equalled; but I suppose he lacked the power of work—a defect which comes out in subsequent life. Copleston, however, when Provost of Oriel, put him above both his brothers.

I quite enter into your remarks upon memory, and its peculiar selection of scenes and occurrences for keeping its hold of, which one cannot always fully account for. But they are very valuable when they are connected with old friends and their tone and character and conversation. They constitute a stock of internal imagery which, in certain states of mind, is very satisfying and soothing. But memory is full of peculiar feats. I was reminded of a strong impress of memory myself the other day, at the ceremonial at Keble College. I saw Miss Yonge the authoress once, when she was fifteen. It so happened I had always remembered her face, but I never saw her again till a week ago; so I had the recollected face and the seen face in clear comparison. And though, of course, time must alter, as I need not say, the face came very well out of the trial.

Edith is a very lively and agreeable niece, and she has plenty of good sense too. She leaves Oxford in a few days now, as soon as her father and mother [Mr. and Mrs. Bonamy Price], whose house she and her husband now occupy, return from their Eastern travels. The girls [his nieces by marriage] have been a great comfort to me all along, and just that sort of interest which is most suitable.—With all kind remembrances, yours most sincerely, J. B. MOZLEY.

TO THE DEAN OF ST. PAUL'S.

CH. CH., *December* 1, 1873.

... The principal event of the term, the Union dinner, I can give no account of, as I had not come up then, but I have heard

from Heurtley the whole account of his treatment by the
Committee, which seems to have been of the very obvious bamboozling kind. Lord Salisbury did the best thing that could
be done on the occasion—insisting on Archbishop Manning
sitting before him; so that a friendly contest of pushing, or
something like it, ensued, which was of course turning the
whole thing into a joke, and covering the degradation of the
Bishops. There has been nothing memorable since, except the
Sunday of Pusey and Stanley. Stanley spoke against *party*
in religion—a daring thing for him to do; for I think of all
men in the world he most uniformly moulds all his statements
about men and things to his own public religious ends. So in
this sermon he called F. Robertson, of Brighton, the greatest
preacher of this century!—a most glaringly party pedestal to
put Robertson upon; done simply to raise his own party by
something which he had at his command—a stroke of praise.—
Yours affectionately, J. B. M.

At this time his nephew, H. W. Mozley, was bringing out
a translation of Dante's *Inferno*, in terza-rima, in the *Monthly
Packet*.

To his Sister.

January 19, 1874.

From my small knowledge of Dante's translators, I should
say that Harry's translation has its decided points of superiority over others. It seems to me the genuine Dantean verve
comes up sometimes more faithfully in it than in any other
translations I have read. The too-constant penultimate rhymes
are perhaps a defect which could not be guarded against, and
which must be taken as included in the difficulty of the original
condition. It is some twenty years since I looked into the
Inferno in the original, but I find the translation often brings
back my first fresh acquaintance with Dante—the keen pictorial outline which the descriptions and similes have so well
preserved.

The Dantean devils are an extraordinary difference from the

Miltonic; but in estimating the magnitude of this difference we must remember that Dante does not describe Satan, or make him speak. I wonder how he would have done it. I think Satan is at the bottom of the great pit, but entirely dumb and stationary. But his devils are the contemptible ones of the Middle Ages. This translation gives them very faithfully and vividly. There is a dreadful emptiness and void in them, and a misery to which cruelty appears the only sedative, and they enjoy a horrible momentary glee while they torture somebody; but they pay for it by a frightful, tormenting, restless vacuity immediately afterwards. There is, however, a sort of humour about them, and a gregariousness which has something social about it, and a kind of obedience to their own authorities.

I hope Harry will publish as a whole; the work will tell more than it does coming out in bits, and it will be a challenge to criticism, which he need not, I think, be afraid of.—Yours affectionately, J. B. M.

To his sister he describes a friend endowed with what he calls a mental physique; that is, gifted with that conversational power from which, all his life, he derived so much pleasure as a listener:—

" She was a remarkable specimen of a person endowed with a mental physique which is something between the world of bodily perfections and mental; that is, it has great gifts of description and imagination, and strength to use them. She could not but be a conspicuous figure in any circle in which she took part. But her sphere of talk was human life. There she was at home, in its domestic points, vicissitudes, and character. One always seemed to be listening to some one who had the threads of history in her hands. She could manage plots and unwind them, and there was a moral tone in her dramas. Such a person accompanies the train of events with which she is concerned like an interpreter—explaining them to outside spectators, who see them with only dim, confused eyes. Indeed, how very meagrely do the mass of people see what goes on around them—in a scattered way, just the bits as they happen, but they cannot put them together. A person cannot fulfil such a position as this without an extraordinary ability to take interest in people around. It is a kind of life led in sympathy with all that happens. How very few care enough about others to spend their breath upon them. . . . She was charged with something to which she gave life, language, and energy; but what work it would have been to anybody but her!"

To his Sister.

July 18, 1874.

I have made a beginning of Patteson. Perhaps more letters are given than is necessary to find out what he is, and how much stuff he has in him. . . . He is certainly a worker, and quick at his work. As near as I can make out, he acquired in one year the Maori language and the art of navigation,—the former enough to preach a sermon, and the latter sufficient to enable him to officiate as captain of a ship in a storm. I confess this, to my mind, raises a high notion of his powers of work. With respect to the Maori sermon, the auditors might perhaps interpose with criticisms, but the feat of navigation is its own evidence. His sense of humour and the picturesque comes out certainly most in contact with savage nature, so as to intimate some secret impulse which took him out there; as, for example, his description of the cliffs of Valua, and the swarming natives clustering upon them, and the curious idea it was to him to find himself "walking arm in arm with a Nongone gentleman stark naked," asking him questions about various ladies, mutual acquaintances. . . .

I read *Unawares* as I came up [a book I had given him to read on a journey]. There is a great deal of good, lively, pleasant description in it, especially of French towns, and very characteristic. Deshoulières is well done, his awkwardness and goodness; and Therese is made interesting by a few touches. The plot is too much gathered up into a knot at the end, and would bear more expansion. . . . Miss Peard's little moral

remarks are very good and striking sometimes.—Yours affectionately,
J. B. M.

To the Dean of St. Paul's.

Ch. Ch., *November* 6, 1874.

My dear Church,—I have to forward to you the particular request of the University Missionary Association, that you would undertake the sermon on the Day of Intercession, which will be this year St. Andrew's Day. . . . This is a new association, set up last term. It is intended to add to the ordinary missionary objects some encouragement of literary and intellectual work and thought, inquiring into the character of native races, attention to language, making acquaintance with natives who show a wish to acquaint themselves with us—rather vague and dim at present, but what may work up into something useful. We have a committee which meets from time to time; we collect books, magazines, native papers, etc., and hope to create an interest in the subject in under-graduates. The Bishop of Zanzibar, as he is to be, is here now, and is taking out one good man—James of Oriel, nephew of the late Bishop Wilberforce. So the Provost resigns. It is quite an historical fact. At present he appears as active as ever, and he has only a prospective regard to his health. . . . Yours affectionately,
J. B. M.

To the Rev. Francis A. Faber.

Old Shoreham, *January* 1875.

My dear Faber,— . . . What a kettle of fish this Archbishop's Bill is! In its present shape I do not see any particular harm in it, or any very striking advantage either. Whatever could have given the Bishops any unfair power seems to have been taken out of the Bill. Roundell Palmer has come out in a manner that suits him—honest and straightforward. I could not but sympathise with his letter, which seemed to me substantially true. One hardly knows what is to become of it all. And Gladstone's resolutions are a smasher. I think what provokes Gladstone is the apparently retrogressive character of the bill, bringing an Act of Parliament again to help the Church. The thing looks obsolete to him.

I find the term at Oxford gets fuller of work. There is so much collateral work of all kinds in which you must join. New societies are set up. We established last term a University Association, which I hope will do good. It aims at collecting a missionary library, and encouraging the residence of natives in the University. . . . Church, at St. Paul's, is in a difficulty with his plan of ornamentation—everything so full of obstructions. Stanley preached twice last term. I thought his tone rather modified and subdued by Burgon's opposition, though it was not successful. He is somewhat tamed, and, in taming him, B. has taken some spirit out of him. Kindest remembrance to Mrs. Faber.—Yours affectionately,

J. B. MOZLEY.

On some personal ground, an old letter having been sent to him, which happened to contain a spirited account of a party of Clarkson's friends discussing the *Life of Wilberforce*, just published by his sons, he writes :—

TO HIS SISTER.

January 19, 1875.

It was quite a treat to read a letter of Mrs. Wayland's. Such perfection of statement, the thought so full and so clear. I always feel proud of her good opinion, and should have regarded it as a great advantage if she had lived longer to act her friendly part. I remember the Clarkson dispute, and this very letter, and the whole impression it made. I think it may be called a permanent impression. For, great man as one of the Wilberforces was, and all of them were superior, there was a certain tendency to insolence in them. The two elder were alone concerned in the publication of the Memoirs. How strange it should be such a failure !

What a transition in the material of public interest ! Gladstone's abdication, then his *Quarterly* article, and the Pope's scurrility ; J. H. N.,[1] etc. etc. Theology certainly is master of

[1] His letter to the Duke of Norfolk, in answer to Mr. Gladstone's "Political Expostulation," entitled, *The Vatican Decrees.*

the scene. Most amusing the articles in *The Times*, especially the one to-day. It is quite a true view of the Pope's style and its origin, and so naturally introduced, and travel made use of. It must have an effect, the head of the Church being brought in to receive such a very rough reception. It must tend to loosen the anchorage of men's ideas.

As for what is to become of Gladstone in politics, it is beyond conjecture. One cannot believe he can sink. He continues in Parliament. I can fancy it ending in a higher position than any he has yet had; he seems to have such elasticity and spring. It must be immensely disagreeable to be Premier (on his own side) under his exclusion. Altogether it is a most singular posture of affairs. The ordinary Liberal statesmen do seem conventional figures compared with Gladstone. . . . Yours affectionately, J. B. M.

To his Sister.

Ch. Ch., *March* 6, 1875.

I saw something of a remarkable girl before I left Shoreham—a daughter of an old friend of Amelia's and mine; I daresay you have heard A. talk of her. The daughter was on her death-bed when I came up at Christmas, having been seized with rheumatic fever, and then with galloping consumption. Everything about her was full of sadness, except herself. She was so natural, so bright, so courageous; it was quite a marvel. I had seen nothing of her for some years, as she had been out at place, and not fine places at all; but she had shot up remarkably. She talked well, had quite a *style*, a peculiarly light touch of everything, and I should almost say elegant; quite a lady in manners, though talking always about things within her sphere. She had ideas—at least I call it thus—getting up in bed to look at the setting sun. She saw quite the proper joke in her brother George nursing his baby. You could not have supposed that anything was impending over her. Yet she saw her weakness growing, and faced all the symptoms of approaching death. She just took up the glass of water on her table, and, looking significantly, said: "It's very heavy." It was the most vivid way of describing weakness in its effects. She had a striking thankfulness about every little thing. It seemed a constant happiness to her. One remembers the expression: "The incense-breathing morn;" there was quite a fragrance in her gratitude. It was like music, every expression of her feelings was so clear. I have not given her name—Louisa Burtenshaw. She was only eighteen.

I have had to entertain a deputation from Liverpool, who came up to appeal to the youth of the University. They want men [missionaries]; money they have, and are ready to supply salaries liberally. Espin, Chancellor of the Diocese, headed them, and spoke at a public meeting. Five young men called and offered themselves—very well as a first-fruits. Two laymen were of the party, pleasant, gentlemanly men, with interests of the highest sort. . . . Yours affectionately,   J. B. M.

It may be remarked, the strong hold the thought of death and its approaches had always had upon my brother, the feeling of equality the thought dwelt upon inspired, and how this feeling gained depth as years went on. The following notes to the dying girl have been preserved by her mother. They show how little directly didactic his turn of mind was, how ready he was to feel himself a learner in the presence of one close on the portals of the unseen.

To LOUISA BURTENSHAW.

February 6, 1875.

MY DEAR LOUISA,—You know we agreed that people might think of one another a great deal, though they might be a long way off. So I write these few lines only to say that I have been thinking much of you. I saw with what sweetness of mind, with what religious courage, with what faith and trust in God you took your great trial. It is the same now, and therefore it is that your peace continues, as you now send me word. And so it will continue; God will ever watch over you to give you happy and good thoughts. "The Shepherd calleth

His own sheep by name, and He goeth before them, and the sheep follow Him; for they know His voice."

Good-bye, and remember me in your prayers, as I always do you in mine.   J. B. M.

Again:—

... I write to you only to let you know how I have you in my thoughts. I like writing to you, for while you are before me, you impart something of your own spirit. You show how God has freed you from gloom and fear, and what compensation He has given for thus early calling you. ... I follow you through your days of restlessness. What experience you have of illness! It came upon you all at once; yet your spirit rose. You knew that in your trial God had given you something to do, and that you could do it, and take everything as coming from a God of Love. Close to my heart is the prayer that you may be carried safe through these last few days of trial into a world of rest.   J. B. M.

In the spring of 1875 I visited my brother at Christ Church—a happy visit. I used the opportunity to press on him the publication of his University Sermons, going into particulars, calculations, etc., in order to engage his interest in the idea. My sister Fanny, who was earnest on the point, writes: "If you can persuade James to publish his sermons you will have done a good work in going to Oxford." This is mentioned to account for his subsequent revival of the point under a change of circumstances.

At this time my brother's Graduate Class, for whom the lectures on the Old Testament were composed, was meeting at his own house—lectures read by members of the class alternating with his own. He took very great pleasure in this class, speaking with strong regard of its members, and forming high hopes of their future, who in their turn showed their appreciation. "James testifies," says one letter, "to the fixity of purpose in Mr. Wordsworth; inexorable in keeping up the meetings through all the distractions of this term."[1]

From Shoreham he paid a short visit to Mrs. Rickards, now settled at Bury St. Edmunds.

TO HIS SISTER.

August 2, 1875.

I had three active talking days with Mrs. Rickards, from Saturday afternoon till Tuesday noon. She was full of mental activity, though slightly impaired bodily, having taken to a chair—calling and receiving calls. She keeps up her connection with her old neighbourhood. . . . Mrs. Rickards' establishment is a remarkable one, as you know, containing one partial lunatic, whom she has had to conquer, and has done it very successfully. She [the lunatic] seems well now, only showing some vestiges of her complaint, in a suppressed dislike of Mrs. Rickards, and also of her sister, the chief servant, but otherwise behaving admirably. . . . I am glad to

[1] The reader will be interested to know the names of some who attended the Graduate Class during the years 1874-1875. The following list has been sent to the Editor:—

R. S. Copleston, Fellow of St. John's College, now Bishop of Colombo.
L. G. Mylne, Tutor of Keble College, now Bishop of Bombay.
E. S. Talbot, Warden of Keble College.
H. S. Holland, Senior Student of Christ Church, now Canon of St. Paul's.
J. Wordsworth, Tutor of Brasenose College, now Oriel Professor of Exegesis.
M. Creighton, Fellow of Merton College, now Professor of Ecclesiastical History at Cambridge.
A. H. D. Acland, Lecturer of Keble College, now Senior Student of Ch. Ch.
J. R. Illingworth, Fellow of Jesus College, now Vicar of Longworth.
F. J. Jayne, Tutor of Keble College, now Principal of St. David's College, Lampeter.
W. Lock, Fellow of Magdalen College, and Tutor of Keble College.
A. C. Madan, Senior Student of Ch. Ch.
R. C. Moberly, Senior Student of Ch. Ch., now Vicar of Great Budworth.
F. Paget, Senior Student of Ch. Ch., now Rector of Bromsgrove.
W. T. Richmond, Lecturer at Keble College, now Warden of Trinity College, Glenalmond.
J. W. Stanbridge, Fellow of St. John's College, now Rector of Bainton.
E. D. Whitmarsh, D.C.L., St. John's College.

have possessed myself of Jemima's work, which is most suitable for our own Sunday wants, and such a fit remembrance of Jemima, and of the quantity of delightful playing which I have heard from her. . . . I shall try to see my friend Faber on Friday, whom I have not seen for some time. . . . Yours affectionately,
J. B. M.

One of the charms of Old Shoreham to my brother was the Downs. The following letter relates to a characteristic of such scenery :—

To his Sister Elizabeth.

September 13, 1875.

My dear Elizabeth,—I must confess it is a long time to go back to attempt to renew the subject of a very small literary conflict which I once had with you. So much so, that I may appear guilty of breaking all the statutes of limitation that ever were framed. Nevertheless, I will state that, I think, about ten years ago, you disputed an allusion of mine to a poetical fact that skylarks enjoyed the title of "Drunken," bestowed upon them in token of their elevated and merry style of singing. I do not know whether it was not taking advantage of such a beautiful extravaganza to insinuate a motive. However, I understood you to doubt the fact that the epithet had been applied. I had an idea that it must be Shelley or Tennyson; it was not in either, and curiously, when he was so obvious a poet to try, I didn't go to Wordsworth. The other day I turned upon his poem to the Lark [1] by mere accident, and saw the veritable epithet, with a capital D., vol. ii. p. 29. The Downs are much favoured with the inspiration of the lark, which accounts for their place in poetry having met with such attention on my part.

In November 1875, during my brother's residence at Christ Church, came the shock of his seizure, which he at once recognised for what it was. He did not lose consciousness, and told the attendant who had been waiting on him at break-

---

[1] The poem beginning "Up with me ! up with me into the clouds !"

fast, and was now robing him, not to be frightened, and that he must have a doctor. The details of illness are not in place here. All that care and tenderness on the part of those around him, and his own patience and submission could do to sustain him under the trial, was done. He was open to every alleviation, though deeply aware of the nature of the attack, and what might be its consequences: still not without cheering hope of recovery as time went on and he gained strength. He now decided, unprompted, to bring out his University Sermons, and early in December wrote to Messrs. Rivington on the subject, saying that his sister would carry on the correspondence with them, of course under his direction. As the University Sermons had undergone his own careful scrutiny, there was no presumption in undertaking such a charge—one most welcome on its own account.

My two youngest sisters, who were with him by turns at this early stage, wrote constant reports, from which I gather notices of the interests that occupied him in the progress of his recovery from the immediate consequences of what was called a slight seizure. Books were, of course, the great resource—sermons and religious books, poetry, and travels which carried his thoughts to remote periods of the world's history: —his approval often varied by clear and pungent criticism of style. Still jealous of looseness and vagueness, " he protests against the clumsiness of construction in much modern poetry: —'a way always to be found; there was a path, but such labour to find it!' Enthusiasm for Gray :—' the ideas firmly welded together like iron.'"

When he was sufficiently recovered for drives and walks, my sister Elizabeth wrote : "He goes pretty often by Littlemore, but it depresses him. He admits he cannot get over the gloomy feeling it and the times it represents to him give him. He sees more light-hearted natures find pleasure in recollections he cannot find. But there is clearly something in the 'rent and chasm' of that time that is dreary to him still." In reporting a visit from his brother Arthur, which he enjoyed, she adds, " It was only general talk : James is of so reserved a nature that only under the greatest pressure can he go beneath the surface." But at times, and as time went on, this reserve gave way, as the following touching letter proves :—

CH. CH., *February* 16, 1876.

MY DEAR CHURCH,—I hear rumours of your coming down. I shall be very glad if the promise is fulfilled. . . .

As for myself, you may perhaps know that I am repaired externally ; but I need not tell you, who are so well up to physical cases, that the outward part of the case here is but a small part of the whole, and that the effect on the brain does not wholly cease with the outward result. I am suffering much from the effect on my mind, and I am told everywhere that is the hardest thing to remedy. At the same time, bodily exercise is something, and I am exhorted to continue it, but the exercise cannot continue to any extent until the bodily power is strengthened and developed. My best wishes for yourself and all yours. I know you have your troubles. May they all issue in the best. As for me, pray for me in my deep weakness.—Ever, my dear Church, yours affectionately,

J. B. M.

My love to your dear wife. Remember me with all the affection of the past to Lord and Lady Blachford.

There lie before me confidential reports of conversations, showing that he was able to speak of the subjects occupying his thoughts; among which was the unbelief of the day. " There ought to be a sermon preached on the nature of God." " With lowered voice and look of horror he spoke of ——'s absolute disbelief; of his assertion that there was no God; of the sort of men Mr. C. meets, who are at the bottom unbelievers ; of the state of opinion in Oxford—his mind, no doubt, dwelling on arguments to meet this scepticism, and on the task so congenial laid on him by his office." Again the heads of another conversation are given:—" The instinctive necessity in our nature for a Cause—a great moral Cause;" " The great evidence that this instinct is;" " The overwhelming nature of the idea of God;" " The demands for verifying evidence impossible to supply;" " The faith that does without it the essential test of Christianity;" " St. Paul, his intellect, and strong sense." Again, a few days later, " The trial of illness;" " The sense of the presence of God the great thing to obtain, such as holy men have felt;" " The importance of attending to the first stirrings of conscience;" " Allusion to trials in early life;" " The attraction of our Lord's teaching—the crowds that followed Him—the power and originality of that teaching."

The notes go on:—" I had been playing hymns to myself, the others being at Cathedral. He wanted me to go on. He spoke of the Morning Hymn, which had additionally struck him as taking all duties, whether simple and daily, or difficult and critical, as being only the obvious duties of the day." " I like," the writer adds, " to remember and put down what he says, when it is evidently the result of fresh thought and perhaps fresh circumstances. I went into his room just now. He was deep in cogitation about the state of belief in Spain,—with *Untrodden Spain* in his hand; and he entered upon the subject for some time, till I was afraid of such thoughts in a morning, which is never his best time." Again:—" I have had a long talk with him, a long religious talk, partly on the Psalms." Such touches of conversation cannot be pursued into those more intimate confidences to which they sometimes led. Only, perhaps, it is well some indication should be given that his mind was still engaged upon those great subjects which had so long occupied his pen.

In January 1876, Mr. Wordsworth, at my brother's request, undertook to be his deputy till he should be able to deliver his own lectures, which he hoped to be able to do—" and he had asked Dr. Jackson before he expressed this hope "—by the summer term. Other thoughts had been in my brother's mind, but having secured the aid of a definite deputy, and one so eminently fitted for that post, his mind was reconciled, and as he gained strength, the hope of returning to the duties of his office came with a sense of reviving power.

Having decided to try change of air and scene, he went early in March to St. Leonard's, where he remained for some months. Before leaving Oxford he wrote to Dr. Pusey taking leave. Some words of the note remained in my sister's memory: " Not knowing in what condition he may return, he asked for his—Dr. Pusey's—prayers, sending his love to ' Liddon, Bright, and King.' ' Under a deep sense of unworthiness I feel that none can suffer without benefit under the Divine rod.'" To this note he received the following reply :—

DR. PUSEY TO J. B. M.

CH. CH.

MY DEAR MOZLEY,—I have not called at your lodgings, knowing that you have to keep quiet. I pray God that we may have you back again in tolerable health. But it must be so difficult for your very active brain to be still; and your work is so unlike mine, of which so much is quiet reading, whereas yours is all thinking, I suppose.

I often think of those young days of yours, when you were in this house, and your brain seemed to me the most active I had ever seen.

It must be a great self-denial to keep it still. Yet, as you feel, it is something to have to give up to our Father's will, to use or not use it, as He will.

We miss its use much in the battle with unbelief; but the quiet yielding of your strong brain to be kept inactive, so long as it shall seem good to Him, may impress those whom you wish to impress more than its active use.

I will not fail to remember you, as you, I hope, will me.

I will give your message to Liddon, Bright, and King.

May God preserve your going out and coming in, until the coming in where there is no going out, in life everlasting.—
Yours affectionately,   E. B. PUSEY.

ASH-WEDNESDAY, *March* 1, 1876.

As has been said, my brother had delayed publishing his sermons in spite of considerable pressure; but it must be granted that the time he at length chose was happy for himself. While he could produce such good work, his office was well represented; and the interest of carrying his two volumes —the University Sermons and the Old Testament Lectures— through the press was an incalculable alleviation, and benefit to his spirits during the period of suspended labour. There was always the work and bustle of proofs going on. Each morning the post brought business for the day—constant employment for judgment and memory. He might feel himself never less laid aside. Everything was done under his eye and direction. Books of reference were hunted through, to verify some statement or quotation, by able though unaccustomed heads and hands, whose pleasure it was to work under his indispensable orders. His study was a busy scene. And when the time came for the first of these volumes to see the light, the unanimous voice of interest and approval, the homage to his powers, might have upset a less resolute humility. What his sister Elizabeth on one occasion wrote of him was true throughout: "James certainly succeeds in keeping hold of his humility in spite of the ovations he receives; and in speculating on the capacity for praise that some have, he really seems to remove it from himself and withdraw from all personal relations to it."

I was with him at St. Leonard's when the sermons came out, and well recall going into his room with a letter Mrs. Johnson had received from Lord Blachford, written on the first warmth of a rapid perusal. My brother was sitting alone and unoccupied; except by his own thoughts, which must often have been sad ones, however resigned he was to the dispensation under which he was suffering. His first words, in being told the subject of the letter, were to the effect that "he would say they reminded him of Newman;" and so it proved, for the letter has this sentence: "It is no bad compliment to say that I feel Bishop Butler and Newman in them. The dry wit of Butler, the rich expansion of Newman, and the searching judgment of both:" the letter going to that discrimination and selection so interesting to an author. "I think the four that took hold of me were, 'The Pharisees,' 'The Reversal of Human Judgment,' 'Duty to Equals,' and 'Strength of Wishes,' though a second reading might change this order." It was the greater pleasure, to those near my brother, to report the general consent of warm approval, whether from private letters or the press, from the impossibility, as there seemed, of awaking in him any vanity of authorship. He was always critical of his own work as though he had an ideal he had never reached. He had to be persuaded into the due amount of satisfaction. His real lasting pleasure in his friends' praise was because it came from them.

On returning to my own home, soon after the publication of the sermons, he wrote to me of a letter he had received from Mr. Gladstone, whose warmth of praise had reached him earlier through friends.

TO HIS SISTER.

May, 1876.

Gladstone's letter is pleasant; in his usual style. He keeps it up with epistolary naturalness. Considering he knows so well that everybody places such a value on his letters, his humility is a real merit, and deserves a reward, which it does not always do.

The reception of his sermons by the press was another enlivening feature of the time. He writes to a sister:—

To F. M.

SHOREHAM, *July* 28, 1876.

I have to thank my reviewers not only for their complimentary papers, but for the solidity of them. This one [from the *John Bull*] is well worked up upon a solid bottom. It has done justice to the pains taken with the argument. I am glad to see a theological sermon, more especially, well and accurately treated, and attention called to the argumentative points.

Nor was the interest of bringing out his volume confined to its first reception. My brother was not unfamiliar with warm praise from a select circle of readers, but he had not been led by the wide experience of those best informed to expect a large demand for a book of sermons. It would perhaps seem to him more to be expected that a few should appreciate warmly than that his work should gain general acceptance; so that there was a pleasant surprise at the early call for a second edition. The book had been published in May, and on July 27 he writes to me "amused" by Messrs. Rivington's *regret* that they cannot send a copy of the first edition (" not a single copy of the first edition of your University Sermons remaining") which he had written for; having a strong preference for octavo over the modern crown octavo form.

The following letter from Dr. Liddon, gratifying from its tone of warm appreciation, would also be valued for its testimony to the good work emanating from the Divinity Chair which he filled :—

DR. LIDDON'S LETTER.

May 12, 1876.

MY DEAR MOZLEY,—I have been reading your recently published volume of sermons, and cannot help writing to say how grateful I am to you for publishing them, and how sure I am that this will be a very general feeling in Oxford. If it were not unfeeling to do so, I should also like to say that I can hardly regret the circumstances which have resulted in their publication, so very sure am I that they will do a great deal of good, and will show that our leading Chair of Divinity is better filled than has been the case at any time since the death of Bishop Lloyd. I should not venture to say so much to you, but in illness, as I know from experience, such assurances may be of use in a way which would not be at all possible in days of health and strength.

It was a great pleasure to me to get a fairly good account of you from the Dean of St. Paul's a few days ago, and a very improved one from the Miss Johnsons to-day. It is delightful to be able to hope that you will again be among us in October. Meanwhile, if I might do so, I would beg you not to be tempted into any sort of premature exertion. As regards the University, the publication of this volume will, of itself, make anything of the sort unnecessary for a long time to come. . . . —Ever very truly yours, H. P. LIDDON.

Another alleviation of a protracted period of inactivity,—of the trial to a mind ever engaged in thought at being cut off from the congenial work of expression, and compelled to dependence on others for carrying out inquiries once his own familiar occupation,—was in the invaluable help and services of Mr. (now Canon) Wordsworth, not only in his office of deputy but in his essential supervision during the bringing out of the volume of Old Testament Lectures; and, more than all, in the affectionate warmth of regard with which these services were rendered. In the letters before me his name constantly occurs, and always as inspiring confidence that all would go well where his help might be relied on.[1]

[1] At the close of 1876 Mr. and Mrs. John Wordsworth visited Dr. Mozley at Old Shoreham. In writing to me my brother speaks of Mrs. Wordsworth's music. "Her Beethoven every night was a great treat." Throughout his life he had been very earnest in his love of music, and it was a lasting pleasure to him. It was indeed so distinct a feature that some mention ought to be made of it. He was an intellectual listener. His mind never lost itself in vague dreams, but was consciously at work upon what he was hearing, and, as in talk, he was content to be a hearer without taking an active part. It was a thoughtful process. His tastes had to be reasoned out to himself—why he liked, why he was indifferent, or suffered positive

With the new year 1877 came out the Old Testament lectures, under the title, *Ruling Ideas in Early Ages*. The preparing it for the press had occupied some months, and, as being my brother's most recent work, had a peculiar interest to him. In fact, he had had the lectures in hand for publication before his illness. On February 16th he writes to his sister of criticisms on the new volume:—

"The *Spectator* had an article a fortnight ago, which took an interest in the argument of the book, though the writer did not see things as we wanted him to see them. As you do not mention the article, I send it you. You call my books tough morsels. You know I labour under a fate to take to tough books. I have extracted my share of interest out of them."

On November 22, 1877, I received his last letter, which begins, "I beg to congratulate you on a new edition of *Ruling Ideas*." But the hand that held the pen had lost its cunning. It is something that its labours during a lifetime brought him this touch of pleasure at the last;—that he might know that his good work would survive him. At the latter end of December came a final seizure, from which he did not recover apparent consciousness, but lay in monumental calm till he passed away amid prayers and tears on the evening of January the 4th, 1878.

A College friend, on occasion of the publication of James Mozley's *Essays* in 1878, wrote an article[1] on them, which not

annoyance. He had moral repugnances, as for instance Chopin, whom he always suspected. Of one of his compositions he spoke during his illness with strong repugnance. "He [Chopin] was a Manichean—certainly a Manichean: he did not believe in God; he believed in some spirit, not in God." The trite, tuneless, often vulgar, modern ballad was one of his antipathies of a less grave type. He never learnt the art of not listening; his attention could not but be kept on the stretch—the music speculated on. This habit gave seriousness to his appreciation. The moral grandeur of Beethoven's genius was always present to him, as, with less force, was also Mendelssohn's; "They believed in God—their music showed it."

[1] *Mozley's Essays*. By the Right Hon. Lord Blachford. *Nineteenth Century*, June 18, 1879.

only entered into the merits and characteristic qualities of the essays, but gave a sketch of the author as he had known him in under-graduate and subsequent days. The character he drew illustrates and bears out the letters here laid before the reader in so remarkable a manner, that I have asked to be allowed to close my task by inserting those passages that relate to my brother's personal character apart from his works :—

"Among Dr. Mozley's youthful characteristics were simplicity of habits, warm but undemonstrative affections, sincerity of thought, an almost stern purity of mind, carelessness of worldly advancement or distinction, and a deliberate desire to attach himself to a worthy object of life. He soon felt that thinking and writing were his vocation; and he found a career in the service of the Anglican Church, and guides in the leaders of what was called the Oxford Movement, with whom circumstances at once made him intimate. To an unmistakable independence of thought he joined a cordial and natural recognition of all those claims for respect, or even provisional submission of belief, which arise from intellect, age, moral character, or social relation. And so under these leaders he fairly enrolled himself as pupil and soldier. He was fond of his friends and of society, conscious of his own powers, without valuing himself on them, and ready and liberal in his appreciation of others. But partly from the modesty of a man who had before him a high standard of excellence, partly because he could not easily do himself justice in spoken words, partly because it was a kind of serious amusement to him to observe and ponder, he did not talk much in company. If he spoke he seemed to speak because there was something which ought to be said and nobody else to say it; expressing himself in short or even abrupt sentences and well-chosen words, which showed even a critical or eager interest in what was going on; but, when this was done, falling back into his normal state of amused or inquiring attention, like a man who has discharged a duty and is glad to have done with it. He was not an artist or a writer of poems, but he had a keen and somewhat analytical appreciation of what was beautiful to the eye or ear, whether severe or florid, and his writings show that his sense of things was as vigorous in point of humour and poetry as in point of philosophy. . . .

"He had not the special excellencies or the defects of a great preacher, and, with all his power of thought and imagery, could scarcely, I think, have become one, even had his delivery been better than it was. He was wholly genuine—in his friendships, his arguments, his measurement of things, and in his devotion to the Church of England—not an imagination of his own mind, nor exactly the Church as it is, but a distinct historical community, having, like his country, its defects and its merits ; and, in spite of those defects, capable of greatness and goodness on the basis supplied by its formularies and great divines.

"With a lively discrimination of characters and situations he had not the flexibility of address, the resource, the practical energy, or the taste for active movement which are required for a leader. His line was thought ; and, in choosing theology as the object of that thought, he approached it on its philosophical side. The details of doctrine, the scholarship, the archæology, or the textual interpretation of Scripture might interest but did not detain him. Appreciating the value of *minutiæ*, he had no taste for them. He was always ambitious of 'a view,' as it was called—an available principle under the light of which *minutiæ* fell into their places as of course,—and spared no thought or reading in attaining it. Thus he found himself particularly at home in tracing the bearing of scriptural teaching on the laws of human nature, or the constitution of the world, or in determining the connection between a particular doctrine and the moral temperament or necessity to which it appealed, or out of which it sprang. It was a pleasure to him to penetrate, whether states of things, states of mind, forms of character, or courses of argument; and in this he was patient of labour and suspense. But once satisfied, he was ready, as the phrase is, to go off at score. No one liked better to give his pen a gallop. No one had greater power of bringing home to a reader that what is obvious is obvious—a matter not always so easy as it may be thought—no one had greater richness of development and illustration. He agreed apparently with Lord Bacon, that a broad and true view should bear down objections by its mere completeness and momentum. . . .

"In this respect his mind was remarkably constituted. To an idea of limited extent—a platitude if you like—or a just and appropriate observation which he fathomed at a glance, he could at once give a profuse and vigorous expression, could develop, illustrate, and enforce it with the utmost force and vivacity, almost off-hand. But if he was called upon to search out what was subtle, doubtful, or involved, or what, clear in itself, had been obscured by the hardy credulity of doubt, and therefore had to be hunted back into what was clearer than clear, he was embarrassed by his fastidious desire to touch the true bottom, and when there to grasp firmly the cardinal truth with a full apprehension of its surroundings. The sense of half knowledge only paralysed him. He had no tincture of that *aimable légèreté qui fait prononcer sur ce qu'on ignore*. If he understood a matter wholly or in part, he could write on that whole or part with force and richness. But if he had only a confused and inchoate understanding of it he could not write at all. A proud disgust at "cram" or make-believe made him incapable of that adroit use of smattering which plays so much part in the examinations of second-rate men."

In its notice of the four biographies, Strafford, Laud, Cromwell, and Luther, which compose the first volume of the essays, and are earliest in date, the article dwells on James Mozley as a "portrait painter," showing how congenial the work of character-drawing was to him, as is shown in the letters:—

"His turn, indeed, for analysis of character, pursues him everywhere, and the theological part of the essay on Luther derives its interest, not from any scriptural or logical argument, but its searching exhibition of the connection between the great Lutheran doctrine and the personal character of its inventor.

"A word in conclusion on one aspect of his works... I wish to notice one pervading strain of thought, which, as it appears in his first works, serves to give depth and force, and life and richness and purpose to his latest. He touches a great variety of subjects, but that which is constantly colouring his narratives, directing his philosophy, and bursting out in a kind of stern poetry, is the position of moral goodness in the world. He inherited this from his teachers. In the earlier part of this century the Calvinistic theology was one of feeling and dogma, almost suspicious of the sounds of duty and desert; the High Churchman was careful about duties, but jealous of enthusiasm; while a literary world and the clergy who belonged to it, maintaining in a tone of apology the compatibility of reason and religion, were apt to enlarge on the supreme authority and dignity of the intellect. The school of which Newman, Pusey, and Keble were the acknowledged heads, if it did nothing else, taught unflinchingly and continually, a religion of the heart and will, of the thoughts and emotions, of the passions and conduct to which everything else was accessory or subordinate. None could accuse them of being blind to the beauty of poetry, the cogency of reason, the value of divine truth, the majesty of the divine dispensations; but one of their peculiarities was, that before beauty, before knowledge, before power, before self-satisfaction, they placed the simple-hearted and determined purification of the will and affections. This unflinching reference to true-heartedness as an avenue to all that Christians hope for, is constantly breaking forth in these earlier works of Dr. Mozley; but it is in some of his later works that his fervent sense of this supremacy is most adequately expressed. In force of language, fertility of illustration, and vividness of conception, they are scarcely superior to what is now published. In maturity of style and balance of thought they are. And in this they are remarkable, that while the author does not shrink from employing the full force of his intellect on the various great questions which our days have brought forth, he most rises above himself when he most directly asserts the inherent and illimitable authority of the central truth of morality, tears all disguise from its counterfeits, and casts the human heart naked at the feet of its Judge."

INDEX.

A.

ABERDEEN, Lord, 208, 216, 244.
Acland, Dr., 88, 177, 225.
Acland, A. H. D., 343.
Albert, Prince, 110.
Alexander, Bishop, 111.
Alford, Dean, 266.
Alison, Sir A., 232.
Allies, Rev. Mr., 202.
Anderson, Sir Charles, 81.
Andrea, Cardinal, 277.
Andrews, Mr., 4, 5, 7, 8, 14, 16, 17, 18, 19.
Antonelli, Cardinal, 290.
Arnold, Dr., 19, 20, 30, 45, 53, 92, 155.
Arnold, Matthew, 248.
Ashwell, Canon, 153.
Ashley, Lord, 127, 163.
Atkinson, Mr., 66.

B.

BADELEY, Edward, 123, 138, 139, 143, 145, 152, 157, 163, 246.
Bagot, Bishop of Oxford, 116, 126, 130.
Balfour, Dr., 258.
Barker, T. F., 94.
Baynes, Mrs., 264.
Beaufort, Captain, 92.
Bellasis, Edward, 96, 130.
Bennett, Rev. W. J. E., 202.
Bentinck, Lord G., 194.
Bernard, Montague, 184.
Bethell (Lord Westbury), 159, 237.
Bieni, 88.
Bismarck, Prince, 314.
Blackwood, John, 311.
Blagrave, Colonel, 199.
Blandy, Rev. F., 164.
Blencowe, T., 34, 35.
Bliss, Dr., 38, 48, 51, 128.
Blomfield, Bishop of London, 62.
Bloxam, Dr., 94, 101, 108, 117, 122, 136, 149.
Bowden, Captain, 146.
Bowden, John, 47.
Bowyer, Sir George, 92, 281.
Bridges, Rev. B. E., 48, 49, 78, 152, 304.
Bright, Canon, 348.
Brougham, Lord, 25, 30, 283.
Bulteel, Mr., 25, 27.
Bulwer, Lytton, 330.
Bunsen, Chevalier, 87, 88, 92.
Burgon, Dean, 193.
Burton, Dr., 45, 50.
Butler, Bishop, 223.

C.

CARDIGAN, Lord, 252.
Cardwell, Dr., 52, 183, 184.
Carlyle, Thomas, 101.
Cartwright, W. R., M.P., 90.
Caswell, Rev. Henry, 135.
Chalmers, Dr., 85.
Chandler, Rev. D., 165.
Cholmeley, Rev. R., D.D., 108, 225, 233.
Christie, Rev. John, 23, 28, 40, 44, 45, 60, 106.
Church, Dean, 145, 150, 161, 203, 220, 226, 243, 284.
Churton, Rev. B. W., 116.
Clarke, Miss, 47.
Clarke, Dr., 267.
Claughton, T. L. (Bishop), 119, 149.
Clyde, Lord, 252.
Cobden, Richard, 244.
Colenso, Bishop, 253.
Coleridge, Rev. Edward, 123, 156.
Coleridge, H., 185.
Coleridge, Hartley, 62.
Coleridge, Lord, 165, 184.
Coleridge, Sir John (Judge), 47, 145, 163, 301.

Coleridge, S. T., 46, 204, 238.
Collinson, Rev. Mr., 129.
Colquhoun, Mr., 65.
Congreve, Mr., 193.
Copleston, R. S. (Bishop), 343.
Copleston, E., Bishop of Landaff, 19, 21, 53.
Copeland, Rev. W. J., 58, 63, 101, 103, 122, 303, 305.
Cornish, Rev. C. L., 60, 190.
Coutts, Mrs., 194.
Cowley, 199.
Coxe, Mr., 44.
Coxwell, Miss, 77.
Craufurd, Captain, 230.
Creighton, Rev. M., 343.
Cumberland, Duke of, 38, 41, 42.

D.

Daubeny, Dr., 122, 156.
Davenport, Mr., 72.
Davison, Rev. John, 33, 265, 301.
Dean, Rev. James, 20, 34, 35 n.
Denison, Rev. G. A., 27, 37, 216, 219.
Derby, Lord, 215, 219, 221 n.
Devon, Lord, 128.
Dickens, Charles, 198.
Digby, Kenelm, 300.
Disraeli, Rt. Hon. B., 221, 333, 292.
Dodson, Mr., 159.
Donkin, Professor, 95, 153, 196, 307.
Donkin, Miss, 199.
Dornford, Rev. Joseph, 26.
Dupanloup, Bishop of Orleans, 280.
Dyson, Rev. Charles, 232.
Dyson, Rev. F., 164, 233.

E.

Eden, Rev. C., 110, 158.
Eldon, Lord, 39, 42.
Elwyn, Mr., 234.
Emerson, R. W., 269 n.
Espin, Chancellor, 341.
Estcourt, Sotheron, 90, 183.

F.

Faber, Rev. Francis, 92, 108, 148, 209, 247, 292, 338.
Faber, Frederick, 209, 261.
Faber, Canon, 124, 125.
Faussett, Dr., 120, 122, 142.
Fitzgerald, Rev. Mr., 299.
Forbes, Lord, 194.

Fowle, Rev. Fuller, 106, 107.
Foy, Rev. Martin Wilson, 129.
Freeman, Miss, 259.
Froude, Anthony, 239.
Froude, Rev. R. Hurrell, 28 n, 32, 34, 45, 61, 67, 70, 75, 102.
Froude, William, 69, 308.
Fuller, Margaret, 269 n.

G.

Garbett, Mr., 123, 126.
Gauntlett, Dr., 192.
Gibbins, Mr., 74.
Gilbert, Bishop, 51, 127.
Gladstone, Right Hon. W. E., 87, 88, 145, 158, 160, 162, 163, 165, 180, 182, 183, 184, 185, 198, 205, 207, 208, 216, 218, 220, 223, 230, 232, 255, 259, 266, 292, 300, 338, 340, 350.
Gleig, Rev. Mr., 88.
Golightly, Rev. C. P., 34, 61, 62, 112, 124, 125, 161, 188.
Gorham, Rev. Mr., 201.
Goulburn, Dean, 333.
Graham, Sir James, 208.
Gresley, Rev. W., 74, 85.
Greswell (Corpus), Rev. E., 51, 185, 187.
Grey, Rev. W., 16 n.
Grey, Lord, 41.
Grey, Sir George, 65, 202.
Guillemarde, Rev. Mr., 165.
Gurney, Judge, 101.

H.

Haddan, A., 185.
Haddan, H., 127, 185.
Halford, Sir H., 128.
Hall, Archdeacon, 183.
Hallam, Henry, 182.
Hamilton, Dr. W. K., 46, 250.
Hampden, Bishop, 39, 50, 51, 52, 53, 54, 55, 60, 131, 132, 134, 151, 164, 187, 188, 248.
Hare, Rev. Aug., 329.
Hare, Rev. Julius, 329.
Harris, H., 185.
Harrison, Rev. B., 40.
Hawkins, Dr., Provost of Oriel, 21, 54, 61, 82, 134, 135, 142, 157, 184.
Hayes, Mr., 181.
Heathcote, G. W., 95.
Heathcote, Sir W., 61, 165, 184, 223.

Index. 361

Herbert, Sidney, 208, 244, 251.
Hervey, Lord Arthur, 268.
Heurtley, Canon, 335.
Hill, Rev. Mr., 74.
Hircher, Dr., 253.
Holland, Rev. H. S., 343.
Hook, Dean, 37, 50, 111, 114, 145, 152, 165, 172.
Hooker, Richard, 204.
Hope, James Robert, 87, 104, 111, 122, 123, 165, 209.
Hopkins, Dr., Bishop of Vermont, 89.
Horne, Bishop, 101 n.
Howley, Archbishop, 33, 61, 153.
Hume, David, 201 n, 211.
Hurd, Bishop, 201 n.
Hussey, Rev. Mr., 158.
Hutton, Rev. Mr., 162.

I.

ILLINGWORTH, J. R., 343.
Inglis, Sir R., 180, 182.
Irons, Rev. Dr., 268.

J.

JACKSON, Dr., 225.
James, G. P. R., 146.
Jayne, F. J., 343.
Jelf, Dr. R. W., 6 n, 142 n, 251.
Jenner, Sir Herbert, 188.
Jenkyns, Dr., 142 n.
Jersey, Lady, 291.
Jeune, Bishop, 206.
Jewell, Bishop, 132.
Johnson, Manuel, (Observer,) 69, 76, 90, 91, 94, 184, 235, 239, 241.
Johnson, Dr., 201 n.
Jowett, Rev. B., 223, 238, 245, 246, 248.
Joyce, Rev. J., 19.

K.

KAYE, Bishop of Lincoln, 39.
Keble, Rev. John, 27, 31, 33, 34, 35 n, 36, 37, 47, 49, 53, 55, 63, 72, 77, 78, 85, 92, 93, 97, 114, 119, 120 n, 123, 125, 154, 155, 156, 161, 170; 191, 195, 201, 202, 216, 223, 239, 251, 265, 301.
Keble, Mrs., 77, 92.
Keen, Miss, 68, 70.
Kelly, Sir Fitzroy, 190.
Kempe, Rev. J. E., 262.
Kettle, J. R. L., 66.

Kidd, Dr., 39.
King, Rev. Canon, 348.
Kingsley, Rev. Charles, 239, 251, 260.
Kynaston, Rev. Dr., 119.

L.

LAKE, Dean, 223.
Laud, Archbishop, 132, 147, 159.
Le Bas, 104.
Lee, Archdeacon, 299.
Lee, Prince (Bishop), 130.
Liddon, Dr., 331.
Lind, Jenny, 195, 196, 197.
Lock, W., 343.
Locke, 223.
Lockhart, John, 64, 218.

M.

MACAULAY, Lord, 30, 101, 234.
M'Ghee, Rev. Mr., 130.
Macmullen, Rev. Mr., 134, 142, 151, 314.
Magee, Mr., 36.
Madan, A. C., 343.
Maitland, Mr. 71.
Manning, Cardinal, 71, 110, 116, 148, 149, 165, 209, 335.
Mansel, Dean, 240.
Marriott, Rev. Charles, 34, 90, 122, 154, 189, 202, 229.
Marshall, Mr., 118.
Matheson, Mr., 64, 65.
Mathison, Mr., 177.
Maurice, J. F. D., 63.
Maurice, Rev. F., 111, 222, 238.
Maynard, M., 212.
Melbourne, Lord, 53.
Merivale, H., 63, 71.
Mill, Dr., 27, 177.
Mill, Stuart, 211.
Mitchell, Dr., 42, 66, 183.
Moberly, Bishop, 161, 216, 307.
Moberly, R. C., 343.
Morris, Rev. Mr., 113.
Mozley, Mr., 2, 14, 19, 44.
Mozley, Mrs., 4, 6, 16, 17, 18, 44, 49, 69, 287, 289.
Mozley, Jane, 3, 17, 18, 20 n, 23, 24, 28, 31 n.
Mozley, John, 40, 59, 70, 87, 93, 101, 253.
Mozley, the Rev. Thomas, 6, 19, 20, 21, 22, 23, 24, 28, 29, 31, 34, 37, 40, 42, 54, 58, 60, 85, 90, 97, 106, 108, 138, 143, 205, 230 n, 251.

2 A

Mozley, Charles, 4, 40, 101, 257.
Mozley, Rev. Arthur, 5, 79, 83, 129, 134, 135, 143, 161, 215, 216, 220, 238, 260, 262 n, 268.
Mozley, Mrs. Thomas, 76, 91, 102, 105, 120 n, 142, 174, 214.
Mozley, Herbert Newman, 209.
Mozley, Mrs. John, 102, 104, 163, 173.
Mozley, J. R., 294.
Mozley, H. W., 335.
Müller, Max, 235.
Murray, Dr., 122, 206.
Murray, John, 229.
Mylne, Bishop, 343.

N.

NARDI, Monsignor, 291.
Neate, Charles, 232.
Newman, J. H., Cardinal, 6, 19, 21, 24, 27, 28, 31, 32, 33, 34, 35, 36, 37, 38, 39, 40, 45, 46, 47, 48, 50, 51, 52, 53, 57, 58, 59, 60, 61, 62, 63, 64, 65, 66, 67, 68, 70, 71, 72, 73, 74, 75, 76, 78, 79, 80, 81, 83, 85, 87, 88, 90, 91, 92, 95, 96, 97, 100, 101, 103, 104, 107, 108, 109, 112, 114, 122, 124, 125, 136, 145, 157, 163, 165, 169, 173, 174, 177, 180, 196, 259, 260, 292, 349.
Newman, Mrs., 28, 48, 49, 58, 59.
Newcastle, Duke of, 208, 215.
Nicholson, Rev. Mr., 131.
Northcote, Sir Stafford, 181, 218.
Norton, Hon. Mrs., 216.

O.

OAKELEY, Rev. F., 104, 133, 148.
Ogilvie, Dr., 27, 33, 37, 142 n, 162, 184.
Ogle, Dr., 98, 188, 230, 235, 237.
Ogle, Dr. John, 258.
Oldham, Mr., 129.
Overton, Rev. J. G., 15.
Owen, Professor, 176.

P.

PAGET, F., 343.
Paley, 248, 250.
Palmerston, Lord, 238, 244, 266.
Palmer, Rev. W. (of Worcester), 51, 113, 150.

Palmer, Rev. W. (of Magdalen), 37, 95, 96, 108, 111, 117, 118, 119, 124, 135, 148, 194, 276, 291.
Palmer, Roundell, (Lord Selborne,) 149, 223, 224, 338.
Parr, Dr., 201.
Park, Judge, 47.
Parker, Mr., 19.
Pascal, 211.
Patteson, Judge, 101.
Patteson, Bishop, 337.
Peard, Miss, 337.
Peel, Sir Robert, 46, 90, 127, 135, 139, 141, 152.
Peel, Dean, 301.
Percival, Mr., 216.
Phillips, L., 136.
Phillpotts, Dr. H., Bishop of Exeter, 46, 92, 153, 163, 209, 262.
Pio Nono, 286.
Poerio, Signor, 281.
Powell, Baden, 158, 246, 248, 249.
Powis, Lord, 138, 139, 140, 152, 153.
Price, Professor Bonamy, 22, 158, 258, 334.
Pugin, Welby, 99, 100, 101, 149.
Pusey, Dr., 27, 50, 57, 58, 60, 62, 64, 66, 68, 69, 70, 71, 72, 74, 76, 78, 80, 81, 88, 94, 95, 97, 108, 111, 115, 119, 125, 129, 130, 141, 142, 143, 144, 145, 156, 158, 163, 169, 172, 181, 196, 202, 229, 286, 290, 310, 330, 348.
Pusey, Mrs., 58, 65, 73, 84.
Pusey, Philip, 93.
Pusey, Philip, M.P., 46, 64.
Pusey, Rev. William, 107, 259.

R.

RASSAM, Ormuzd, 194, 200 n.
Rawlinson, Rev. Canon, 223.
Redesdale, Lord, 128, 215.
Renan, 291.
Richards, Dr., 113.
Richmond, W. T., 343 n.
Rickards, Rev. S., 55, 131, 132, 143, 151, 152, 158, 186, 253, 263.
Rickards, Mrs., 181, 264, 265, 343.
Rivington, Mr., 109, 146, 148.
Robertson, Rev. F., 335.
Rose, Rev. Edward, 294.
Rose, Rev. Hugh James, 33, 34, 37, 39, 45, 52.
Round, C. G., M.P., 184.

Round, Rev. Mr., 27.
Russell, Lord John, 188, 205, 206, 207, 230, 244, 265.
Rogers, F. (Lord Blachford), 48, 50, 58, 65, 74, 75, 80, 85, 95, 104, 105, 122, 146, 163, 183, 184, 229, 259, 290, 294, 349.
Routh, Dr., President of Magdalen, 39, 55, 98, 116, 136, 169, 200 n, 205, 208, 209, 219, 225, 226, 330.
Ryder, T. D., 26, 55, 78, 144.

S.

SADLER, Miss, 25.
Salisbury, Lord, 335.
Saunders, Rev. Dr., 182.
Scaliger, 10.
Scott, Rev. W., 150, 155, 165, 166, 224, 228, 321.
Scott, Sir Walter, 85, 312.
Scott, Thomas, 213, 284.
Selwyn, Bishop, 122, 292.
Sewell (Fellow of Magdalen), 97, 98, 101.
Sewell, Miss, 91.
Sewell, Rev. Wm., Fellow of Exeter, 40, 71.
Shaftesbury, Lord, 265.
Sharpe, Martin, 179.
Shepherd, Mrs., 194.
Shipley, Rev. Orby, 266.
Shrewsbury, Lord, 100, 131.
Sibthorpe, Rev. Mr., 136, 149.
Sidmouth, Lord, 90.
Small, Mrs., 93.
Smith, Adam, 201 n.
Smith, Goldwin, 239, 240, 248, 320.
Southey, 203.
Spencer, Rev. G. (Father Ignatius), 95.
Spooner, Mr., M.P., 177.
Spranger, Mr.
Spry, Dr. Hume, 55, 182.
St. John, Rev. A., 146.
Stanbridge, J. W., 343 n.
Stanley, Dean, 193, 194, 240, 241 n, 151, 255, 257, 259, 260, 262, 286, 291, 292, 295, 300, 335.
Stanley, Bishop of Norwich, 195.
Stowell, Rev. Hugh, 161.
Symons, Rev. B. P., D.D., 112, 142 n, 153, 154.

T.

TALBOT, Rev. E. S., 343 n.
Talfourd, Serjeant, 153.
Taylor, Jeremy, 73.
Thackeray, W. M., 311.
Thomas, Vaughan, 54, 134, 188.
Thurland, Rev., F., 106.
Todd, Dr., 74, 299.
Townsend, Mr., 291.
Trench, Archbishop, 257.
Trower, Rev. Dr., 55.
Tyler, Rev. J. Endell, 182.
Tyndall, John, 292.

W.

WALES, Prince of, 261.
Walker, Professor, 110.
Wall, Rev. H., 154, 183.
Waller, Mr., 309.
Walter, John, M.P., 185.
Ward, George (of Balliol), 116, 118, 123, 135, 137, 157, 161, 164, 165.
Ward, Mr. (of Trinity), 97, 98, 101.
Wayland, Mrs., 3.
Wayland, Dr., 117.
Wayland, Rev. D., 117, 242.
Wellington, Duchess of, 252.
Wellington, Duke of, 38, 41, 109, 128, 140, 152, 215.
Wesley, Dr., 192.
Westbury, Lord, 159, 237.
Wetherell, Sir C., 128.
Whately, Dr., 6 n, 24, 53, 54, 164, 205, 232, 258.
Wheeler, Rev. Mr., 129.
Wheeler, Rev. Mr., 235.
Whitmarsh, E. D., D.C.L., 343 n.
Wilberforce, Rev. H., 24, 26, 42, 53, 55, 63, 74, 78, 146, 165, 172, 334.
Wilberforce, Rev. R. J., 25, 55, 154, 192, 224.
Wilberforce, Bishop S., 22, 53, 55, 63, 73, 74, 80, 81, 88, 95, 116, 131, 160, 162, 188, 191, 219, 220, 221, 232.
Williams, George, 310.
Williams, Rev. Isaac, 63, 97, 102, 119, 120 n, 123, 124, 126, 154, 216.
Williams, Rowland, 295.
Williams, R., M.P., 65.
Wilson, Professor, of Exeter, 110.
Wilson, Rev. R. F., 27, 65, 76, 174, 240.

Wilson, Rev. H. B., 116.
Wilson, Rev. Mr. (of Magdalen), 119.
Wiseman, Cardinal, 117, 118, 119, 131, 136, 137, 158, 206, 268.
Wodehouse, Rev. the Hon. W., 215.
Wood, Rev. F., 119.
Wood, Rt. Hon. Sir Charles, (Lord Halifax,) 52, 53, 65, 88.
Woolcombe, E. C., 185.
Wootton, Dr., 84, 148.

Wordsworth, Bishop C., 131, 179, 259.
Wordsworth, Rev. John (Canon), 343 n.
Wordsworth, W., 28, 62, 92, 236.
Wynter, Dr., 142 n, 153, 158.

Y.

YONGE, Miss, 91, 334.
Yonge, Mr., 77.
Yonge, Mrs., 78.

THE END.

Edinburgh University Press
THOMAS AND ARCHIBALD CONSTABLE, PRINTERS TO HER MAJESTY.

NEW BOOKS AND NEW EDITIONS

IN COURSE OF PUBLICATION BY

Messrs. RIVINGTON

WATERLOO PLACE, LONDON

NOVEMBER, 1884.

●●

Letters of the Rev. J. B. Mozley, D.D.,
late Canon of Christ Church, and Regius Professor of Divinity in the University of Oxford.
Edited by his Sister.

8vo. 12s.

The World as the Subject of Redemption.
Being an attempt to set forth the Functions of the Church as designed to embrace the Whole Race of Mankind.
Eight Lectures delivered before the University of Oxford in the year 1883 on the Foundation of the late Rev. John Bampton, M.A., Canon of Salisbury.
By the Hon. and Rev. W. H. Fremantle, M.A., Canon of Canterbury, and Fellow of Balliol College, Oxford.

8vo. [*In the Press.*

Footprints of the Son of Man, as traced
by S. Mark. Being Eighty Portions for Private Study, Family Reading, and Instruction in Church.
By Herbert Mortimer Luckock, D.D., Canon of Ely; Examining Chaplain to the Bishop of Ely; and Principal of the Theological College.

Two Vols. Crown 8vo. [*Nearly ready.*

3, WATERLOO PLACE, LONDON.

Life of S. Francis of Assisi.

By H L. Sidney Lear, Author of "Life of Lacordaire," &c.

Crown 8vo. [*In preparation.*

Monte Carlo and Public Opinion.

Edited by **A Visitor to the Riviera.** With Illustrations.

Crown 8vo. 3s. 6d.

Maxims and Gleanings from the

Writings of the Rev. **T. T. Carter**, M.A. Selected and arranged for daily use.

By **C. M. S.**, Compiler of "Daily Gleanings of the Saintly Life," "Under the Cross," etc. With an Introduction by the Rev. **M. F. Sadler**, Rector of Honiton, Devon.

Crown 16mo. 2s.

Modern Doubt and Unbelief: Its Extent,

Causes and Tendencies.

By **Edward Bickersteth Ottley**, M.A., Minister of Quebec Chapel.

Crown 8vo. [*In preparation.*

A Treatise on the Church of Christ.

By **William Palmer**, M.A., of Worcester College, Oxford.

New and Revised Edition. Two Vols. 8vo. [*In preparation.*

The Four Holy Gospels according to the

Authorized Version.

With variations of type in the use of Capital letters, and with Marginal Notes, containing selections from various Readings of the Earlier English Translators, of the Authorized Version, of the Revisers of 1881, and others.

By the Rev. **Edwd. Thos. Cardale**, late Rector of Uckfield.

Crown 8vo. 5s.

De Vitâ Pastorali.

The Office and Work of a Priest in the Church of God.

By the **Lord Bishop of Lichfield.**

Crown 8vo. [*In preparation.*

3, WATERLOO PLACE, LONDON.

A Life of Edward Bouverie Pusey, D.D.,

Regius Professor of Hebrew, and Canon of Christ Church, Oxford.
By H. P. Liddon, D.D., Canon Residentiary of S. Paul's.

8vo. [*In preparation*

The Apostolic Fathers.

The Epistles of S. Clement, S. Ignatius, S. Barnabas, S. Polycarp, together with the Martyrdom of S. Ignatius and S. Polycarp. Translated into English, with an Introductory Notice.
By Charles H. Hoole, M.A., Student of Christ Church, Oxford.

Second Edition. Crown 8vo. [*Nearly ready*.

The Gospel according to S. Matthew,

With Explanatory Notes for the Use of Teachers.
By Henry Herbert Wyatt, M.A., Principal of Brighton Training College, and Vicar of Bolney, Sussex; Author of "Principal Heresies relating to Our Lord's Incarnation."
With Commendatory Preface by the Archbishops' Inspector of Training Colleges.

Crown 8vo. 2s. 6d.

From Morn to Eve.

A Companion Poem to "Yesterday, To-day, and For Ever."
By the Rev. E. H. Bickersteth, M.A., Vicar of Christ Church, Hampstead, and Rural Dean.

18mo. [*In preparation*

The Profitableness of the Old Testament

Scriptures.
A Treatise founded on 2 Timothy, iii., 16, 17.
By W. A. Bartlett, M.A., Vicar of Wisborough, Sussex.

Crown 8vo. 7s. 6d.

Good Friday.

Being Addresses on the Seven Last Words delivered at St. Paul's Cathedral, on Good Friday, 1884.
By the Rev. H. S. Holland, M.A., Canon Residentiary of St. Paul's, and Senior Student of Christ Church, Oxford.

Small 8vo. 2s.

3, WATERLOO PLACE, LONDON.

The Missioner's Hymnal.

Edited by the Rev. A. G. Jackson, Resident Chaplain of the Farm School, Redhill, Surrey.

Royal 32mo. Sewed, 1d.; cloth boards, 3d. With Music, Small 4to. 2s. 6d.

The One Mediator.

The Operation of the Son of God in Nature and in Grace. Eight Lectures delivered before the University of Oxford in the year 1882, on the Foundation of the late Rev. John Bampton, M.A., Canon of Salisbury.

By Peter Goldsmith Medd, M.A., Rector of North Cerney; Hon. Canon of S. Albans, and Examining Chaplain to the Bishop; late Rector of Barnes; formerly Fellow and Tutor of University College, Oxford.

8vo. 16s.

Selections from the Writings of H. P.

Liddon, D.D., Canon Residentiary of S. Paul's.

Second Edition. Crown 8vo. 3s. 6d.

Selections from the Writings of John

Keble, M.A., Author of "The Christian Year."

Crown 8vo. 3s. 6d.

Selections from the Writings of Edward

Bouverie Pusey, D.D., late Regius Professor of Hebrew, and Canon of Christ Church, Oxford.

Crown 8vo. 3s. 6d.

Selections from the Writing of John

Mason Neale, D.D., late Warden of Sackville College.

Crown 8vo. 3s. 6d.

The Hymn "Te Deum Laudamus."

Observations upon its composition and structure, with special regard to the use, Liturgical and Choral, of this and other Canticles and Psalms, and to the true character of the Chant. Together with the Canticles carefully printed, pointed, and accented in accordance with their poetical structure for antiphonal chanting.

By the Rev. Francis Pott, B.A., Rector of Northill, Bedfordshire.

8vo. 3s.

The Three Hours' Agony of our Blessed

Redeemer. Being Addresses in the form of Meditations delivered in S. Alban's Church, Manchester, on Good Friday, 1877.

By the Rev. W. J. Knox Little, M.A., Canon Residentiary of Worcester, and Rector of S. Alban's, Manchester.

New Edition. Small 8vo. 2s.; or in Paper Cover, 1s.

Letters and Sermons of the Rev. Lewis

M. Hogg, M.A., sometime Rector of Cranford, Northamptonshire.

8vo. 4s.

Maigre Cookery.

Edited by H. L. Sidney Lear.

16mo. 2s.

Practical Reflections on every Verse of

the New Testament.

By A Clergyman. With a Preface by H. P. Liddon, D.D., Canon Residentiary of S. Paul's.

Crown 8vo.

Vol. I. THE HOLY GOSPELS. *Third Edition.* 4s. 6d.
Vol. II. ACTS TO REVELATION. 6s.

Of the Five Wounds of the Holy Church.

By Antonio Rosmini. Edited, with an Introduction by H. P. Liddon, D.D., Canon Residentiary of S. Paul's.

Crown 8vo. 7s. 6d.

Second Series of Sermons preached be-

fore the University of Oxford, 1868-1882.

By H. P. Liddon, D.D., Canon Residentiary of S. Paul's.

Third Edition. Crown 8vo. 5s.

Lectures and other Theological Papers.

By J. B. Mozley, D.D., late Canon of Christ Church, and Regius Professor of Divinity in the University of Oxford.

8vo. 10s. 6d.

A Lent with Jesus.

A Plain Guide for Churchmen.

Third Edition. 32mo. 1s., or in Paper Cover, 9d.

3, WATERLOO PLACE, LONDON.

Logic and Life, with other Sermons.
By H. S. Holland, M.A., Canon Residentiary of S. Paul's.
Second Edition. Crown 8vo. 7s. 6d.

A Review of the Baptismal Controversy.
By J. B. Mozley, D.D., late Canon of Christ Church, and Regius Professor of Divinity in the University of Oxford.
Second Edition. Crown 8vo. 7s. 6d.

The Reformation of the Church of
England ; its History, Principles, and Results.
By John Henry Blunt, D.D., F.S.A., Editor of "The Annotated Book of Common Prayer," etc., etc.
Two Vols. 8vo. Sold separately.
Vol. I. A.D. 1514-1547. Its progress during the reign of Henry VIII. *Fifth Edition.* 16s.
Vol. II. A.D. 1547-1662. From the Death of Henry VIII. to the Restoration of the Church after the Commonwealth. 18s.

A Companion to the New Testament;
being a Plain Commentary on Scripture History from the Birth of our Lord to the End of the Apostolic Age.
By John Henry Blunt, D.D., F.S.A., Editor of "The Annotated Book of Common Prayer," etc., etc.
With Maps. Small 8vo. 3s. 6d.

Studies in the History of the Book of
Common Prayer. The Anglican Reform—The Puritan Innovations—The Elizabethan Reaction—The Caroline Settlement. With Appendices.
By Herbert Mortimer Luckock, D.D., Canon of Ely, etc.
Second Edition. Crown 8vo. 6s.

Counsels of Faith and Practice.
Being Sermons Preached on Various Occasions.
By the Rev. W. C. E. Newbolt, M.A., Vicar of S. Matthias, Malvern Link.
8vo. 7s. 6d.

Sunrise. Noon. Sunset.
A selection from various Authors.
By H. L. Sidney Lear, Editor of "For Days and Years," "Precious Stones,' etc., etc.
Three Vols., with red borders, 48mo, 1s. each.
Also a superior Edition, printed on Hand-made Paper, 2s. each ; or Bound in Parchment, 3s. each.

3, WATERLOO PLACE, LONDON.

Plain Sermons on the Catechism.
By the Rev. Isaac Williams, B.D., late Fellow of Trinity College, Oxford; Author of a "Devotional Commentary on the Gospel Narrative."
Two Vols. New Edition. Crown 8vo. 5s. each. Sold separately.

Sermons preached for the most part in Manchester.
By the Rev. W. J. Knox Little, M.A., Canon Residentiary of Worcester, and Rector of S. Alban's, Manchester.
Second Edition. Crown 8vo. 7s. 6d.

Manuals of Religious Instruction.
Edited by John Pilkington Norris, D.D., Archdeacon of Bristol, and Canon Residentiary of Bristol Cathedral.
  I. THE CATECHISM AND PRAYER BOOK.
  II. THE OLD TESTAMENT.
  III. THE NEW TESTAMENT.
New and Revised Editions. Small 8vo. 3s. 6d. each. Sold separately.

Sermons, Parochial and Occasional.
By J. B. Mozley, D.D., late Canon of Christ Church, and Regius Professor of Divinity in the University of Oxford.
Second Edition. Crown 8vo. 7s. 6d.

Thoughts on Personal Religion.
Being a Treatise on the Christian Life in its Two Chief Elements, Devotion and Practice.
By Edward Meyrick Goulburn, D.D., D.C.L., Dean of Norwich.
New Presentation Edition, elegantly printed on Toned Paper.
Two Vols. Small 8vo. 10s. 6d.
An Edition in one Vol., 6s. 6d.; also a Cheap Edition, 3s. 6d.

A Plain Exposition of the Thirty-nine
Articles of the Church of England, for the Use of Schools.
By William Baker, D.D., Head Master of Merchant Taylors' School, and Prebendary of S. Paul's.
16mo. 2s. 6d.

Lyra Apostolica.
[Poems by J. W. BOWDEN, R. H. FROUDE, J. KEBLE, J. H. NEWMAN, R. I. WILBERFORCE, and I. WILLIAMS; with a New Preface by CARDINAL NEWMAN.]
New Edition. With red borders. 16mo. 2s. 6d.

3, WATERLOO PLACE, LONDON.

Prayers for a Young Schoolboy.
By the Rev. E. B. Pusey, D.D. Edited, with a Preface, by H. P. Liddon, D.D., Canon Residentiary of S. Paul's.
Large type. Second Edition. 24mo. 1s.

Maxims and Gleanings from the
Writings of Edward Bouverie Pusey, D.D. Selected and arranged for daily use.
By C. M. S., Compiler of "Daily Gleanings of the Saintly Life," "Under the Cross," etc. With an Introduction by the Rev. M. F. Sadler, Rector of Honiton, Devon.
Second Edition. Crown 16mo. 2s.

Under the Cross.
Readings, Consolations, Hymns, etc., for the Sick; original and selected. Compiled by C. M. S. Edited by the Rev. M. F. Sadler, Prebendary of Wells, and Rector of Honiton, Devon.
Crown 8vo. 5s.

Lovest thou Me?
Thoughts on the Epistles for Holy Week.
By L. C. Skey, Author of "Comforted of God," "All your Care," etc. With an Introduction by the Rev. W. H. Hutchings, M.A., Rector of Kirkby Misperton, Yorkshire.
Crown 16mo. 2s.

Voices of Comfort.
Edited by the Rev. Thomas Vincent Fosbery, M.A., sometime Vicar of S. Giles's, Reading.
Sixth Edition. Crown 8vo. 7s. 6d.

The Beginnings of the Christian Church.
Lectures delivered in the Chapter-room of Winchester Cathedral.
By William Henry Simcox, M.A., Rector of Weyhill, Hants; late Fellow of Queen's College, Oxford.
Crown 8vo. 7s. 6d.

The Life of Christ.
By S. Bonaventure. Translated and edited by the Rev. W. H. Hutchings, M.A., Rector of Kirkby Misperton, Yorkshire.
Crown 8vo. 7s. 6d.

Life of Robert Gray, Bishop of Cape
Town, and Metropolitan of Africa.
Edited by his Son, the Rev. Charles N. Gray, M.A., Vicar of Helmsley, York.
With Frontispiece. New Edition, abridged. Crown 8vo. 7s. 6d.

3, WATERLOO PLACE, LONDON.

The Litany and the Commination Service.
From the Book of Common Prayer.
With Rubrics in red. Royal 8vo. 4s. 6d.

A Commentary on the Office for the
Ministration of Holy Baptism. Illustrated from Holy Scripture, Ancient Liturgies, and the Writings of Catholic Fathers, Doctors and Divines. By the Rev. H. W. Pereira, M.A., M.R.I.A., formerly Scholar of Trinity College, Dublin.
8vo. 14s.

The Mystery of the Passion of our Most
Holy Redeemer. By the Rev. W. J. Knox Little, M.A., Canon Residentiary of Worcester, and Rector of S. Alban's, Manchester.
Second Edition. Crown 8vo. 3s. 6d.

The Lord's Table; or, Meditations on
the Holy Communion Office in the Book of Common Prayer. By the Rev. E. H. Bickersteth, M.A., Vicar of Christ Church, Hampstead, and Rural Dean.
16mo. 1s.; or Cloth extra, 2s.

Five Minutes.
Daily Readings of Poetry. Selected by H. L. Sidney Lear, Editor of "For Days and Years," "Christian Biographies," etc.
Second Edition. 16mo. 3s. 6d

The Children's Saviour.
Instructions to Children on the Life of our Lord and Saviour Jesus Christ. By **Edward Osborne** (of the Society of S. John Evangelist), Assistant Minister of the Church of the Advent, Boston, Mass.
With Outline Illustrations. 16mo. 3s. 6d.

Precious Stones.
Collected by H. L. Sidney Lear. PEARLS—Grace. RUBIES—Nature. DIAMONDS—Art.
Three Vols. 32mo. 1s. each; or in Paper Cover, 6d. each.
Also a superior Edition, printed on Dutch Hand-made Paper, with red borders, Crown 16mo. 2s. each.
Also an Edition in One Volume, with red borders, 16mo. 3s. 6d.

3, WATERLOO PLACE, LONDON.

The Collects of the Day.

An Exposition, Critical and Devotional, of the Collects appointed at the Communion. With Preliminary Essays on their Structure, Sources, and General Character; and Appendices containing Expositions of the Discarded Collects of the First Prayer Book of 1549, and of the Collects of Morning and Evening Prayer.
By Edward Meyrick Goulburn, D.D., D.C.L., Dean of Norwich.
Two Vols. Third Edition. Crown 8vo. 8s. each. Sold separately.

Thoughts upon the Liturgical Gospels

for the Sundays, one for each day in the year. With an introduction on their origin, history, the modifications made in them by the Reformers and by the Revisers of the Prayer Book, the honour always paid to them in the Church, and the proportions in which they are drawn from the Writings of the Four Evangelists.
By Edward Meyrick Goulburn, D.D., D.C.L., Dean of Norwich.
Two Vols. Crown 8vo. 16s.

Yesterday, To-Day, and For Ever.

A Poem in Twelve Books.
By Edward Henry Bickersteth, M.A., Vicar of Christ Church, Hampstead, and Rural Dean.
*One Shilling Edition, 18mo; With red borders, 16mo, 2s. 6d.
The Small 8vo. Edition may still be had, 3s. 6d.*

Weariness.

A Book for the Languid and Lonely.
By H. L. Sidney Lear, Editor of "For Days and Years," "Christian Biographies," etc.
Large Type. Third Edition. Small 8vo. 5s.

The Apostolic Liturgy and the Epistle

to the Hebrews: Being a Commentary on the Epistle in its Relation to the Holy Eucharist, with Appendices on the Liturgy of the Primitive Church.
By John Edward Field, M.A., Vicar of Benson.
Crown 8vo. 12s.

After Death.

An Examination of the testimony of Primitive Times respecting the State of the Faithful Dead, and the Relationship to the Living.
By Herbert Mortimer Luckock, D.D, Canon of Ely, &c.
Fourth Edition. Crown 8vo. 6s.

3, WATERLOO PLACE, LONDON.

The Organization of the Early Christian Churches.
Eight Lectures delivered before the University of Oxford in the year 1880. On the Foundation of the late Rev. John Bampton, M.A., Canon of Salisbury.

By **Edwin Hatch**, M.A., D.D., Vice-Principal of S. Mary Hall, Grinfield, Lecturer on the Septuagint, Oxford, and Rector of Purleigh.

Second Edition. 8vo. 10s. 6d.

A Narrative of Events connected with
the Publication of the "Tracts for the Times." With an Introduction and Supplement extending to the Present Time.

By **William Palmer**, Author of "Origines Liturgicæ," etc.

Crown 8vo. 7s. 6d.

Corpus Christi.
A Manual of Devotion for the Blessed Sacrament.

With a Preface by the Rev. **H. Montagu Villiers**, Vicar of S. Paul's, Wilton Place.

With red borders. Royal 32mo. 2s.

All your Care.
By **L. C. Skey**, Author of "Comforted of God: Thoughts for Mourners." With a Preface by the Rev. **R. W. Randall**, M.A., Vicar of All Saints, Clifton.

32mo. 1s.

Maxims and Gleanings from the
Writings of **John Keble**, M.A. Selected and arranged for daily use.

By **C. M. S.**, Compiler of "Daily Gleanings of the Saintly Life," "Under the Cross," etc. With an Introduction by the Rev. **M. F. Sadler**, Rector of Honiton, Devon.

Crown 16mo. 2s.

Guides and Goads,
An English Translation of ETHICA et SPIRITUALIA. Being short Sayings from the Fathers and other Ancient Authors.

By **Chr. Wordsworth**, D.D., Bishop of Lincoln.

Crown 16mo. 1s. 6d.

Here and There.
Quaint Quotations. A Book of Wit.

Selected by **H. L. Sidney Lear**, Editor of "For Days and Years," "The Life of S. Francis de Sales," etc., etc.

Crown 8vo. 5s.

3, WATERLOO PLACE, LONDON.

The Children's Hymn Book.

For use in Children's Services, Sunday Schools, and Families, arranged in order of the Church's Year.

Published under the revision of the Right Rev. **W. Walsham How**, Bishop Suffragan for East London; the Right Rev. **Ashton Oxenden**, late Bishop of Montreal and Metropolitan of Canada; and the Rev. **John Ellerton**, Rector of Barnes.

    A. *Royal 32mo, Sewed*, 1d.; *Cloth limp*, 2d.
    B. *Royal 32mo, Cloth*, 1s.; *Cloth extra*, 1s. 6d.
    C. *With Music, Crown 8vo, Cloth*, 3s.; *Cloth extra*, 3s. 6d.

The Vision of the Holy Child.

An Allegory.

By **Edith S. Jacob**, Author of "The Gate of Paradise."
With Illustration. Square 16mo. 1s. 6d.

Characteristics and Motives of the

Christian Life. Ten Sermons preached in Manchester Cathedral in Lent and Advent, 1877.

By the Rev. **W. J. Knox Little**, M.A., Canon Residentiary of Worcester, and Rector of S. Alban's, Manchester.
Third Edition. Crown 8vo. 3s. 6d.

The Annotated Bible.

Being a Household Commentary upon the Holy Scriptures, comprehending the Results of Modern Discovery and Criticism.

By **John Henry Blunt**, D.D., F.S.A., Editor of "The Annotated Book of Common Prayer," etc.

Three Vols. With Maps, etc. Demy 4to. Sold separately.

    Vol. I. (668 pages.) Containing the GENERAL INTRODUCTION, with Text and Annotations on the Books from GENESIS to ESTHER. 31s. 6d.
    Vol. II. (720 pages.) Completing the OLD TESTAMENT and APOCRYPHA. 31s. 6d.
    Vol. III. (826 pages.) Containing the NEW TESTAMENT and GENERAL INDEX. 21s.

Henri Dominique Lacordaire.

A Biographical Sketch.

By **H. L. Sidney Lear**, Author of "Christian Biographies," etc.
With Frontispiece. Second Edition. Crown 8vo. 7s. 6d.

3, WATERLOO PLACE, LONDON.

The Witness of the Passion of our Most
Holy Redeemer.
By the Rev. W. J. Knox Little, M.A., Canon Residentiary of Worcester, and Rector of S. Alban's, Manchester.
Crown 8vo. 3s. 6d.

Thoughts for Holy Days and Vigils.
Original and Selected.
With a Preface by the **Lord Bishop of Derry.**
16mo. 2s. 6d.

The Confessions of S. Augustine.
In Ten Books.
Translated and Edited by the Rev. W. H. Hutchings, M.A., Rector of Kirkby Misperton, Yorkshire.
Cheap Edition. 16mo. 2s. 6d.
Also with red borders. Small 8vo. 5s.

The Life of Justification:
A Series of Lectures delivered in Substance at All Saints', Margaret Street.
By the Rev. **George Body**, M.A., Canon of Durham.
Sixth Edition. Crown 8vo. 4s. 6d.

The Life of Temptation:
A Course of Lectures delivered in Substance at S. Peter's, Eaton Square; also at All Saints', Margaret Street.
By the Rev. **George Body**, M.A., Canon of Durham.
Fifth Edition. Crown 8vo. 4s. 6d.

Christian Womanhood and Christian
Sovereignty.
By **Chr. Wordsworth**, D.D., Bishop of Lincoln.
Crown 16mo. 1s.

A Church History.
By **Chr. Wordsworth**, D.D., Bishop of Lincoln.
Four Vols. Crown 8vo. Sold separately.
Vol. I. To THE COUNCIL OF NICÆA, A.D. 325. *Third Edition.* 8s. 6d
Vol. II. To THE COUNCIL OF CONSTANTINOPLE, A.D. 381. *Second Edition.* 6s.
Vols. III. & IV.—FROM THE COUNCIL OF CONSTANTINOPLE, A.D. 381, TO THE COUNCIL OF CHALCEDON, A.D. 451; WITH INDEX TO THE WHOLE WORK. 6s. *each Volume.*

3, WATERLOO PLACE, LONDON.

Thoughts on the prescribed use of Bread

and Wine in the Lord's Supper. By a Communicant. Edited by the Rev. R. W. Johnson, M.A., Vicar of S. Giles', Packwood, Warwickshire.

8vo. Paper Cover. 1s.

Edward Bouverie Pusey.

A Sermon preached in St. Margaret's Church, Prince's Road, Liverpool, in Aid of the Pusey Memorial Fund, on Sunday, January 20, 1884. By H. P. Liddon, D.D., D.C.L., Canon Residentiary of S. Paul's.

8vo. Paper Cover. 6d.

The S.P.C.K. and the Creed of Saint

Athanasius. Remarks upon some recent action of the Christian Knowledge Society, together with a digest of evidence proving the Creed to be earlier than the Ninth Century.

By G. D. W. Ommanney, M.A., Vicar of Draycot, Somerset; Author of "The Athanasian Creed: an Examination of Recent Theories respecting its Date and Origin," and of "Early History of the Athanasian Creed."

8vo. Paper Cover, 1s.

Solitude and Sympathy in the presence of

Death. A Sermon preached in Quebec Chapel on Sunday, March 30, 1884, with reference to the Death of H.R.H. Prince Leopold, Duke of Albany.

By the Rev. Edward Bickersteth Ottley, M.A., Minister of Quebec Chapel.

8vo. Paper Cover. 6d.

What says the Bible as to Marrying a

Deceased Wife's Sister.

By the Rev. Daniel A. Beaufort, M.A., formerly Rector of Lymn-with-Warburton, Cheshire.

Crown 8vo. Sewed. 3d.

True Temperance, as taught by the Bible.

By M. A. Austen Leigh.

Crown 8vo. Sewed. 3d.

Sobriety.

Teachings of Holy Scripture on this subject applied to recent developments of the Temperance Movement.

By the Rev. C. Lambert Coghlan, M.A., Vicar of Marchwood, Hants.

Crown 8vo. Sewed. 3d.

3, WATERLOO PLACE, LONDON.

The Fiftieth Year of the Reformation of
the Nineteenth Century. A Sermon, in three parts, preached in the Church of All Saints', Margaret Street, on the first three Sundays of November, 1883. By **Berdmore Compton**, Vicar.
8vo. Paper Cover, 1s.

Marriage, as affected by the Proposed
Change in the Marriage Laws. A Letter addressed to English Wives. By **Edith Mary Shaw**.
8vo. Paper Cover. 1s.

A Charge.
Delivered at his third Triennial Visitation to the Clergy of the Diocese of St. David's, October 17-24, 1883. By **William Basil Jones**, D.D., Lord Bishop of St. David's.
8vo. Paper Cover, 1s.

The Church in Wales.
A Retrospect and a Defence. By **John Morgan**, Rector of Llanilid and Llanharan, Glamorganshire.
8vo. Paper Cover, 1s.

The Foreign Church Chronicle and
Review. Published Quarterly.
8vo. 1s. 6d. each Number.

The Church Builder.
A Quarterly Record of the work of the Incorporated Church Building Society, and of other works of Church extension.
8vo. 3d. each Number.

The Question of Incest relatively to
Marriage with Sisters in Succession. By **Henry H. Duke**, Rector of Brixton Deverill, Wilts.
Second Edition. 8vo. Paper Cover, 6d.

3, WATERLOO PLACE, LONDON.

The Annotated Book of Common Prayer.

Being an Historical, Ritual, and Theological Commentary on the Devotional System of the Church of England.

Edited by the Rev. John Henry Blunt, D.D., F.S.A., Author of "The History of the Reformation," "The Annotated Bible," etc., etc.

Revised and Enlarged Edition. 4to. £1 1s.;
or, *Half-bound in Morocco,* £1 11s. 6d.

Private Prayers.

By the Rev. E. B. Pusey, D.D. Edited, with a Preface, by H. P. Liddon, D.D., Canon Residentiary of S. Paul's.

Second Edition. Royal 32mo. 2s. 6d.

Conjectural Emendations of Passages in Ancient Authors, and other Papers.

By Chr. Wordsworth, D.D., Bishop of Lincoln.

8vo. 4s.

Lectures on the Industrial Revolution in England. Popular Addresses, Notes, and other Fragments.

By the late Arnold Toynbee, Tutor of Balliol College, Oxford. Together with a Short Memoir by B. Jowett, Master of Balliol College, Oxford.

8vo. 10s. 6d.

The Limits of Individual Liberty.

An Essay.

By Francis C. Montague, M.A., Fellow of Oriel College, Oxford.

8vo. [*In the Press.*

Sophocles.

Translated into English Verse.

By Robert Whitelaw, Assistant Master in Rugby School; late Fellow of Trinity College, Cambridge.

Crown 8vo. 8s. 6d.

The Annual Register.

A Review of Public Events at Home and Abroad, for the Year 1883.

8vo. 18s.

3, WATERLOO PLACE, LONDON.

www.ingramcontent.com/pod-product-compliance
Lightning Source LLC
Chambersburg PA
CBHW032032220426
43664CB00006B/450